Inside/Outside
Teacher Research and Knowledge

Marilyn Cochran-Smith and Susan L. Lytle

TEACHERS COLLEGE PRESS

Teachers College, Columbia University
New York and London

Published by Teachers College Press, 1234 Amsterdam Avenue, New York, N.Y. 10027

Inside/outside : teacher research and knowledge / [edited by] Marilyn
    Cochran-Smith and Susan L. Lytle.
        p.   cm — (Language and literacy series)
    Includes bibliographical references and index.
    ISBN 0-8077-3236-2 (alk. paper). — ISBN 0-8077-3235-4 (pbk.:
alk. paper)
        1. Action research in education—United States. I. Cochran-
Smith, Marilyn, 1949–   . II. Lytle, Susan L. (Susan Landy), 1942–   .
III. Title: Inside outside. IV. Title: Teacher research and
knowledge. V. Series: Language and literacy series (New York, N.Y.)
LB1028.24I67   1992
370'.78—dc20   92-31875

ISBN 0-8077-3236-2
ISBN 0-8077-3235-4 (pbk.)

Printed on acid-free paper
Manufactured in the United States of America
99 98 97 96 95 94 93 92   8 7 6 5 4 3 2 1

Contents

FOREWORD

"Research is just like searching." That is what Angel said. He and other students from a middle school in the Bronx were reflecting on community studies they had been doing as student researchers led by their teacher, Marcelina. They were reporting their work at the Ethnography in Education Forum, which is held each year at the University of Pennsylvania.

Angel was even more on target in a formal sense than I had realized when I first heard his definition. Etymology shows us that *search* derives from the Latin *circum*. Hence, searching means not only to look intently for something we really want to find—it also connotes *looking around* at things. To research, then, is to take a second look around; to pay attention in especially thorough ways. Because we are all so busy doing life we often don't take the time for careful scrutiny.

This book is about teachers taking second looks around their teaching, their students, and their schools. It is thus about searchings, re-searchings, and findings. In the first part of the book Cochran-Smith and Lytle tell of their searchings for what teacher researchers have been doing as such research becomes a movement within the profession of education. In the book's second part, elementary, secondary, and adult literacy teachers tell us of their own searchings and findings.

The volume is remarkable for the comprehensiveness of the connections it makes. In the first chapters, Lytle and Cochran-Smith provide the most complete survey and analysis of teacher research that is currently available. They have sketched the recent history of teacher research, the scope of teacher inquiry, and the range of genres and audiences within which this work is being shared. Their discussion of the field as a whole provides a framework for the approaches and findings of particular studies by the teachers whose contributions compose the second part of this volume.

Cochran-Smith and Lytle have not only provided here a fresh and incisive review of a developing field, they have been active in helping that field to develop. By creating preservice and continuing educational settings that center upon teacher inquiry, they have encouraged individual teachers to do research and have fostered networks of discourse within which teachers can share searchings and findings, encouraging one another in their work. This is tricky business. Lytle and Cochran-Smith challenge and provide support as teachers become active agents in research on their own practice; yet as scholars in the university, they must not upstage the teachers or appropriate their voice. The authenticity of this collaboration with teachers is evidenced by the clarity and force of authorial voice in the essays the teacher researchers have contributed here.

This book is also comprehensive in that the teachers whose research is brought together are remarkable in their diversity. They vary in race, in gender, and in the grade levels and subjects they teach. Their practice takes place in inner city and suburban communities, in public and private schools, and in adult literacy centers. Thus, the comprehensiveness of the essays by Cochran-Smith and Lytle in this volume is matched by the range of teaching practice of their collaborators.

In the contributors' essays, the knowledge gained is about particulars—a particular way of teaching writing, a particular child's discovery. The more common social research moves from the general to the specific, from principle or covering law to a particular instance and back again. But the contributors here do not present what they have found as instantiation—mere examples of something else more fundamental and interesting. Their practice and their understanding of it are shown to us as a phenomenon of significance in its own right.

This is not because the contributors do not deal with abstraction, but because in their work *the concrete has an irreducible centrality and dignity.* I think this has to do with the vantage point from which their knowing develops. In research by a visiting outsider, knowledge about teaching is gained by observational records and reporting that, whether quantitative or qualitative, usually take the form of statements such as, "The teacher did/said/attempted. . . ." In the research reports by teachers in this volume, that kind of statement appears in reference to students. But when the teacher and teaching itself are in the foreground of research attention, then what is usual are statements of the form, "I did . . . I wondered . . . I was trying to. . . ." This is to portray the teacher as agent in a way that cannot be portrayed in research conducted by intermittent visitors to the classroom, however sensitive they may be as observers and reporters. The teacher comes to know teaching from within the action of it, and a fundamentally important aspect of that action is the teacher's own intentionality.

Yet these studies also show compellingly that insiders' knowledge does not develop in isolation. Repeatedly, the teacher researchers have drawn on the views of others as they developed distinctively owned views from another teacher who visited their classroom, or from conceptual or empirical research literature, or from discussion in an oral inquiry group, or from a workshop with someone who inspires and guides reflection, such as Patricia Carini. Lytle and Cochran-Smith make a fundamental claim in saying that teacher research needs communities of discourse in order to thrive. The essays by the teacher researchers attest to that insight.

The book tells us that "outside" and "inside" are not related simply as opposites but as voices that engage one another in dialogue. In discovering their own voices, teacher researchers take in the views of various outsiders and, in a Vygotskyan sense, the voices of others become integrated in one's own. I do not mean to imply that appropriating outsider perspectives within a dialogue that becomes increasingly internal is done without any inner or outer conflict, as if it were only sweet singing with others in close harmony. There are unsettling discords as those voices engage and combine — discrepancies between the stance of outsider and insider, of participant observer and observant participant.

Neither the outsider nor the insider is granted immaculate perception. In objectivist moments we may think of this as a curse, but it can be seen as a great blessing. Culture in the anthropological sense liberates us from the burden of nonselective attention. Through custom and routine we can learn to see and hear—and not see and hear—strategically, which is the only way we can do it. Plato complained of this, but his metaphor for the limits of common sense put the knower inside the cave all alone. The partiality of knowing need not limit us in the ways he feared if we bring companions along who see and hear differently from us. Through teacher research, then, in the development of external and internal reflective dialogue, teaching can become something profoundly other than a solitary profession whose practice is driven by unexamined routine.

Cochran-Smith and Lytle and their colleagues in this volume have become outsiders and insiders for each other. This book in all its parts is the result of the conversation they are creating together during their searchings and findings. As readers we are invited into their discourse, within which we can learn to hear teaching not only as insightful but as agentive. If we begin by listening carefully with them, we may come to hear and speak our own teaching in new ways. Their dialogue is already in progress. Let us join them in it now.

Frederick Erickson
University of Pennsylvania

PREFACE

For many years, we have been negotiating the uncertain borders of educational practice and scholarship, struggling to compose professional and personal lives that connect what has often been divided. Working with others to alter traditional relationships between practice and theory and between schools and universities has profoundly shaped our roles as university-based teachers and researchers and has compelled us to wrestle with the fundamental questions about teachers, research, and knowledge that this book explores. Here we have tried to question the common assumption that knowledge for teaching should be primarily "outside-in"—generated at the university and then used in schools—a position that suggests the unproblematic transmission of knowledge from a source to a destination. In contrast, this book is based on the notion that knowledge for teaching is "inside/outside," a juxtaposition intended to call attention to teachers as knowers and to the complex and distinctly nonlinear relationships of knowledge and teaching as they are embedded in the contexts and the relations of power that structure the daily work of teachers and learners in both the school and the university.

This book has emerged from the dialectic of our experiences as both practitioners and researchers and from our unwillingness to privilege one role over the other. In so doing, we have worked both inside and outside the culture of a large research university, acutely conscious of the ways that efforts to merge practice and research have sometimes made us marginal in both worlds. As efforts of this sort have accelerated in schools and universities across the country, we have come to understand even more deeply that the transformation of schools has far-reaching implications for—and indeed requires—the parallel and reciprocal transformation of universities. Our work with others over the years has taught us that legitimating the knowledge that comes from practitioners' research on their own practice—whether in schools or universities—is a critical dimension of change in both cultures.

Although we have been colleagues and friends for more than a decade, we mark the inception of this book with our concurrent efforts to create new school-university communities committed to collaborative inquiry into language, literacy, and learning. Some 6 years ago, we worked with Philadelphia-area teachers to invent both Project START (Student Teachers As Researching Teachers), a community of beginning elementary teachers and their school and university mentors, and the Philadelphia Writing Project (PhilWP), a community of experienced urban teachers and their university colleagues. From the beginning, we regarded these projects as strategic sites for both research and practice, positioned to prompt the rethinking of fundamental assumptions about the intellectual project of teaching and to explore the prospects for reconstructing practice as inquiry across the professional life span. And from the beginning, these communities were rich sites for exploring language itself—the ways that children, adolescents, and adults learn across classrooms, age groups, and cultures; the ways that communities of beginning and experienced teachers use writing, reading, and oral language to explore and rethink their theories of practice; and the ways that groups of teacher researchers come to function as literacy communities, drawing on diverse interpretive frameworks and discourses to construct their own distinctive ways of knowing.

The essays that compose Part 1 of this book are adaptations of presentations we have given at the University of Pennsylvania's Ethnography and Education Forum, a conference that promotes conversations about qualitative research among an unusually wide range of participants, both local and national, including graduate students, school- and program-based teachers and administrators, and university faculty. Because the conference brings together students, teachers, and academics, it has challenged us to talk across traditional boundaries that often seem to divide practitioners from researchers, doers from thinkers, and actors from analysts. Reframing our essays for presentation in more conventional academic settings such as the American Educational Research Association's annual meetings and for publication in a variety of journals, newsletters, and books (Cochran-Smith & Lytle, 1990, 1992a, 1992b; Lytle & Cochran-Smith, 1990, 1992) has heightened our need to find a discourse about teacher inquiry that speaks to more than one audience. Over the years, the forum has become a place and an occasion for participants in our projects and for other teacher groups to present their work to one another, to deepen the conversation about teaching as research, and as a consequence to bolster the local culture of communities for teacher inquiry. Many of the pieces of teacher research that we include in Part 2 of this book came from work in our local communities and were originally presented at the forum. In taking their texts from classroom to local community to wider arenas, the teacher researchers whose work appears in this volume contribute to the ongoing national conversation about school reform, teacher professionalism, multicultural curriculum and pedagogy, and language and literacy education.

For us, writing essays over a period of 6 years has become the primary context in which we simultaneously wrestle with the daily dilemmas of practice and build conceptual frameworks for the emerging domain of teacher research. Although not a particularly efficient way to write, composing every sentence together at the keyboard has demanded close scrutiny of each assumption and idea. Over time, this way of writing collaboratively has exposed our vulnerabilities as both researchers and practitioners and has forced us to confront issues of participation and hierarchy, generation and imposition, and diversity and uniformity. In each essay we have tried to address a particular question or set of questions that has been problematic in our daily work as teachers, teacher educators, and researchers. Thus, in a very real sense, the contradictions in our own practice oriented our research, while at the same time the distinctions we made in our writing have provided new lenses on our practice. Our essay on the genres of teacher research, for example, grew out of our extensive reading of the varied forms in which teachers write about their daily work and out of our participation with teachers in a range of structured oral inquiry processes. These experiences contributed to our growing discontent with the assumption that research by school-based teachers should be expected to follow the conventions of method and presentation developed in the university. In the working typology of teacher research that resulted from our deliberations, we tried to provide a framework that pushed the edges of what counts as research by teachers. We have also used the framework as a heuristic when we worked with our colleagues to design and redesign the social and organizational structures of Project START and PhilWP.

Throughout this volume, the examples of teachers' work and our projects' histories serve as illustrations of and sources for the broader conceptual frameworks we propose. These examples also reveal our stance as practitioner researchers whose daily work with teachers and student teachers is our primary source of knowledge about teaching. In drawing on teachers' work, however, we are not presuming to speak for or to represent the viewpoints of teachers and student teachers on teacher research. Rather, we write from our own perspectives as university teachers, teacher educators, and researchers committed to a view of teacher research as a radical alternative to traditional epistemologies of research on teaching and teacher education.

In the literature and in popular usage, terms such as "research," "action," "collaborative," "critical," and "inquiry" have been combined with one another and with the term "teacher" to signal a wide range of meanings and purposes. These terms and the various ways they are connected seem to us to reflect surface as well as deeper differences: contrasting paradigms for research, conflicting conceptions of professional development for beginning and experienced teachers, and different assumptions about the roles of teachers in the production and use of knowledge. They also reflect different emphases on individual and institutional growth and on the promotion of teacher research as a means to problem solving, to technical improvement, or to strategic social change. This admixture of terms is not surprising given the complex ideological, multinational, and sociocultural history of efforts by teachers and their school- and university-based colleagues to document, understand, and alter practice. Each participant in the work of teacher research is somewhat differently positioned in the power structures of schools and universities and thus becomes involved in teacher research to further different agendas or outcomes. Our own perspectives on teacher research emerge from our intellectual histories in the fields of language, literacy, and learning and from commitments to activist scholarship and practice.

In this volume, we propose that as teacher research of various kinds accumulates and is more widely disseminated, it will present a radical challenge to current assumptions about the relationships of theory and practice, schools and universities, and inquiry and reform. As the pieces in Part 2 of this volume demonstrate, research by teachers represents a distinctive way of knowing about teaching and learning that we believe will alter—not just add to—what we know in the field. Because we see teacher research as both interpretive and critical, however, we do not mean to suggest that its contribution will be in the form of generalizations about teaching (this time from the "inside" perspective), nor do we mean that teacher research is benign and evolutionary, a process of accumulating "new knowledge" and gradually admitting "new knowers" to the fold. Rather, we have come to see teacher research as a challenge and as a critique, often emerging from but also causing conflict when the traditionally disenfranchised begin to play increasingly important roles in generating knowledge and in deciding how knowledge ought to be interpreted and used.

It is our intention in this book to argue that teacher research is a form of social change wherein individuals and groups labor to understand and alter classrooms, schools, and school communities and that this project has important implications for research on teaching, preservice and inservice teacher education, and language and literacy education. Because teacher research interrupts traditional assumptions about knowers, knowing, and what can be known about teaching, it has the potential to redefine the notion of a knowledge base for teaching and to challenge the university's hegemony in the generation of expert knowledge for the field. Because teacher research challenges the dominant views of staff development and preservice training as transmission and implementation of knowledge from outside to inside schools, it has the potential to reconstruct teacher development across the professional life span so that inquiry and reform are intrinsic to teaching. And finally, because teacher research makes visible the ways that teachers and students co-construct knowledge and curriculum, it has the potential to alter profoundly the ways that teachers use language and literacy to relate to their colleagues and their students, and it can support a more critical and democratic pedagogy.

The design of this book reflects the dialectic that is involved when school- and university-based professionals work to construct lives that connect practice and research. Part 1 includes five essays that build a conceptual framework for teacher research, considering its definition, its relationship to university-based research on teaching, its epistemology, its role in preservice and in-service teacher education, and the social and organizational structures that support teacher research communities. Part 2 includes 21 pieces written by teacher researchers who work in schools, colleges, and adult literacy programs in the Philadelphia area. Originally written for a range of audiences and purposes, these address practice-centered issues related to language, learning, and literacy; the cultures of teaching; and teacher research as a mode of inquiry. It is our hope that taken together, the two parts of this volume will speak to some of the questions of teachers and student teachers, university-based researchers and teacher educators, administrators, and policymakers concerned with the relationships of inquiry and change.

In *Composing a Life,* Mary Catherine Bateson tells us, "Writing a book with someone is a curious kind of sharing in the creation of a new life, an intimacy that establishes a permanent link even when one moves on to other interests." The intimacy that we have come to share as we have worked together over the past 6 years has significantly shaped and sustained our intellectual and personal lives as women seeking connected ways of working and living in the world. We think that the bond and the energy that come from close collaborative work—for us as coauthors, for teachers as members of communities, and for anyone who struggles along with others to bring about educational change—make it possible to renegotiate the boundaries of research and practice and reconfigure relationships inside and outside schools and universities.

REFERENCES

Cochran-Smith, M., & Lytle, S. L. (1990). Research on teaching and teacher research: The issues that divide. *Educational Researcher, 19* (2), 2–11.

Cochran-Smith, M., & Lytle, S. L. (1992a). Communities for teacher research: Fringe or forefront? *American Journal of Education, 100* (3), 298–324.

Cochran-Smith, M., & Lytle, S. L. (1992b). Interrogating cultural diversity: Inquiry and action. *Journal of Teacher Education, 43* (2), 104–115.

Lytle, S. L., & Cochran-Smith, S. L. (1990). Learning from teacher research: A working typology. *Teachers College Record, 92* (1), 83–103.

Lytle, S. L., & Cochran-Smith, S.L. (1992). Teacher research as a way of knowing. *Harvard Educational Review, 62* (4).

Acknowledgments

We would like to thank a number of people and organizations who supported us individually and collectively during the six years that we worked on this project. First and foremost, we acknowledge the contributions of our colleagues in Project START and The Philadelphia Writing Project with whom we struggled to understand the potential of teacher inquiry as a way of knowing about teaching and learning.

We also want to thank the various organizations and funders whose inspiration and support made this project possible: the Philadelphia Teachers Learning Cooperative, the School District of Philadelphia, the Fund for the Improvement of Post-Secondary Education (U.S. Office of Education), the Philadelphia Partnership for Education (PATHS/PRISM), the National Writing Project, the National Council of Teachers of English, the National Center for Adult Literacy, the Philadelphia Schools Collaborative, the Milken Family Foundation, and Joseph L. Calihan. We owe a special debt of thanks to the faculty and staff of the Graduate School of Education at the University of Pennsylvania, in particular to Dean Marvin Lazerson, who forwarded our vision and our work; Frederick Erickson, the organizer of the Ethnography in Education Forum; and Elizabeth Deane who helped us organize and who formatted the manuscript.

Finally we both want to thank our families—Brad, Michael, and Karen Smith, and Torch, Sarah, and Jenny Lytle—for their love, their patience, and their belief that this project someday really would be completed.

Part I

CONCEPTS AND CONTEXTS FOR TEACHER RESEARCH

For much of the 50-year history of research on teaching, teachers and their work have been the topics of study. They have been the researched rather than the researchers. As subjects of research conducted by university-based scholars, teachers have been in effect the objects of study. Their classrooms have served as sites for the collection of data on classroom management and climate, patterns of classroom behavior, personality attributes, social interactions, and instruments of instruction. More recently, research on teaching has looked explicitly at teachers' thought processes and has begun to give prominence to the complex interplay of teachers' content and pedagogical knowledge and the ways that these are used in diverse classroom contexts. This movement toward recognizing teachers' knowledge and thinking as critical components in teaching, however, continues to objectify teaching and often ignores teachers' roles as theorizers, interpreters, and critics of their own practice. Although teachers have been regarded as decision makers in their own classrooms, they have rarely been included in decisions about research as knowledge generation.

Teachers are also expected to be the eventual recipients of the knowledge generated by professional researchers. That is, they are expected to acknowledge the value of researchers' work for their own professional practice and to accept its validity for their day-to-day decisions. Consequently beginning as well as in-service teacher education programs are typically organized to disseminate a knowledge base constructed almost exclusively by outside experts. This means that throughout their careers, teachers are expected to learn about their own profession not by studying their own experiences but by studying the findings of those who are not themselves school-based teachers.

1

In the first part of this book, we question some of the conventional relationships of teachers, knowledge, and research. We argue that it is possible to imagine a different knowledge base for teaching—one that is not drawn exclusively from university-based research but is also drawn from research conducted by teachers, one that is not designed so that teachers function simply as objects of study and recipients of knowledge but also function as architects of study and generators of knowledge. This radical shift from receivers to researchers, users to knowers, and subjects to participants transforms the current notion of research on teaching and makes necessary a redefinition of what we mean by a professional knowledge base.

In the five essays that follow, we argue for this shift by examining the nature of teacher research, its relationship to research on teaching by university-based scholars, its role in knowledge generation in the field, the prospects for reconstructing teacher education as inquiry across the professional life span, and the social and organizational structures that support communities for teacher research. In addressing these questions about teacher research and its definition, position, epistemology, role in professional development, and structure of communities, as listed in Figure I.1, it is our intention to explore the implications of altered relationships among knowers, knowing, and what can be known about teaching.

Chapter 1 argues that although several critical issues divide research on teaching from teacher research, it is best understood as its own genre with a number of distinctive features. In Chapter 2, we develop this idea, proposing a four-part working typology of teacher research that includes both empirical and conceptual work by teachers. In Chapter 3, we argue that teacher inquiry is a significant way of generating both local and public knowledge for teaching. Chapter 4 argues for a reconceptualization of teacher education at both preservice and in-service levels, suggesting that inquiry and reform ought to be regarded as integral parts of the activity and of the intellectual project of teaching. Finally, Chapter 5 provides a framework for considering the social and organizational structures that support and sustain communities for teacher research at all levels of professional development. Taken together, these five essays both provide an analytic framework for understanding teacher research and make the case that research by teachers in their own schools and classrooms represents a radical challenge to current assumptions about how teachers learn and about what constitutes a knowledge base for teaching.

Figure I.1. Issues and Questions Toward a Theory of Teacher Research

DEFINING TEACHER RESEARCH	***What is the nature of teacher research?***

- Is teacher research, "research"?
- What are its critical features?
- Who conducts it, reads it, and uses it?
- What kinds of questions, theories, and frameworks does it stem from and/or generate?

What are the range and variation of the types, methods, and topics of teacher research?

- What types of teacher research are there?
- How does teacher research vary in methods of data collection, analysis, and interpretation?
- What topics do teacher researchers explore?

POSITIONING TEACHER RESEARCH

What is the relation of teacher research to research on teaching?

- How are they similar/different with regard to research questions, theoretical frameworks, and documentation/analysis?
- How do they differ in the relationship of the researcher to the researched?
- To what extent are they institutionalized?
- From what sources do research problems emerge?

EPISTEMOLOGY OF TEACHER RESEARCH

Is teacher research a way of knowing about teaching, learning, and schooling?

- What distinguishes teachers as knowers from researchers on teaching?
- In what contexts and for what purposes is the knowledge generated through teacher research useful?
- What are the implications of teacher research for the knowledge base on teaching?
- What can be learned about teachers from teacher research?

(cont'd. on next page)

Figure I.1. *(cont'd.)*

TEACHER RESEARCH ACROSS THE LIFE SPAN

What does it mean to redefine teaching as inquiry across the professional lifespan?

- How do beginning teachers and experienced teachers use inquiry to reconsider what they already know and what they observe in their schools and classrooms?
- How can schools and classrooms be research sites and sources of knowledge for teachers, parents, administrators, and community members?
- What organizational and social structures are needed to support teaching as a form of inquiry at preservice and inservice levels?
- What learning opportunities, themes, and strategies support the notion of teaching as inquiry and reform?

COMMUNITIES FOR TEACHER RESEARCH

What contexts support and sustain the inquiries of teachers and teacher groups?

- How are communities for teacher research established and maintained within and across schools and universities?
- How do communities for teacher research organize time and talk, construct and use texts, and regard the goal of teaching?

1

Research on Teaching and Teacher Research: The Issues That Divide

Although current educational research has placed considerable emphasis on developing a systematic and rigorous body of knowledge about teaching, little attention has been given to the roles that teachers might play in generating a knowledge base. Lack of significant teacher participation in codifying what we know about teaching, identifying research agendas, and creating new knowledge is problematic. Those who have daily access, extensive expertise, and a clear stake in improving classroom practice have no formal ways for their knowledge of classroom teaching and learning to become part of the literature on teaching.

In the first part of this essay, we argue that efforts to construct and codify a knowledge base for teaching have relied primarily on university-based research and have ignored the significant contributions that teacher knowledge can make to both the academic research community and the community of school-based teachers. As a consequence, those most directly responsible for the education of children have been disenfranchised. We propose that teacher research, which we define as systematic, intentional inquiry by teachers, makes accessible some of the expertise of teachers and provides both university and school communities with unique perspectives on teaching and learning. In the second part of the essay, we identify a number of critical issues that divide research on teaching from teacher research and thus make it extremely difficult for the academic community to recognize the contribution that teacher research can make. Finally, we touch on the value of teacher research for the school and university communities, claiming that a broader context for research on teaching requires the systemic reform of school structures. This is discussed in more detail in Chapter 5. In this essay, we explore audiences for teacher research in the academy and in schools, and we argue for the potential of teacher research to help in the reform of schooling.

THEORETICAL AND RESEARCH FRAMEWORKS

Research on Teaching

Two paradigms have dominated research on teaching over the last two decades (Shulman, 1986a). The first, which has been characterized as process-product research, accounts for the majority of studies. For more than 15 years, researchers have been exploring effective teaching by correlating particular processes, or teacher behaviors, with particular products, usually defined as student achievement as measured by standardized tests (Brophy & Good, 1986; Denham & Lieberman, 1980; Dunkin & Biddle, 1974). Underlying this research is a view of teaching as a primarily linear activity wherein teacher behaviors are considered causes and student learnings are considered effects. This approach emphasizes the actions of teachers rather than their professional judgments and attempts to capture the activity of teaching by identifying sets of discrete behaviors reproducible from one teacher and one classroom to the next. Research of this kind has been associated with the view of teacher as technician (Apple, 1986), wherein the teacher's primary role is to implement the research findings of others concerning instruction, curriculum, and assessment. With this view, the primary knowledge source for the improvement of practice is research on classroom phenomena that can be observed. This research has a perspective that is "outside-in"; in other words, it has been conducted almost exclusively by university-based researchers who are outside of the day-to-day practices of schooling.

The second paradigm includes a diverse group of qualitative or interpretive studies that Shulman (1986a) refers to as studies of "classroom ecology." This family of inquiries draws from anthropology, sociology, and linguistics and from the traditions of qualitative, interpretive research (Cazden, 1986; Erickson, 1986; Evertson & Green, 1986). Research from these perspectives presumes that teaching is a highly complex, context-specific, interactive activity in which differences across classrooms, schools, and communities are critically important. Interpretive research provides detailed, descriptive accounts of customary school and classroom events that shed light on their meanings for the participants involved. For example, many interpretive studies explore the perspectives and experiences of teachers and students through extensive interviews, and some studies are conducted cooperatively by classroom teachers and university-based researchers (Bussis, Chittenden, & Amarel, 1976; Erickson, 1989; Perl & Wilson, 1986; Yonemura, 1986). Although a small number of research reports are coauthored by university-based researchers and school-based teachers (Edelsky & Smith, 1984; Heath & Branscombe, 1985; Smith & Geoffrey, 1968), most are published singly by university researchers and are intended for academic audiences. Cooperative research provides valuable insights into the interrelationships of theory and practice but, like more traditional interpretive research, often constructs and predetermines teachers' roles in the research process, thereby framing and mediating teachers' perspectives through researchers' perspectives.

We propose that current research on teaching within both process-product paradigms and interpretive paradigms constrains and at times even makes invisible teachers' roles in the generation of knowledge about teaching and learning in classrooms. The contents of the *Handbook of Research on Teaching* (Wittrock, 1986), widely viewed as the most comprehensive synthesis of research in the field, is indicative of this exclusion. Described on the book jacket as "the definitive guide to what we know about teachers, teaching, and the learning process," this 1,037-page handbook contains 35 research reviews. Although a few of these include studies carried out by university researchers in cooperation with teachers and several focus explicitly on teachers' thinking, knowledge, and the cultures of teaching (Feiman-Nemser & Floden, 1986; Clark & Peterson, 1986), none are written by school-based teachers themselves or, as far as we can determine, are published accounts of teachers' work cited. Rather, in most of the studies included, teachers are the objects of researchers' investigations and are ultimately expected to be the consumers and implementors of these findings. What is missing from the handbook are the voices of teachers themselves, the questions that teachers ask, and the interpretive frames that teachers use to understand and to improve their own classroom practices.

Teacher Research

We take here as a working definition for teacher research systematic and intentional inquiry carried out by teachers. We base this definition in part on the work of Lawrence Stenhouse (1985), who defines research in general as "systematic, self-critical enquiry," and in part on an ongoing survey of the literature of teacher writing. We derive this definition from an ongoing survey of the literature of teacher writing, including journal articles written by teachers, in-house collections of teachers' work in progress, and monographs about teachers' classroom experiences as well as published and unpublished teachers' journals and essays. With this definition, we wish to emphasize that there already exists a wide array of writing initiated by teachers that is appropriately regarded as research. (Chapter 2 presents a more detailed discussion of the working typology and an analysis of the contribution of teacher research in these categories to the university-based and school-based educational communities.)

The term "teacher research" has been used as a kind of umbrella to describe a wide range of activities, which many trace to the "action research" notion of the 1950s and 1960s. Characterized by Lewin (1948) as "comparative research on the conditions and effects of various forms of social action, and research leading to social action" (pp. 202–203), action research presented an implicit critique of the usefulness of basic research for social change. One of the most influential interpretations of action research is found in the work of Stenhouse and his colleagues, who established the Center for Applied Research in Education at the University of East Anglia in 1970. The goal of the center was to "demystify and democratize research which was seen as failing to contribute effectively to the growth of professional understanding and to the improvement of professional practice" (Stenhouse in Rudduck & Hopkins, 1985, p. 1). Stenhouse and, later, his colleagues (Elliott & MacDonald, 1975; Nixon, 1981; Rudduck & Hopkins, 1985) encouraged teachers to become intimately involved in the research process. They believed that through their own research, teachers could strengthen their judgments and improve their own classroom practices. Stenhouse's argument was radical: He claimed that research was the route to teacher emancipation and that "researchers [should] justify themselves to practitioners, not practitioners to researchers" (Stenhouse in Rudduck & Hopkins, 1985, p. 19). (For more extensive discussions of the historical roots of action research, see Kyle and Hovda [1987] and Oja and Smulyan [1989]).

Like action research, the work of Patricia Carini and her teacher colleagues at the Prospect Center and School in Bennington, Vermont, is related to the current concept of teacher research. For almost two decades, the Prospect group has worked to develop a number of processes for documenting children's learning in school contexts, for helping teachers to uncover and clarify their implicit assumptions about teaching, learning, and schooling, and for solving a variety of school-based educational problems (Carini, 1975, 1979, 1986). Carini's work is unique; it not only provides formats for teacher research and collaboration, but also, through the Prospect Archives of children's work and records of teachers' deliberations, serves as a living resource for the study of children's development over time. The work of the Prospect group has influenced many teachers to document and reflect on their classroom practices. Similarly, the North Dakota Study Group on Evaluation, guided by Vito Perrone and many teachers, has long provided a forum for collaborative teacher inquiry into their own and children's work. (See, for example, North Dakota Study Group monographs on children's thinking and language, teacher support systems, inservice training, and the school's relationship to the larger community.)

Although the terms "teacher research" and "action research" are relatively new, their underlying conceptions of teaching and the role of teachers are not. Early in the century, Dewey (1904) criticized the nature of educational devel-

opment, pointing out that it tended to proceed reactively by jumping uncritically from one new technique to the next. He argued that the only remedy for
this situation was teachers who had learned to be "adequately moved by their
own ideas and intelligence" (p. 16). Dewey emphasized the importance of
teachers' reflecting on their practices and integrating their observations into
their emerging theories of teaching and learning. He urged educators to be
both consumers and producers of knowledge about teaching—both teachers
and students of classroom life. Dewey's notion of teachers as students of learning prefigures the concept of teachers as reflective practitioners, which was
more recently developed in the work of Schön. Unlike those who characterize
teaching as the acquisition of technical skills, Schön (1983, 1987) depicts professional practice as an intellectual process of posing and exploring problems
identified by teachers themselves.

Some teacher researchers model their classroom and school-based
inquiries on more traditional university-based social science research. Myers
(1985) has been influential in arguing for the adaptation of basic and applied
social science research paradigms to teacher research. He suggests that the
norms of generalizability, tests of significance, and optimization of control of
problems apply to teacher research but must be defined differently by classroom teachers. Myers calls for teacher researchers to be well grounded in
problem definition, research design, and quantitative data analysis and suggests that they begin by replicating the studies of university-based researchers.
In contrast to Myers, Mohr and Maclean (1987) and Bissex and Bullock (1987)
argue that teacher research is essentially a new genre not necessarily bound by
the constraints of traditional research paradigms. They urge teachers to identify their own questions, document their own observations, analyze and interpret data in light of their current theories, and share their results primarily with
other teachers. Berthoff (1987) puts little emphasis on data gathering and
instead asserts that teachers already have all the information they need and
should reexamine—or, in her words, "REsearch"—their own experiences.
Kincheloe (1991), Carr and Kemmis (1986), and others whose perspective is
grounded in critical social theory emphasize the liberatory function of teacher
research as part of a larger effort toward more participatory democracy.

Each of these sets of recommendations for teacher research contains an
image of what the genre might look like: an approximation of university-
based research; a more grass-roots phenomenon that has its own internal standards of logic, consistency, and clarity; a reflective or reflexive process that is
for the benefit of the individual; or a dialectical process of action and reflection aimed at social change. Each of these images, although quite different,
also implicitly compares teacher research with university-based research on
teaching. In the section that follows, we argue that several critical issues
underlying these comparisons account for the exclusion of teacher research
from research on teaching.

The Issues That Divide

We argue in this section that comparison of teacher research with university-based research involves a complicated set of assumptions and relationships that act as barriers to enhancing our knowledge base about teaching. Researchers in the academy equate "knowledge about teaching" with the high-status information attained through traditional modes of inquiry. They fault teachers for not reading or not implementing the findings of such research even though teachers often view these findings as irrelevant and counterintuitive. Yet teacher research, which by definition has special potential to address issues that teachers themselves identify as significant, does not have a legitimate place. If simply compared with university research, it can easily be found wanting. Regarding teacher research as a mere imitation of university research is not useful and is ultimately condescending. As Figure 1.1 suggests, it is more useful to consider teacher research as its own genre, not entirely different from other types of systematic inquiry into teaching yet with some quite distinctive features.

Figure 1.1, which contrasts research on teaching with teacher research, outlines the comparisons we draw in this essay. By research on teaching, we refer to the large body of literature accumulated over the last several decades that has attempted to open "the black box" of classroom teaching and learning. Much of this work has been critically reviewed and analyzed in the three volumes of the *Handbook of Research on Teaching* (Gage, 1963; Travers, 1973; Wittrock, 1986) and other syntheses of research in various domains of teaching (Flood, Jensen, Lapp, & Squire, 1991; Reynolds, 1989; Richardson-Koehler, 1987). The features of research on teaching outlined on this chart are not intended to capture the distinctive qualities of particular studies but rather to represent the broad contours of the field as a whole. By teacher research, we refer to the growing body of literature that has accumulated over the last decade and that has attempted to represent teachers' work from teachers' own perspectives. Unlike research on teaching, teacher research has just begun to be collected (Alaska Teacher Researchers Group, 1991; Bay Area Writing Project, 1990; Bissex & Bullock, 1987; Goswami & Stillman, 1987; Mohr & Maclean, 1987; Peitzman, 1991) and has not yet been synthesized or systematically critiqued. The qualities of teacher research listed in Figure 1.1 are derived from our own analysis of the genre.

To elaborate on our comparison of teacher research and research on teaching, we turn now to two of the most important issues in educational research: (1) institutionalization, including content and ownership as well as supportive structures, and (2) standards for methodological rigor, including research questions, generalizability, theoretical frameworks, and documentation and analysis. Exploring teacher research along these lines points out some of the salient features of this genre, suggests questions raised by the comparison of university-based research and teacher research, and identifies conflicting conceptions of the nature and purposes of teacher research.

Institutionalization

Origins and Content. Although some teacher researchers are university teachers who reflect on their own teaching at the university level (Duckworth, 1987; Freeman, 1989; Kutz, 1989; Rorschach & Whitney, 1986), most of those engaged in teacher research are K–12 classroom teachers or student teachers who have participated in some institute, inservice, or graduate program based at a university where they have been exposed to particular ideas about teaching and learning. They do teacher research as dissertations, as graduate coursework projects, as part of their work as cooperating teachers or student teachers, or as ongoing work in teacher collaborative projects. Some teacher researchers work on collaborative research projects with university-based researchers or teacher educators (Buchanan & Schultz, 1989; Edelsky & Boyd, 1989; Lytle & Fecho, 1991); others form research partnerships with their teacher colleagues (Philadelphia Teachers Learning Cooperative, 1984; Boston Women's Teachers' Group, 1983) or with their own students (Branscombe, Goswami, & Schwartz, 1992; Cochran-Smith, Garfield, & Greenberger, 1992).

Encouraged by the widespread activities of the National Writing Project, the Breadloaf School of English, and the work of influential researchers/practitioners such as Donald Graves and Lucy Calkins, the focus of much of the K–12 teacher research of the last decade has been writing: children's development as writers (Avery, 1987), classroom environments that support students' progress (Atwell, 1987), classroom and schoolwide strategies for writing assessment (*Making Room for Growth: A Documentary Portrait of the 1987–1989 Writing Assessment Program in the School District of Philadelphia,* 1989), teachers' own writing and classroom inquiry processes (Frutkoff, 1989), and the generation of theory through sustained reflection on classroom practice (Johnston, 1989). Other teacher researchers have focused on classroom teaching and learning more broadly by looking, for example, at the interrelationships of children's oral and written language development (Strieb, 1985); the complexities of a single class or a teacher's experience over time (Harris, 1989); the corpus of a single child's artistic or written work (see Buchanan in Chapter 8); children's growing and changing conceptions of the world and how these are expressed in their stories, play, and drama (Paley, 1981); and thematic analyses of teachers' curriculum theory and design (Wiggington, 1985). Many of these address the interactive relationships of students' language, literacy, and learning (Ashton-Warner, 1963), while others focus on the acquisition of discipline-based knowledge (Tierney, 1981) and a few center on more general issues of school organization, policy, and multicultural education (Palonsky, 1986). The range of topics addressed by teacher researchers is described in more detail in Chapter 3.

Supportive Structures. Recently, a number of organizations have begun to focus their efforts on teacher research. For example, both the National Coun-

Figure 1.1. Research on Teaching and Teacher Research

	RESEARCH ON TEACHING	TEACHER RESEARCH
Ownership	Professional researchers: university-based or R&D center-based	Teachers: K–12 school-based, college/university-based, or adult program-based
Supportive Structures	Academic community organized to provide formal/informal support for research: monetary, work load, scheduling, and institutional support, as well as local and national forums for dissemination and publication	Teaching organizations (school or university) lack formal/informal support for research: inflexible work loads and teaching schedules, little monetary support or release time, and few local or national forums for dissemination/publication
Research Questions	Generally emerging from study in a discipline (or multiple disciplines) and/or analysis of theoretical and empirical literatures; referenced to the major work in some area(s) of the field	Generally emerging from problems of practice: felt discrepancies between intention and reality, theory/research and practice; reflexive and referenced to the immediate context
Generalizability	Findings intended for application and use outside of the context in which they were developed: either specific teaching procedures correlated with increased student learning or interpretations/ analyses of the social and cultural construction of teaching and learning	Findings intended for application and use within the context in which they were developed: enhanced conceptual frameworks, altered practice, and/or reconstructed curricula; often useful beyond the immediate context (see Chapter 3)
Theoretical Frameworks	Derived from disciplines related to teaching, learning, and schooling (e.g., psychology, linguistics, anthropology, sociology, and literature) Generating theories related to teaching, learning, and schooling	Derived from the knowledge of professional practice and from disciplines related to teaching, learning, and schooling Generating theories related to teaching, learning, and schooling

Documentation & Analysis	**RESEARCH ON TEACHING**	**TEACHER RESEARCH**
	Quantitative studies and interpretive studies: professional detachment/ objectivity of the researcher, standard paradigms and means of data collection, analysis, and rules of evidence	Predominantly interpretive studies: professional involvement/systematic subjectivity of the researcher, new paradigms and alternative kinds of discourse and analysis

cil of Teachers of English (NCTE) and the U.S. Department of Education's Office of Educational Research and Improvement (OERI) have begun to sponsor national efforts to support and sanction teacher research through direct funding. These two funding efforts represent different approaches to supporting teacher research.

The guidelines for OERI's funding require that teachers be the principal investigators and that proposed projects address issues important to local school improvement. Specified topics are broad, including teachers' roles and functions, instructional processes and materials, subject matter teaching, assessment, professional development, alternative patterns of school management and organization, and ways for schools to find, understand, and use research and practice-based knowledge. This represents a significant federal effort to institutionalize teacher research in planning and decision making at the school and district levels. Funding efforts like those of OERI seem very promising, but for these initiatives to make a difference, those in positions of power in school districts would need to believe and operate on the following: (1) that the questions that teachers ask about theory and practice ought to be the starting points for classroom inquiry; (2) that teachers can and should play a central role in the creation of new knowledge about teaching and learning; (3) that the benefits of this new knowledge would outweigh the problems inherent in altering standard school routines and practices; and (4) that power in decision making can and ought to be distributed among teachers, specialists, and administrators across the school system.

In contrast, NCTE provides funds for individual teacher researchers who are asked to identify a study based on concerns directly relevant to their own work. NCTE's guidelines for would-be teacher researchers specify that funds may not be used for teacher released time, travel, or other organizational changes or staffing arrangements. Furthermore, to support their proposals, teacher researchers are asked to include evaluations by three knowledgeable reviewers who may or may not include school-based personnel. Unlike OERI's efforts, which require school-level commitment and the creation of systemic structures that support changing roles for teachers, the emphasis of NCTE's program is on the professional development of individual teachers inside their own classrooms. However, the structures of NCTE as an organization, as well as those of the Breadloaf School of English and the national and local sites of the National Writing Project, function as infrastructures that make it possible for teachers to present their work at conferences and publish their writing.

There are no obvious and simple ways to create systemic supports for teacher research that on one hand encourage teacher autonomy and initiative but on the other hand recognize that teacher research occurs within the context of broad-based efforts of school improvement. Unlike the academic research community, which is organized to provide formal and informal structures to support research on teaching, the community of teacher researchers is disparate, and few structures support their work. Variations in the efforts of OERI, NCTE, and other organizations reflect the complexity of the problem.

Standards for Methodological Rigor

Research Questions. It may appear to be self-evident that the research questions in teacher research emanate from the day-to-day experiences of teachers themselves, but this is not a trivial issue. In traditional university-based classroom research, researchers' questions reflect careful study of the existing theoretical and empirical literature and sometimes negotiation with the teachers in whose classrooms they collect data. On the other hand, teachers' questions often emerge from discrepancies between what is intended and what occurs: Initially, these may be experienced as a concern about a student's progress, a classroom routine that is floundering, conflict or tension among students, or a desire to try out a new approach. This questioning process is highly reflexive, immediate, and referenced to particular children and classroom contexts: What happens when my "high-risk" second graders shift from a basal reading program to a whole language curriculum? How will I know when my students are on the way to thinking like mathematicians and not simply learning new routines? How do my digressions from lesson plans contribute to and/or detract from my goals for the students? How do my students' theories of teaching and learning shape and become shaped by writing conferences?

Although these questions are not framed in the language of educational theory, they are indeed about discrepancies between theory and practice. Although they are not always motivated by a need to generalize beyond the immediate case, they may in fact be relevant to a wide variety of contexts. The questions of teacher researchers are simultaneously more general than questions that concentrate on the effectiveness of specific techniques, materials, or instructional methods and more specific than interpretive questions that explore the meanings of customary school and classroom events. Teachers' questions are not simply elaborated versions of "What can I do Monday morning?" or "What will work in my classroom?" Embedded within the particular questions of teacher researchers are many other implicit questions about the relationships of concrete, particular cases to more general and abstract theories of learning and teaching. For example, when a teacher asks, "What will happen if I use journals with my first graders at the beginning of the school year before they have begun to read?" she is also asking more generally: How does children's reading development relate to their writing development? Does some explicit instruction in letter-sound relationships have to precede children's expressive uses of those relationships? Do children have knowledge of these relationships before they begin formal reading instruction? If they do, where does this knowledge come from? How does collaboration influence writing? What kinds of contexts support sharing? Whom do children imagine is their audience? What is the relationship between "errors" and growth in writing? For which students are particular writing activities effective and useful, and for which students are they not? Why? The unique feature of the questions that prompt teacher research is that they emanate from neither theory nor practice alone but from critical reflection on the intersection of the two.

Generalizability. The criterion of generalizability has been used to discount the value of research prompted by the questions of individual teachers and conducted in single classrooms. However, as Zumwalt (1982b) effectively argues, there is a growing realization in the research community that the positivistic paradigm that attempts to formulate general laws is probably not the most useful for understanding educational phenomena. Zumwalt points out that generalizations about teaching and learning are by definition context free. She quotes Guba's (1980) assertion that "it is virtually impossible to imagine any human behavior which is not mediated by the context in which it occurs" (Zumwalt, 1982b, p. 235) to make the case that rather than laws about what works generically in classrooms, we need insight into the particulars of how and why something works and for whom it works within the contexts of particular classrooms.

A similar argument is made by interpretive researchers who demonstrate that understanding one classroom helps us to understand better all classrooms. Teachers are uniquely situated to conduct such inquiries: They have opportunities to observe learners over long periods of time and in a variety of academic and social situations; they often bring many years of knowledge about the culture of the community, school, and classroom; and they experience the ongoing events of classroom life in relation to their particular roles and responsibilities. This set of lenses sets the perspectives of teachers apart from those of others who look into classrooms. Knoblauch and Brannon (1988) make a related point in their discussion on the phenomenological basis of teacher research:

> The story-telling of the teacher-inquirer in a classroom devoted to language prac-
> tices has its peculiar features and makes a distinctive contribution to our knowl-
> edge of school experience. . . . The telling aims not at selectivity or simplification
> but at richness of texture and intentional complexity. (p. 24)

John Holt did not use the phrase "teacher research" in 1964 when he called
for teachers to observe more closely their children's classroom activities and
then meet together to talk about their observations, but his words are very
much in keeping with its spirit:

> Once we understand that some of the things we teachers do may be helpful, some
> merely useless, and some downright harmful, we can begin to ask which is which.
> But only teachers can ask such questions and use their daily work with students to
> test their answers. All other kinds of research into ways of improving teaching lead
> mostly to expensive fads and nonsense. (p. 54)

Although Holt's critique probably responds to the experimental research of the
1950s and early 1960s, his point about the unique potentialities of teacher
questions and classroom inquiry remains significant.

Theoretical Frameworks. Not only is the status of teacher questions at
issue, but there is also considerable disagreement about the way in which
teacher research is theoretically grounded. In a discussion of practical theories
of teaching, Sanders and McCutcheon (1986) argue that teaching requires
intentional and skillful action within real-world situations. The success of these
actions depends on the ability to perceive relevant features of complex, problematic, and changeable situations and to make appropriate choices. The
knowledge necessary to perform these professional tasks has been called "theories of action" (Argyris, 1982). Rather than make a distinction between professional knowledge and educational theory, as is usually done, Sanders and
McCutcheon make the case that professional knowledge is essentially theoretical knowledge.

This position contrasts with North's recent analysis of practitioners' knowledge in composition (1987). North calls professional knowledge "lore" and
defines it as "the accumulated body of traditions, practices, and beliefs in terms
of which practitioners understand how writing is done, learned and taught" (p.
22). Although North seems critical of the fact that practitioner knowledge has
been devalued, conceptions like his may contribute to its devaluation by suggesting that the structure of this knowledge is experiential and driven only by
pragmatic logic. We wonder how "lore," which North claims is a "very rich and
powerful body of knowledge," can be, as he also points out, totally unselec-
tive, self-contradictory, and framed only in practical terms. From North's perspective, teachers' knowledge would hardly qualify as theory; indeed, in
North's discussion of practical inquiry—his version of teacher research—there
is little mention of theory.

Juxtaposing North's concept of "lore" with the recent work of Shulman

(1986b, 1987) and colleagues, which explores the knowledge base for teaching, reveals a major discrepancy among views of teachers' knowledge and theories. By working intensively with beginning and experienced teachers, Shulman's group is exploring the wide variety of categories of knowledge that teachers have and use. His work suggests that the base for teaching is complex, encompassing knowledge of content, pedagogy, curriculum, learners and their characteristics, educational contexts, purposes and values, and philosophical and historical grounds (p. 8). Our own work with teachers leads us to believe that all of Shulman's categories of knowledge can be seen as leading to theoretical frameworks that teachers not only bring to the identification of their research questions but also utilize in the analysis and interpretation of their findings.

These debates demonstrate that the status and role of theory are central issues in teacher research. Just as our earlier discussion indicated that there are controversies within the academic community about the feasibility of discovering generalizable laws, similar questions are raised about the kinds of theory appropriate to applied fields like education. In these fields, various combinations of facts, values, and assumptions may better capture the state of knowledge than conventional scientific theories (House, 1980; Zumwalt, 1982b). It may be that the notion of theory as a combination of perspectives will be particularly compatible with and productive for the emerging genre of teacher research. Indeed, how and whether teachers theorize are empirical questions currently being explored in a variety of interesting ways (Clark & Peterson, 1986; Elbaz, 1983; Munby, 1987; Shavelson & Stern, 1981; Shulman, 1987). Teacher research itself may provide evidence of the unique theoretical frameworks that underlie teachers' questions and decisions and are grounded in their classroom practice. If we regard teachers' theories as sets of interrelated conceptual frameworks grounded in practice, teacher researchers are both users and generators of theory. If, however, we limit the notion of theory to more traditional university-based definitions, research by teachers may be seen as atheoretical, and its value for creation of the knowledge base on teaching may be circumscribed.

Documentation and Analysis. In many respects, the forms of documentation in teacher research resemble the forms used in academic research, particularly the standard forms of interpretive research. Field notes about classroom interactions, interviews with students and teachers, and classroom documents (e.g., students' writing and drawing, test scores, and teachers' plans and handouts) are commonly collected by teacher researchers. In addition, teacher researchers often keep extensive journals and audiotape or videotape small and large group discussions, peer and teacher-student conferences, students' debates, and role plays and dramatic productions, as well as their own classroom presentations. Like university-based qualitative research, a strength of teacher research is that it often entails multiple data sources that can be used to confirm and/or illuminate one another.

Questions about the demands of rigorous documentation emerge from both teacher researchers and university researchers. Although many teachers collect some of these data in the course of the normal activity of teaching, as teachers readily point out, the complex and extensive demands on teachers' time and attention place obvious limitations on what teachers can manage to do. Some university researchers, who equate data collection with training in the traditions of social science research, question whether teachers' data can be sufficiently systematic and teacher researchers sufficiently well prepared as classroom observers. However, as we have demonstrated elsewhere, many teachers have sophisticated and sensitive observation skills grounded in the context of actual classrooms and schools. In analyzing the patterns and discrepancies that occur, teachers use the interpretive frameworks of practitioners to provide a truly emic view that is different from that of an outside observer, even if that observer assumes an ethnographic stance and spends considerable time in the classroom.

Teacher Research: Contributions and Future Directions

Underlying much of the debate about methodological rigor in teacher research is a limited concept of what kinds of research can contribute to our knowledge about teaching. This limited concept is the basis of our critique of the contents of the *Handbook of Research on Teaching* (Wittrock, 1986), "the definitive guide to what we know about teachers, teaching, and the learning process." As we have shown, "we" refers only to the academic community and privileges its particular ways of knowing about, writing about, and publishing about teaching. In this arena, the academy decides what counts as knowledge according to its own traditions. We have been arguing that teacher research constitutes another legitimate arena of formal knowledge about teaching. The status and value of teacher research, however, have yet to be determined by school-based teachers, the interpretive community for whom it is primarily intended. Just as academics have evolved a complex set of criteria and standards for judging the quality and contribution of research in the academic community, teachers over time will develop a similarly complex set of standards for evaluating the research generated in and for their community.

Value for the Teaching Community

There is little disagreement that teachers who engage in self-directed inquiry into their own work in classrooms find the process intellectually satisfying;

they testify to the power of their own research to help them better understand and ultimately to transform their teaching practices. In *Reclaiming the Classroom: Teacher Research As an Agency for Change*, one of the earliest and most widely disseminated collections of conceptual pieces about teacher research as well as studies by teachers, Goswami and Stillman (1987) provide a compelling summary of what happens when teachers conduct research as a regular part of their roles as teachers:

1. Their teaching is transformed in important ways: they become theorists, articulating their intentions, testing their assumptions, and finding connections with practice.
2. Their perceptions of themselves as writers and teachers are transformed. They step up their use of resources; they form networks; and they become more active professionally.
3. They become rich resources who can provide the profession with information it simply doesn't have. They can observe closely, over long periods of time, with special insights and knowledge. Teachers know their classrooms and students in ways that outsiders can't.
4. They become critical, responsive readers and users of current research, less apt to accept uncritically others' theories, less vulnerable to fads, and more authoritative in their assessment of curricula, methods, and materials.
5. They can study writing and learning and report their findings without spending large sums of money (although they must have support and recognition). Their studies, while probably not definitive, taken together should help us develop and assess writing curricula in ways that are outside the scope of specialists and external evaluators.
6. They collaborate with their students to answer questions important to both, drawing on community resources in new and unexpected ways. The nature of classroom discourse changes when inquiry begins. Working with teachers to answer real questions provides students with intrinsic motivation for talking, reading, and writing and has the potential for helping them achieve mature language skills. (Preface)

Similar claims about the value of teacher research for teachers themselves have been made by a number of groups of teacher researchers and university researchers working together (Bissex & Bullock, 1987; Mohr & Maclean, 1987; Strickland, Dillon, Funkhouser, Glick, & Rogers, 1989). It is likely that when more teachers have opportunities to collaborate across classrooms, schools, and communities and when they develop their own set of evaluative standards, they will find avenues for broader dissemination and the value of their work will increase dramatically.

Value for the Academic Community

Just as teachers read and use the research of university-based researchers, many academics committed to teacher education and/or the study of teaching and learning undoubtedly will find the research of teachers a rich and unique source of knowledge. We can imagine at least four important ways in which the academic community can learn from teacher research. Teachers' journals, for example, provide rich data about classroom life that can be used by academics to construct and reconstruct theories of teaching and learning. In this capacity, teachers serve primarily as collectors of data, but their data are unlike other classroom descriptions that have been selected, filtered, and composed in the language of researchers. Second, because teacher research emanates from teachers' own questions and frameworks, it reveals what teachers regard as the seminal issues about learning and the cultures of teaching. Third, as Shulman (1986a) argues, both "scientific knowledge of rules and principles" and "richly described and critically analyzed cases" need to constitute the knowledge base of teaching. Teacher research provides these rich classroom cases. Because cases are often more powerful and memorable influences on decision making than are conventional research findings in the form of rules and generalizations (Nisbett & Ross, 1980; Shulman, 1986a), teacher educators can use teachers' cases to study how practitioners learn from the documented experiences of others. Finally, through their research, teachers can contribute to the critique and revision of existing theory by describing discrepant and paradigmatic cases, as well as providing data that ground or move toward alternative theories. The value of teacher research for both the academic community and the teaching community is elaborated in Chapter 3. What teachers bring will alter and not just add to what is known about teaching. As the body of teacher research accumulates, it will undoubtedly prompt reexamination of many current assumptions about children, learning, and classroom processes.

Communities for Teacher Research

Participation in teacher research requires considerable effort by innovative and dedicated teachers to stay in their classrooms and at the same time carve out opportunities to inquire and reflect on their own practice. It is unlike university-based research, which occupies an unquestioned position at the center of the institution's mission. Furthermore, the academic research community is organized to provide formal and informal opportunities for response and critique. On the other hand, teacher research struggles on the margins of K–12 schools and programs, and teacher researchers often work outside school systems. The Philadelphia Teachers Learning Cooperative, which has met weekly in private homes for more than a decade to reflect on classroom practices (Philadelphia Teachers' Learning Cooperative, 1984), and the Boston Women's Teachers' Group, which comes together to study the effects of teaching on teachers throughout their professional careers (Boston Women Teachers' Group, 1983), are good examples of self-initiated and sustained teacher inquiry groups.

Cautioning against the problem of simply adding research to teachers' work loads, Myers (1987) has argued persuasively for the institutionalization of teacher research by making inquiry an integral part of the professional lives of teachers. Recently, a few school districts have moved in this direction by establishing new positions that combine teaching and researching responsibilities such as lead teachers, teacher mentors, or peer supervisors. For example, the Pittsburgh public school system has created positions for researchers in residence, who collect and manage data for the school principal and faculty (LeMahieu, 1988), and in the Philadelphia public schools, teacher consultants combine classroom teaching with teacher research through a unique cross-visitation program initiated by teachers in the Philadelphia Writing Project (Fecho, 1987; Lytle & Fecho, 1991). These efforts are part of a trend to differentiate teachers' roles in schools and capitalize on teacher expertise. It is unclear at this time what the impact of innovations like these will be. It would be unfortunate, however, if they inadvertently buttressed the traditional association between gaining increased power and responsibility in the school system and abandoning the classroom.

A variety of arrangements have been proposed to enable teachers to do research. These include reduced loads, released time, paid overtime, and summer seminars or institutes in which teachers can write about and reflect on their teaching practices (Mohr & Maclean, 1987); collaborative networks, study groups, or research teams; opportunities to visit voluntarily the classrooms of teachers in other grade levels, subject areas, schools, and school districts; financial support for their research projects; and a variety of formal and informal channels for the dissemination of teachers' work. It is our contention that the most important factor in determining where and how these arrangements work is whether school systems allow teachers on a voluntary basis to participate in designing and revising these new structures. This will come about if schools and school systems realize that there is a direct connection between supporting the systematic inquiries of teacher researchers and improving the quality of teaching and learning in schools.

In many school systems, however, teachers have not been encouraged to work together on voluntary, self-initiated projects or to speak out with authority about instructional, curricular, and policy issues. When groups of teachers have the opportunity to work together as highly professionalized teacher researchers, they become increasingly articulate about issues of equity, hierarchy, and autonomy and increasingly critical of the technocratic model that dominates much of school practice. This notion of highly professionalized teachers is consonant with Aronowitz and Giroux's (1985) concept of teachers as "transformative intellectuals" who have the potential to resist what Apple (1986) refers to as "deskilling" mandates and to change their own teaching practices. In a recent collection of case studies by teachers of writing, editors Bissex and Bullock (1987) suggest that "by becoming researchers teachers take control over their classrooms and professional lives in ways that confound the traditional definition of teacher and offer proof that education can reform itself from within" (p. xi). In the same vein, they also argue that teacher research is a natural agent of change: "doing classroom research changes teachers and the teaching profession from the inside out, from the bottom up, through changes in teachers themselves. And therein lies the power" (p. 27).

Although we agree with the direction of these claims, we are concerned about school reform efforts that depend primarily on the efforts of teachers without school restructuring. Because many structural features of school systems constrain bottom-up, inside-out reform, it seems unlikely that school systems traditionally organized to facilitate top-down change will readily acknowledge and build on the potential impact of teacher-initiated reforms. Furthermore, as teachers empower themselves by adopting a more public and authoritative stance toward their own practice, they are more likely to create the contexts for their own students to be empowered as active learners. Ironically and indeed unfortunately, many school systems are slow to realize the potential link between teacher research and enhanced student learning.

For teachers to carry out the systematic and self-critical inquiry that teacher research entails, teachers will need to establish networks and create forums so that ongoing collaboration is possible. These networks begin to function as intellectual communities for teachers who are more typically isolated from one another. Teacher research has the potential to play a significant role in the enhanced professionalization of teaching, but it will certainly not be the entire agenda for school reform. As we have shown, complex problems are involved in even calling for teacher research. As Myers (1985) rightly argues, "telling teachers they should do teacher research is . . . an inadequate way to begin" (p. 126). To encourage teacher research, we must first address incentives for teachers, the creation and maintenance of supportive networks, the reform of rigid organizational patterns in schools, and the hierarchical power relationships that characterize most schooling. Likewise, to resolve the problematic relationship between academic research and teacher research, it will be necessary to directly confront controversial issues of voice, power, ownership, status, and role in the broad educational community. We are not arguing that teacher research ought to occupy a privileged position in relation to research on teaching. Rather, we are suggesting that exploration of the issues that divide research on teaching and teacher research may help raise critical questions about the nature of knowledge for teaching and hence enhance research in both communities.

2 | Learning From Teacher Research: A Working Typology

In arguing for the inclusion of teacher research in the knowledge base for teaching, we are not simply equating teacher research with practitioner knowledge or with any kind of writing by a teacher, nor are we attempting to attach to the term "teacher" the higher status term "researcher" in order to alter common perceptions of the profession. Rather, we are proposing that teacher research makes accessible some of the expertise of teachers and provides both university and school communities with unique perspectives on teaching and learning.

In this essay, we propose a working typology for teacher research that includes both empirical and conceptual work: teachers' journals, oral inquiries, classroom studies, and essays. By looking closely at examples of each of these four types, we demonstrate that teacher research takes a variety of forms, each of which provides rich and distinctive perspectives on teaching and learning. In constructing this typology, we are arguing for the importance of a broader notion of teacher research that incorporates some existing teacher writing, prompts wider participation by teachers in classroom inquiry, and generates new knowledge on teaching. Taken seriously, teacher research represents a radical challenge to assumptions about the relationships of theory and practice, school and university partnerships, and school structures and educational reform.

TEACHER RESEARCH: A DEFINITION

We have found it useful to take the following as a working definition for teacher research: systematic, intentional inquiry by teachers about their own school and classroom work. Even though their meanings overlap to a certain extent, it is helpful to begin by clarifying the three terms. By systematic, we refer primarily to ordered ways of gathering and recording information, documenting experiences inside and outside of classrooms, and making some kind of written record. Systematic also refers to ordered ways of recollecting, rethinking, and analyzing classroom events for which there may be only partial or unwritten records. By intentional, we signal that teacher research is an activity that is planned rather than spontaneous, although we do not mean to suggest that important insights about teaching are only generated when planned. Our emphasis on intention is in keeping with Boomer's (1987) argument that "to learn deliberately is to research" (p. 5) and with Britton's (1987) notion that "every lesson should be for the teacher an inquiry, some further discovery, a quiet form of research" (p. 15). By inquiry, we suggest that teacher research stems from or generates questions and reflects teachers' desires to make sense of their experiences—to adapt a learning stance or openness toward classroom life. According to Berthoff (1987), it is not even necessary that teacher research involve new information but rather that it interpret the information one already has—what she calls "REsearching."

In commenting on the nature of knowledge building in the scientific community, Thomas (1974) argues that each little bit of information may not be significant in and of itself but that when connected to many other bits it can achieve a kind of "corporate, collective power that is far greater than any one individual can exert." Thomas continues:

> We like to think of exploring in science as a lonely, meditative business, and so it is, in the first stages, but always, sooner or later, before the enterprise reaches completion, as we explore we call to each other, communicate, publish, send letters to the editor, present papers, [and] cry out [our] finding. (p. 15)

Connecting this concept to our definition, we can see that teacher research, like all forms of research (educational or otherwise), is a fundamentally social and constructive activity. Not only can each separate piece of teacher research inform subsequent activities in the individual teacher's classroom, but also each piece potentially informs and is informed by all teacher research past and present. Although teacher research is not always motivated by a need to generalize beyond the immediate case, it may in fact be relevant for a wide variety of contexts.

Corey (1953), one of the first to use action research in education, emphasized that its major value was in increasing the individual teacher's effectiveness with subsequent classes in similar situations over time rather than in extending generalizations across educational contexts. Schaefer (1967) on the other hand asserted that schools could be organized as centers of inquiry, actively producing knowledge in the field of education. In the 1960s and early 1970s, action research by teachers was typically carried out in collaboration with consultants, partly in response to critique that action research was not scientifically valid. Many of the action research initiatives have aimed both to improve school and classroom practice and to contribute to knowledge about teaching and research itself (Elliott, 1985; Oja & Smulyan, 1989; Tikunoff, Ward, & Griffin, 1979).

Following the earlier work in action research, we take the position that teacher research should be valued not simply as a heuristic for the individual teacher. Rather, if it is to play a role in the formation of the knowledge base for teaching, teacher research must also be cumulative and accessible to different people over time for a variety of purposes. Furthermore, school-based teachers as well as university-based teachers and researchers must develop standards of value and evaluation for teacher research that are appropriate to various segments of the educational community.

TEACHER RESEARCH: A WORKING TYPOLOGY

In its recent iterations, teacher research has been thought of almost exclusively as classroom- or school-based empirical studies that resemble university-based studies in conventions, methods, and forms. Equating teacher research with empirical studies limits in at least two ways what we can learn from teachers about their work. First, teachers inquire about their work in a number of forms other than classroom studies that, we argue, can be appropriately regarded as empirical. Our working typology, which acknowledges a wider range of teachers' empirical research, provides a broader view. It allows us to reclaim and reexamine more of the existing empirical work on teaching conducted by teachers themselves and enables us to make distinctions about a variety of teacher-researcher texts and about the contexts in which they are produced and used. Second, teachers also generate conceptual work about the assumptions and characteristics of teaching, learning, schooling, and research on teaching. Teachers' conceptual work articulates theoretical and philosophical perspectives, making distinctions and connections from the stance of insider and participant. In short, we are arguing that acknowledging both conceptual research and several types of empirical research by teachers makes visible much of the work that already exists and helps to organize the field.

Following the distinction commonly made in the field of education, we group four types of teacher research into two broad categories: empirical and conceptual. Teachers' empirical research, which involves the collection, analysis, and interpretation of data gathered from their own schools and classrooms, includes journals, oral inquiries, and studies. Journals are both published and unpublished. Oral inquiries are usually written records of formalized inquiry procedures and other discussions convened specifically for reflection and questioning. Studies use the documentation and analysis procedures of university-based classroom research. Teachers' conceptual research, which consists of theoretical work or the analysis of ideas, includes teachers' essays on classroom and school life or on the nature of research itself. In essays, teachers draw on examples and insights from empirical and conceptual research, from a wide range of their own and others' teaching and learning experiences, and from published texts, both literary and informational. Figure 2.1 outlines the typology.

In the remainder of this essay, we examine each of the four types as systematic, intentional inquiry, and we demonstrate that each makes a contribution to the knowledge base on teaching, learning, and schooling.

EMPIRICAL RESEARCH

Type 1: Teachers' Journals

Journals are accounts of classroom life in which teachers record observations, analyze their experiences, and reflect on and interpret their practices over time. Journals intermingle description, record keeping, commentary, and analysis. Similar in some ways to ethnographic field notes, journals capture the immediacy of teaching: teachers' evolving perceptions of what is happening with the students in their classrooms and what this means for their continued practice. Furthermore, because journals stand as a written record of practice, they provide teachers with a way to revisit, analyze, and evaluate their experiences over time and in relation to broader frames of reference. And they provide access to the ways that teachers' interpretive perspectives are constructed and reconstructed using data from their classrooms.

During the 1980–1981 school year, Lynne Strieb, then a first-grade teacher with 13 years of experience, began keeping a narrative journal to supplement her daily notes and records about individual children. Published by the Center for Teaching and Learning at the University of North Dakota, *A (Philadelphia) Teacher's Journal* (1985) contains selections from that narrative. Working at a large Philadelphia public elementary school, Strieb had a class of 33 children: 22 black, 9 white, and 2 who spoke only Spanish when the year began. One way to read and understand Strieb's journal is as a teacher's attempt to make sense of her daily work life as a teacher. In it she addresses how she connects with her students, how students learn to make sense of the world around them, and how she uses writing to perceive and understand her evolution as a teacher. In Strieb's (1985) words:

> The more I wrote, the more I observed in my classroom and the more I wanted to write. As I reread my journal I got more ideas for teaching. I expanded the journal to include other aspects of teaching—anecdotes, observations of children and their involvement in activities, interactions with parents both in and out of school, my

Figure 2.1. Teacher Research: An Analytic Framework

TEACHER RESEARCH:

Systematic and intentional inquiry about teaching,
learning, and schooling carried out by teachers in
their own school and classroom settings

Empirical Research	**Conceptual Research**
(collection, analysis, and interpretation of data)	(theoretical/philosophical work or the analysis of ideas)

Type 1: Journals

Teachers' accounts of classroom life over time
• records of observations
• analyses of experiences
• reflections & interpretations of practices

Type 2: Oral Inquiries

Teachers' oral examinations of classroom/school issues, contexts, texts, and experiences
• collaborative analyses and interpretations
• explorations of relationships between cases and theories

Type 3: Classroom/School Studies

Teachers' explorations of practice-based issues using data based on observation, interview, and document collection
• stems from, or generates, questions
• individual or collaborative work

Type 4: Essays

Teachers' interpretations of the assumptions and characteristics of classroom and school life and/or research itself
• recollections and reflections on students' and teachers' work in classrooms and/or on published texts (including curricula, empirical and conceptual research, and literature)
• selection of specific examples that warrant the general assertions

---

plans, descriptions of the pressures on public school teachers. I also wrote about my continuing education through my own reflections and the questions that emerged, through books, and through association with colleagues in the Philadelphia Teachers Learning Cooperative, and at the Prospect Summer Institutes. (p. 3)

In Strieb's journal (1985), we find records of lessons, conversations, children's questions, and detailed descriptions of specific interactions with particular children. In some entries, Strieb provides a narrative account of the ongoing daily stream of classroom events. In others, she consciously breaks that frame to review and synthesize her efforts in a particular area. For example, when Strieb had a non-English-speaking child enter her classroom in October of the school year, she responded intuitively to the situation. Later she intentionally made visible her intuitive actions by reviewing in her journal all the things she had done to help the child:

> [Use a] soothing voice, hold his hand, chant to calm him. Assign a child to help, one who speaks the same language if possible. Use the child's language together with English if possible. Have lots of interesting objects in the room to provide common experiences which bring all the children together. Help him to see some familiar faces in an unfamiliar place at lunch by pointing to his sisters, introducing him to the lunch aide, assigning someone to help him, and staying with him for a while. (p. 14)

The journal functioned here as a way for Strieb to step back from the daily stream, take stock of what was happening, and assess the ways that the children responded. Repeatedly, Strieb used her journal to search for meaning: the patterns or structures that organized her own teaching and that characterized the children's efforts to learn and cope with the classroom environment.

As inquiry, Strieb's (1985) journal contains many implicit and some explicit questions: How can I help children learn English? How can I make children feel comfortable in my class? How can I help this class become a community? What counts as play, what counts as work, and how do children figure out the differences in my classroom? What do I do about issues of race and gender in my classroom? As a teacher, what is my role in helping children to develop attitudes about diversity? What does it mean to learn to read in this class, and how do children learn to do it? What roles do they play in each other's learning? When should I go with a child's ideas, when should I intervene? How can I connect with children's emotions? Strieb used her journal to articulate and clarify her own questions and to search for evidence to address them.

The following excerpt, one of many about children's early reading experiences, reveals both Strieb's (1985) questions about how children learn to read and some of the frameworks she used to interpret and assess their progress as readers:

> January 28. My sustained Reading Time is not silent because the children help each other so much when they read together. I would like to have a real Sustained Silent Reading Time (SSR), but it would have to be separate from this. I'm not willing to take away the help that the children give one another as beginning readers. So many have begun by reading with friends: Benjamin helped Paul, Maria helped Anita, Bethann helped Atiya, Leonard helped Henry, Jimmy helped William, William helped Ali.

Whenever a kid is on the brink of reading or is reading slowly, I suggest he or she read with someone. That usually pulls the child into reading. With my limited time (a conference with each child every other week), I need the kids to teach each other. I've also noticed that some kids are more relaxed with friends than with me. Still, I'd also like an SSR period. . . . (p. 39)

About 6 weeks later, she continued to ask questions about how the children in her classroom were learning to read:

March 6. Sustained reading must be getting to me. I see lots of kids reading the Bank Street Primer *Around the City*. They don't know all the words, but they usually read together and they figure them out, or at least get the meaning of the stories. But when they are finished with that book, they want to go on to the next one, and it's really too hard. Many of the kids can't get meaning from that. But no matter how I try to suggest that they try other books at about primer level (and I have many), they want to stick with the "series." They've seen other kids follow the progression, and they want to do the same. Should I let them do it and struggle? (p. 57)

Strieb's journal reveals her sense of the push and pull of independent and collaborative learning—of the children's ability to scaffold each other's reading and provide emotional support for one another in a way that differed from what she, as teacher, could offer. In the March 6 entry, Strieb compared her own view of progress in reading with that of the children: She understood the need for the children's emerging skills to gel, but to the children, progress in reading was signified by movement from one level of text to the next. Strieb's interpretation of these classroom events center around her struggle to make sense of the discrepancy between what she thought might be most appropriate for children's learning and their own social and intellectual agendas. Her interpretation alerts us to the complexity of conflicting notions of "progress" in learning to read and reminds us that the knowledge that children bring to the classroom includes expectations about traditional symbols of school success. Her journal provides insider information about teachers' dilemmas and their consequences for classroom learning.

Another first-grade teacher, a teacher educator, a language and learning researcher, and Lynne Strieb herself obviously learn different "lessons" from these journal entries. There are rich data here about many of the central issues of schooling: how a classroom becomes a community; how a teacher uses children's questions to build, plan, and interweave class discussions; how a teacher connects with the interests and needs of individual children; and how a teacher's routines express what counts most to her in her unique context. Strieb's journal also reveals the inherent uncertainty and tentativeness of teaching. The restless questioning that punctuates her journal contrasts rather dramatically with the certainty of the instructional principles asserted by the literature in effective teaching.

Strieb's account helps to make clear that teachers' journals are more than anecdotal records or loose chronological accounts of particular classroom activities. As systematic intentional inquiry, journals provide windows on what goes on in school through teachers' eyes and in teachers' voices and on some of the ways that teachers use writing to shape and inform their work lives. Other journals ask other questions and are guided by different interpretive frames. Palonsky's (1986) *900 Shows a Year: A Look at Teaching From the Teacher's Side of the Desk* focuses on structural constraints, issues of power and authority, and teacher-student relationships in suburban high school, while Natkins' (1986) *Our Last Term: A Teacher's Diary* emphasizes the dilemmas of urban high school teaching. Teachers' journals provide a unique blend of observation and analysis in which classroom vignettes are juxtaposed with more general assertions and interpretations.

Type 2: Oral Inquiry Processes

Oral inquiry processes are procedures in which two or more teachers jointly research their experiences by examining particular issues, educational concepts, texts (including students' work), and other data about students. These processes are unique in our typology of teacher research in that they are by definition collaborative and oral. During oral inquiry, teachers build on one another's insights to analyze and interpret classroom data and their experiences in the school as a workplace. We wish to emphasize that oral inquiry is not synonymous with teacher talk, just as teacher research is not synonymous with teacher writing. Rather, oral inquiry processes often follow specific theoretically grounded procedures and routines, require careful preparation and collection of data, and rely on careful documentation that enables teachers to revisit and reexamine their joint analyses. For teachers, oral inquiries provide access to a variety of perspectives for problem posing and solving. They also reveal the ways in which teachers relate particular cases to theories of practice.

The reflective-descriptive processes developed by Patricia Carini and her colleagues at the Prospect Center and School in Bennington, Vermont, provide a good example of formalized teacher inquiry procedures that are documented through thorough note taking. Carini and the many teachers with whom she has worked over the years do not necessarily refer to these processes as teacher research, nor are the records of their inquiries typically available to an audience beyond the participants. However, in constructing a working typology of teacher research, we feel it is important to include oral inquiry processes even though they are the least visible of the types of teacher research that are currently occurring.

Since the school was founded in 1965, an important dimension of Carini's (1986) work has been the development of research and evaluation methods, called documentary processes, which promote understanding of children's learning and both inform and are informed by teaching practices. Carini's introduction to the processes makes the point that oral inquiry is theory based as well as grounded theory:

> The Documentary Processes depend on immersion in the focus of interest—a child, a drawing, a setting—and they make available a mode of inquiry with which one can describe and explore a complex human occasion, such as a school, or a child's expressiveness, without interference or manipulation. The child, or the event, is studied "as is," with respect for the integrity and privacy of the person. Regular recording of observations and collecting of children's work gather and preserve events at the Prospect School. The Documentary Processes are ways to re-enter those events in order to grasp, in concentrated form, what occurred at disparate points in time. (p. ii)

Three major processes structure the oral interactions of groups of practitioners who convene specifically for the purpose of exploring teachers' and children's learning: the reflective conversation, the description of children's work, and staff review of a child.

In the reflective conversation, the goal is to explore from teachers' perspectives the various "meanings, images, and experiences" (Carini, 1986, p. 1) embodied in words that are central to understanding teaching and learning. For example, a group might participate in a reflective conversation on "retention," "composition," "basal," or "community." The outcome of the process for the group is a richer understanding of the words and enhanced respect and appreciation for the ways that others' contributions build new understandings; the outcome for the individual is more divergent thinking that leads to more "refined and nuanced observations" (p. 2).

In the description of children's work (Carini, 1986), participants concentrate on children's drawings, writings, or constructions to make accessible both the inherent structures and meanings of the work and the perspective of the child. The inquiry process begins with impressionistic responses to a child's work that is read aloud or viewed. After the chair has noted and restated connections among participants' impressions, the group begins several individual-by-individual rounds of description, moving from surface details to the integrative elements of style, tone, rhythm, and form. The process very intentionally respects careful description and guards against premature interpretation.

Staff review of a child entails the use of multiple perspectives to explore a question posed by the teacher about a particular child. The process is extremely systematic. It specifies not only the categories according to which a child is described but also the roles taken by participants and the steps used as the procedure unfolds (see Kanevsky, Chapter 7). The data include close observations and rich examples organized around six categories that describe children in school. Although each staff review focuses on a single child, each teacher participant draws from the single case some specific teaching strategies that may apply to other situations as well as generalizations about language, literacy development, and other overarching concerns. Over time, teachers become more acute observers of children in their own classrooms, and they learn how to learn from the children whom they teach.

As examples of systematic intentional inquiry, Prospect's documentary processes are based on a phenomenological view of knowledge and learning. By participating in these experiences, teachers grapple with children's meanings as expressed in their projects and with the varied meanings that their colleagues find in these. Preparing for documentary processes often entails selection and collection of students' work and classroom observations. These serve as the data for the group's analyses. Furthermore, an important part of the procedure is that a recorder keeps almost verbatim notes that are used to create periodic summaries and statements of the organizing concepts perceived in the work at hand. The result is an unusually rich and complex rendering of patterns that invites rather than forecloses further interpretations.

Like teachers' journals and essays, oral inquiry processes such as these represent teachers' self-conscious and often self-critical attempts to make sense of their daily work by talking about it in planned ways. The processes developed by Carini and her colleagues are not the only examples of this type of teacher research, although they may be the most formalized and best documented. In addition, teacher seminars such as those conducted by Bill Hull (1978) or Margaret Yonemura (1982) and teacher groups like the Philadelphia Teachers Learning Cooperative (1984) and the Boston Women's Teachers' Group (1983) regularly convene to explore issues and practices across contexts by examining particular cases. Oral inquiry processes are unlike teacher's journals and essays, which may be completed by a teacher-researcher writing alone. The primary outcomes of oral inquiries are the conjoined understandings of the participants.

When documentary records are preserved, teachers can return to the texts of their deliberations to REsearch their own knowledge and insights, which acquire additional significance over time as teachers confront new situations in their own classrooms and schools. Like the archive of children's work preserved at the Prospect Center, records of teachers' oral inquiry processes have the potential to be of great value for the broader community of teachers, teacher educators, and university researchers. Buchanan (1988b) and a group of Philadelphia teachers are currently working toward this end by proposing the development of an urban archive of teachers' writing and oral inquiry as well as the children's work from which it stems. Buchanan makes an eloquent case for the need for an archive:

> Every day teachers' observations and reflections on the teaching process, on their students, and on educational issues are irretrievably lost because there is no provision for preserving them. Such materials are essential for shaping and recording the evolution of the profession. Similarly the day-to-day writing, art work and number work of students is rarely saved in a systematic manner. What children don't take home is often thrown away. Other than the presentation of test scores, there are few large-scale efforts to demonstrate what and how children are learning in

school. The Archive will serve as a rich resource for teachers, researchers and other professionals who are interested in the long view of what is happening to children in our society. (pp. 1–2)

Buchanan's (1988b) proposal emanates from a decade of work with the Philadelphia Teachers Learning Cooperative and association with the Prospect Center and from her frustration about the relationship between academic research and teacher knowledge. The first purpose of an archive is to provide a way to make teachers' work in classrooms visible to other teachers. However, as she points out, the systematic collection of teacher's inquiries and children's work will also "give scholars an unobtrusive, 'inside view' of classrooms [that] is currently not available" (pp. 1–2) and that is, we believe, sorely needed.

Type 3: Classroom Studies

In our own typology, classroom studies encompass most of what others currently term teacher research. Several volumes that describe this work have recently been published. In *Reclaiming the Classroom: Teacher Research As an Agency for Change,* Goswami and Stillman (1987) trace the roots of this concept among British and American educators who have called for teacher inquiry into practice, provide guidance in planning classroom research, and offer as examples the work of Bread Loaf's teacher-researchers. They characterize teacher research as an activity in which teachers and their students:

> . . . formulate questions about language and learning, design and carry out inquiries, reflect on what they have learned, and tell others about it. In other words, teachers and students are conducting inquiries that are necessary to provide contexts for, and help us make sense (and reject or use), the findings of quantitative, experimental projects. (preface)

Two other volumes have recently been authored by leaders of sites of the National Writing Project: Mohr and Maclean's (1987) *Working Together: A Guide for Teacher Researchers* and Myers' (1985) *The Teacher Researcher: How to Study Writing in the Classroom.* Mohr and Maclean show how a teacher-researcher group works together to design and conduct classroom studies and provide examples of various forms of the reports of teacher research. Myers references his suggestions about teacher research to the assessment of writing in order to promote teacher research more generally. Bissex and Bullock (1987), faculty members of the writing programs at Northeastern University, compiled *Seeing for Ourselves: Case Study Research by Teachers of Writing* from work by graduate students in the English department and teachers who attended a writing institute. In addition to the studies, Bissex and Bullock include roundtable discussions of the value of these studies for teachers.

Our definition of classroom studies is essentially the same as the definitions common to these volumes. However, we see classroom studies as one among at least four types of teacher inquiry that ought to be termed teacher research. Within the teaching and university research communities, there seems to us to be a great deal of ambivalence about the extent to which teacher studies resemble or ought to resemble studies conducted by university researchers. As we pointed out in Chapter 1, there are conflicting conceptions in these communities about methodological rigor, theory, documentation, or value to the teaching community itself. It is our position that these questions will need to be resolved in two contexts. The first is the teaching community itself, where teachers will gradually develop a set of criteria or standards to evaluate the usefulness of teacher research for teachers individually or collectively. Second, if and when the university community recognizes the need for an expanded knowledge base, it will need to consider the ways that teacher research contributes to and perhaps alters what we know about teaching, learning, and schooling.

"Relearning to Teach: Peer Observation as a Means of Professional Development for Teachers" is a college classroom study of freshman writing courses conducted by Elizabeth Rorschach and Robert Whitney (1986), then doctoral candidates in English Education at New York University. We use an example from a postsecondary teaching situation to emphasize that teacher research is not limited to teachers who work in K–12 schools but is instead an activity that is relevant to all teachers. Rorschach and Whitney shared what they believed were fundamentally similar goals for their writing courses. For 15 weeks, they attended each other's twice-weekly classes, taking the role of students by participating in discussions, drafting assignments, and sharing writing with other students. They met weekly to share observations, focusing initially on what they liked about each other's teaching and carefully moving toward comparison of what was happening in the two classes. Rorschach and Whitney point out that "this duality of viewpoints by the same observers reversing roles in parallel cultures . . . led [them] to the most important new learnings and insights" (p. 161). Eventually, Rorschach and Whitney tape-recorded discussions in each other's classes, contrasted lesson plans and assignments, and tried out new classroom strategies as they began to theorize about what might be happening in the two classrooms. Both teachers better understood their classrooms as a result of their research; Whitney dramatically changed the culture of his classroom by altering some of his strategies.

The value of doing collaborative classroom study for the teachers themselves is eloquently expressed by the authors:

> We set out to learn some things which would be useful in our own teaching, and we felt that we succeeded. For that, casual and exploratory methodology was much more appropriate, perhaps even necessary. Indeed, a great deal of what we learned is not in this paper, nor even as yet consciously conceptualized in our own minds—it exists in the realm of what Michael Polanyi calls "tacit knowledge" and informs our decisions in the classroom without our even being aware of what it is.

One of the richest aspects of this project was the direct experience of another teacher's classroom over a period of time, and a chance to think and talk about that experience with another teacher who was present. This is holistic learning of a kind that perhaps can never be understood in the abstract. Though we do not now consider ourselves ethnographers . . . we do understand something of the lure of that discipline, the power of the direct experience of another culture with the goal of understanding its workings. (p. 171)

Classroom studies like that of Rorschach and Whitney exemplify the potential of teacher research to reform classroom practice by prompting powerful intellectual critique of assumptions, goals, and strategies. Their work further demonstrates the recursiveness of the classroom study process, wherein questions are continuously reformulated, methods are revised, and analysis is ongoing.

The value of teachers' classroom studies like that of Rorschach and Whitney is not necessarily self-evident to the academic research community. In this case, the authors address several significant issues that academics are also researching, among them discrepancies between the intended and the enacted curriculum; authority, power, and autonomy in writing classrooms; and the culture of the classroom as a social construction of students and teachers. Rorschach and Whitney's evolving questions suggest avenues of inquiry about these issues that the university community may have not considered or found important. Finally, collaborative studies like this provide, as Rorschach and Whitney (1986) point out, a powerful "means of professional development for teachers" as well as "a method of faculty development for institutions which train teachers or want to support the improvement of teaching" (p. 170).

CONCEPTUAL RESEARCH

Type 4: Teachers' Essays

In conceptual research, teachers recollect and reflect on their experiences to construct an argument about teaching, learning, and schooling. Drawing on students' work and classroom observations, for which there may or may not be complete written records, teachers write essays to convince others about particular ways to teach and understand the processes of teaching and learning. They also theorize about children's learning and development, the school as workplace, professional growth across contexts, and sources of knowledge for teaching. Unlike journals and oral inquiries, which are initially intended only for the participating teachers themselves, essays select examples that provide for a more public audience a kind of "evidentiary warrant" for the general assertions that are made (Erickson, 1986).

We include in the category of conceptual research some full-length essays such as Dennison's *The Lives of Children* (1970), Kohl's *36 Children* (1967),

Ashton-Warner's *Teacher* (1963), Wigginton's *Sometimes a Shining Moment: The Foxfire Experience* (1985) and Paley's *White Teacher* (1979) and *Wally's Stories* (1981). Briefer essays are regularly published in academic or professional journals such as *Harvard Educational Review, Language Arts, English Journal,* and *Educational Leadership;* in national publications of teacher or school organizations such as the National Education Association (NEA), the American Federation of Teachers (AFT), or the National Association of Independent Schools; in occasional papers and newsletters such as the *National Writing Project's Quarterly;* and in school bulletins such as *Studies in Education,* produced by the faculty at Germantown Friends School in Philadelphia.

Despite these many forums, teachers' conceptual research is not generally counted as part of the formal knowledge base about teaching, perhaps because it is often personal, retrospective, and based on the "narrow" perspective of a single teacher. Rather than disqualifying this work from the knowledge base, however, these characteristics seem to us to be part of what recommends it. All of it is systematic intentional inquiry. It draws on the data of teachers' experiences and reflections, often over long periods of time. To explore teachers' questions, conceptual research selects and analyzes significant events and features from the ongoing stream of classroom and school life. It locates a single teacher's experience in relationship to the teacher's own practices, to what he or she knows of the practices of other teachers, and sometimes to the conclusions of university-based research. By selecting particular questions or problems to write about, teachers reveal in their essays what matters from their perspectives. Unfortunately, teachers' essays infrequently contain citations to the work of other teachers, partly because much of this work is published only locally and there is little exchange among the diverse communities that read this literature.

In conceptual research, teachers connect practice to overarching concepts and show us how broad theoretical frameworks apply to particular contexts. By analyzing the patterns and discrepancies that occur, teachers use their own interpretive frameworks as practitioners to provide a truly emic view that is different from that of an outside observer, even if that observer assumes an anthropological stance and spends considerable time in the classroom. Teachers' essays attempt to answer questions through systematic investigation and reflection on experience.

Eliot Wigginton's (1985) monograph on 20 years of high school English teaching serves as a highly visible example of an extended essay written from a teacher's point of view. *Sometimes a Shining Moment: The Foxfire Experience* is an essay in three parts: a narrative analysis of the Foxfire story from its inception as a high school English class writing activity; an exposition of the principles distilled out of the 20-year experience; and a description of a sample grammar/composition course that demonstrates the philosophy explained in the previous section and includes suggestions for bringing other courses in line with this philosophy (p. xii).

As Wigginton (1985) points out, the book attempts to answer the broad set of questions that he encountered in talking about his work and to encourage other teachers to continue asking questions of themselves, their students, and others: "For I have found that it is the constant, unrelenting examination and revision of approach—not a package of answers to packaged questions—that makes the better teachers among us the best" (pp. 37–41). To tell the story of Foxfire, Wigginton draws heavily on his own journals, letters, in-school memos and directives, passages from students' writing, and the writing assignments he set for himself.

Like other teacher researchers, Wigginton (1985) comments in his essay on the fact that for him, writing functioned as a primary way to make meaning of his daily teaching life. For example, Wigginton recounts that he was once disappointed and chagrined when he asked his students to recall positive and negative school experiences. When they could recall very few positive experiences to share, Wigginton himself tried the same writing assignment. He discovered that his own memorable experiences were few but could be grouped into several broad categories:

> Times when there were visitors to our class from the world outside the classroom . . . times when as students we left the classroom on assignments or field-trips . . . times when things we did as students had an audience beyond the teacher . . . times where we, as students, were given responsibility of an adult nature, and were trusted to fulfill it . . . times when we as students took on major independent research projects that went far beyond simply copying something out of an encyclopedia, or involved ourselves in periods of intense personal creativity and action. (p. 308)

This written analysis allowed him to compare what stood out for him during 13 years of school and the opportunities he was offering his own students. Through this process, he realized there was a great deal he wanted to change about his teaching.

Reflections like these reveal Wigginton's intense, continuous, and systematic interrogation of his personal experience as both teacher and student. These processes of selection, organization, and interpretation are essential to REsearching one's own experience through conceptual research. In this case, writing the Foxfire monograph required Wigginton to add another layer to his teaching, which was already a many-layered and reflexive research process. In his classes, Wigginton's students used writing to explore their roots and to form a community. Wigginton studied their writing to examine the ways in which they were developing as writers and learners, and he wrote constantly and to a wide variety of audiences, including the school principal, his colleagues inside and outside the school, community people, and granting institutions. He wrote as a way to make things happen, to make sense of what was happening, and, although perhaps without a clear end product in mind at first, to document the entire experience for a wider audience.

Sometimes a Shining Moment: The Foxfire Experience contains many explicit and implicit questions. All of these seem to be subsumed by the search to understand how teachers can make schools work for adolescents. Among his questions are: How can teachers get students to come together for a "common cause"? How can teachers integrate innovative projects into the normal curriculum? How do schools relate to communities? What is power in education? Who has it and who doesn't? What is the extent of the teacher's power? How can teachers help adolescents to understand the problems of the world outside the school? How can teachers help students to move beyond themselves and their new understandings into a caring and active relationship with others? What are the purposes of public high schools? How can teachers find compelling activities that serve all the goals of education simultaneously? Structured by Wigginton's questions, the essay moves from a primary focus on students to concerns about teaching and the assumptions of teachers in general and then to an exploration of curriculum and schooling. At least two themes function as interpretive frames throughout the book: the discontinuities and connections between life inside and outside of school and the forces that constrain and support the integration of adolescents' lives and the school curriculum.

The centerpiece of *Sometimes a Shining Moment* is a long chapter that Wigginton calls "Some Overarching Truths." In this chapter, he proposes a number of characteristics common to effective teaching that he has generalized from 20 years of experience. The evidence for each proposition is Wigginton's skillful synthesis of events and interactions that occurred within his own classroom and school as well as his reading of educational philosophers and theorists. The validity of Wigginton's generalizations is shown by the extent to which they resonate with the experiences of other teachers, his primary audience for this analysis. As Fenstermacher (1986) reminds us, only some educational research improves educational practice. This happens, he suggests, "if [the research] bears fruitfully on the premises of practical arguments in the minds of teachers." Wigginton's compelling essay, richly textured with narrative analysis, theory, and speculation, has unusual potential to inform the "practical arguments" that teachers use to understand, articulate, and ultimately improve their own practices.

Sometimes inquiry itself becomes the subject of teachers' conceptual research. For example, in two recent essays, Hahn (1991a, 1991b) explores teacher research as a catalyst for teacher change and the problems and possibilities of institutionalizing teacher research. Using as cases the experiences of teacher-research groups in a variety of school settings, Hahn (1991b) argues that local knowledge is critical. For teacher research to be institutionalized within diverse contexts, programs need site-specific forms of support from leaders, group membership, and the institution itself. In his essay on teacher change, Hahn (1991a) discusses teacher research in relation to constructivism:

> When we begin to look at teachers as active learners, constructing and reconstructing their ideas about students, classrooms, learning and teaching, as well as

learning about the various aspects of the subjects they teach, we can see that class-room research is a natural activity for teachers to pursue, not an additional burden to be added to an overwhelming workload. In fact, teacher research can become the one way teachers make sense of their often chaotic lives as teachers. Because teacher research is a constructivist activity, it is a good model for real learning in the context of the classroom. It is not something that is learned elsewhere that then needs to be applied to the classroom. The teacher's knowledge is conceived in the classroom and it lives in the classroom. (p. 2)

Drawing on the experiences of individual teacher researchers and the groups with which they worked, Hahn (1991b) describes in some detail the evolution of teachers' questions as they document classroom interactions, share their observations with colleagues over time, and develop plans to reconstruct curriculum and instruction in their own settings. Hahn distinguishes this form of professional development from traditional models:

If one of the goals of staff development is to "get everyone to do the same thing," then teacher research would be a bad model to follow. If, however, the goal is to get each teacher to look more critically at teaching and learning (rather than acting as thoughtless drones who "implement the program"), then enabling teachers to become reflective practitioners could be one of the best forms of staff development. (p. 1)

Taking the research of teachers as his subject, Hahn's work links rich illustrations to broader themes in teaching and learning to teach. Teachers' conceptual research on inquiry leads to the development of conceptual frameworks for the activities of teacher research from teachers' own perspectives. These frameworks are different from those of university-based teacher educators and researchers.

Often, teacher essays explicitly consider the relationships of theory and practice and the ways that these reciprocally influence one another. Ashton-Warner's (1963) full-length essay, *Teacher*, for example, focuses on her construction of a theory of child development grounded in her observations and experimentation with children in a Maori village school. Ashton-Warner proposes a child-centered view of the acquisition of literacy by language-minority children that foregrounds the relationships between cultural background and experience and the materials and processes for literacy instruction. Ashton-Warner's work and the work of other teacher researchers suggest that research by teachers about their own practices can be theoretical, abstract, and generalizable.

The value of teachers' conceptual research for the authors themselves and for the broader community of teachers is obvious. However, their value for the university-based research community is not quite so clear. Wigginton and Ashton-Warner are well-known writers whose work has been acknowledged in many circles as ground breaking and who are frequently cited. This does not mean, however, that their work fits within the accepted paradigms for research on teaching nor that it is part of the official knowledge base. Shulman (1986a) forcefully makes this point when he notes in his discussion of Dunkin and Biddle's landmark study of teaching that Philip Jackson's *Life in Classrooms* is omitted from their review of research even though it is one of the references most often cited in their conceptual analysis of teaching. Shulman explains its absence by pointing out that members of a particular community of researchers generally acknowledge and build on the work of those whom they perceive as peers in their field. Teachers' research clearly contributes to the understanding of other teachers. However, it can also contribute to university research efforts, a fact that is currently ignored and sometimes invisible.

Teachers' conceptual work uses vivid, concrete experiences to build an argument about teaching and learning. This is possible because of teachers' long-term, intimate knowledge of teaching and the rich perspectives they bring to observing and understanding students' learning. With opportunities to observe learners over time and in a variety of academic and social situations, teachers often bring to their analyses many years of knowledge about the culture of the community, school, and classroom. The essay form, which builds on the dialectic between argument and evidence, provides a unique context for teacher research.

CONCLUSION

Teacher research addresses a wide range of subjects and takes a variety of forms. We imagine that there are many useful ways to categorize the work, and we do not regard the typology proposed here as an exhaustive or definitive one. However, as we have shown, when the notion of teacher research is broadened to include more of the writing of teachers, it is possible to see the range and variation of questions, types of evidence, modes of analysis, interpretive frameworks, and arguments for implications in classroom work. As more teachers become researchers in their schools and classrooms, they explore innovative forms and formats for documenting classroom activities, interrogating conventional assumptions about the research itself, and questioning relationships between researchers and the researched. These conversations raise many questions about teacher research as a way of knowing: what can be known about teaching, who can know it, how it can be known, and how that knowledge can be used. We explore these questions in Chapter 3.

3

Teacher Research: A Way of Knowing

In 1989, the American Association of Colleges for Teacher Education (AACTE) released the charter edition of a volume intended to define the knowledge that beginning teachers should have and to close the gap between what they refer to as the state of the art and the state of practice in teaching. Entitled *Knowledge Base for the Beginning Teacher* (Reynolds, 1989), the volume begins with a statement of assumptions, each of which implicitly takes a position on ways of knowing about teaching:

1. [W]hat is known and worth knowing about teaching . . . should be related to the practical knowledge possessed by teachers of how and when to act in actual teaching situations.
2. [K]nowledge about teaching will never be absolute or complete. . . . [T]eachers should be prepared for a career in which they are continuously involved . . . in making adaptations in their work in accord with the changing knowledge base and their own teaching situations.
3. [T]he knowledge base for teaching takes a variety of forms and is drawn from many disciplines and other sources, including research, inventions, tested practice (maxims), and value principles held by the community. . . . [T]his knowledge base, when mastered, will provide teachers with a unique fund of knowledge. . . .
4. [T]eaching is a profession. Knowledgeable teachers are not technicians, but professionals, worthy and able to make reflective decisions or judgments and plans based on principled knowledge that is adapted to the particulars of their teaching situations, their students, their unique experiences, and their own special insights, self knowledge, values, and commitments. They have a body of understandings, knowledge, skills, and dispositions: a set of constructs that can be invoked for the explanation of cognitive phenomena . . . Professional judgment is required. Knowledge . . . enlarges the range and quality of discretionary judgments made by professional teachers in the performance of their complex work.

5. [T]here is no single taxonomy or correct way of structuring the knowledge base for teaching . . . the particular structure [of the volume] probably will be revised in the future on the basis of added knowledge and improved professional insights. . . .
6. Although [the volume] would provide a means for presenting a number of seemingly discrete areas of knowledge, the importance of the volume to teachers [is] the understanding of how professional knowledge is organized, validated, and used. (p. x)

By synthesizing and making accessible a wide range of important ideas about teaching, learning, and schooling, the volume provides a valuable resource for teacher education not only at the preservice level but across the developmental continuum. As Griffin (1989) emphasizes in the closing chapter, the contributors to the volume emphasize that knowledge for teaching is mutable and that theories, research, and practical wisdom all play influential roles in school programs.

Although we do not wish to take issue with the ideas presented in the individual chapters of this volume, we think it is important to question some of the assumptions about knowledge and teachers' roles in the creation and use of knowledge that frame the volume as a whole. Since John Dewey's writings at the beginning of this century, scholars and researchers have devoted considerable attention to understanding the relationships of knowledge and teaching. From various disciplinary perspectives and research paradigms, they have asked what it means to know about teaching: what can be known, how it can be known, who has the authority to know, and how knowledge can or should be used for theoretical and practical purposes. What the editors of the AACTE volume seem to be saying is that the knowledge that makes teaching a profession comes from authorities outside of the profession itself. What makes teachers professional is using this knowledge base in their practice. In this epistemology, teachers are knowledgeable in that they have "insights" as well as "knowledge, skills, and dispositions," which they call on to explain phenomena and to make judgments about practice, but they do not participate in the generation of Knowledge (with a capital K) or official, "principled," "discipline"-based knowledge.

We are not suggesting here that the knowledge contained in this volume or in other similar publications is of no use to teachers. To the contrary, we agree that a rich body of information that ought to inform the practice of teaching has been generated by university researchers and that making that knowledge accessible for teachers' critical appraisal and adaptation is an essential endeavor. The epistemology embodied in these assumptions, however, is exclusionary and disenfranchising. It stipulates that knowing the knowledge base for teaching—what university researchers have discovered—is the privileged way to know about teaching. Knowing the knowledge base is, as the preface to the volume suggests, what "distinguishes more productive teachers from less productive ones" (p. ix).

In this essay, we argue that we need to develop a different theory of knowledge for teaching, a different epistemology that regards inquiry by teachers themselves as a distinctive and important way of knowing about teaching. From this perspective, fundamental questions about knowing, knowers, and what can be known would have different answers. Teachers would be among those who have the authority to know—that is, to construct Knowledge (with a capital K) about teaching, learning, and schooling. And what is worth knowing about teaching would include teachers' "ways of knowing" (Belenky, Clinchy, Goldberger, & Tarule, 1986) or what teachers, who are researchers in their own classrooms, can know through systematic subjectivity.

Teacher researchers are uniquely positioned to provide a truly emic, or insider's, perspective that makes visible the ways that students and teachers together construct knowledge and curriculum. When teachers do research, they draw on interpretive frameworks built from their histories and intellectual interests, and because the research process is embedded in practice, the relationship between knower and known is significantly altered. This obviates the need to "translate findings" in the conventional sense and moves teacher research toward praxis, or critical reflection on practice (Lather, 1986). Furthermore, because teacher researchers often inquire with their students, students themselves are also empowered as knowers. In this different epistemology, teacher research, currently marginalized in the field, would contribute to a fundamental reconceptualization of the notion of knowledge for teaching. Through inquiry, teachers would play a role in reinventing the conventions of interpretive social science, just as feminist researchers and critical ethnographers have done by making problematic the relationships of researcher and researched, knowledge and authority, and subject and object (Crawford & Marecek, 1989; Noffke, 1990).

Our aim in this essay is to explore the contribution of teacher inquiry to a new theory of knowledge for teaching. This paper is not an analysis of the forms and domains of teachers' knowledge, however, although this area has yielded rich discussions in the field (Fenstermacher, 1986; Schön, 1983; Shulman, 1986b), nor is it merely a rhetorical argument in favor of teacher research as part of a growing popular movement. Our question here is not, Is teacher research research? or even, What kind of research is teacher research? Rather, it is our intention to contribute to the conversation about teaching and knowledge by arguing that research by teachers is a significant way of knowing about teaching. As Figure 3.1 indicates, we examine teacher research as a way of generating both local knowledge and public knowledge about teaching, learning, and schooling—that is, knowledge developed and useful to teachers themselves and their immediate communities as well as knowledge useful to the larger school and university communities. We show that inquiry by individual teachers and communities of teacher researchers realigns their relationships to knowledge and to the brokers of knowledge and also necessitates a redefinition of the notion of a knowledge base for teaching.

Figure 3.1. Teacher Research and Knowledge Generation

LOCAL KNOWLEDGE		PUBLIC KNOWLEDGE

Through inquiry, teacher researchers generate knowledge:

for their own practice	*for the immediate community of teachers*	*for the larger community of educators*
How teachers and their students co-construct teaching and learning in their particular classrooms	A contextualized knowledge based on teaching and learning within a specific community	New knowledge in many of the domains of research on teaching and learning
<ul><li>how knowledge functions</li><li>interactions of teachers and students</li><li>how the curriculum is enacted</li><li>how students learn</li></ul>	<ul><li>how teachers and students co-construct teaching and learning across classrooms and contexts</li></ul>	<ul><li>case studies of students, classrooms, and schools</li><li>how curricula and practice are constructed, enacted, and altered</li><li>relationships of classrooms and communities to cultural and institutional contexts</li><li>conceptual frameworks</li><li>questions for further inquiry</li></ul>
Development of the curriculum	Development of curricula for particular programs or institutions	New knowledge about teacher inquiry, knowledge, thinking, and professional growth
Relationships of the classroom to institutional cultures and to larger communities	Relationships of teacher researchers' classrooms and the teacher researcher community itself to institutional cultures	New knowledge about the relationships among teacher inquiry, knowledge, and school reform
Rationales and consequences for students and teachers of altering practice	Rationales and consequences for the community of altering practice	
Conceptual frameworks for teaching, learning, and schooling	Conceptual frameworks for teaching, learning, and schooling	

Realign practitioners' relationships to knowledge generation and to the brokers of knowledge	*Redefine the notion of knowledge for teaching and alter the locus of the knowledge base*

In our analysis, we draw on a wide range of texts written by teachers—published and unpublished empirical and conceptual research; accounts of teachers' groups that have appeared in national and local journals, newsletters, and booklets; and edited collections of teachers' work. We have selected examples from a range of K–12 grade levels and contexts as well as university settings. We quote at length from these texts because we think it is important to provide direct access to teachers' ways of explaining and representing relationships between inquiry and knowledge. Although we are drawing heavily on their texts, we do not presume to speak for teachers. Rather, this essay represents our efforts to understand and present publicly what we are learning from teacher research from our perspectives as university-based teacher educators and researchers.

TEACHER RESEARCH AND LOCAL KNOWLEDGE

In his volume of essays on interpretive anthropology, Geertz (1983) talks about the difficulties involved in representing emic, or insider, knowledge and meaningful perspectives. He suggests that ultimately anthropologists can't really represent "local knowledge"—what native inhabitants see—but can only represent what they see through—that is, their interpretive perspectives on their own experiences. Borrowing Geertz's term, we use local knowledge to signal both what teachers come to know about their own knowledge through teacher research and what communities of teacher researchers come to know when they build knowledge collaboratively.

Knowing One's Own Knowledge

We begin with the assumption that through their interactions, teachers and students together construct classroom life and the learning opportunities that are available (Bloome & Green, 1984; Cochran-Smith, 1984; Cochran-Smith, Paris, & Kahn, 1991; Erickson, 1986). Essentially, teachers and students negotiate what counts as knowledge in the classroom, who can have knowledge, and how knowledge can be generated, challenged, and evaluated. We are arguing here that through inquiry, teachers come to understand how this happens in their own classrooms and how their own interpretations of classroom events are shaped. To make the case that teacher inquiry is a way for teachers to know their own knowledge, we consider six cases that suggest some of the range and variation that occur.

Case 1: Becoming Mean and Sensitive. Prompted by the realization that there was a discrepancy between his intentions and what was going on in the classroom, Fecho (1989), for example, began an empirical study of teacher-student writing conferences after viewing videotapes made in his classroom. Fecho was dissatisfied with what he saw:

> While some students were able to advance their own agendas and seek answers to their own questions, far too many students sat and waited for me to question, to figure out, and to change their writing. Although conferencing was successful in altering my relationships with the students, what occurred between us was still much too close to a teacher-centered classroom. . . . Provoked by these stimuli and supported by my colleagues . . . I resolved to take a more systematic look at my conferencing. Aside from the generic ethnographic question of, "What happens?" specifically, I was interested in what occurred in the conferences over the course of one school year—did the structure and work change or remain static? Did similarities and differences exist across conferences? Did the passing of time allow students to develop as conference participants? (pp. 3–4)

Although Fecho (1989) was intrigued by the arguments of academic researchers (Florio-Ruane, 1986; Michaels, Ulichney, & Watson-Gegeo, 1989) about the need to interrupt the replication in writing conferences of teachers' classroom dominance, his work was not simply about implementing the conferencing strategies that one might derive from the literature. Rather, he set out to understand how face-to-face talk about writing functions and varies over time when a white teacher works with 30-some African-American adolescents in an urban comprehensive high school. Fecho concluded the report of his research with these words:

> In one of our interviews, Geeman [one of Fecho's students] mentioned that our conferencing experience had led him to take second looks at writing he did for other classes. He liked the idea that he could be his own critic, that he could [in his words] be "mean and sensitive" to himself. I understood exactly what he meant. For myself, in the conference I had to be "mean" in order to resist my student's reliance on my expertise, but also "sensitive" to their needs and opinions. But looking at the phrase again, I realized that it also comments on my teacher research. As I find myself getting woozy watching tapes and reading transcripts, I know that I must continue looking for what the tapes may reveal, must continue to separate the real from the imagined, must continue seeing my practice with mean and sensitive eyes. For if I don't, who will? (pp. 20–21)

Although Fecho initiated and conducted the research, his students' inquiries brought unexpected insights into his own work. As Fecho wrestled with the implications of sharing power, both he and his students came to view knowledge differently. They came to a similar realization that while others can support, inform, challenge, and provide a context for learning, only learners themselves (whether teachers or students) can come to know or assume responsibility for making meaning of their work in the classroom.

Case 2: Balancing Structure and Freedom. Like Fecho, student teacher Crouse (1990) wanted to explore empirically classroom structures that provide a predictable format for discussion but also create opportunities for students to take responsibility for their own ideas. Unlike Fecho, who had been teaching for more than a decade, Crouse was for the first time wrestling with ways to engage her third-grade students in active construction of knowledge:

> In thinking about my literature study group before the unit began, I realized that a lot of my thoughts related to the issue of teacher-directed instruction versus child-centered education. I wanted the third graders in my group to discover and experience the wonderful world of Fantastic Mr. Fox on their own, but I wasn't sure how to do that without providing some sort of structure. I wanted to have a series of "grand conversations" à la Edelsky, but I wasn't sure that I understood or agreed with this approach to literature in the classroom. I began to realize that I thought of teaching as the art of finding the right balance between providing a clear and cohesive structure that facilitates learning and giving children the freedom to construct knowledge themselves. Children need direction, as well as freedom of choice, and the teacher needs to be careful not to give too much of either. For me, this unit was going to be about, in part, playing with that balance. (p. 7)

It is clear that Crouse sees her classroom as a site of inquiry into children's learning and that she approaches the planning of a literature unit with central questions about the teacher's role. Within this larger agenda framed by issues around child centeredness and teacher direction, Crouse also articulates a set of more specific questions about children's understanding of characterization, author's point of view and how children's moral development is reflected in their responses to texts:

> During my discussions with [my cooperating teacher] about our plans for the unit on Fantastic Mr. Fox, I became interested in the presence of good characters who do bad things in Roald Dahl's books. I became interested in knowing what sense the children made of who was a good character and who was a bad character. More specifically, I wanted to know whether or not they could determine whose side Roald Dahl was on, and whether they viewed these good characters who did bad things as heroes. I was very curious to know, for example, how the children would feel about the fact that Mr. Fox stole from the farmers and did so in sneaky ways. Basically, I was interested developmentally in where children, age 8, are in terms of their moral development. (p. 9)

Crouse's questions do not take the form of "What works in my classroom?" but, rather, "How can I learn with the children about what is going on here?" Implicit in Crouse's account is a belief that children and teachers together construct the curriculum and that the teacher can only come to know how to teach and how to learn from teaching by being attentive to their interactions. As a student teacher but like the more experienced teachers whose work we mention here, Crouse seems to regard knowledge generation as both the purpose of teaching and the subject of her own research.

Case 3: The Making of Hindsight. Like Crouse, Baum-Brunner (chapter 8) also looked at literacy, but in this case, at the writing workshops that occurred in her 12th-grade classroom. When she analyzed the data, Baum-Brunner discovered that her assumptions about several of her students had been largely incorrect. Writing about the study in retrospect, she reflected:

> As teacher, I taught this class, and consciously shaped it through my beliefs, training, choice of teaching techniques, [and] understanding of the genre. I even believed I understood consciously or intuitively most of what was occurring as I taught. Yet, by audiotaping the class and taking field notes at the time, and analyzing the interactions that had taken place, I realized I had not, in fact, accurately interpreted the interactions that had occurred. With the researcher's view, I saw that I had originally viewed as counter-productive [one student's] imitation [of the language of others during workshop discussions]; later I saw that his imitative style [had] helped him rehearse a kind of talk he didn't know. Had I to do it over again, I would not have discouraged his imitative talk. Instead I would have accepted the imitation, perhaps even have encouraged him to imitate more.
>
> The making of this insight was born out of my hindsight—my misjudgments and erroneous assumptions placed beside my view of the facts from another point in time. An outside researcher would have gotten a different . . . view. This hindsight was born out of my own experiences and . . . reflection about the feelings, assumptions, even myths that . . . shaped the teaching I did. Through analysis of disparities between [my original] feelings and [what I later realized] had occurred, I . . . created new pedagogy and theory about response and revision. (p. 209)

Baum-Brunner not only observed stylistic differences among students' patterns of participation in the workshop context, but she also expanded her interpretive framework—her notion of where to look and what to look at in order to understand students' efforts to respond and revise their writing. As she points out, when teachers treat classroom occurrences as data, they see discrete and sometimes disparate events as parts of larger patterns of behavior and interpretation. Rereading the texts of their classrooms allows teacher researchers to make visible their own characteristic ways of interpreting students' behavior and allows them to revisit and revise them.

Case 4: Untracking English. Also a 12th-grade English teacher, Cone (1990) and her colleagues had for several years experimented unsuccessfully with ways to make advanced placement (AP) English accessible to nonhonors students and to more minority students. In the spring of 1988, student teachers and master teachers were invited to the University of California at Berkeley to see a private showing of *Stand and Deliver* and to meet Jaime Escalante. After watching the film, teachers decided that what was wrong with their AP selection process was that they—rather than students—took full responsibility for selecting the class. In their words, they turned the AP selection process on its head. Reflecting on the year's experience designed so that a wider range of students would qualify and succeed in the AP curriculum, Cone commented:

> For a long time I have been concerned about the damage done by academic ability grouping. I worried that schools label students and never allow them to get unlabeled or relabeled. As early as second grade, students are tested for gifted. If they pass the test, they are tracked into gifted classes for the rest of their school

years. Students who are not tested or who do not pass the test, generally do not take honors classes. Ability grouping creates not only honors tracks: [it also creates] a two-tiered educational system of learners and non-learners, an elite academic class and an underclass that mirrors the social, racial, and economic underclass of our society as a whole. What would happen if the labels—"honors," "college prep," "average," "remedial"—came unglued? What would happen if students got to label themselves? What would happen if students got to choose the most academic class in the school if they wanted to—even if they weren't "gifted"?

Opening up AP English to all students who were willing to commit to a rigorous summer and year-long regimen of writing and reading allowed me to study first hand what does happen when students are given choices in their schooling. I discovered [that students] with combined SAT scores of 690 and 740 can learn with students with scores of 1290 and 1350; that students with SAT verbal scores of 460 and 490 can earn a 4 and a 5 on the national Advanced Placement English Language and Composition test; that students with SAT verbal scores of 290 and 380 can pass the University of California Subject A Exam. I discovered that gifted and nongifted students can discuss sophisticated literature with each other and can respond to each other's writing in ways that lead to thoughtful revision, and I discovered that giving them the chance to elect to work at the highest academic levels empowers them to see themselves as learners.

Opening up AP English also allowed me to see the kinds of changes I had to make as a teacher when students had accepted the challenge of a mixed-ability AP English class. Almost immediately, I saw that I had to move away from the front of the room, I had to turn classroom talk over to my students, I had to use writing to beget talk and talk to beget writing in ways that I had never used before. I had to give my students real choices about their education. Who did they want in their writing response group? How were they going to organize literary discussions? Which books were they going to read? Were they going to take the AP test? More than anything I had to learn how to shift the control of the class to my students in a way that suited my need for structure and their need to take control of their education. (pp. 27–28)

Cone was studying a complex and recursive set of interventions that took place over a full year as she and her students and colleagues constructed and reconstructed the curriculum. As a researcher, she explored the dynamic relationships that evolved among talk, writing, choice, changing roles, and student achievement. Cone's inquiry involved working with her students to renegotiate the meaning of student ability, construct new routes to textual understanding, and alter views about knowers and knowing in English classrooms. Like other teacher researchers, Cone diminished traditional distinctions between researcher and researched by making her agenda for the class public and by involving students in ongoing analysis of the data.

Case 5: The Middle Ground. In a conceptual essay on teaching and knowledge, elementary teacher Howard (1989) blended close descriptions with analysis of the role of the teacher in creating the circumstances that make it possible for children to generate knowledge. Using what she calls "the middle ground" as a metaphor, Howard explains how teachers mediate between children's interests and the broader world around them:

As a teacher, it is my opportunity and responsibility to provide for children the . . . time, tenderness, and recognition that can nurture growth and broaden perspectives. To do that, I have to gauge the moment to set self-knowledge against other perspectives. I have to balance the child's need for privacy and time to put down roots against the broadening to be gained by a more public participation in the give-and-take of group activity. In a related way, I provide the lens between the "very now" and the "larger now": the "now" we're living in at this time in our classroom, and the "now" of the past and future that expands around us. As the middle ground, I have to bridge all these states of being. It's hard to do. I am always aware of the connections I have failed to make—with children individually, between a child and the ideas he or she is pursuing, among the children as a group and their mutual interests, between the knowledge the children are making and both cultural and disciplinary knowledge. I am not as effective, for example, in connecting children with physics and foreign languages as I am in connecting them with nature and literature. No one can do or be all things.

My own limitations don't worry me the way they used to, because I have come to trust the vitality and thought of the children. I know I am doing a good job when some child says to me, equal to equal: "That's a good idea. . . ." Then I know the recognition I have given to the child's ideas has created a sense of equality; we are connected through our mutual pursuit of knowledge. We are, for the moment, colleagues in our respective pursuits. (p. 228)

In Howard's reflective essay is an articulated view of knowledge as something "that arises between the inner impulses, interests, and qualities of the child and the physical and cultural world of which he or she is a part" (p. 229). With rich examples, Howard explores how knowledge arises in one classroom, how she works to give children room to make knowledge, and how she and the children construct knowledge together.

Case 6: Rethinking Resistance. Although worlds apart in one sense, college teacher Lewis (1989) is like Howard in that she analyzes the process of constructing knowledge with the students in her classroom, in this case an undergraduate sociology course for preservice teachers intended to raise questions about social relations from a critical perspective. In her writing, Lewis made it clear that she is committed to feminist politics and pedagogy in the academy. Through studying her own teaching, she analyzed how students' responses to feminist theory emerged from conflicts between their own previous experiences and the discourse of the class. Lewis identified critical issues in a feminist pedagogy in part through analysis of her students' resistance. Lewis both researched her own teaching and taught as a way of doing research—that is, her research informs her practice and her teaching functions as an important site of inquiry for her larger project:

I want to examine the potential basis of feminist teaching that does more than address the concerns of the already initiated. For me, the urgency of this issue arises from my own teaching. On the one hand the often chilling stories of experiences women students share with me and each other in the context of our relations within the classroom point to their clear understanding of the politics of gender subordination: experiences that have affected them profoundly and yet which have no outlet for expression (often even understanding) within the confines of traditional academic practices.

On the other hand, I hear that young woman who speaks to me in anger, who derides me for being the bearer of "bad news" and who wants to believe that our oppression/subordination is something we create in our own heads. It has been my experience that, for many women, working through and coming to a feminist perspective is not easy. This journey often generates anger and ultimately a politicization of every moment of our personal and public lives until we can come to grips with the positive political potential of our anger—an anger that is freed by the uncovering/unbinding of centuries of powerlessness and the denial of the conditions for speaking, what we know, in terms circumscribed by our own desires and interests.

Women don't need to be taught what we already know. . . . Nor do we need to be taught the language through which to speak what we know. Rather we need to find ways of understanding what we are already saying and how we are saying it. (pp. 18–19)

Lewis' position is reminiscent of Berthoff's (1987) notion of teaching as "REsearching." Berthoff suggests that we do not need new information, but new ways to think about the information we already have:

Educational research is nothing to our purpose, unless we formulate the questions; if the procedures by which answers are sought are not dialectic and dialogic, that is to say, if the questions and the answers are not continually REformulated by those working in the classroom, educational research is pointless. (pp. 29–30)

Classrooms with a feminist pedagogy, which explicitly make issues of knowledge, authority, and institutional hierarchies parts of the curriculum (Ellsworth, 1989; Lather, 1991; Miller, 1987), provide strategic sites for understanding what it means for teachers to know their own knowledge through inquiry.

It is clear from their own words that these six teachers use inquiry as a way of knowing about teaching. Fecho examines what it means to both lead and follow students. Crouse explores the delicate balance between structure and spontaneity in classroom talk. Baum-Brunner enlarges her understanding of the social nature of writing. Cone explores the consequences for achievement of empowering adolescents to make choices. Howard articulates a conceptual framework for students' and teachers' roles in constructing classroom knowledge. And Lewis demonstrates the inseparability of teaching and inquiry in the enactment of a critical pedagogy.

Teacher research is a powerful way for teachers to understand how they and their students construct and reconstruct the curriculum. By conducting inquiry on their own practices, teachers identify discrepancies between their theories of practice and their practices, between their own practices and those of others in their schools, and between their ongoing assumptions about what is going on in their classrooms and their more distanced and retrospective interpretations. Inquiry stimulates, intensifies, and illuminates changes in practice. Out of inquiry come analytic frameworks as well as questions for further inquiry. Obviously, one does not have to engage in teacher research to make decisions about or changes in classroom practice. Teachers revise and reflect on their strategies regularly as part of the ongoing cycle of teaching (Paris, in press; Schön, 1983). Nor is teacher research in the sense we mean it here necessarily instrumental: It may involve deliberate change, but it may just as likely entail a deliberate attempt to make more visible what is already going on.

Thus, in contrast to the implications of the AACTE volume, what "distinguishes more productive teachers" (p. ix) may not be mastery of a knowledge base, but rather standing in a different relationship to one's own knowledge, to one's students as knowers, and to knowledge generation in the field. Freire (1971) has argued that educators and their students are "knowing subjects," constantly learning from the process of teaching. For him, "education is a pedagogy of knowing" (p. 217). Knoblauch and Brannon (1988) have built on Friere's notion that teaching itself is a knowledge-generating process and suggest that the defining characteristic of teacher researchers is their "knowledge of the making of knowledge" (p. 27). When we regard teaching as a process of generating knowledge with students, we need to understand teacher research as a significant process of coming to know one's own knowledge and understanding how knowledge is constructed. There is a dynamic interaction among teachers' stances toward themselves as knowers, their students as knowers and learners, and their knowledge of disciplinary/subject matter (Lyons, 1990). In the texts of teacher research, we see that teachers have the legitimate authority to know about teaching. When teachers redefine their own relationships to knowledge about teaching and learning, they often begin to reconstruct their classrooms and to offer different invitations to their students to learn and know. When they change their relationships to knowledge, they may also realign their relationships to the brokers of knowledge and power in schools and universities.

Building Knowledge in the Community

We think of intellectual communities of teacher researchers as networks of individuals who enter with other teachers into "a common search for meaning" in their work lives (Westerhoff, 1987) and who regard their research as part of larger efforts to transform teaching, learning, and schooling. Through inquiry, groups of teachers conjoin their understandings to create local knowledge in and for their own communities. Because teachers in different settings have diverse goals, activities, and ways of doing research, there is considerable variation in the knowledge constructed in different groups. We argue that just as the knowledge generated by individual teachers ought to count in an epistemology of teaching, so should the knowledge generated by communities of teachers.

To understand how teacher research is a way of knowing for the local community, we will look at groups of teachers working together within a single institution as well as groups of teachers coming together from several institutions to form a community. Groups of teachers from one institution often use inquiry as a way to build curriculum.

Phelps (1991), for example, describes the work of the community of university teachers involved in the Syracuse Writing Program:

> [T]eaching depends for its richness on a community of shared practice constituted through exchanges of talk and writing about curriculum. We are working actively to create such a sense of community among a mixed group (numbering close to 150) including full-time research faculty, part-time professional writing teachers, and graduate teaching assistants—largely young, inexperienced, and from disciplines other than composition. Our modes of interaction include "teacher talk" in weekly meetings of small groups, co-teaching and mentoring arrangements, varied professional development activities, task forces and working groups on curriculum, and a remarkable amount of writing including an in-house journal.
>
> The business of such a community is curriculum development as a form of knowledge-making. . . . Part of the work of the community is to make visible to itself (and to colleagues at the university) the ecology of curricular contexts in which any teaching decision is embedded, not merely abstractly, but as vivid, particular realities. This requires . . . practical investigations that go beyond classroom observations of one's own teaching to specify how actions fit together on the programmatic or institutional scale. . . . Through its talk, writing, inquiry, and action, members of the Writing Program, are imagining and shaping its writing courses as a developmentally related sequence; translating the university curricula into a particularized range of writing, reading, thinking and learning tasks set for students; profiling the students themselves as unpredictably diverse and heterogeneous despite their apparent typicalities. . . .
>
> The Syracuse Writing Program, with its particular history of teaching practices and the heterogeneous composition of its thinkers and practitioners, presents both an extraordinarily difficult [and] complex context and a richly rewarding matrix for experiments and reflection on teachers' (and students') ways of knowing. (pp. 863–865)

A group of faculty at Michigan State University (MSU) is involved in a similar process of reconstructing their teacher education curriculum by drawing on data collected by all those teaching different sections of an introductory course on teaching (Feiman-Nemser & Featherstone, 1992). Like the community at Syracuse, MSU group members share knowledge of particular classroom events to articulate a vision of the teacher education curriculum as a whole.

Moving back and forth between collaborative curriculum building and data gathering in individual classrooms occurs in teacher-researcher groups at all levels of the educational continuum. Colgan-Davis (see chapter 7), for example, describes a curriculum development project at Friends Select Lower School, where a group of teachers met regularly over a year to build a curriculum that would meet the needs of diverse groups of learners:

The unifying factor was that we all saw diversity in how our students learned and found this diversity a challenge. Some teachers who were originally attracted to Friends Select School because of its economic, cultural, and racial diversity found the differences in how children learn exciting, and came to the group to expand their skills in responding to children's needs. Others felt the school had lost sight of its mission, had accepted children who should not be in a private, academic school, and wanted the school to narrow its focus, clarify its standards, and begin to sift out those children whom they felt did not belong. Other teachers were mystified by how children learn, saw it as a "hidden act" and did not know how to respond when the student did not succeed. . . .

Through a series of descriptions of students' work, reflections on key concepts, descriptive reviews, and analyses of other classroom data, the group explored its own values and assumptions about learners' appropriate behavior and made specific recommendations for working with individual children in classrooms:

[The group came] to understand how our own values and assumptions clouded [our] abilities to accurately perceive children's struggles and interfered with our ability to meet their educational and emotional needs. Had we not reflected upon [our] own values, perceptions, and experiences, we would not have been able to push past our own biases and see the topic of learning diversity in a new light.

Using collaborative inquiry to design a curriculum responsive to diversity is also the goal of a group of Philadelphia Writing Project teachers who plan a yearly summer institute for adolescents participating in the school district's desegregation program. Their process, like the processes of other groups involved in curriculum construction, allows for comparative interpretations of texts, students' work, and styles of teaching.

Developing curriculum through analysis of data is radically different from the process of curriculum development typically used by many schools and school districts. Often, there are preestablished calendars and formal procedures for reviewing the curriculum in each subject area. These generally involve discussion of objectives and goals as well as close examination and comparison of published materials. When curriculum construction is conceptualized as a process of inquiry and systematic consideration of data, however, it is qualitatively different from consideration of topics, books, or sequences of activities. When groups of teachers develop curriculum through inquiry, they use data from their own classrooms (e.g., students' work, actual lesson and unit plans, descriptions of individual learners, syllabi, texts, and teacher-made materials and assignments) to pose problems, sort out commonalities and differences in perspectives and values, and build instructional frameworks. Teacher groups involved in charter schools such as Crossroads (Fecho, 1990; Hiller, 1991), a school within Gratz High School in Philadelphia, intend to make curriculum construction that is based on observation, interviews, and collection of student work an ongoing dimension of their work.

Any time groups of teachers from the same institution come together to consider issues of curriculum and instruction, there is the potential for building knowledge for the local community. Self-studies for accreditation purposes, pupil support teams, supervisory sessions, and even department, faculty, and committee meetings could be reconceptualized as sites of inquiry, and their practices could be transformed to emphasize the formulation of questions, data collection, analysis, and interpretation. This is similar to earlier propositions that schools and school systems have the potential to be centers for inquiry (J. Lytle, 1992; Myers, 1987; Schaefer, 1967) and to recent calls for school-university partnerships wherein experienced and beginning teachers work together with university faculty in professional development schools (Holmes Group, 1990). And of course, the notion that curriculum construction is a form of knowledge making is an essential part of the history of teacher research. Stenhouse (1985) reminds us:

> Curriculum is the medium through which the teacher can learn his art. Curriculum is the medium through which the teacher can learn knowledge. Curriculum is the medium through which the teacher can learn about the nature of education. Curriculum is the medium through which the teacher can learn about the nature of knowledge. (p. 98)

In a certain sense, the typical curriculum committee and the teacher-research group seem worlds apart. It is difficult to imagine the shift from problem solving to problem posing, from quick closure to deeper exploration, and from making judgments to discovering relationships based on data. On the other hand, some of the contexts in which inquiry would be powerful already exist, particularly the new structural arrangements created as schools divide into teams, houses, and other smaller organizational units.

Rather than a shared physical and institutional context, other teacher groups cross institutional boundaries and share a broad intellectual agenda, which sometimes sets them apart from one another. Teachers who have been associated with Pat Carini, the Prospect School, and the North Dakota Study Group, for example, have organized a number of local communities such as the Philadelphia Teachers Learning Cooperative that are committed to the perspectives of progressive education in public schools. In *Speaking Out: Teachers on Teaching,* a collection of Prospect Institute teachers' essays, Kanevsky and Traugh (1986) comment on the ways that communities of teachers know about teaching:

> Our classrooms are complicated. . . . They generate lives of their own but they also include and respond to the lives people lead outside their walls. They are the setting for the exploration and implementation of ideas. They support the having of new ideas. . . . As teachers, we are temporarily immersed in this busy life, a part of what occurs. The question is: How do we lift our heads up out of the stream, which in its movement, carries us along, to see where we are going and look back at where we have been? And, if we are able to see, how do we keep track of what we see? How do we make sense of it and see the patterns in it?

Taking advantage of the classroom's potential as a source of knowledge which will nurture and feed the quality of work done in that classroom requires special efforts and energy. However the means we can use to pull what is important out of the vague, undifferentiated background of experience are readily available to us and indeed, they have long histories in the ordinary human effort to keep track and make sense of our wo̤k lives: conversations, journals, interviews, and stories are among the most useful of these modes. (p. 6)

The work of the Prospect community is based on a phenomenological view of knowledge and learning wherein teachers grapple with children's meanings as expressed in their projects and with the varied meanings that their colleagues find in children's work.

While the Teachers Learning Cooperative explores issues in urban education, teachers and administrators in the Biographic Literacy Profiles Project (Taylor, 1990) explore multiple literacies and alternative ways of assessing students' literacy development. They document children's literacy behaviors by writing descriptive biographic literacy profiles. In describing the work of the group, Taylor shows how the group's process became a way of knowing about teaching:

At the second institute that took place . . . teachers and administrators who had been participating in the project for one year met to share their experiences, advance their own training, and begin the training of a new group of teachers. . . . Much of our time was spent in observing ourselves in complex problem-solving situations—observing the ways in which we, as learners, generate and reconstitute problems through the use of the social, symbolic, technical, and material resources at our disposal, and then go on to invent new procedures and arrive at instrumental solutions. Some teachers and administrators participated in the collaborative problem-solving situations, while others observed and took notes which were later shared and analyzed by all those who participated in the institute. In this way, we advanced our own understanding of the social construction of cognitive tasks, while at the same time the teachers new to the project had the opportunity to think about the possibilities of establishing classroom environments in which they could observe children engaged in solving the problem of problem-solving literacy. (p. 10)

Cross-institutional communities of teachers pose distinctive problems for themselves and hence build knowledge in domains different from one another. Often, this is a reflection of their origins and their affiliations with various programs, universities, and institutes or with particular ideologies. In each case, the community of teachers constructs knowledge for its own consideration and use. By investigating the function of talk in classrooms across the grades and curriculum, for example, participants in the Brookline Teacher Researcher Seminar, affiliated with the Literacies Institute in Boston, build their own distinctive knowledge base about classroom discourse. Teacher-researcher groups at the Breadloaf School of English (Goswami & Stillman, 1987) and other graduate programs in writing and language (Bissex & Bullock,

1987; Calkins, 1991) as well as groups associated with sites of the National Writing Project—in the Bay Area, Philadelphia, Detroit, Northern Virginia, and Baltimore—focus on the interrelationships of language, literacy, and learning. Finally, inquiry-centered preservice programs, such as Project START (Student Teachers As Researching Teachers) (Cochran-Smith, 1991a, 1991b) and the University of Wisconsin elementary education program (Zeichner, 1986), and inservice teacher communities (Evans, 1989; Lytle & Fecho, 1991; Yonemura, 1982) explore the processes of learning to teach across the developmental continuum and thus build knowledge for the local community about teacher knowledge, teacher thinking, and professional socialization.

When teachers build knowledge in these and other domains of research on teaching and learning, they begin to develop local criteria for evaluating questions, evidence, and interpretive frameworks. Furthermore, they develop a different stance toward knowledge itself and toward those who have been traditionally regarded as keepers and distributors of knowledge for teaching.

TEACHER RESEARCH AND PUBLIC KNOWLEDGE

In addition to its function as a way of knowing for teacher researchers in their local communities, teacher research has the potential to be a significant way of knowing for the larger communities of both school-based teachers and university-based researchers and teacher educators as well as policymakers and school administrators. There have been relatively few forums for the presentation and publication of teacher research, and there is an even smaller subset of these in which school- and university-based teachers and researchers join together. Furthermore, there have been limited opportunities to explore empirically the ways that teachers' texts are being read and interpreted by university-based researchers and teacher educators and whether and how teacher research is beginning to alter understandings of classroom practice.

Increasingly, communities of teacher researchers from different parts of the country are disseminating their work to one another and developing a classroom-grounded knowledge base from the collective inquiries of teachers across contexts. Growing networks of teacher researchers have thus begun to provide access to their teaching colleagues through conferences and publications. When teachers are the audience for teacher research, the task, as Fecho (1990) has suggested, is "to read like a teacher," or to bring teachers' analytic frameworks to bear on the questions, issues, and interpretations presented by other teachers. As teacher research becomes public knowledge, teachers—not university-based researchers or teacher educators—will determine its value for the broader community of school-based teachers.

From our perspectives as researchers, however, we would argue that teacher research has particular potential for transforming the university-generated knowledge base. In a recent address to the American Educational Research Association, Jackson (1990) discussed the changing venue of educational research and the potential for linking the contextual emphasis of much of current research with its orientation toward conclusions. He points out:

> In recent years we have witnessed a growing interest within our research community in the use of techniques and scholarly traditions that provide a close look at the everyday affairs of educational practitioners and those they serve. . . . [There has also been] a decline of interest on the part of many of us in what used to be looked upon as our main business, which was the discovery of rules and principles of teaching and of running schools that would prove to be universal or nearly so in application and invariant or nearly so over time. That dream of finding out once and for all how teaching works or how schools ought to be administered no longer animates nearly as many of us as it once did. In its place we have substituted the much more modest goal of trying to figure out what's happening here and now or what went on there and then. This does not mean that we have given up trying to say things that are true from situation to situation or that we are no longer interested in making generalizations. But the kind of truth in which more and more of us seem interested these days takes a very different form than it once did. (p. 7)

Jackson's comment suggests that teacher research might provide several ways of knowing for the larger community of both school-based and university-based teachers and researchers. Just as critical scholarship has challenged many of the norms of interpretive social science, teacher research makes problematic in a different way the relationships of researcher and researched, theory and practice, knower and knowledge, process and product. When teachers do research, the gap between researcher and researched is narrowed. Notions of research subjectivity and objectivity are redefined: Subjective and local knowing rather than objectified and distanced "truth" is the goal. The teacher researcher is a native inhabitant of the research site—not a participant observer over a bounded period of time but a permanent and "observant participant" (Florio-Ruane & Walsh, 1980) who knows the research context in its richest sense of shared "webs of significance" (Geertz, 1973).

Because teacher research investigates from an emic perspective topics that are already widely researched by university-based researchers, it is a source of new knowledge in many of the domains of teaching and learning and also has the potential to open up new areas of study. Furthermore, because teaching requires simultaneous attention to many agendas and because it also provides the opportunity for constant observation of particular phenomena such as children's drawings or writings, teacher researchers' analytic frameworks are extraordinarily rich and complex. What we mean here is that when teacher researchers turn their attention to something like children's drawings, they bring a historical framework based on a thousand other drawings and what these drawings meant for particular children in real school time. Hence they ask questions that other researchers may not ask, and they see patterns that others may not be able to see.

Teacher research is concerned with the questions that arise from the lived experiences of teachers and the everyday life of teaching expressed in a language that emanates from practice. Teachers are concerned about the consequences of their actions, and teacher research is often prompted by teachers' desires to know more about the dynamic interplay of classroom events. Hence teacher research is well positioned to produce precisely the kind of knowledge currently needed in the field.

Almost by definition, teacher research is case study: The unit of analysis is typically the individual child, the classroom, or the school. Whether and how case studies function in knowledge generation is part of a larger set of questions about the relationships between qualitative research and practice, which have long been topics of considerable debate. As Eisner (1991) points out, this debate hinges on what is meant by the accumulation of knowledge in a field— on whether we mean that knowledge accumulates in the sense that dollars and garbage do, a view that presumes that knowledge is an "inert material" that can be collected, stored, and stockpiled (p. 210). Rather, Eisner argues that knowledge growth in the social sciences is "more horizontal than vertical," not at all like building with blocks: It yields multiple conceptual frameworks that others can use to understand their own situations:

> My point . . . is not to claim that the products of research have no bearing on each other, or that they do not connect in any way. It is, rather, to challenge the notion that all researchers must use a common intellectual currency whose profits are additive in the same way in which money accumulates in the bank. Research studies, even in related areas in the same field, create their own interpretive universe. Connections have to be built by readers, who must also make generalizations by analogy and extrapolation, not by a water-tight logic applied to a common language. Problems in the social sciences are more complex than putting the pieces of the puzzle together to create a single, unified picture. (p. 210)

We think that with teacher research, knowledge will accumulate as communities of school-based and university-based teachers and researchers read and critique one another's work, document and perhaps disseminate their responses, and create a network of citations and allusions, and hence begin to build a different kind of "interpretive universe."

Teacher researchers have been especially active in the area of language and literacy. Teachers have studied their own and their students' experiences in reconstructing the traditional language/literacy curriculum, including writing and oral history (Wiggington, 1985), oral history and cultural identity (Stumbo, 1989), self-initiated writing (Atwell, 1987), dialogue writing (Five, 1987), and culturally responsive reading curriculum (Ashton-Warner, 1963). In addition, Lumley (1987) explored social interaction and peer group dialogue journals; Holmstein (1987) studied students' interpretations of writing with word processing; Branscombe (1987) studied students as language researchers; Buchanan (1989) studied the language of whole language; Johnston (1989)

studied the social scenes of reading; Ray (1986) studied talk and writing conferences; Starr (see Chapter 8) studied deaf children's composing processes;
Headman (see Chapter 8) studied parents' and teachers' perspectives on literacy; Morizawa (1990) studied writing, dramatization, and children's social
worlds; Wilson (1990) studied students' and teachers' talk and writing; and
Farmbry (see Chapter 9) studied dialect and standardization. In addition, a
number of National Writing Projects publish collections on various aspects of
teaching and learning writing.

What we know from each domain of teacher research is not simply a series
of discrete findings. Instead, we get a sense of the multiple perspectives that
teachers bring to their work, which together generate unique interpretive uni-
verses. Other domains of active teacher research include progressive education [Howard, 1989; Kanevsky (see Chapter 7); Kanevsky & Traugh, 1986;
Philadelphia Teachers Learning Cooperative, 1984; Strieb, 1985]; critical pedagogy [Brown (see Chapter 9); Ellsworth, 1989; Lather, 1991; Lewis, 1989; Miller,
1987]; teaching and learning to teach [Brody et al. (see Chapter 9); Cochran-
Smith, Garfield, & Greenberger, 1992; Colgan-Davis (see Chapter 7); Dicker,
1990; Dunstan, Kirscht, Reiffer, Roemer, & Tingle, 1989; Fecho, 1989; Guerin,
1985; Harris (see Chapter 8); Kean, 1989; Pincus (see Chapter 9); Reither, 1990;
Rotchford, 1989; Wunner (see Chapter 8); Yagelski, 1990]; adult literacy education (Lytle, 1991; Lytle & Wolfe, 1989); and theories of teacher research itself
(Burton, 1991; Hahn, 1991; Queenan, 1988; Schwartz, 1990).

None of the examples of teacher research that we have mentioned are
what Calkins (1985) has referred to as "field-testing" research, in which practitioners test out new ideas that they are already convinced are exemplary. The
goal of teacher research is not product testing, but "the development, assessment, and revision of theories that inform practice" (p. 143). As Calkins
reminds us, teacher researchers like Freud, Erikson, and Bettelheim are practitioners as well as theory builders:

> Through working with patients and through related study they developed theories
> that informed their practices. They also acted as researchers, observing their own
> work and the results of it and letting these observations guide them as they stud-
> ied. This constant interaction between practice, reflection, and study led them to
> flesh out and refine their theories. . . . Each case report provides a forum for inte-
> grating theory and practice. (p. 143)

Teacher research, then, is a way of knowing for the larger communities of
teachers and researchers because it contributes both conceptual frameworks
and important information about some of the central domains of the knowledge base.

Finally, the texts of teacher research provide data about teacher knowledge
itself, a burgeoning area of study since 1975, when researchers turned their
attention to teaching as a cognitive activity. Research conducted by preservice
and inservice teachers provides a window into the nature of their perspectives

on teaching, learning, and schooling. This method of data collection contrasts with some of the more common methods of exploring teachers' thinking and knowledge, including stimulated recall, policy capturing, and repertory grid techniques, which are often supplemented by interviewing, observation, and narrative descriptions (Clark & Peterson, 1986). Of necessity, these methods typically focus on simplified and researcher-created tasks, constructs, or a priori categories. Consequently, these techniques do not account for the ways in which teacher inquiry is mediated by and essentially embedded in the cultures of classrooms, schools, school districts, and teacher-research communities. Because teacher research emerges from praxis and because it preserves teachers' own words and analyses, it has the potential to be a particularly robust method for understanding whether and how preservice and inservice teachers construct their knowledge and theories of practice, how these may change and develop over time, and what impact these may have on teaching and learning.

For example, there is considerable discussion in the field about the content and form of teacher knowledge (Shulman, 1986b, 1987; Sockett, 1987), especially about the nature of teachers' practical knowledge (Fenstermacher, 1986; Sanders & McCutcheon, 1986). Teacher research often reveals teachers' explorations of the discrepancies they perceive between their theories of practice and their actual practices. If university-based researchers use as data the texts written by teachers themselves, it is likely that the domain of teacher knowledge will be refined and eventually redefined as a field of study.

Although we see clear advantages to understanding teachers' knowledge through teachers' own representations, we also have reservations about what might happen if teacher research were the object of others' interpretations without serious attention to the ethical and epistemological issues that this form of inquiry entails. What seems to us most important is that each case be regarded on its own terms, with members of both school- and university-based communities participating in identifying the issues, making arguments, and deciding how teachers' texts are to be used for different purposes.

REDEFINING THE KNOWLEDGE BASE

In conclusion, we return to the AACTE volume with which we began. In the epistemology implied in that volume, knowledge is something received by teachers who adapt it to their particular situations and who are not themselves a source of knowledge generation for the field. We have been trying to sketch a different theory of knowledge for teaching—one in which teachers are among those who are knowers. As we have shown, inquiry conducted by teachers is a way to build knowledge both locally and more publicly—for the individual teacher, for communities of teachers, and for the larger field of university-based researchers and teacher educators, policymakers, and school administrators. We want to be clear that a different theory of knowledge would not simply add new knowers to the same knowledge base but would redefine the notion of knowledge for teaching and alter the locus of the knowledge base and the practitioner's stance in relation to knowledge generation in the field. We are not hoping for simply the inclusion of teachers in academic arenas—as authors of chapters in "knowledge base" handbooks, for example—but for a grander arena that privileges local as well as public knowledge generated by school-based as well as university-based researchers.

4 | Learning From Teaching: Inquiry Across the Life Span

Throughout this volume, we have proposed that teacher researchers stand in a different relationship to their own knowledge, to their students as knowers, and to knowledge generation in the field. As Freire (1971) has suggested, they are "knowing subjects," constantly learning from the process of teaching. Here we take the more radical position that learning from teaching ought to be regarded as the primary task of teacher education across the professional life span. By "learning from teaching," we mean that inquiry ought to be regarded as an integral part of the activity of teaching and as a critical basis for decisions about practice. Furthermore, we mean that classrooms and schools ought to be treated as research sites and sources of knowledge that are most effectively accessed when teachers collaboratively interrogate and enrich their theories of practice. This argument is based in part on the assumption that the increasing diversity of America's schools and schoolchildren and the increasing complexity of the tasks that educators face render global solutions to problems and monolithic strategies for effective teaching impossible. Hence, what is required in both preservice and inservice teacher education programs are processes that prompt teachers and teacher educators to construct their own questions and then begin to develop courses of action that are valid in their local contexts and communities.

When learning from teaching is taken to be the primary task of teachers across the life span, a distinctive set of assumptions about knowledge, collaboration, and inquiry obtains. Teachers are assumed to be among those who have the authority to know—that is, to construct knowledge about teaching, learning, and schooling—and their research becomes a significant part of a redefined knowledge base for teaching. Knowledge from the academy is not accepted unproblematically but is taken to be rich and generative, providing conceptual frameworks, detailed information from other contexts, new problems and dilemmas, confirming and disconfirming evidence, and grist for further deliberations. This stance on knowledge is interdependent with a concept of teachers as collaborators (Florio-Ruane, 1986; Little, 1987) rather than simply coworkers or cooperators. More and less experienced teachers as well as teacher educators labor together to construct their understandings of individual learners (Clay, 1975; Philadelphia Teachers Learning Cooperative, 1984), classroom interactions, and the cultures of schooling by closely observing students (Bussis, Chittenden, Amarel, & Klausner, 1985; Goodman, 1985), reflecting on experiences (Carini, 1986; Hollingsworth, 1989), and reading and writing widely in content and pedagogy. As many of the teacher researchers who have contributed to this volume have argued, conducting research is a powerful way for teachers to understand how they and their students construct and reconstruct the teaching and learning that occur in their classrooms and schools. When teachers themselves conduct research, they make problematic what they think they already know, what they see when they observe their own students as learners, and what they choose to do about the disjunctions that often exist in their classrooms, schools, and communities.

In the first part of this essay, we draw on our experiences in two teacher education projects to describe some of the intellectual, social, and organizational structures that support and sustain a teacher-research-based curriculum at both the preservice and inservice levels. We demonstrate how the link between inquiry and professional development can be played out at these two levels by providing some detail about the structures of Project START (Student Teachers As Researching Teachers) and the Philadelphia Writing Project (PhilWP)—teacher education projects located in urban Philadelphia and affiliated with the University of Pennsylvania. Next, we argue for the power of inquiry in the teacher education curriculum by focusing on one of the most critical issues in education today: how to prepare beginning and experienced teachers to respond appropriately to the increasing cultural and linguistic diversity in American education. By providing examples from the writing of both beginning and experienced teachers as they struggle with the issues of race, class, and ethnicity, we analyze the ways that teachers can use inquiry to make problematic their own knowledge about diversity, their observations about differences across learners and classrooms, and their own roles in reform. We conclude by asserting that no one can empower teachers to respond to cultural diversity or to the many other complex challenges that face today's teachers. Instead, we argue that only teachers themselves can interrogate their assumptions and their interpretive frameworks and then decide on the actions that are appropriate for their local contexts.

STRUCTURES FOR INQUIRY IN PRESERVICE AND INSERVICE TEACHER EDUCATION

If inquiry is to be an integral part of teaching across the professional life span, we need social and organizational structures supportive of beginning and experienced teachers' learning and collaboration. Some of these structures, as well as many of the themes and strategies for inquiry, are similar at the preservice and inservice levels of teacher development.

Both Project START and PhilWP, for example, are designed to provide a range of intellectual opportunities for teachers to examine dimensions of race, class, gender, and ethnicity as they relate to teaching, learning, and schooling. Indeed, both projects are based on the assumption that it is impossible to understand these phenomena apart from the ways that they structure and are structured by each other. Inquiry into cultural diversity is thus woven into and not taken as a separate strand of a wide range of themes in the curriculum. Furthermore, participants in both groups rely on a number of structured oral and written inquiry strategies that promote systematic and intentional study of classroom and school data. Figure 4.1 provides an overview of the organizations and their goals, their social structures and roles, and the intellectual opportunities for inquiry that are the hallmarks of these two teacher education programs.

Preservice Teacher Education: Project START

Organizational Goals and Structures. At the University of Pennsylvania, preservice teacher education is viewed as both liberal art and professional practice. It is assumed that teachers make curricular and instructional decisions, construct their own interpretations through the processes of inquiry, and play significant roles in the shaping of policy and practice. Project START, a 5th-year program in elementary education for liberal arts graduates, was conceived 5 years ago by Philadelphia area teachers and University of Pennsylvania teacher educators to provide intensive, year-long student teaching experiences and closer links between university and schools. Working within long-standing traditions of research- and theory-based methods and foundation courses in teacher education, project designers took what Dewey (1904) calls a "laboratory" view of the practical work in teacher education, which emphasizes the intellectual strategies of teachers, in contrast to an "apprenticeship" view, which has the more immediate goal of training students to perform as efficient workers in the classroom.

The major intention of Project START is to invite student teachers into a community of school-based and university-based learners, and essentially a way of life as teachers, by emphasizing reform and inquiry across the profes-

Figure 4.1. Inquiry Across the Life Span: Two Examples

PROJECT START UNIVERSITY OF PENNSYLVANIA	Philadelphia Writing Project UNIVERSITY OF PENNSYLVANIA

GOALS

• Build close links between schools and university • Invite student teachers into a community of learners and a way of life as teachers by emphasizing reform, research, and renewal across the professional life span	• Build professional networks of teachers and administrators • Create intellectual community through emphasis on practitioners as writers, researchers, and reformers in classrooms, schools, programs, and universities • Support school and program restructuring and reform efforts

ORGANIZATIONAL STRUCTURES

12-Month Post-Baccalaureate Program	
• MS in education, state certification K–6 • Student cohort progresses through program together • Cooperating teachers and university supervisors stable over time	***School-University Collaborative*** • Ongoing network of K–12, college, and adult literacy teachers and administrators, university faculty, and students • Continuous development of new programs responsive to local needs
Core University Components • 3 Semesters of coursework promote critical perspectives on teaching, learning, and schooling and frameworks for learning from children and for constructing curriculum • Publications/presentations of work (local, regional, and national) • Monthly teaching and learning seminars for all participants	***Core University Components*** • Institutes, seminars, and study groups for teachers, administrators, and students • Publications/presentations of work (local, regional, and national forums) • PhilWP Scholar Program • Integration with reading/writing/literacy graduate programs
Core School Components • 2 Semesters of student teaching with subcohorts of student teachers at each school site (student teaching in same classroom with the same teacher for a full year) • Weekly school-site teacher-researcher meetings • Cross-visitation program of observation/participation at contrasting school sites and joint reflections with other school-site groups	***Core District/Program Components*** • Teacher-consultant program that provides opportunities for cross-visitation and leadership in staff development, curriculum, and policy • Teacher inquiry communities within and across school and program sites • Collaboration with other organizations that support district and adult literacy program initiatives

PROJECT START UNIVERSITY OF PENNSYLVANIA	Philadelphia Writing Project UNIVERSITY OF PENNSYLVANIA

PARTICIPANTS' ROLES

• *Redefinition of roles:* All participants regarded as learners, researchers, and collaborators • *Student teachers:* 25–35 students per cohort (liberal arts BAs, usually with some work experience) • *Cooperating teachers:* Involved in reform, research, school restructuring, and teacher collaboratives at diverse school sites/school district sites • *University supervisors/teacher educators:* Facilitate school-site meetings, research their own practice, and engage in supervision as inquiry • *Program planning:* Teachers, teacher educators, and student teachers assess and plan collaboratively	• *Redefinition of roles:* All participants regarded as learners, researchers, and collaborators • *Teachers:* 250 teacher-consultants in 90 schools and 40 adult literacy teachers in 20 Philadelphia programs • *Administrators:* Involved in institutes, writing groups, and inquiry communities • *University faculty and students:* Facilitate, participate in, and document all project activities • *Project planning:* Governance through steering committee and school-university-corporate advisory board

LEARNING OPPORTUNITIES

Themes for Inquiry

• Language and literacy • Curriculum and pedagogy • Race, class, and gender • Modes of assessment • Cultures of teaching and schooling	• Inquiry within and across disciplines • Professional development and educational reform • Community-school relationships

Strategies for Inquiry

• Documentary processes: Reflection, description of a child's work, and descriptive review (Carini, 1986) • Critical discussion/writings about experiences and common readings • Collaborative analyses of classroom data	• Cross-grade, cross-school, cross-school system observations, discussion, and writings • Journals (individual and collaborative) • Case studies of students, classrooms, and schools • Literature studies • Personal and academic exploratory essays

sional life span. Prospective teachers are assumed to be part of a larger struggle with a responsibility to reform—not just replicate—standard school practices by "teaching against the grain" (Cochran-Smith, 1991b), a skill learned by struggling along with experienced teachers to be reformers in particular schools and classrooms. Toward this end, students progress through the 12-month program as a cohort, participating simultaneously in university-based coursework and school-based field work experiences. Courses prompt critical perspectives on teaching, learning, and schooling as well as theoretical frameworks for learning from children and constructing subject matter curriculum. Monthly university seminars provide a context for student teachers, experienced teachers, and teacher educators to meet over the course of a year to raise questions about teaching and learning across grades, schools, and school systems. Three locally distributed publications—a newsletter, a collection of autobiographical essays, and a booklet of writings on teaching and learning to teach—help members to understand one another's professional perspectives and work lives.

Each student teacher works in the same classroom over the course of one school year, beginning on the first teacher day and working 2 days per week for the first 4 months and then 5 days per week for the next 4 months. Student teachers attend school-based and outside-school professional development activities such as inservice workshops, faculty meetings, parent-teacher conferences, and teacher collaboratives with their cooperating teachers. The key school-site structure is the teacher-researcher team meeting, a weekly session of each subcohort of student teachers, cooperating teachers, and university supervisors. In these meetings, which feature classroom and school inquiries into topics selected by the individual group, participants share observations, raise questions, and suggest different ways of looking at and thinking about the social life of classrooms.

Participants' Roles. It is the intention of Project START to interrupt the role expectations of the novice-expert model common to many teacher education programs. Rather than imitate the instructional styles of their mentors, student teachers are expected to construct their own knowledge of teaching and learning, question theory-practice relationships, write about their work, and participate with their experienced mentors as inquiring professionals. Likewise, the primary role of cooperating teachers is not to demonstrate model teaching techniques and effective language. Rather, cooperating teachers—who are selected for their commitment to curricular redesign, teacher research and publication, progressive education, grass-roots parent-teacher community groups, teacher collaboratives, or other teaching and school reform efforts—are expected to bring an inquiry-centered perspective to their roles as mentors and to articulate their own questions and frameworks to student teachers as they support students' initial forays into inquiry. Finally, the university supervisor, who spends 1 day per week learning the culture of the school site, getting to know school personnel, and observing in classrooms, is expected to function as co-learner and colleague rather than as evaluator and broker of knowledge. In addition to regular consultations with students and cooperating teachers, supervisors share resources, facilitate weekly teacher-researcher meetings, and meet regularly with the other university staff members to inquire into their own work as teacher educators. Student teachers work with school and university mentors who inquire about their own work, call policies and procedures into question, and seek out ways to meet regularly with their colleagues. This provides student teachers with powerful role models for learning from teaching across the life span.

Based on a series of group interviews with graduating students, cooperating teachers, and supervisors as well as information from questionnaires designed to assess various components of the program, a group of cooperating teachers, university supervisors, and project directors meets several times yearly to revise program structures and plan for the following year. The group collaboratively constructs inquiry assignments that student teachers complete by collecting data in their field work classrooms, plans seminar topics and reading/writing selections for the year, and revises structures for cross-visitation and collaboration across grade levels and schools.

Learning Opportunities, Themes, and Strategies. Course assignments, school- and university-site activities, in-house and regional publications and professional forums, and the larger professional community give START participants opportunities to engage in many kinds of inquiry about early literacy, schools, and schooling. Inquiry strategies include critical discussion of common readings; descriptive reviews of individual children; reflective conversations; cross-grade and cross-school observations; literature studies; journal writing; and collaborative analysis of children's work, anecdotal records, and excerpts from essays. In weekly school-site meetings and monthly university-site seminars, student teachers have the chance to be both close observers and participants in the inquiry process.

At monthly seminars, for example, members of the START community consider teaching and learning from perspectives that cut across grade level, school, school system, and disciplinary perspectives. Seminar topics over the last 2 years have included teaching mathematics for understanding; teaching as research (presentations of teacher-research projects by several START teachers and former student teachers); journal writing (readings from the published and unpublished journals of START and PhilWP teachers); mentoring as inquiry (reflection/discussion among more experienced and less experienced cooperating teachers and supervisors); learning from a child (analysis of one child's writing over time, led by a cooperating teacher); giving reason to children (demonstration and discussion of clinical interviewing); alternatives in urban education (presentations and discussion led by Central Park East teachers); descriptive review of a child (with review co-presented and co-chaired by teams of cooperating teachers and student teachers); multicultural education and teacher education (lecture and discussion of approaches to multicultural teaching); race, class, and gender in the work lives of teachers (presentations/small discussion groups led by START teachers in contrasting urban schools); children's understanding of science concepts (reflection/ analysis of children's conversations about scientific phenomena, led by a cooperating teacher); and learning to teach against the grain (1st-year teachers' stories and struggles shared by former START students).

In cooperation and consultation with their cooperating teachers, START student teachers also conduct small-scale classroom studies that provide opportunities for both active teaching and research on teaching. For example, student teachers collect data from their teaching to compare conventional and alternative methods of reading instruction, explore children's responses to various kinds of texts, examine the preconceptions that children bring to controversial social and historical issues, compare the question and response patterns during math lessons that include manipulative materials with those that occur during paper-and-pencil lessons, and investigate the contrasting profiles of children that emerge with test-based and observation-based modes of assessment. Small-scale studies like these offer students opportunities to construct curriculum and develop pedagogy as well as to formulate questions and collect and analyze observational, documentary, and interview data. With their mentors as partners, student teachers also write in and reflect on double-entry dialogue journals over the course of the year. Also, all participants in Project START write essays, which give form and voice to theories of practice as well as provide opportunities to connect diverse classroom incidents and examine underlying assumptions.

Inservice Teacher Education: PhilWP

Organizational Goals and Structures. Located at a graduate school of education at a research university in a major urban area, PhilWP is a school-university partnership and a site of the National Writing Project that reflects its origins and ongoing affiliation with a national model as well as the distinctive and dynamic features of a local culture. Begun by School District of Philadelphia teachers, University of Pennsylvania faculty, and other educators working to build a writing-across-the-curriculum initiative in the city schools, the project is a teacher collaborative designed primarily to provide an intellectual community for urban teachers in the city system and to strengthen the district's efforts to reform and restructure schools. It shares with the national model fundamental assumptions about teacher-to-teacher inservice education, collaboration between schools and universities as partners, cross-grade and cross-discipline writing, staff development across the professional life span, teachers as writers, and practice as an important source of knowledge for teaching. As the project has evolved, participants have come to include not only K-12 teachers but also college teachers, school administrators, and adult literacy practitioners as well.

PhilWP emphasizes the roles of teachers as writers, researchers, and reformers who seek ways to develop and provide leadership in writing and literacy, broadly conceived. The project focuses on building an intellectual community wherein teachers' explorations into language and learning support the gradual transformation of the cultures of teaching and schooling for urban children, adolescents, and adults. To provide contexts for investigating issues and practices that relate writing and literacy, collegial learning, and urban school reform, PhilWP's structures and activities center on teacher inquiry. Teachers' own classrooms, schools, and relationships with other teachers provide critical sites for observation, and their ongoing research functions as a powerful medium for sharing daily experiences and learning from one another. To further the work of the both the project and the district, PhilWP is also organized to study itself so that teachers become engaged in collaborative research on project activities and write about those activities for local as well as national audiences.

The writing project supports structures that connect and ultimately work to realign relationships between the schools and the university. The initial and advanced summer institutes, for example, provide a unique environment for intensive talking, reading, and writing about practice. Drawing on the prior knowledge and experience of teachers in the group and on the writings of other teachers, these institutes also use the research literature as a source of knowledge. This juxtaposition enables participants to investigate deeply their own histories as learners, particularly what they have experienced as raced, classed, and gendered readers and writers. At the conclusion of these invitational institutes, all participants become teacher consultants in the school district, with periodic access to one another's and to experienced teacher consultants' classrooms during the school day through a program of cross-visitation supported by the School District of Philadelphia. In addition to these components of the project, teachers provide leadership in year-long inservice courses on language and literacy, participate in a variety of inquiry communities and study groups, engage in project planning and governance, and present and publish their work in district, regional, and national contexts.

Participants' Roles. The writing project provides a context in which school-, program-, and university-based educators work to redefine and restructure their roles in both the field and the university. It is the intention of PhilWP to interrupt role expectations associated with teachers as isolated practitioners and as recipients or implementors of expert knowledge and to reframe the roles of university researchers as generators of knowledge and as transmitters to or trainers of others. As an organization that involves teachers, administrators, university faculty, and students, the project invites all participants to construct and reconstruct their own knowledge of teaching and learning, question theory-practice relationships, and contribute to the creation of a new image of professionalism and of scholarly work that makes activist inquiry fundamental. To do so, educators involved in PhilWP mediate between the immediate daily life of teaching or administering in schools and programs and their commitment to the larger political project of educational reform. Roles in the project are typically multiple and developed over time, reflecting the dynamics of the system as a whole as well as specific school or program contexts.

Teachers in PhilWP regard restructuring their own roles in classrooms as central, drawing on the collegial network and other project resources to craft learning environments relevant and responsive to their particular school and community contexts. In these contexts, students and their teachers as well as parents and others function as active and critical inquirers and constructors of knowledge and curriculum. Using writing and literacy as primary foci, teacher consultants in the district become leaders in school-based reform by participating in and facilitating planning and policy groups at all levels of the system. They also create, facilitate, and document the work of teacher inquiry communities within and across schools, including grade level, discipline-based or interdisciplinary focus groups, district- or university-sponsored inservice courses, charter schools within schools at the high school level, and cross-school study groups.

At the university, teachers from schools and literacy programs design and facilitate institutes for their peers, mentor new teachers, present their research in graduate courses, offer their own classrooms as sites for collaborative inquiry, and contribute to the literature of the field by disseminating their own research on practice. Further blurring the boundaries between teachers and learners, PhilWP in conjunction with the Graduate School of Education provides support for advanced study in reading, writing, and literacy, including a special fellowship and role for PhilWP Scholars, who come to the university to study full-time and to help develop the project during the summer and the school year. The project also offers opportunities for teachers to assume new roles as writers and collaborators on grants, proposals, curricula, and school-university research projects. And finally, by bringing together teachers and administrators in innovative formats through institutes, advisory boards, and the teacher-consultant program, the project creates contexts for redefining roles and relationships in the system as a workplace.

Learning Opportunities, Themes, and Strategies. In PhilWP, the most common structures for collaborative inquiry are diverse teacher inquiry communities that emerge from particular project affiliations and commitments. Participants include project teachers and others who share an interest in topics such as interdisciplinary thematic curriculum, whole language as a theory of practice, issues of cultural and linguistic diversity, critical and intergenerational literacy and pedagogy, performance-based assessment, and/or collegial learning and teaching. Often, the investigation of these themes through writing, reading, talking, and observing (Lytle & Botel, 1988) involves efforts to make the classroom a learning community and to make the communities in which the schools or programs are situated rich sources for teaching and learning. Teacher inquiry groups vary in size, duration, leadership, activities, and supportive structures that link them to larger reform efforts such as comprehensive high school restructuring, the national urban teachers' network, or the movement to professionalize the adult literacy work force. They have in common a participatory organization and collaborative teacher leadership with a particular emphasis on writing and inquiry as powerful modes of learning about teaching, students, and school and program improvement.

Processes used in PhilWP inquiry communities vary according to the specific purpose of the group but often center on different forms of structured oral inquiry—using, adapting, and often developing new versions of the documentary processes designed by Patricia Carini and teachers at the Prospect School and brought to PhilWP by teachers who have worked closely with these approaches over many years. Drawing on journals, field notes, work portfolios, and other classroom artifacts and documents, participants use data from one another's workplaces to investigate common themes and interests and to learn about learners and the specific settings that make the demands of teaching distinctive. Reading one another's practices as well as the texts of other school-, program-, and university-based teachers enables participants to create literacy communities. Using documentation of their own learning as a primary source, these groups provide a context for teachers and administrators to investigate their own questions, document and alter daily practice, and support one another's efforts to disseminate their work to local and more public audiences through presentation and publication.

INTERROGATING DIVERSITY

In this section, we demonstrate the power of inquiry as the intellectual centerpiece of teacher education across the professional life span by describing the ways that teachers struggle with cultural diversity by making knowledge, difference, and reform problematic. Using a variety of excerpts from teachers' essays, journals, and studies, we identify some of the similarities and common themes in the inquiries of beginning and experienced teachers. All of the examples in this section are excerpts from the writings of student teachers in Project START and of experienced teachers in PhilWP, and are used with permission.

Making Knowledge Problematic

Teacher research both stems from and generates questions. When teachers take an inquiry stance on diversity, they make problematic much of what is usually taken for granted about culture, learning, language, and power. They question common practice, deliberate about what is regarded as expert knowledge, examine underlying assumptions, interrogate educational categories, and attempt to uncover the values and interests served by the common arrangements and structures of schooling (Beyer, 1986; Carr & Kemmis, 1986; Smyth, 1987; Zeichner, 1986). In the process, they pay attention "not only to what is included in a world view but also what is left out and silenced" (Giroux, 1984, p. 35)—not only to what they as teachers believe but also to what they need to do.

In Project START, student teachers are invited to make problematic what they know about cultural diversity by examining typically unexamined assumptions about their own histories and the cultural and linguistic backgrounds of others; about the motivations and behaviors of children, parents, and other teachers; and about the most appropriate pedagogies for particular groups of learners. A variety of contexts are provided for individual and small- and large-group inquiries into these issues. In the following excerpt from an essay, white student teacher Dionne Enea draws on her own experiences as a raced, classed, and gendered learner as well as on her own experiences in student teaching. This assignment was one of several designed to promote critical response to readings by addressing the generic question: What do you think you think about ____? The intent of this kind of assignment, in which student teachers pose their own questions about assigned readings, is to have teachers use others' research to uncover their own interpretive frameworks and to explore the implications of these connections in ways that are tentative, evolutionary, and personal:

I found Lisa Delpit's article, "The Silenced Dialogue: Power and Pedagogy in Educating Other People's Children" [1988] to be very disturbing, and I've linked this to the way that I felt when we read in class Peggy McIntosh's "White Privilege: Unpacking the Invisible Knapsack" [1989]. The fact that something called "white privilege" exists in our society is easy for someone who is white to ignore, and I think that it made me uncomfortable to have to face up to these truths that I otherwise never consider in my everyday experiences. . . .

It is easy for me to simply say that I do not judge individuals in terms of race, but after thinking about the validity of Lisa Delpit's [1988] and Bernardo Ferdman's [1990] articles I realize that this is nowhere near enough. If cultural identity does indeed play a role in how a child learns, as Ferdman claims in "Literacy and Cultural Identity," then as a teacher my responsibility goes far beyond treating people as equals. Am I one of those white liberals whom Delpit believes ignores the fact that a culture of power and its rules exist, and who tries in vain to address successfully issues of race in an educational system designed by white males to perpetuate a society that holds them in a dominant and advantaged position?

If the bottom line is, "We teach who we are," how can I effectively teach those who are not like myself? How much will "who I am," make me blind to the needs and experiences of those who are different from me? I fear that Lisa Delpit's article, which seems to make so much sense, is right. Does the fact that I am white leave me with my hands tied because I will never be able to escape my position in the "culture of power" to teach those who do not hold this power? . . .

Written in October, this essay provides a window into the way that one preservice teacher begins to construct the dilemmas of race and gender in teaching. Part of what is important here is that Enea is struggling to formulate questions rather than moving too quickly to premature conclusions. Perhaps even more significant, however, is her effort to move beyond the belief often held by beginning teachers that educational equity requires teachers to be color blind in their classrooms. In doing so, she implicitly takes on the responsibility for educating herself about the cultural and linguistic resources that her children bring to school. Finally, she begins to recognize that her efforts to respond to cultural diversity in the classroom are inevitably located in her own preconceptions, experiences, and assumptions about learning and teaching.

When experienced teachers such as those in the PhilWP inquire into cultural diversity, they also get in touch with and then interrogate their deep personal histories of cultural difference and inequity. Particularly in urban environments, where both student and teacher populations are increasingly diverse, there is a critical need to create contexts in which experienced teachers have access to the richness of one another's cultural frameworks and the ways that these inform pedagogical decisions across classrooms, schools, and communities. In PhilWP, urban teachers read and respond to current theory and research about linguistic and cultural diversity. However, they also share fiction, poetry, and biography selected to tap into experiences that are otherwise unexamined or forgotten and that help to provide lenses for close observation and learning from their own students.

In the PhilWP summer institute, teachers are invited to write about "a time when school didn't fit your culture." In response, Puerto Rican Teresa Alvarez chose to describe what happened when a school policy clashed with the needs of a young girl newly arrived in Philadelphia from Puerto Rico. The policy stipulated that new students be placed initially in the English-only classroom with the lowest enrollment, regardless of the language needs of the child:

Ten minutes later [after the child had been placed in an Anglo classroom], a call came to the office. It was Virgin's new teacher, "Please have someone take this *new* girl out of my room, she is disrupting my class, she won't stop crying or screaming!"

I was asked to go talk to the *new* girl and calm her down. As I reached the door, I could hear the screams and sobbing. Virgin looked at me and pleaded, "Sacame de aqui, por favor." (Please take me out of here.) I took this frightened child out to the hallway, she grabbed my waist, I hugged her and let her cry. Through sobs she said, "Yo odio esta escuela y a esa maestra, yo no hablo ingles, yo no entiendo nada de lo que ella dice. Yo no se lo que ella esta diciendo. Por favor busca a mi mami." (I hate this school and that teacher, I do not speak English, I do not understand anything of what she is saying. I do not know what she is saying. Please get my mother.) I tried to calm her down by explaining that this class might not be a permanent assignment, that she would be tested, and most likely be assigned to the bilingual class. Virgin wanted no part of that reasoning. "Por favor, sacame de ese salon, si me pones en ese salon otra vez yo me mato!" (Please take me out of that room, if you put me back in that room, I will kill myself!) she cried. I took it upon myself and spoke to the bilingual second grade teacher. I explained the problem and she allowed Virgin to sit in the class until she was tested. Two weeks later Virgin was tested and was permanently assigned to that room.

I sit and wonder: How can organization of a school take priority over our students' needs? How can everyone in the school make learning a wonderful experience? How can we as educators make that first day a happy and memorable experience for that frightened student?

I think of Virgin: What possible negative effects did that first day in a *new* school have on her?

This piece does not contain lengthy analysis or elaboration of the obvious issues involved in providing appropriate school experiences for linguistically different students. Rather, the recollection shows in vivid detail the experience of a child caught in the often contradictory logic of school policy and highlights the critical need for an advocate who navigates that system on behalf of the child. Teresa's story provides grist for experienced teachers to deliberate about the choices that adults make for children and to interrogate the potential in their own classrooms and schools for unintentional insensitivity to cultural differences. In inservice teacher education programs where teacher research is central, stories like these often serve as occasions for experienced teachers to confront their own racism and to work together to imagine more culturally responsive curricula and school policies. In both of these examples, teachers interrogate their previous experiences and prior knowledge about cultural differences and about school practices that may constrain opportunities for learning and reproduce inequities.

Making Difference Problematic

A second way to make cultural diversity problematic is to provide preservice and inservice contexts in which difference itself is interrogated. When teachers from different ethnic groups and races, community and school contexts, subject areas and grade levels, and years of experience work together, there is a rich mix of perspectives, personalities, and school practices. Opportunities for elementary and secondary teachers to work together are relatively rare in school district inservice programs, as are opportunities for urban and suburban experienced and student teachers to work together in preservice programs. When these worlds are juxtaposed, however, one consequence is that some of the inequities of schools as workplaces and of children's opportunities to learn are foregrounded. In addition, by watching others work, experienced teachers question their own stereotypes about particular age groups and add new images of language and literacy instruction across classrooms. Seeing firsthand the cultures of teaching and learning in other classrooms, schools, and communities provides data for contrastive analysis and thus a deeper analysis of one's own place and possibilities.

Cross-visitation within and across schools and school districts is a central activity that makes difference problematic in both Project START and PhilWP. In Project START, each school-site teacher-researcher group is paired with another group at a school that differs in terms of size, structure, and/or racial, ethnic, and economic composition of the communities served. Teams of students and supervisors are hosted by their partner teams for several day-long visitations, followed later in the year by a 2-week exchange in which student teachers trade places. Student teachers conduct close observations of students and teachers; talk to students, parents, and school personnel; and observe across grade-level settings. School-site groups prepare and follow up on cross-visits by reading, writing, and talking together about the cultures of teaching, children's and teachers' language and cultural differences, and similarities in and differences between large and small, private and public, and urban and suburban schools. Group discussions are intended to help student teachers to develop frameworks for making sense of differences that are highlighted during the cross-visits. Student teachers raise questions provoked by their experiences in cross-visiting and heightened by the contrasts they observe on returning to their home schools, as the following brief excerpts from journals reveal:

Student Teacher 1: Throughout the day I kept wondering how children from my [urban, public] home school would function at my [urban, private] cross-visit school. The teachers at my home school feel that the kids they work with require a very structured environment. The classroom of [the teacher I visited] was structured but in a different way. The children were given choices to make within distinct limits.

Student Teacher 2: I am struck by the casualness at my cross-visit [private] school. Even changing classes is slow and unhurried. I've only been here a few hours, but I don't see the kids working hard. Maybe it's there and I can't see it.

Student Teacher 3: After being at my cross-visit [suburban, private] school for two full weeks, being in my home [urban] classroom for one day was in many ways a "new" experience because I was looking at it in a different way. I keep wondering if that change means that I have been doing too much judging and comparing, but I think really that it just means that I am looking more critically now, or at least from a broader experience.

Making difference problematic through student teacher cross-visitation is tricky. Traveling between two worlds heightens student teachers' awareness of many features of schools: class size, facilities and resources, teachers' modes of discipline, and children's attitudes as well as school norms of collegiality and professionalism. Students raise thoughtful questions that are not likely to arise without the comparative framework. On the other hand, there is a risk that crossing cultures reinforces stereotypes about families and communities, and prompts students to assign too readily personal blame for the inadequacies of schools or systems, or to accept uncritically that what works effectively in one environment ought to work in another. Despite the risks, however, over time START student teachers, cooperating teachers, and university supervisors agree that making difference problematic through cross-visitation is critical to learning from teaching. By creating situations in which students write about their own biases and preconceptions, it is possible to revisit and interrogate these over the course of time. In addition, cross-visitation helps students to begin to see the power of context—that every child's educational experience is deeply embedded in particular social, economic, and political structures.

At the inservice level, teacher-to-teacher cross-visitation functions both to reduce the culture of isolation and to interrupt the widely held assumption that professional development is a process wherein more knowledgeable teachers or specialists deliver expertise and provide models for imitation by those who are less knowledgeable. The cross-visitation program in PhilWP is one component of a teacher-consultant program developed with the school district to alter the location and expectations of traditional staff development models. Each subdistrict in Philadelphia has a writing support teacher, a long-term substitute hired for this program by the central administration. The writing support teacher makes it possible for teacher consultants to visit other teachers in their own building, in other schools in the subdistrict, or across the district as a whole. Cross-visitation provides the opportunity for inservice teachers to make sense of and improve their everyday practice, not by imitating routines and strategies but rather by questioning, observing, documenting, and discussing their own work in relation to the work of other urban teachers. Although cross-visitation occurs primarily in pairs, teachers also share experiences through research logs and discussions, and cross-visitation itself is studied by members of the project as a form of professional development.

For inservice teachers in a large urban school system, cross-visitation provides structures for teachers who may differ from one another in race and ethnicity to observe, share field notes, and even teach one another's students. Although the schools in urban Philadelphia have in common some demographic similarities, they are also dramatically different from each other in student ethnicity, school culture, and the culture of the immediate community. The opportunity for experienced teachers to come to know students who may differ from their own in age, race, and ethnicity prompts them to raise new questions about pedagogy and curriculum that are responsive to the needs of different populations at different developmental periods. In PhilWP, for example, Lynne Strieb, a white primary-grade teacher who had taught for many years in classes with primarily African-American children, decided to visit the classroom of Deborah Jumpp, an African-American middle school teacher whose students were white, Hispanic, and African-American (see Chapter 6 for more detail). In notes about the cross-visitation, Strieb wrote:

[We] had been in the same journal group in the second Summer Institute. . . . I was fascinated with the ideas about literacy, about non-dominant English, about young teenagers which Deborah was expressing, but which were somewhat new to me. I knew that I wanted to see her in action in the classroom. So, when she asked for someone to come and observe the children at their journal time, I jumped at the chance.

In her journal, Strieb described her first impressions of the middle school:

Jones Junior High was built in the 1930s. Its halls are lined with marble and granite, and it gives a clean, grand appearance. The school population is mixed white (German, Irish, Polish), Hispanic, and African-American. It is truly a desegregated school. Deborah has told me that the children with whom she works are all "at risk" for failure and dropping out of school altogether. They are, in some cases, older than they should be for their grades, having been retained two or more times in lower grades.

Both during and after her visit, Strieb wrote detailed field notes, which she later shared with Jumpp. These captured some of the richness of oral interactions, the subtlety of nonverbal behaviors, and Jumpp's deft weaving of many separate curricular strands. Congruent with Jumpp's strong emphasis on writing in the classroom, she invited Strieb, a published author, to share multiple drafts of her writing and to talk with the students about her own processes as a writer. Later Strieb herself reflected on the experience of visiting Jumpp's class, not as a critic or a passive observer but as a participant in the widening community of adolescent and adult learners:

I learned a lot from that visit. I saw two groups of children who are traditionally considered difficult working calmly, quickly, and with purpose at writing. I saw a wonderful teacher at work. She turned my visit into an effective lesson, a lesson to which the children listened attentively. I saw a teacher who skillfully got the children to work together quietly and seriously.

Jumpp later wrote a response to these field notes:

What I saw in Lynne's journal was a very different observation than I've ever gotten from my principal, and the class I saw was a different class from the class I'd been seeing. Before the Writing Project, I had never had another teacher in my class-room. . . . It was an alienated and lonely existence. What could mean more to me than a fellow colleague saying something about my teaching? Things really change when teachers start observing. . . . You can really learn something when you have another perspective in your classroom.

One of the most striking aspects of interactions such as these is that both observer and observed play the dual roles of teacher and learner. Both take an inquiry stance, raising questions, collecting and interpreting classroom data in a specific context, and considering the implications of these for their own practice and for the larger struggles they face as urban teachers. More impor-tant, perhaps, is that cross-visitation provides an opportunity for urban teach-ers to "cross the boundaries" (Rose, 1989) of school cultures, student cultures, and their own cultural perspectives and experiences. When teachers research their own practice by cross-visiting, they begin to envision alternative config-urations of human and material resources to meet the needs of culturally diverse groups of students, teachers, and administrators. And they are willing to invest more of their own resources and professional energy in larger efforts to reform classrooms and schools.

Making Reform Problematic

As a consequence of interrogating knowledge and differences, both preservice and inservice teachers become increasingly committed to school and peda-gogical reform, increasingly conscious of their own efficacy as individual teachers, and increasingly involved in concrete efforts to alter the educational prospects of culturally diverse populations of students. The START curriculum, for example, is designed to help student teachers to become aware of their potential roles as change agents in their own classrooms and schools, and questioning is assumed to be part of the process of teaching and learning from teaching—even for beginners. PhilWP is intended to provide an intellectual community for experienced teachers who seek to restructure their own class-room practices and to work actively for reform in a variety of contexts within the school district. Both programs make problematic the teacher's role in reform—that is, they prompt inquiry that leads to critical perspectives on the social, economic, and political bases of educational systems and on the limited roles that teachers have been expected to play in the transformation of schools. Participation in teacher-research positions teachers to examine and take action on issues of equity, access, and culturally appropriate pedagogy and curriculum.

At the preservice level and for beginning teachers, learning to meet the social, emotional, and academic needs of culturally diverse groups of students means making problematic rather than accepting common assumptions. These include beliefs about student motivation and potential for achievement, families' capacity for supporting children's learning, the appropriateness of the curriculum, and the efficacy of teachers in ameliorating what often appear to be insurmountable problems. The exploratory essay excerpted in the following was written by Jennifer Eastman, a white teacher and recent START graduate. It was intended for an audience of current student teachers considering urban teaching. In it, Eastman grapples with what it means to be successful in an urban school. The excerpts suggest that a research-centered preservice program predisposes new teachers to evaluate their practice, knowing that the school success of urban schoolchildren depends on changing the status quo and that individual teachers play a part—either by design or by default—in that change:

This essay is based on my own experiences as a new teacher in a public school in a very poor section of Philadelphia, where I do not feel defeated and do not see the staff or the school or the children as defeated. . . .

As a new teacher in a new system, new school, new neighborhood, I believed that caring about these children, and getting through the first year without quitting or leaving them was one success. And even this was not easy. The first year, many days I felt incompetent, silly, not in control, unable to figure out simple lesson plans, afraid of any kind of change, nervous about trips, worried about parent meetings and conferences, and so on. I was also faced with the possibility of being transferred to another school due to a change in the allotment of teachers at Hunter. . . . I also discovered that I need to operate on several different levels of involvement: in my classroom, with other teachers on joint projects, on school-wide projects, and on community/political issues. These different involvements keep me from feeling too much despair at any one problem by seeing hope for change in all these areas. . . . So I want the best for [my children], and at the same time I see a very difficult, bleak path for them in this society and this neighborhood. I find, for my own sake, ways to respond. It was not until I wrote this article that I realized very clearly that my way of coping is to create some concrete project in response.

In the essay, Eastman goes on to describe her responses to particular problems and even tragedies that had occurred in her school during her first year:

In response to [a teaching] assistant's shooting death, I wrote and received a grant for a school-wide study of Puerto Rican culture, with a library corner of books and materials on Puerto Rico in [the assistant's] name. . . .

In response to the family problems encountered by some of the children, I invited four children to participate in an origami club on Mondays, which gives me the opportunity to show some special attention to children who lack attention at home.

In response to the needs of families, I helped to write a grant . . . to provide family-oriented services after school. . . .

In response to a need to form connections with other teachers, I am currently writing another grant with the other kindergarten teacher on a circus theme, culminating in taking our children and their parents to the circus. . . . .

In response to the difficulty communicating with parents, I initiated monthly parent meetings. . . . We write a monthly newsletter and calendar . . . and in our meetings we have translators as we go over the monthly schedule and school-related information.

This essay makes it clear that there are many ways for beginning teachers to take a proactive stance toward reforming the school environment for culturally diverse populations. In this case, the preservice teacher education program had provided Eastman with many opportunities to read and critique the literature on multicultural education and urban schooling. But it had also prompted her to enter the teaching force as a learner, not expecting to apply ready-made answers to complex, situation-specific problems. She needed to observe, talk with other teachers and parents, get to know the community, and build her own networks of resources, projects, and services. In this way, she built her own agenda for reform both within her classroom and within the school community.

In teacher education projects for experienced teachers—just as for preservice teachers—making reform problematic means questioning assumptions and common practices in classrooms and schools and seeking ways to take action individually and collectively. PhilWP's Seminar on Teaching and Learning was established to provide a context in which experienced teachers could conduct collaborative inquiry in three schools that were part of the school district's larger efforts to reform comprehensive high schools in the city. Together, participants in the multiyear seminar explored issues of cultural diversity among teachers and their students by reading, writing, and jointly interpreting data collected in their schools and classrooms. These inquiries focused on cultural diversity through the lenses of alternative assessment, interdisciplinary thematic teaching, and teacher and student collaboration.

A concern that emerged from their collaborative inquiry was that many of the administrative, curricular, and programmatic structures of high schools failed to provide or even subtly constrained students' access to current and future educational opportunities. In inquiry projects that they completed for the seminar, five African-American women teachers attempted to make these structures more visible by questioning premises and practices about placement, course selection, counseling, and appropriate pedagogy for learners in urban schools. The teachers were not simply tinkering with instructional and organizational routines but instead were envisioning and creating new environments within which their students could interrogate the social structures of their own lives. Through their research, teachers in five different disciplines chose to make issues of access problematic by looking more closely at school and classroom practices and by beginning to take action to address these problems.

A computer teacher, for example, investigated the procedures that led to the labeling and tracking of college-bound and non-college-bound students by developing alternative methods of self-assessment for her keyboarding classes. Disturbed by inequities between college- and non-college-bound students' access to career counseling, a business teacher initiated a program of earlier and more intensive career counseling that was integrated into the business curriculum. In an attempt to be responsive to the needs of "at-risk" ninth graders, a humanities teacher collaborated with a reading teacher to restructure her curriculum to focus on the lives and career obstacles of African-American males in religion, sports, art, jazz, and acting. A special education teacher who was concerned about the social and emotional needs of a mildly handicapped multiracial group of ninth-grade girls studied their interactions with a black woman attorney whom she invited to lead discussion sessions about their social lives.

Finally, by examining rostering, counseling, teacher expectations, student attitudes, and administrative policies, math teacher Joan McCreary sought explanations for why so few African-American and Hispanic students, who represented more than 60% of the population in the school, were enrolled in academic mathematics classes. What follows are several excerpts from a report of her research:

The late bell rings to commence second period and the slow, somber procession of General Mathematics students enters the room . . . the same four or five male African-American youth must be peeled from the wall and personally invited to class each day. It takes them another ten to twenty minutes for everyone to get ready (pencil or pen, paper, book, materials, in groups, and on task). Needless to say, the lesson is heavily peppered with reminders. . . .

My concern initially was focused on the disproportionate number of African-American and Hispanic students in non-academic mathematics classes, in particular General Mathematics II. Why weren't more of our youth excelling in higher level mathematics classes such as Algebra II, Elementary Functions, and Geometry? . . . Didn't they understand the importance of such studies? Didn't they know of our proud legacy in the sciences?

Based on extensive reading and informal interviewing with teachers, McCreary found that teachers' responses fell primarily into two groups: those who perceived the students as incompetent and those who thought that the students were capable of doing the work but did not do it. In both cases, the students were blamed for the problem. Based on her research, McCreary made many recommendations about how teachers could take action on this situation:

Involve ourselves in the political structure and work to effect change. . . .
Involve ourselves in educational research. . . .
Keep abreast of current issues in educational theory, psychology, economics, and politics as they may impact on our children's education not just on our "jobs." . . .
Relinquish some of [teachers'] authority in the classroom to students. . . .
Correlate subject matter to the students' world and their career options. . . .
Recognize and address the different learning styles of students. . . .

As she completed her research project, McCreary noted that she often experienced anger and despair, but she also came to a new understanding of how racism functions to deny students access to educational opportunities. That certain academic courses function as gatekeepers to higher education for minority students is well documented (J. Lytle, 1990). What this teacher's own research contributes to her learning about cultural diversity, however, is a fuller understanding of the problem, how it is played out in the context of her own high school, and how all teachers might interrupt this system by changing their behaviors and attitudes. Like the other teachers who investigated issues of access and equity, she has not only strategies and recommendations to make to other educators but also a stronger sense of her own voice in the larger conversation about school reform.

The increasing cultural diversity of America's schools and schoolchildren demands that every teacher, whether new or experienced, thoughtfully examine the local meanings of disjunctions between home and school, community and school system, and teacher and student and then responsibly take action to improve the educational choices and life chances of his or her students. As Huebner (1987) reminds us:

Teachers must act in an imperfect world. To postpone action until the knowledge and technique makers establish the educational millennium is sheer irresponsibility, based on illusions of progress. We have no choice but to risk ourselves. The choice is to consider the risk private or to build a community that accepts vulnerability and shares risks. (p. 26)

In communities that support teacher research, beginning and experienced teachers may be willing to confront their own histories, hear the dissonance within their own profession, and begin to construct working alliances with colleagues, students, parents, and communities.

5

Communities for Teacher Research: Fringe or Forefront?

There is growing support for the notion that research by teachers about their own classroom and school practices can function as a powerful means of professional development and can also contribute to the knowledge base in education (Erickson, 1986; Goswami & Stillman, 1987; Stenhouse in Rudduck and Hopkins, 1985). In this volume, we have been positing the stronger position that research by teachers represents a distinctive way of knowing about teaching and learning that will alter—not just add to—what we know in the field. Furthermore, we have argued that as it accumulates and is more widely disseminated, research by teachers will represent a radical challenge to our current assumptions about the relationships of theory and practice, schools and universities, and inquiry and reform. Despite its potential, there is widespread agreement that there are no obvious and simple ways to create the conditions that support teacher research and that, in fact, major obstacles constrain this activity in schools and make it difficult to redefine teaching as a form of inquiry. Although many current proposals for school reform involve innovative arrangements of time, space, and resources intended to enhance teachers' autonomy and their opportunities for collaboration and inquiry, structural rearrangements are not sufficient for teacher research to contribute fully to the burgeoning national movement for the professionalization of teaching. Innovative structures are necessary but not sufficient to realize the potential of teacher research as a legitimate and unique form of knowledge generation and a profound means of professional growth that can radically alter teaching and learning.

In this chapter, we briefly consider some of the obstacles to teacher research in schools, teacher groups, school-university partnerships, and regional and national forums. We argue that overcoming these obstacles requires the building and sustaining of intellectual communities of teacher

85

researchers or networks of individuals who enter with other teachers into "a common search" for meaning in their work lives (Westerhoff, 1987) and who regard their research as part of larger efforts to transform teaching, learning, and schooling. Drawing on examples from a number of teacher and student teacher groups in the greater Philadelphia area, we develop a framework for analyzing and evaluating the work of communities for teacher research according to four perspectives: the ways in which communities organize time, use talk, construct texts, and interpret the tasks of teaching and schooling. A framework based on time, talk, text, and task provides a way to critique systematically the various structures and strategies intended to foster teacher inquiry that are currently in place or are being developed in teacher organizations, partnerships, and schools. It may be used as a heuristic to help existing and prospective teacher groups to plan their collaborative work and to raise questions about the cultures of school and university organizations as sites of inquiry.

ON THE FRINGE: SOME OBSTACLES TO TEACHER RESEARCH

The various commission reports on the state of schools and teachers have chronicled a now familiar list of reasons why teaching has failed to become a major profession, including poor preservice preparation, absence of clearly articulated standards of performance, lack of public confidence, flatness of the career ladder, and failure of teachers to remain current in theory and research on teaching. However, the obstacles to teacher research are more subtle than the items on this familiar list. They are deeply embedded in the cultures of school and university organizations, in pervasive assumptions about the nature of teaching and learning, and in the traditions involved in the generation of new knowledge. Four of the most important obstacles to teacher research are described in the following.

Teacher Isolation

As a profession, teaching is defined primarily by what teachers do when they are not with other teachers. When teachers are evaluated, it is individual classroom performance that is scrutinized. When contracts are negotiated, it is the amount of instructional time that is often a key issue. In fact, when teachers are out of their classrooms or talking to other teachers, they are often perceived by administrators, parents, and sometimes even by teachers themselves as *not* working. The isolation of teachers at all stages of their careers is well documented (Goodlad, 1984; Lieberman & Miller, 1984; Lortie, 1975), and it is clear that the daily rhythms of schools typically provide little time for teachers to talk, reflect, and share ideas with colleagues (Little, 1987; Lytle & Fecho,

1991). On the other hand, teacher research is by definition a collaborative and social activity that requires opportunities for sustained and substantive intellectual exchange among colleagues (Cazden, Diamondstone, & Naso,1989; Goswami & Stillman, 1987). It also requires time within the school day to perform the fundamental tasks that researchers in all other professions take for granted—observing and documenting phenomena, conducting interviews, and gathering artifacts and supporting data. Tacit images of teaching as a solo performance carried out on the classroom stage mitigate against the institutionalization of inquiry (Myers, 1987) both as an integral part of teaching (Britton, 1987) and as a way for teachers to interact professionally (Schaefer, 1967).

On the other hand, isolation from other teachers is not a condition that is simply imposed on teachers by outside forces or is always perceived by teachers as a problem. Rather, isolation has two sides: It makes for privacy as well as loneliness, autonomy as well as separation. As Little (1987) points out, isolation often safeguards teachers from the scrutiny of others: They may "forfeit the opportunity to display their successes, [but they also] reserve the right to conceal their failures" (p. 60). We are suggesting that even when teachers have opportunities to collaborate with one another to conduct teacher research, they may be hesitant to do so. Isolation acts as a deterrent by secluding teachers from each other and creating a cycle in which teachers may view teacher research as hazardous—a high stakes game in which collaboration comes at the price of exposure and loss of autonomy (Lytle & Fecho, 1991).

Occupational Socialization

In many schools, the competent teacher is assumed to be self-sufficient, certain, and independent (Lortie, 1975). Asking questions and being uncertain are inappropriate behaviors for all but the most inexperienced teachers, and even they have only brief periods of grace during which they may ask a limited number of questions (Richardson-Koehler, 1988). Teachers are not encouraged to talk about classroom failures, ask critical questions, or openly express frustrations. In short, the occupational culture perpetuates the myth that good teachers rarely have questions that they cannot answer about their own practices or about the larger issues of schools and schooling (Lortie, 1975).

Researching teachers, on the other hand, are noted for their questions (Berthoff, 1987; Knoblauch & Brannon, 1988). They may indeed be self-sufficient, competent, and sometimes certain. However, they also pose problems, identify discrepancies between their theories and their practices, challenge common routines, and attempt to make visible much of what is taken for granted about teaching and learning. They often count on other teachers for alternative perspectives on their work (Cochran-Smith, 1991a). They seek help not because they are failing but because they are learning (Traugh et al., 1986).

And they regard struggle and self-critical questioning as integral parts of their intellectual lives (Lather, 1986; Miller, 1987). Going public with questions, seeking help from colleagues, and opening up one's classroom to others go against the norms of appropriate teaching behavior (Lytle & Fecho, 1991). Taking a stance as a learner and researcher involves risks that may change a teacher's status and have unintended consequences (Lewis, 1989). Furthermore, it is difficult to combine teaching and teacher research. Some teachers worry that research will require that they give less time to their students, and they are not persuaded that time spent in inquiry will have sufficient payoff for learning.

The Knowledge Base for Teaching

A third obstacle to the creation of communities for teacher research, which is closely related to the second, is the push to make teaching a legitimate profession by the generation of what Pellegrin (1976) calls "a systematic codified technology that is universally known to practitioners" (p. 348). The question here is not whether we need a knowledge base for teaching but rather what kind of knowledge base is needed, who constructs it, and what roles teachers play in its formation. If the generation of a knowledge base is primarily associated with a technical view of teaching (Apple, 1986) and if it is constructed only by university-based researchers, the teacher's role is clear. He or she is expected to learn the skills of effective teaching and also learn how to apply them to practice. When the professionalization of teaching is linked to this technical view, staff development is regarded as a vehicle for transmitting skills to teachers rather than as a process for collaborative inquiry (Lambert, 1989), and the teacher has no role to play in the generation of a knowledge base.

In contrast to the technical model of professionalization wherein the teacher is an increasingly sophisticated consumer of other people's knowledge, the teacher-researcher movement is based on the notion that a professional plays a participatory role in the creation and use of knowledge in the field. This relationship involves ways of knowing about teaching in which the teacher develops theories to "interpret, understand, and eventually transform the social life of schools" (Smyth, 1987, p. 12).

The Reputation of Educational Research

Finally and somewhat ironically, the reputation of educational research itself tends to function as an obstacle to promoting teacher research. Teachers' suspicions and even contempt for educational research are hardly surprising given that research has been used to blame teachers for the failings of the larger educational and sociopolitical systems. Research is often called on as the rationale for school systems to train and retrain teachers in a wide variety of areas and as the grist for countless checklists, scripts for teaching, and evaluation schemes (Lieberman, 1986; Zumwalt, 1982a), which have deskilled teachers (Apple, 1986) by regarding them as replaceable and fixable parts in the larger educational machinery.

Unfortunately, even when educational researchers have addressed problems that are of interest to teachers, their findings have frequently been reported in ways that are inaccessible, seemingly unrelated to the everyday realities of teaching, and counterintuitive to lessons learned from experience. Furthermore, educational research has frequently been presented to teachers as "uncovered truths" about the most effective ways to teach and as "definitive procedures" for assessing students' learning. As Howe and Eisenhart (1990) recently pointed out, there is an emerging consensus even in the scientific community that no research can be accurately regarded as value neutral or completely objective. However, because educational research is rarely presented to teachers as value laden and socially constructed, teachers are not encouraged to interrogate its premises and relevance for their own situations. The fact that most educational research is perceived by teachers as irrelevant to their daily work lives spills into and contaminates their willingness to believe both that teacher research has the potential to be relevant and that they themselves might want to be researchers. To many teachers, research is more or less by definition something that is distant, uninteresting, and impenetrable. Furthermore, because few teachers have had the opportunity in their own graduate and professional training to become acquainted with alternative conventions and paradigms of research, they have little reason to identify with a professionalization movement that is based on the notion of teachers as researchers (see Fecho and Pincus in Chapter 9).

We argue that to encourage wider involvement of teachers in research, it is necessary to overcome the serious obstacles caused by teacher isolation, a school culture that works against raising questions, a technical view of knowledge for teaching, and the negative reputation of educational research. Overcoming these obstacles requires the building of communities for teacher research.

TO THE FOREFRONT:
COMMUNITIES THAT SUPPORT TEACHER RESEARCH

There has been a growing effort over the past decade to provide organizational structures that enable groups of teachers to come together to talk about their work, learn from one another, and address curricular and instructional issues. In-school and school-university structures include cross-visitation, teacher study groups, schools within schools, writing projects, student teacher–cooperating teacher discussion groups, and on-site courses and seminars that focus on teacher inquiry. Some teacher groups meet outside of the auspices of schools or school systems, and local, regional, or national networks provide forums for teachers to exchange ideas with colleagues from across the country. All of these structures have in common the purpose of enabling teachers to reflect on their work, and some of them are explicitly intended to encourage teacher research or action research.

Using examples from a number of teacher groups, we provide an analytic framework that describes the qualities of such communities and can be used to raise questions about current school and university efforts to promote teachers' participation in research. Represented in Figure 5.1, our framework provides four perspectives on teacher-research communities: the ways in which communities organize time, use talk, construct texts, and interpret the tasks of teaching and schooling. Although the interrelationships of these four perspectives will vary in particular communities, the framework can be used as a heuristic to help existing and prospective teacher groups to plan their collaborative work and to raise questions about the cultures of school and university organizations as sites of inquiry.

Organizing Time

It is no accident that one of the most common characteristics of fantasy literature for both children and adults is the manipulation of time. In novels, we can wrinkle in and out of time, make time fly, drag and stand still, shift back and

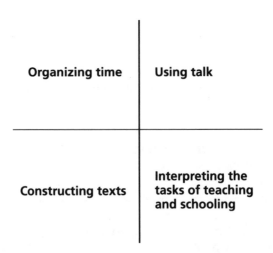

Figure 5.1. Communities for teacher research: A framework for analysis.

forth between time spheres, and ultimately surpass time's boundaries altogether. Unfortunately, some of the harshest contrasts to literary images of unbounded time are real-life images of the factory and the schoolroom. In schools, teachers and students are organized according to whether they are on time, behind time, out of time, killing time, saving time, serving time, watching their time, or moving double time. Teachers are often evaluated according to how they manage transition time, allocated time, academic time, and time on task. Clearly, time is a dimension that is central to the work lives of teachers.

Time is also one of the most critical factors in the formation and maintenance of learning communities for teacher research. Unlike other professions, which are organized to support research activities, teaching is a profession in which it is extraordinarily difficult to find enough time to collect data and it is almost impossible to find time to reflect, reread, or share with colleagues (Goodlad, 1984; Griffin, 1986; Zeichner, 1986). When groups of teachers come together as researchers, they need sufficient chunks of time in which to work and sufficient longevity as a group over time (Little, 1987). When the pace of a community's work is unhurried and members of the group make a commitment to work through complicated issues over time, ideas have a chance to incubate and develop, trust builds in the group, and participants feel comfortable raising sensitive issues and risking self-revelation. These ways of organizing time are frequently identified in the feminist literature as critical to fostering collaborative ways of knowing and constructing knowledge (Belenky et al., 1986). Over time, communities that support teacher research develop their own histories and, in a certain sense, their own culture—a common discourse, shared experiences that function as touchstones, and a set of procedures that provide structure and form for continued experience. Longevity makes it possible for teacher researchers to engage in inquiry that is both systematic and spontaneous.

On the other hand, maintaining teacher-research communities over relatively long periods of time also presents a number of challenges. How can a group meet the needs of both new and experienced members? Can a group become too large or too small? What happens to a group as members come and go? How can a group avoid becoming locked into procedures and continue to be receptive to critique and change even when many members feel satisfied with the status quo? How can teacher-researcher groups be increasingly responsive to special interests without fragmenting the organization? If teacher-researcher groups are to be more than the latest educational fad or the newest theme of staff development programs, they must be analyzed and reconceptualized as enduring structures subject to many of the same problems as other voluntary organizations that exist over time.

For example, in a Network of New and Experienced Urban Teachers (NNEUT) (Cochran-Smith, Larkin, & Lytle, 1990), a program that combines inservice and preservice teacher education, longevity is a mixed blessing. In contrast to more typical student teaching terms, which range from 10 to 14 weeks, NNEUT's full-year student teaching period allows supervisors, cooperating teachers, and student teachers to work together in a variety of stable groups to reflect on their work and write about their practices. Although each year, student teachers who are by definition new to the group have many of the same needs, new and returning cooperating teacher mentors bring more diverse backgrounds and differing previous experiences with the notions of reflective practice, teacher research, and urban education. This means that project activities need to be redesigned continuously to meet the needs of preservice and inservice teachers with varying degrees of readiness to be teacher researchers. Some have been teacher researchers in their own classrooms and published their work in local and national publications, while others are less familiar with the notion of critique and analysis of their own practice. Finding activities that are intellectually exciting and useful to all members of the community can be a tricky balancing act. However, unlike more typical modes of staff development, teacher research both generates and is generated by individual and collective questions about practices and theories that evolve over time. The activities of teacher researchers therefore change qualitatively over time even though inquiry structures remain the same.

One of the most salient issues concerning time in teacher-research communities is how much control teachers have over their time. Forming and maintaining communities that support teacher research within schools requires attending to the constraints and conflicts about the construction and interpretation of time by both teachers and administrators. Hargreaves (1989), for example, argues that control of teachers' time is a highly contested arena in the school as workplace. Three of the dimensions of time that Hargreaves identifies help us to understand how little control teachers actually have. "Micropolitical" time refers to ways that time is distributed according to power and status relationships. Although all teachers' work is defined by time spent in the classroom, high school teachers have more time allotted to planning outside the classroom than do their elementary and middle school colleagues. This suggests that it might be easier to form teacher-research communities in secondary schools or that secondary teachers might have more discretionary time to allot to research activities.

Hargreaves' category of "phenomenological" time refers to the ways that time is lived or experienced by different members of the school. Using Hall's (1984) categories, Hargreaves (1989) argues that operating within a "monochronic" view of time means working on one task at a time, complying with a schedule, and giving priority to procedures rather than relationships. Operating within a "polychronic" perspective on time, on the other hand, means doing several tasks at once, being highly sensitive to context, and being oriented primarily to people and relationships rather than procedures. Hargreaves argues that a polychronic conception of time is more common among women than men and is more likely in smaller organizations with a personal rather than an official style of leadership. Many of the activities of teacher researchers who work in schools require pursuing several tasks simultaneously, attending to complex relationships between and among teachers and students, and recognizing the multiple layers of context in which learning and teaching are embedded. Monochronic time frames dominate education because they are, as Hargreaves argues, the "prerogative of the powerful" (p. 19)—not necessarily because they are effective administratively or pedagogically. The issue is whether a teacher-research community can exist within a monochronic time frame or whether it is necessary to examine and attempt to alter the ways that time is constructed in school settings.

"Sociopolitical" time refers to the ways that teachers' time is allocated and used in schools. Sometimes, as Hargreaves (1989) points out, administrators "colonize" teachers' time by claiming more and more of it for formal purposes and leaving teachers with less and less discretionary or flexible time. Supporting teacher-research communities may entail redistributing some of the time during the school day that is already allotted for other purposes, adding to the contracted amounts of time for research purposes and enabling teachers to make different arrangements of class, preparation, and meeting times. For example, in Crossroads, a charter school within a school at Gratz High school in Philadelphia, eight teachers have reorganized the school day so that they share students and planning periods to construct an integrated interdisciplinary curriculum. By redistributing time across the school day, they have reframed and reconstructed their own teaching lives and significantly altered the learning opportunities of their students. As part of the continuous cycle of inventing, enacting, and evaluating the curriculum, they collect, share, and interpret data about the effects of these innovations (Fecho, Pincus, & Hiller, 1989).

Teacher research cannot simply be an additional task added to the already crowded teacher's day. It has become increasingly evident from our work with teacher researchers that building communities requires that teachers have more discretion over how they spend in-classroom and out-of-classroom time. Increased control over time enables teachers to engage in research by analyzing data gathered in their own classrooms as well as by documenting learning in one another's classrooms and schools, team teaching, and scheduling classes to accommodate informal and formal group meetings. If teacher groups are to become communities, participants will have to integrate research more fully into the ongoing activities of the school day and work out some of the difficult issues associated with the politics of time.

Using Talk

A second factor critical to the formation and maintenance of learning communities for teacher research is talk—particular ways of describing, discussing, and debating teaching. In communities that support teacher research, groups of teachers engage in joint construction of knowledge through conversation. Through talk, they make their tacit knowledge more visible (Polanyi, 1958), call into question assumptions about common practice (Giroux, 1984), and generate data that make possible the consideration of alternatives. We have pointed out that teacher research is not limited to classroom studies carried out by teachers but also includes essays, journals, and oral inquiries. Oral inquiry, which we defined in Chapter 2 as teachers' self-conscious and often self-critical attempts to make sense of their daily work by talking about it in planned and formally structured ways, is one type of teacher research that is only beginning to be recognized as a research process. Some teacher-research groups regularly conduct oral inquiries such as reflections on practice or descriptive reviews of students (Carini, 1986), literature studies (Edelsky, 1988), and doubting/believing discussions (Elbow, 1973). Other communities do not use formal oral inquiry formats, but they still talk in distinctive ways about their teaching.

In communities that support teacher research, all talk does not contribute directly to the joint construction of knowledge about teaching. Rather, teachers swap classroom stories, share specific ideas, seek one another's advice, and trade opinions about issues and problems in their own schools and the larger educational arena. In most professional contexts, these exchanges are typically considered "small talk," which implies that they are pleasant but unimportant relative to the "big talk," or the more serious purposes for which the group has convened. In communities that support teacher research, these "smaller" conversations have an important function: They create and sustain the interpersonal relationships necessary for the larger project of the joint construction of knowledge. When teachers describe encounters with individual students or the responses of their classes to particular texts or activities, for example, they provide rich information about their day-to-day work and the ways that they construct their worlds inside and outside their classrooms. Stories swapped casually acquire more significance when recalled in a different context; advice sought and received may solve an immediate problem, but it may also percolate for a time and then reappear as a different kind of question. In communities for research, teachers use small talk to enter into one another's frames of reference.

Two interrelated ways of talking about teaching are central to building communities for teacher research both inside and outside of school. The first is similar to Geertz's (1973) notion of "thick description," with which he emphasizes that what researchers often call data are really their own constructions of what others are saying, doing, and meaning. Thick description is a process of "grasping" and "rendering" the multiple and complicated "webs of significance" (p. 5) that people themselves have created. In teachers' communities, this kind of rich descriptive talk helps make visible and accessible the day-to-day events, norms, and practices of teaching and learning and the ways that different teachers, students, administrators, and families understand them. Talk of this kind transforms what is ordinarily regarded as "just teaching" (Little, 1989, p. 23) into multi-layered portraits of school life that depend on diverse and sometimes conflicting interpretations. Structured formats such as Prospect School's documentary processes (Carini, 1986) are particularly powerful ways for teachers to make explicit what is often implicit, to remember by drawing on past experiences, to formulate analogies between seemingly unrelated concepts and experiences, and to construct from disparate data patterns in students' learning. When teachers' conversations build thick description, they conjointly uncover relationships between concrete cases and more general issues and constructs.

During one session of the year-long Seminar in Teaching and Learning of the Philadelphia Schools Collaborative, for example, a group of African-American and white urban high school teachers talked about tracking, inquiring into the many ways that students are typically grouped within and across classes. Together, they raised questions about race, class, and gender and the short- and long-term impacts of tracking on educational opportunities, including access to courses, programs, and higher education. Using the format of a "reflective conversation" (Carini, 1986), in which participants explore the range of meanings and experiences associated with key educational terms, teachers wrote and then shared their individual images, which they analyzed through integrative summaries from several perspectives. Notes from the session convey some of the images that participants shared as they explored their understandings (Philadelphia Schools Collaborative, 1989):

- tracks which leave a trace or mark, as do animal or needle tracks
- tracking down those who could excel and making them mediocre
- running on a track, around and around without a goal—just stuck there only being able to ride one track at a time
- the tracks on 69th Street and what it would take to switch tracks—the early railroads, using cars on tracks to carry coal, everything had to be standardized to make it easier
- tracks as having known destinations, placing limits on where you can go.

Through this talk, teachers shared poignant and even painful memories of being tracked themselves. Some expressed personal sadness and anger at being labeled. Others were outraged as they recounted the all too apparent connection they perceived between race and track upon first walking into the school as beginning teachers 20 years earlier. The personal and collective experiences of the group helped uncover ways that their expectations for students in their own classrooms might be reinforcing differences rather than interrupting differences. Although the individual and collective experiences of teachers always figure significantly in the ongoing construction and interpretation of knowledge about teaching and school culture, these experiences are rarely interrogated and then used to generate plans for further inquiry and action. The joint construction of knowledge in teacher-research communities is not a neat or bounded process that leads to consensus (Cochran-Smith, 1991b). When teachers are working together to construct greater understanding about teaching, their conversations are recursive and reflect a fluid, changing view of knowledge.

Closely related to the first, the second way of talking about teaching that is central to building communities for teacher research is broadly termed critique. In using this term to describe teacher researchers' talk, we call attention to conversations in which teachers question common practice, deliberate about what is regarded as expert knowledge, examine underlying assumptions, interrogate educational categories, and attempt to uncover the values and interests served by the common arrangements and structures of schooling (Beyer, 1986; Carr & Kemmis, 1986; Smyth, 1987; Zeichner, 1986). This way of talking makes problematic much of what is usually taken for granted about teaching and learning.

In teacher-research communities, making teaching problematic means calling into question labels, practices, and processes that are so ingrained in our language and metaphors for teaching and learning that they have become reified. The givens of schooling compose a long list, including reading groups, rostering, inservicing, tracking, abilities, disabilities, mastery, retention, promotion, giftedness, disadvantage, special needs, departmentalization, 47-minute periods, coverage, standards, Carnegie units, detention, teacher-proof instructional materials, and homework. Making the givens of education problematic requires asking interpretive questions, which rarely take the form, "What's the best way to teach reading to first graders?" or "Is this child reading 'on grade level'?" but are instead phrased, "What do reading and learning to read mean in this classroom?" or "Under what circumstances does this particular child ask for particular kinds of help?" Talking like this is a way for teacher-research communities to "learn to struggle collectively" (Lieberman, 1986), a process that is rarely aimed at or ends in single or definitive conclusions.

The following excerpt from the discussion of a small group of preservice and inservice teacher researchers in Project START (Student Teachers As Researching Teachers) reveals the ways that they struggled together to uncover and call into question some of their assumptions about race and class (Project START, 1989). A cooperating teacher, who was white and female, began the conversation:

COOPERATING TEACHER (WHITE, FEMALE): [One thing we've been trying to learn at our school is how] the qualities we use to describe ourselves are often the qualities we recognize [most] easily in kids. But it's children who have *opposite* qualities or *different* qualities that we have the most to learn from. On our [grade level] team [we've been trying] to identify kids whom we feel we have difficulty with or who are a challenge to us in some way. And often [it turns out that] they are children of a different race or a different class or a different social background. And we try to look closely at those children, really describe them as carefully as we can, to see what they [can] teach us about learning and about us as people and what we project on to other people. And that has been a really helpful thing for us as a first step in thinking about all the things that we assume as middle class white women.

STUDENT TEACHER (AFRICAN-AMERICAN, MALE): I was thinking of a black girl [in my kindergarten class] who is very intelligent, but she has a tendency to be very quiet at times. And she uses a lot of slang and says, "Jesus" and words like that. And then I think of another little boy, a White boy, who's also very intelligent, who sometimes is a management problem. But in terms of the whole issue of culture and power—I realize that even when he's difficult, he's coming from a whole environment where I assume that they're extremely bright. . . . It's almost as if when I see him, I see a child who will probably be all right. But when I see this black girl, I always say she's as intelligent, but I don't assume the same things. . . . I feel some confusion because [when] I think of this little boy, I figure that he'll get a [high] score on tests, and that will just smooth [over] any of the behavior problems.

STUDENT TEACHER (WHITE, MALE): I think class differences are related to some of the cultural differences which cause the problems [in the ways we look differently at kids]. But what [he] was [just] saying about things being smoothed out for a white middle-class male, that's you know, [something] that could go on forever—definitely. Some things in my life I don't think I could have gotten away with as a black male.

STUDENT TEACHER (AFRICAN-AMERICAN, MALE): I guess what I mean is that it's almost as if the little [White] boy is already on the track—to an Ivy League university [or something]. . . .

Through conversations such as these, beginning and experienced teachers have opportunities to articulate and then to question their own assumptions about children's abilities and prospects based on variables of race, class, and gender. Describing classroom experiences and analyzing their own responses depended on the evolving trust of the group and individual participants' willingness to disclose their previously unexamined ways of categorizing and interpreting their observations.

The co-construction of knowledge through talk is a public process. In spontaneous conversation, participants build on one another's ideas in ways that are not possible in solitary situations. Teacher-research communities are often composed of teachers from different schools and school systems, grade levels, and subject matter areas. When teachers meet at regional or national conferences, these differences provoke analyses of commonalities and contrasts across dramatically different contexts. Their varying experiences make it impossible for teacher researchers to rely on habituated ways of talking, seeing, and thinking about teaching. Instead they have to work consciously to make their frames of reference clear as they describe and interpret their practices and theories to others in the community.

Using Texts

A third factor relates to the critical role of texts in forming and maintaining communities for teacher research. Communities use a wide range of texts, not all of which are published or disseminated but are still essential to teachers' individual and collective gathering, recording, and analysis of data. Texts include teacher-researcher reports in the form of journals, essays, and studies as well as selections from the extensive theoretical and research literatures in the fields related to teaching and learning. Texts used by teachers in their communities also include written records of teachers' deliberations, informal writing used to facilitate the talk of teacher groups, transcripts of classroom interactions and interviews, notes made of classroom observations, and drafts of teachers' plans and work in progress. In addition, teachers have access to students' work, including writings, drawings, and other materials; school forms, documents, and records; demographic data; and curriculum guidelines and materials. Although some schools and districts collect some of these texts for management and research purposes, teachers in research communities regard all of these texts as potential data and attempt to examine their interrelationships from the perspective of the classroom teacher.

Communities play a critical role in making texts accessible and usable by teachers. The Philadelphia Writing Project (PhilWP) community, for example, made accessible Philadelphia teacher Lynne Strieb's published journal (Strieb, 1985) to another teacher, Mickey Harris. After reading and discussing Strieb's journal with a group of PhilWP teachers, Harris was prompted to reclassify and thus reclaim her own private teaching journal of some 20 years as a "text" that might be of interest to other teachers. In writing about her journal and revisiting her own experiences over time, Harris punctuated her text with references to James Britton, Eudora Welty, Alexander Pope, and Lynne Strieb—the "tacit tradition" of her field (Emig, 1983)—and in so doing located her own work in relation to a longer history of writers and scholars. This makes it clear that teacher research need not be a loose collocation of individual efforts. Each separate piece of teacher research can not only inform subsequent activities in an individual teacher's classroom but also inform and be informed by all teacher research past and present. As the number and modes of communication among teacher-research communities increase, it is more likely that the full potential of teacher research to inform the profession will be realized.

Teacher research, like all forms of knowledge-building, educational or otherwise, is a fundamentally social and constructive activity that depends on the dissemination and use of texts. In the teacher-research community, the generation and critical use of texts make teachers' inquiries accessible to other teachers. There is further evidence for this collective and cumulative power within the community when members generate and then use texts about their own work. For example, student teachers and cooperating teachers in Project START read essays and studies written by teachers presently and previously in the program. Teacher consultants in PhilWP read research conducted by other participating teacher consultants about their program of teacher-to-teacher cross-visitation. In both cases, teachers used the research of other teachers to stimulate discussion of teacher development and collaboration as well as further action and research.

When a wide range of texts are used over time, teacher-research communities function as discourse communities. From the perspective of the field of composition, Harris (1989) has suggested that the concept of discourse community draws on the everyday meaning of community as a group with common goals and interests as well as the literary concept of interpretive community and the sociolinguistic notion of speech community. "Interpretive community," as used by literary theorists Fish (1980) and others, refers to a network of people with similar meaning perspectives, while "speech community," as used by Hymes (1974), Gumperz (1982), and other linguistic anthropologists, refers to a group of people who engage in face-to-face interaction within a specific context. Teacher-research communities often function as discourse communities in all three of the ways suggested by Harris: They are "real groupings of writers and readers," they share a kind of larger mission, and they become networks of "citations and allusions," which refer to texts both within the speech community and outside of it.

Participants in teacher-research communities are often part of several of the discourses of their profession: the school, the school system, the union, and the university. Thus they are "always committed to a number of conflicting beliefs and practices" (Harris, 1989, p. 19). As we suggest above, this means that teacher-research communities are not and should not be grounded in consensus; rather, they are sites of critical reflection on the discourses themselves. For example, Buchanan (1988a), a Philadelphia teacher, juxtaposes two images of teaching: the media notion of "burnout" and what she calls "handling fire." Buchanan's essay demonstrates that teachers' texts often simultaneously speak to and critique the discourses of several communities, including school administrators, university researchers, their students, and their teacher colleagues. Buchanan writes:

> These differing images underscore two ways of viewing the struggles which go on in contemporary classrooms. Sometimes I think the gulf is so wide between these ways of looking at teachers and classrooms that dialogue between educational researchers and practitioners, between administrators and teachers, is almost impossible.

The students enter my classroom each fall with various fires burning within them. For some of them it is rage, for others it is the lamp of learning, for still others it is only a few glowing embers which need to be carefully fanned. The complex community within the classroom requires looking closely at what individuals need, building on the varied strengths of the students, and struggling with their weaknesses. Depending on the issues, there may be support from university research or from school administration, but I have to reach outside of the classroom to find it. When I try to explain my point of view, it is often lost or incorporated into strengthening theirs. . . .

Those outside the classroom need to hear what we know and understand. We are told what others think of us, but we are rarely asked to explain what we really know to others. Educational reform requires that teachers change. Yet the plans for changing who teachers are and what they know still operate within the old language of educational hierarchy and with the old images of teachers' knowledge. (pp. 40–43)

Texts like Buchanan's are beginning to reach new audiences. The publication and dissemination efforts of teacher-research communities are effectively widening the discourse about schools and schooling to include the knowledge and perspectives of teachers, long disenfranchised from the professional and academic processes of building the knowledge base for teaching. On the other hand, many texts of the teacher-research community remain inaccessible because they are not disseminated beyond the local group. When teachers publish and present their work at regional and national levels, however, they demonstrate the power of their texts to make the familiar strange, to link teachers' work, and to challenge the status quo.

Defining the Tasks of Teaching

We have been suggesting that communities for teacher research have particular ways of spending time, talking, and using texts. Research communities are also committed to a common task, which is ultimately the reform of schooling. Underlying this task is a set of assumptions about teaching, learning, and organizations. One critical assumption of participants in communities for teacher research is that teaching is primarily an intellectual activity that hinges on what Zumwalt (1982b) calls the "deliberative" ability to reflect on and make wise decisions about practice. Teaching is regarded as a complicated and intentional activity that requires a great breadth and depth of professional knowledge and judgment in conditions that are inherently uncertain (Shulman, 1986b 1987, 1989). In contrast to a more technical view that teaching hinges on the use of particular techniques applied in various situations, a deliberative view of teaching regards teachers as professionals who use their knowledge to construct perspectives, choose actions, manage dilemmas, interpret and create curricula, make strategic choices, and to a large extent define their own teaching responsibilities (Cochran-Smith, 1989; Lambert, 1985). Teacher researchers regard these tasks as opportunities for systematic, intentional inquiry and regard the inquiries of others in the community as opportunities for rethinking their own assumptions and practices.

When teachers redefine their own relationships to knowledge about teaching and learning, they reconstruct their classrooms and begin to offer different invitations to their students to learn and know. A view of teaching as research is connected to a view of learning as constructive, meaning centered, and social. Here we emphasize the reciprocal relationship between theories about teaching and theories about learning. Teachers who are actively researching their own practices provide opportunities for their students to become similarly engaged (Johnston, 1990; Schwartz, 1988). This means that what goes on in the classrooms of teacher researchers is qualitatively different from what typically goes on in classrooms (Goodlad, 1984). Researching teachers create classroom environments in which there are researching students (Branscombe, Goswami, & Schwartz, 1992). Students ask—not just answer—questions, pose—not just solve—problems, and help to construct curriculum out of their own linguistic and cultural resources rather than just receive preselected and predigested information. Britton (1987) reminds us that "every lesson should be for the teacher, an inquiry, some further discovery, a quiet form of research" (p. 13). Our point here is that in every classroom where teachers are learners and all learners are teachers, there is a radical but quiet kind of school reform in process.

It is well documented that instruction is the most difficult aspect of schooling to control or change within the normal bureaucratic procedures. In fact, despite numerous efforts to govern classroom instruction from the outside—by prescriptive materials, training and inservicing programs, and elaborate schemes for evaluation—these strategies ultimately fail and teachers retain relative autonomy over what goes on in their own classrooms (Joyce, Showers, & Rolheiser-Bennett, 1987). To bring about instructional reform, teachers' potential to be thoughtful and deliberate architects of teaching and learning in their own classroom must be tapped and supported. We are not suggesting that complete independence for teachers is the answer to radical school reform but that true reform depends on members of the teaching profession developing their own systematic and intentional ways to scrutinize and improve their practices.

In teacher-research communities, the task of teachers is not simply to produce research, as some have argued is the case in the academic research community (Jackson, 1990). Rather, the commitment of teacher researchers is change: in their own classrooms, schools, districts, and professional organizations. At the base of this commitment is a deep and often passionately enacted responsibility to students' learning and life chances. The Philadelphia Teachers Learning Cooperative, for example, has met weekly for more than a decade to raise questions about their work and improve their practices with the students in their classrooms. Often, this entails descriptive reviews of individual children, a process in which a teacher presents a focusing question and data about a student's learning and others in the group raise questions and make recommendations for action. Outsiders regard the work of the cooperative as teacher research and its activities as testimony to a long-standing commitment to systematic, intentional oral inquiry. However, until recently, members of the group did not refer to their work together as research, and their central purpose was (and still is) not to produce publications. Rather, teachers in the cooperative referred to their inquiry activities as simply teaching. As the following excerpt from a collaboratively written article about their work makes clear, their aim is to meet the needs of their students by making more visible their children's progress:

> Especially during late-spring descriptive reviews, we are startled by the growth that is there to see if we only take the time to look. In May, Edna presented her concerns about Mike. He was failing first grade, scheduled to repeat it next year. She needed our recommendations on how she could penetrate his shell to find ways to help him improve academically. She described the stiff, blank-faced loner who couldn't hold a pencil last fall. We asked her about things he seemed to enjoy. She went through his reactions to the year's holiday celebrations, and we began to see a pattern as Mike began to loosen up, to enjoy color and cutting, and even handwriting. We thought of ways she could write down the fingerplays he likes so he and the other ten "readiness" children might have their own texts to read from. We noticed a hidden strength—Mike's pride in working quietly at something until he can finally produce a product comparable to his classmates'. The two hours in May illuminated a pattern of hope, stretching from the dim days of shame and truancy last fall to a more promising future of involvement in school. . . .
>
> Teachers' Learning Cooperative helps teachers look for a way to accept and work with a diversity of learners, often suggesting that they wait for a year or more to see how the "slow learner" might develop. We do have a luxury of time to ask and wonder what will happen to a child. Last September Barbara asked us for ways to help Billie control her outbursts. What has happened to Billie since then? We often schedule a review of a review. Somehow it makes yesterday's temper tantrums and tomorrow's fight less anxious for us as teachers if we can look at Billie again. Billie is on her way toward greater awareness and control. (Philadelphia Teachers Learning Cooperative, 1984, p. 733)

Groups like the Philadelphia Teachers Learning Cooperative see a very clear connection between inquiry and making a difference in the lives of their children. When teachers work together to construct knowledge about children's patterns of growth and development and to generate teaching strategies, they are involved in an ongoing process of altering the social and intellectual life of their classrooms.

In our discussion of the task of communities for teacher research, we have been suggesting that there can be powerful connections between teacher research and school reform. As we have indicated, the activities of teacher research provide the grist for ongoing instructional revision and improvement. Furthermore, teacher researchers identify and help establish priorities for the critical areas of school policy and practice that need to be reexamined.

Teacher research ensures that the agenda for school change is informed by teachers' emic perspectives on everyday school life as well as by the perspectives of academic researchers, policymakers and funders, and the media. When teachers play an active role in shaping the agenda and in the implementation of school reform efforts, it is inevitable that "reform" itself will become a contested notion. As teachers are called on to play increasingly important roles in school-based and district-level decision making, their research provides systematic evidence for and raises serious questions about what goes on in schools. When teachers themselves accumulate data and share it across school and community contexts, they not only change their relationships to knowledge about teaching but also dramatically realign their relationships to the brokers of knowledge and power in their schools, in the university, and even in the corporate community.

The most fundamental issue is whether teacher research will remain on the fringe of educational reform or whether it will be at the forefront. Our argument is that communities for teacher research—communities with particular ways of organizing time, using talk, constructing texts, and interpreting the tasks of teaching and schooling—have the potential to move teacher research from fringe to forefront by fostering reforms that amount to more than tinkering with or reinforcing existing structures. Communities of teacher researchers can play an essential role in school reform. Not only does their work add to the knowledge base on teaching, but their collective power as knowledge-generating communities also influences broader school policies regarding curriculum, assessment, school organization, and home-school linkages. Through teacher-research communities, teachers' voices play a more prominent part in the dialogue of school reform.

Part I: References

Alaska Teacher Researchers Group. (1991). *The far vision, the close look.* Junea: Alaska State Board of Education.

Apple, M. (1986). *Teachers and texts: A political economy of class and gender relations in education.* New York: Routledge and Kegan Paul.

Argyris, C. (1982). *Reasoning, learning and action: Individual and organizational.* San Francisco: Jossey-Bass.

Aronowitz, S., & Giroux, H. (1985). *Education under siege.* New York: New World Foundation.

Asante, M. K. (1991). The Afro-centric idea in education. *Journal of Negro Education, 62,* 170–180.

Ashton-Warner, S. (1963). *Teacher.* New York: Simon & Schuster.

Atwell, N. (1987). *In the middle: Writing, reading and learning with adolescents.* Upper Montclair, NJ: Boynton/Cook.

Avery, C. S. (1987). Traci: A learning-disabled child in a writing-process classroom. In G. Bissex & R. Bullock (Eds.), *Seeing for ourselves.* Portsmouth, NH: Heinemann.

Bay Area Writing Project. (1990). *Research in writing: Working papers of teacher researchers.* Berkeley, CA: Bay Area Writing Project, University of California.

Belenky, M. F., Clinchy, B. M., Goldberger, N. R., & Tarule, J. M. (1986). *Women's ways of knowing.* New York: Basic Books.

Berthoff, E. (1987). The teacher as researcher. In D. Goswami & P. R. Stillman (Eds.), *Reclaiming the classroom: Teacher research as an agency for change.* Upper Montclair, NJ: Boynton/Cook.

Beyer, L. (1986). Critical theory and the art of teaching. *Journal of Curriculum and Supervision, 1,* 221–232.

Bigelow, W. (1990). Inside the classroom: Social vision and critical pedagogy. *Teachers College Record, 91,* 437–446.

Bissex, G., & Bullock, R. (1987). *Seeing for ourselves: Case study research by teachers of writing.* Portsmouth, NH: Heinemann.

Bloome, D., & Green, J. (1984). Directions in the sociolinguistic study of reading. In P. D. Pearson (Ed.), *Handbook of reading research.* New York: Longman.

Boomer, G. (1987). Addressing the problem of elsewhereness: A case for action research in schools. In D. Goswami & P. Stillman (Eds.), *Reclaiming the classroom: Teacher research as an agency for change.* Upper Montclair, NJ: Boynton/Cook.

Boston Women's Teachers' Group (Freeman, S., Jackson, J., & Boles, K.). (1983). Teaching: An imperiled "profession." In L. Shulman & G. Sykes (Eds.), *Handbook of teaching and policy.* New York: Longman.

Branscombe, A. (1987). I gave my classroom away. In D. Goswami & P. Stillman. *Teacher research as an agency for change.* Upper Montclair, NJ: Boynton/Cook.

Branscombe, A., Goswami, D., & Schwartz, J. (Eds.) (1992). *Students teaching, teachers learning.* Portsmouth, NH: Boynton/Cook, Heinemann.

Britton, J. (1987). A quiet form of research. In D. Goswami & P. Stillman (Eds.), *Reclaiming the classroom: Teacher research as an agency for change.* Upper Montclair, NJ: Boynton/Cook.

Brophy, J. E., & Good, T. L. (1986). Teacher behavior and student achievement. In M. C. Wittrock (Ed.), *Handbook of research on teachers* (3rd ed.). New York: Macmillan.

Buchanan, J. (1988a). *Handling fire: Work in progress, 3.* Philadelphia: Philadelphia Writing Project.

Buchanan, J. (1988b). Preliminary proposal for an urban archive of teachers' and children's work. Unpublished ms.

Buchanan, J. (1989). The language of whole language. *The Voice of the Philadelphia Writing Project, 1,* 1–2.

Buchanan, J., & Schultz, K. (1989, March). *Looking together: Communities of learners in an urban third-fourth grade classroom.* Paper presented at the spring conference of the National Council of Teachers of English, Charleston, SC.

Burton, F. (1991). Teacher-researcher projects: An elementary school teacher's perspective. In J. Flood, J.N. Jensen, D. Lapp, & R. Squire (Eds.), *Handbook of research on teaching the English language arts.* New York: Macmillan.

Bussis, A. M., Chittenden, E. A., & Amarel, M. (1976). *Beyond surface curriculum.* Boulder, CO: Westview.

Bussis, A. M., Chittenden, T., Amarel, M., & Klausner, E. (1985). *Inquiry into meaning: An investigation of learning to read.* Hillsdale, NJ: Lawrence Erlbaum.

Calkins, L. M. (1985). Forming research communities among naturalistic researchers. In B. McClelland & T. Donovan (Eds.), *Perspectives on research and scholarship in composition.* New York: Modern Language Association.

Calkins, L. M. (1991). *Living between the lines.* Portsmouth, NH: Heinemann.

Carini, P. (1975). *Observation and description: An alternative methodology for the investigation of human phenomena.* Grand Forks, ND: University of North Dakota Press.

Carini, P. (1979). *The art of seeing and the visibility of the person.* Grand Forks, ND: University of North Dakota.

Carini, P. (1986). *Prospect's documentary processes.* Bennington, VT: The Prospect School Center.

Carr, W., & Kemmis, S. (1986). *Becoming critical.* London: Falmer Press.

Cazden, C. (1986). Classroom discourse. In M. C. Wittrock (Ed.), *Handbook of research on teaching* (3rd ed.). New York: Macmillan.

Cazden, C., Diamondstone, J., & Naso, P. (1989). Teachers and researchers: Roles and relationships. *The Quarterly of the National Writing Project, 2,* 1–3, 25–27.

Clark, C. C., & Peterson, P. L. (1986). Teachers' thought processes. In M. C. Wittrock (Ed.), *Handbook of research on teaching* (3rd ed.). New York: Macmillan.

Clay, M. (1975). *What did I write?* Auckland, New Zealand: Heinemann.

Cochran-Smith, M. (1984). *The making of a reader.* Norwood, NJ: Ablex Publishing.

Cochran-Smith, M. (1989, April). Of questions, not answers: The discourse of student teachers and their school and university mentors. Paper presented at American Education Research Association Annual Meeting, San Francisco.

Cochran-Smith, M. (1991a). Reinventing student teaching. *Journal of Teacher Education, 42,* 104–118.

Cochran-Smith, M. (1991b). Learning to teach against the grain. *Harvard Educational Review, 61,* 279–310.

Cochran-Smith, M., Garfield, E., & Greenberger, R. (1992). Student teachers and their teacher: Talking our way into new understandings. In A. Branscombe, D. Goswami, & J. Schwartz (Eds.), *Students teaching, teachers learning.* Portsmouth, NH: Heinemann.

Cochran-Smith, M., Larkin, J. M., & Lytle, S. (1990). *Network of new and experienced urban teachers.* First annual report to Fund for the Improvement of Post-Secondary Education, Washington, DC.

Cochran-Smith, M., Paris, C. L., & Kahn, J. L. (1991). *Learning to write differently: Teachers, children, and word processing.* Norwood, NJ: Ablex Publishing.

Comer, J. P. (1989). Racism and the education of young children. *Teachers College Record, 90,* 352–361.

Cone, J. (1990). *Untracking advanced placement English: Creating opportunity is not enough: Research in writing: Working papers of teacher researchers.* Berkeley, CA: Bay Area Writing Project, University of California.

Corey, S. (1953). *Action research to improve school practices.* New York: Teachers College Press.

Crawford, M., & Marecek, J. (1989). Feminist theory, feminist psychology: A bibligrapy of epistemology, critical analysis and applications. *Psychology of Women Quarterly, 13,* 477–491.

Crouse, M. R. (1990). *Fantastic Mr. Fox: What about the farmers?* Unpublished manuscript, University of Pennsylvania, Philadelphia.

Cummins, J. (1986). Empowering minority students: A framework for intervention. *Harvard Educational Review, 56,* 18–36.

Delpit, L. (1988). The silenced dialogue: Power and pedagogy in educating other people's children. *Harvard Educational Review, 58,* 280–298.

Denham, C., & Lieberman, A. (Eds.). (1980). *Time to learn.* Washington, DC: National Institute of Education.

Dennison, G. (1970). *The lives of children.* New York: Random House.

Dewey, J. (1904). *The relation of theory to practice in education: The third NSSE yearbook* (pt. 1). Chicago: University of Chicago Press.

Dicker, M. (1990). Using action research to navigate an unfamiliar teaching assignment. *Theory Into Practice, 29,* 203–208.

Duckworth, E. (1987). *The having of wonderful ideas.* New York: Teachers College Press.

Dunkin, M. J., & Biddle, B. J. (1974). *The study of teaching.* New York: Holt, Rinehart, & Winston.

Dunstan, A., Kirscht, J., Reiffer, J., Roemer, M., & Tingle, N. (1989). Working in the classroom: Teachers talk about what they do. *English Education, 21,* 39–52.

Edelsky, C. (1988). Living in the author's world: Analyzing the author's craft. *The California Reader, 21,* 14–17.

Edelsky, C., & Boyd, C. (1989). *Collaborative research.* Keynote address presented at the spring conference of the National Council of Teachers of English, Charleston, SC.

Edelsky, C., & Smith, K. (1984). Is that writing or are those marks just a figment of your curriculum? *Language Arts, 61,* 24–32.

Eisner, E. (1991). *The enlightened eye.* New York: Macmillan.

Elbaz, F. (1983). *Teacher thinking: A study of practical knowledge.* New York: Nichols Publishers.

Elbow, P. (1973). *Writing without teachers.* New York: Oxford University Press.

Elliott, J. (1985). Facilitating action research in schools: Some dilemmas. In R. Burgess (Ed.), *Field methods in the study of education.* London: Falmer Press.

Elliott, J., & MacDonald, B. (1975). *People in classrooms* (occasional paper no. 2). Norwich, UK: University of East Anglia, Center for Applied Research in Education.

Ellsworth, E. (1989). Why doesn't this feel empowering? Working through the repressive myths of critical pedagogy. *Harvard Educational Review, 59,* 297–324.

Emig, J. (1983). *The web of meaning.* Upper Montclair, NJ: Boynton/Cook.

Erickson, F. (1986). Qualitative methods in research on teaching. In M. C. Wittrock (Ed.), *Handbook of research on teaching* (3rd ed.). New York: Macmillan.

Erickson, F. (1989). Research currents: Learning and collaboration in teaching. *Language Arts, 66,* 430–442.

Evans, C. (1989, April). *The educators' forum: Teacher-initiated research in progress.* Paper presented at the annual meeting of the American Educational Research Association, San Francisco.

Evertson, C. M., & Green, J. L. (1986). Observation as inquiry and method. In M. C. Wittrock (Ed.), *Handbook of research on teaching* (3rd ed.). New York: Macmillan.

Fecho, R. (1987). *Folding back the classroom walls: Teacher collaboration via cross visitation: Work in progress.* Philadelphia: Philadelphia Writing Project, University of Pennsylvania.

Fecho, R. (1989). *On becoming mean and sensitive: Teacher to student writing conferences in the secondary classroom.* Report prepared for the National Council of Teachers of English Research Foundation.

Fecho, R. (1990). *Reading like a teacher.* The Voice of the Philadelphia Writing Project, 1, 14–16.

Fecho, R., Pincus, M., & Hiller, N. (1989). *"Crossroads" proposal to Philadelphia Schools Collaborative.* Philadelphia: Philadelphia Schools Collaborative.

Feiman-Nemser, S., & Featherstone, J. (1992). *Adventures in teaching.* New York: Teachers College Press.

Feiman-Nemser, S., & Floden, R. E. (1986). The cultures of teaching. In M. C. Wittrock (Ed.), *Handbook of research on teaching (3rd ed.).* New York: Macmillan.

Fenstermacher, G. (1986). Philosophy of research on teaching: Three aspects. In M. C. Wittrock (Ed.), *Handbook of research on teaching (3rd ed.).* New York: Macmillan.

Ferdman, B. M. (1990). Literacy and cultural identity. *Harvard Educational Review, 60,* 182–201.

Fish, S. (1980). *Is there a text in this class: The authority of interpretive communities.* Cambridge, MA: Harvard University Press.

Five, C. L. (1987). Fifth graders respond to a changed reading program. *Harvard Educational Review, 56,* 395–405.

Flood, J., Jensen, J. M., Lapp, D., & Squire, J. R. (1991). *Handbook of research on teach-*

ing the English/language arts. New York: Macmillan.

Florio-Ruane, S. (1986, April). *Taking a closer look at writing conferences.* Paper presented at the American Educational Research Association, San Francisco.

Florio-Ruane, S., & Walsh, M. (1980) The teacher as colleague in classroom research. In H. Trueba, G. Guthrie, & K. Au (Eds.), *Culture in the bilingual classroom: Studies in classroom ethnography.* Rowley, MA: Newbury House.

Fordham, S. (1988). Racelessness as a factor in black students' school success: Pragmatic strategy or pyrrhic victory? *Harvard Educational Review, 58,* 54–84.

Foster, M. (1991). The politics of race through African-American teachers' eyes. *Journal of Education, 172,* 123–141.

Freeman, C. (1989, February). *The case study method in teacher education: A teacher researcher study.* Paper presented at the Ethnography in Education Forum, University of Pennsylvania, Philadelphia.

Freire, P. (1971). *Pedagogy of the oppressed.* New York: Herder and Herder.

Frutkoff, J. (1989, February). *Journal keeping: A teacher looks inward and backward.* Paper presented at the Ethnography in Education Forum, University of Pennsylvania, Philadelphia.

Gage, N. L. (1963). *Handbook of research on teaching.* Chicago: Rand McNally.

Geertz, C. (1973). *The interpretation of cultures.* New York: Basic Books.

Geertz, C. (1983). *Local knowledge: Further essays in interpretive anthropology.* New York: Basic Books.

Giroux, H. (1984). Rethinking the language of schooling. *Language Arts, 61,* 33–40.

Giroux, H. (1985). Intellectual label and pedagogical work: Rethinking the role of teachers as intellectuals. *Phenomenology and Pedagogy, 3,* 20–31.

Goodlad, J. (1984). *A place called school.* New York: McGraw-Hill.

Goodman, Y. (1985). Kid watching: Observing in the classroom. In A. Jagger & M. Smith-Burke (Eds.), *Observing the language learner.* Newark, DE: International Reading Association.

Goswami, D., & Stillman, P. (1987). *Reclaiming the classroom: Teacher research as an agency for change.* Upper Montclair, NJ: Boynton/Cook.

Griffin, G. (1986). Clinical teacher education. In J. V. Hoffman & S. A. Edwards (Eds.), *Reality and reform of teacher education.* New York: Random House.

Griffin, G. (1989). Coda: The knowledge-driven school. In M. C. Reynolds (Ed.), *Knowledge base for the beginning teacher.* Oxford: Pergamon Press.

Guba, E. G. (1980, April). *Naturalistic and conventional inquiry.* Paper presented at the American Educational Research Association, Boston.

Guerin, K. (1985). "Bounced around": Teachers and leftover children. *Education and Urban Society, 17,* 284–291.

Gumperz, J. (1982). *Discourse strategies.* Cambridge, England: Cambridge University Press.

Hahn, J. (1991a, February). *Teacher research as a catalyst for teacher change.* Paper presented at the Ethnography in Education Forum, University of Pennsylvania, Philadelphia.

Hahn, J. (1991b). Institutionalizing teacher research: There is no substitute for local knowledge. Paper presented at American Education Research Association Annual Meeting, Chicago.

Hale-Benson, J. (1986). *Black children: Their roots, culture, and learning styles.* Baltimore, MD: Johns Hopkins University.

Hall, E. (1984). *The dance of life.* New York: Anchor Press/Doubleday.

Hargreaves, A. (1989). *Contrived collegiality and the culture of teaching.* Paper presented at the Canadian Society for Studies in Education Conference, University of Laval, Quebec.

Hargreaves, A., & Dawe, R. (1989, April). *Coaching as unreflective practice: Contrived collegiality or collaborative culture?* Paper presented to the American Educational Research Association, San Francisco.

Harris, J. (1989). The idea of community in the study of writing. *College Composition and Communication, 40,* 11–22.

Heath, S. B. (1982). What no bedtime story means: Narrative skills at home and school. *Language in Society, 11,* 49–76.

Heath, S. B., & Branscombe, A. (1985). "Intelligent writing" in an audience community: Teacher, students, and researcher. In S. Freedman (Ed.), *The acquisition of written language: Response and revision.* Norwood, NJ: Ablex.

Hiller, N. (1991). *A year in transition.* Unpublished manuscript, Philadelphia Writing Project, University of Pennsylvania.

Hollingsworth, S. (1989). Prior beliefs and cognitive change in learning to teach. *American Educational Research Journal, 26,* 160–189.

Holmes Group. (1990). *Tomorrow's schools: A report of the Holmes Group.* East Lansing, MI: The Holmes Group, Inc.

Holmstein, V. (1987). We watched ourselves write: Report on a classroom research project. In D. Goswami & P. Stillman (Eds.), *Teacher research as an agency for change.* Upper Montclair, NJ: Boynton/Cook.

Holt, J. (1964). *How children fail.* New York: Dell.

House, E. R. (1980, April). *Mapping social disconcensus onto social theory.* Paper presented at the American Educational Research Association, Boston.

Howard, J. (1989). On teaching, knowledge, and "middle ground." *Harvard Educational Review, 59,* 226–239.

Howe, K., & Eisenhart, M. (1990). Standards for qualitative (and quantitative) research: A prolegomenon. *Educational Research, 19,* 2–9.

Huebner, D. (1987). The vocation of teaching. In F. Bolin & J. M. Falk (Eds.), *Teacher renewal, professional issues, personal choices.* New York: Teachers College Press.

Hull, B. (1978). *Teachers' seminars on children's thinking.* Grand Forks, ND: North Dakota Study Group on Evaluation, North Dakota Press.

Hymes, D. H. (1974). *Foundations in sociolinguistics.* Philadelphia: University of Pennsylvania Press.

Jackson, P. (1990). The functions of educational research. *Educational Researcher, 19,* 3–9.

Johnston, P. (1989). A scenic view of reading. *Language Arts, 66,* 160–170.

Johnston, P. (1990, February). *A shift in paradigm: As teachers become researchers so goes the curriculum.* Paper presented at the Ethnography in Education Forum, University of Pennsylvania, Philadelphia.

Joyce, B., Showers, B., & Rolheiser-Bennett, C. (1987). Staff development and student learning: A synthesis of research on models of teaching. *Educational Leadership, 45,* 77–87.

Kanevsky, R., & Traugh, C. (1986). Classroom life: Some interpretations. In C. Traugh (Ed.), *Speaking out: Teachers on teaching*. Grand Forks, ND: University of North Dakota.

Kean, E. (1989). Teachers and administrators eyeing each other (No one stops to clap). *The Teachers' Journal, 2*, 1–7.

Keizer, G. (1988). *No place but here: A teacher's vocation in a rural community*. New York: Penguin.

Kincheloe, J. (1991). *Teachers as researchers: Qualitative inquiry as a path to empowerment*. London: Falmer Press.

Knoblauch, C. H., & Brannon, L. (1988). Knowing our knowledge: A phenomenological basis for teacher research. In L. Z. Smith (Ed.), *Audits of meaning: A festchrift in honor of Ann E. Berthoff*. Portsmouth, NH: Boynton/Cook, Heinemann.

Kohl, H. (1967). *36 children*. New York: Signet Books.

Kutz, E. (1989, February). *Preservice teachers as researchers: Developing practice and creating theory*. Paper presented at Ethnography in Education Forum, University of Pennsylvania, Philadelphia.

Kyle, D., & Hovda, R. (Eds.). (1987). The potential and practice of action research: Parts I and II. *Peabody Journal of Education, 64*.

Ladson-Billings, G. (1990, April). *Making a little magic: Teachers talk about successful teaching strategies for black children*. Paper presented at the American Educational Research Association, Boston.

Ladson-Billings, G., & Henry, A. (1990). Blurring the borders: Voices of African liberatory pedagogy in the United States and Canada. *Journal of Education, 172*, 72–88.

Lambert, L. (1985). The end of an era of staff development. *Educational Leadership 18*, 78–83.

Lambert, L. (1989). How do teachers manage to teach? Perspectives on problems in practice. *Harvard Educational Review, 55*, 178–194.

Lather, P. (1986). Research as praxis. *Harvard Educational Review, 56*, 257–277.

Lather, P. (1991). *Getting smart: Feminist research and pedagogy with/in the postmodern*. London: Routledge, Chapman, and Hall.

LeMahieu, P. (1988). Personal correspondence.

Lewin, K. (1948). *Resolving social conflicts*. New York: Harper & Row.

Lewis, M. (1989, April). *Politics, resistance, and transformation: The psycho/social/sexual dynamics in the feminist classroom*. Paper presented at the annual meeting of the American Educational Research Association, San Francisco.

Lieberman, A. (1986). *Rethinking school improvement*. New York: Teachers College Press.

Lieberman, A., & Miller, L. (1984). *Teachers, their world and their work*. Washington, DC: Association for Supervision and Curriculum Development.

Little, J. (1987). Teachers as colleagues. In V. Richardson-Koehler (Ed.), *Educators' handbook*. New York: Longman.

Little, J. (1989, April). *The persistence of privacy: Autonomy and initiative in teachers' professional relations*. Paper presented at the annual meeting of the American Educational Research Association, San Francisco.

Lortie, D. (1975). *School teacher: A sociological study*. Chicago: University of Chicago Press.

Lumley, D. (1987). An analysis of peer group dialogue journals for classroom use. In D.

Goswami & P. Stillman (Eds.), *Teacher research as an agency for change*. Upper Montclair, NJ: Boynton/Cook.

Lyons, N. (1990). Dilemmas of knowing: Ethical and epistemological dimensions of teachers' work and development. *Harvard Educational Review, 60*, 159–180.

Lytle, J. (1990). *Minority student access to and preparation for higher education*. Washington, DC: Counsel of Great City Schools and the College Board.

Lytle, J. (1992). Using ethnography for organizational development: Administrators learn about their students (and schools). Unpublished ms.

Lytle, S. L. (1991). Living literacy: Rethinking development in adulthood. *Linguistics in Education, 3*, 109–138.

Lytle, S. L., & Botel, M. (1988). *Pennsylvania framework: Reading, writing, and talking across the curriculum*. Harrisburg: State Department of Education.

Lytle, S., Christman, J., Cohen, J., Countryman, J., Fecho, R., Portnoy, D., & Sion, F. (1991, February). *Learning in the afternoon: Teacher inquiry as school reform*. Paper presented at the Ethnography in Education Forum, University of Pennsylvania, Philadelphia.

Lytle, S. L., & Cochran-Smith, M. (1989, March). Teacher researcher: Toward clarifying the concept. *National Writing Project Quarterly*, pp. 1–3, 22–27.

Lytle, S. L., & Fecho, R. (1991). Meeting strangers in familiar places: Teacher collaboration by cross-visitation. *English Education, 23*, 5–28.

Lytle, S., & Wolfe, M. (1989). *Adult literacy: Program evaluation and learner assessment*. Columbus, OH: ERIC Clearinghouse on Adult, Career and Vocational Education.

Making room for growth: A documentary portrait of the 1987–1989 writing assessment program in the School District of Philadelphia. (1989). Philadelphia: Paths/PRISM in Partnership with the School District of Philadelphia.

McCarthy, C. (1990). Multicultural education, minority identities, textbooks, and the challenge of curriculum reform. *Journal of Education, 172*, 118–129.

McConaghy, J. (1990). *Children learning through literature*. Portsmouth, NH: Heinemann.

McIntosh, P. (1989). White privilege: Unpacking the invisible knapsack. *Peace and Freedom*, 10–12.

Michaels, S., & Cook-Gumperz, J. (1979). A study of sharing time with first grade students: Discourse narratives in the classroom. In C. Chairello (Ed.), *Proceedings of the Fifth Annual Meeting of the Berkeley Linguistic Society*. Berkeley, CA: Berkeley Linguistic Society.

Michaels, S., Ulichney, P., & Watson-Gegeo, K. (1989). Writing conferences: Innovation or familiar routine? Unpublished manuscript, Harvard University, Cambridge, MA.

Miller, J. (1987, November). *Points of dissonance in teachers/researchers: Openings into emancipatory ways of knowing*. Paper presented at the Bergamo Conference on Curriculum Theory and Classroom Practice, Dayton, OH.

Mohr, M., & Maclean, M. (1987). *Working together: A guide for teacher-researchers*. Urbana, IL: National Council of Teachers of English.

Morizawa, G. (1990). *Acting out: Research in writing: Working papers of teacher researchers*. Berkeley, CA: Bay Area Writing Project, University of California.

Munby, H. (1987). Metaphors and teachers' knowledge. *Research in the Teaching of English, 21*, 337–397.

Myers, M. (1985). *The teacher-researcher: How to study writing in the classroom*. Urbana, IL: National Council of Teachers of English.

Myers, M. (1987). Institutionalizing inquiry. *National Writing Project Quarterly, 9,* 1–4.

Natkins, L. G. (1986). *Our last term: A teacher's diary.* Lanham, MD: University Press of America.

Nisbett, R. E., & Ross, L. (1980). *Human inference: Strategies and shortcomings of social judgment.* Englewood Cliffs, NJ: Prentice Hall.

Nixon, J. (Ed.). (1981). *A teacher's guide to action resarch.* London: Grant McIntyre.

Noffke, S. (1990, April). *Knowers, knowing, and known in action research.* Paper presented at the annual meeting of the American Educational Research Association, Boston.

North, S. (1987). *The making of knowledge in composition: Portrait of an emerging field.* Upper Montclair, NJ: Boynton/Cook.

Ogbu, J. (1978). *Minority education and caste.* New York: Academic Press.

Oja, S., & Smulyan, L. (1989). *Collaborative action research: A developmental approach.* London: Falmer Press.

Paley, V. (1979). *White teacher.* Cambridge, MA: Harvard University Press.

Paley, V. (1981). *Wally's stories.* Cambridge, MA: Harvard University Press.

Palonsky, S. B. (1986). *900 shows a year: A look at teaching from a teacher's side of the desk.* New York: Random House.

Paris, C. (in press). *Teacher agency in curriculum change: Processes, contexts and meanings.* New York: Teachers College Press.

Peitzman, F. (Ed.). (1991). *The power of context: Studies by teacher researchers.* Los Angeles: Center for Academic Interinstitutional Programs, Regents of the University of California.

Pellegrin, R. J. (1976). *Schools as work settings.* In R. Dubin (Ed.), *Handbook of work, organizations, and society.* Skokie, IL: Rand McNally.

Perl, S., & Wilson, N. (1986). *Through teachers' eyes.* Portsmouth, NH: Heinemann.

Phelps, L. W. (1991). Practical wisdom and the geography of knowledge in composition. *College English, 53,* 866–867.

Philadelphia Schools Collaborative. (1989). *Notes from the seminar on teaching and learning.* Philadelphia: Author.

Philadelphia Teachers Learning Cooperative. (1984). On becoming teacher experts: Buying time. *Language Arts, 6,* 731–735.

Polanyi, M. (1958). *Personal knowledge: Towards a post-critical theory.* Chicago: University of Chicago Press.

Project START. (1989). *Notes from teacher-student teacher seminar on learning to teach.* Philadelphia: Author.

Queenan, M. (1988). Impertinent questions about teacher research: A review. *English Journal, 77,* 41–46.

Ray, L. (1986). Reflections on classroom research. In D. Goswami & P. Stillman (Eds.), *Teacher research as an agency for change.* Upper Montclair, NJ: Boynton/Cook.

Reither, J. A. (1990). The writing student as researcher: Learning from our students. In D. Diaker & M. Morenberg (Eds.), *The writing teacher as researcher.* Portsmouth, NH: Boynton/Cook, Heinemann.

Reynolds, M. C. (Ed.). (1989). *Knowlege base for the beginning teacher.* Oxford: Pergamon Press.

Richardson-Koehler, V. (Ed.). (1987). *Educators' handbook: A research perspective.* New York: Longman.

Richardson-Koehler, V. (1988). Barriers to the effective supervision of students: A field of study. *Journal of Teacher Education, 39,* 28–34.

Rodriguez, R. (1982). *Hunger of memory: The education of Richard Rodriguez.* New York: Bantam.

Rorschach, E., & Whitney, R. (1986). Relearning to teach: Peer observation as a means of professional development for teachers. *English Education, 18,* 159–172.

Rose, M. (1989). *Lives on the boundary.* New York: Penguin.

Rotchford, M. (1989). Student teachers focus on their students. *The Teachers' Journal, 2,* 42–52.

Rudduck, J. (1985). Teacher research and research-based teacher education. *Journal of Education for Teaching, 11,* 281–289.

Rudduck, J., & Hopkins, D. (1985). *Research as a basis for teaching: Readings from the work of Lawrence Stenhouse.* London: Heinemann.

Sanders, D., & McCutcheon, G. (1986). The development of practical theories of teaching. *Journal of Curriculum and Supervision, 2,* 50–67.

Schaefer, R. J. (1967). *The school as a center of inquiry.* New York: Harper and Row.

Schön, D. A. (1983). *The reflective practitioner.* San Francisco: Jossey-Bass.

Schön, D. A. (1987). *Educating the reflective practitioner.* San Francisco: Jossey-Bass.

Schwartz, J. (1988). The drudgery and the discovery: Students as research partners. *English Journal, 77,* 37–40.

Schwartz, J. (1990). On the move in Pittsburgh: When students and teacher share research. In D. Daiker & M. Morenberg (Eds.), *The writing teacher as researcher: Essays in the theory and practice of class-based research.* Portsmouth, NH: Boynton/Cook, Heinemann.

Shavelson, R. J., & Stern, P. (1981). Research on teachers' pedagogical thoughts, judgments, decisions and behaviors. *Review of Educational Research, 51,* 455–498.

Shulman, L. (1986a). Paradigms and research programs in the study of teaching: A contemporary perspective. In M. C. Wittrock (Ed.), *Handbook of research on teaching* (3rd ed.). New York: Macmillan.

Shulman, L. (1986b). Those who understand: Knowledge growth in teaching. *Educational Researcher, 15,* 4–14.

Shulman, L. (1987). Knowledge and teaching: Foundations of the new reform. *Harvard Educational Review, 51,* 1–22.

Shulman, L. (1989, January). *Teaching the disciplines liberally.* Paper presented at the third annual meeting of the Holmes Group, Atlanta, GA.

Smith, K. (1990). Entertaining a text: A reciprocal process. In K. Short & C. Pierce (Eds.), *Talking about books: Creating literature communities.* Portsmouth, NH: Heinemann.

Smith, L. H., & Geoffrey, W. (1968). *The complexities of an urban classroom: An analysis toward a general theory of teaching.* New York: Holt, Rinehart and Winston.

Smyth, W. I. (1987). *A rationale for teachers' critical pedagogy: A handbook.* Victoria, Australia: Deakin University Press.

Sockett, H. T. (1987). Has Shulman got the strategy right? *Harvard Educational Review, 57,* 208–219.

Stenhouse, L. (1985). *Research as a basis for teaching.* London: Heinemann.

Strickland, D., Dillon, R. M., Funkhouser, L., Glick, M., & Rogers, C. (1989). Research currents: Classroom discourse during literature response groups. *Language Arts, 66,* 192–200.

Strieb, L. (1985). *A (Philadelphia) teacher's journal: North Dakota Study Group Center for Teaching and Learning*. Grand Forks, ND: North Dakota Study Group Center for Teaching and Learning.

Stumbo, C. (1989). Beyond the classroom. *Harvard Educational Review, 59*, 87–97.

Taylor, D. (1990). Teaching without testing. *English Education, 22*, 4–74.

Taylor, D., & Dorsey-Gaines, C. (1988). *Growing up literate: Learning from inner city families*. Portsmouth, NH: Heinemann.

Thomas, L. (1974). *The lives of a cell: Notes of a biology watcher*. New York: Bantam Books.

Tierney, R. (1981). Using expressive writing to teach biology. In A. Wotring & R. Tierney (Eds.), *Two studies of writing in high school science: Classroom research study #5*. Berkeley, CA: Bay Area Writing Project, University of California.

Tikunoff, W. J., Ward, B. A., & Griffin, G. A. (1979). *Interactive research and development on teaching study: Final report*. San Francisco: Far West Regional Laboratory for Educational Research and Development.

Traugh, C., Kanevsky, R., Martin, A., Seletzky, A., Woolf, K., & Strieb, L. (1986). *Speaking out: Teachers on teaching*. Grand Forks, ND: University of North Dakota.

Travers, R. M. W. (1973). *Second handbook of research on teaching*. Chicago: Rand McNally.

Westerhoff, J. H. (1987). The teacher as pilgrim. In F. S. Bolin & J. M. Falk (Eds.), *Teacher renewal*. New York: Teachers College Press.

Wiggington, E. (1985). *Sometimes a shining moment: The Foxfire experience*. Garden City, NY: Archer Press/Doubleday.

Wilson, S. (1990). *Spinning talk into writing: Behind the scenes of a research project: Research in writing: Working papers of teacher researchers*. Berkeley, CA: Bay Area Writing Project, University of California.

Wittrock, M. C. (1986). *Handbook of research on teaching* (3rd ed.). New York: Macmillan.

Yagelsky, R. P. (1990). Searching for "sloppy trees": How research shapes teaching. In D. Daiker & M. Morenberg (Eds.), *The writing teacher as researcher: Essays in the theory and practice of class-based research*. Portsmouth, NH: Boynton/Cook, Heinemann.

Yonemura, M. (1982). Teacher conversations: A potential source of their own professional growth. *Curriculum Inquiry, 12*, 239–256.

Yonemura, M. (1986). *A teacher at work: Professional development and the early childhood educator*. New York: Teachers College Press.

Zeichner, K. (1986). Preparing reflective teachers: An overview of instructional strategies which have been employed in pre-service teacher education. *International Journal of Educational Research, 7*, 565–575.

Zumwalt, K. K. (1982a). Are we improving or undermining teaching? In L. N. Tanner (Ed.), *Critical issues in curriculum: 87th yearbook of National Society for the Study of Education*. Chicago: University of Chicago Press.

Zumwalt, K. K. (1982b). Research on teaching: Policy implications for teacher education. In A. Lieberman & M. McLaughlin (Eds.), *Policy making in education: 81st yearbook of the National Society for the Study of Education*. Chicago: University of Chicago Press.

Part II

TEACHERS ON TEACHING, LEARNING, AND SCHOOLING

When teachers study and write about their work, they make their own distinctive ways of knowing about teaching and learning more visible to themselves and others. The questions about practice that prompt further inquiry, the aspects of school life that teachers regard as evidence, and the interpretive frameworks that teachers bring to bear on classroom data alter what we know about teaching and learning. As a body of work, teachers' research has the potential to call into question the assumptions we make about teachers, research, and knowledge and, over time, to redefine the knowledge base itself. Taken together, this research makes a powerful argument for the emic perspectives that teachers are uniquely positioned to provide.

The second part of this volume includes 21 pieces of teacher research written by teachers who work in elementary, middle, and secondary schools as well as adult learning contexts. The pieces are arranged according to the working typology of teacher research we proposed in Chapter 2: journals, oral inquiries, classroom and school studies, and essays. Contributors include experienced and new, urban and suburban, and public and private school teachers who work in large as well as small schools and programs. Some contributors are long-time teacher researchers while others are new to the endeavor. A few have written and published their work over many years, others have written for a long time but have not been previously published, and still others are writing about their work for the first time. Many of the pieces emerged from the work of teacher-researcher groups or were developed initially for local publications, institutes, conferences, and graduate school programs. Several were originally written with no audience in mind other than the teacher writing.

As a collection, the pieces have many commonalities as well as important features that distinguish them from one another. Although many of the authors work in schools that have not yet institutionalized inquiry as an integral part of professional practice, most of them are members of cross-school, school-university, or unaffiliated teacher communities wherein inquiry is regarded as a central task of learning from teaching across the professional life span. As these pieces demonstrate, teacher research is deeply contextualized in the everyday events of schools and classrooms and in the lived experiences of teachers and their students. Their variation in formality, mode of presentation, style of writing, ways of presenting and analyzing data, and use of interpretive frameworks reflects the diversity of their origins as well as the contrasts in their function and use. These variations demonstrate that teacher research is an emerging genre wherein researchers are striving to render their ongoing analyses of classroom and school data in ways that are inventive rather than imitative and that are accessible and meaningful for multiple rather than specific audiences. Although many pieces emerged from collaborative work with other teachers, each piece represents its author's distinctive way of wedding research processes to practice.

To understand how these pieces enrich the knowledge base, it is useful to consider them not just by type but by the questions they raise in relationship to ongoing conversations in teaching and teacher education. The 21 pieces in this section address three major topics widely researched in the literature. The first area—language, learning, and literacy—includes pieces that explore how teachers, students, and even parents jointly construct the language and literacy curriculum as they learn from and with each other. Pieces in the second area—the cultures of teaching—address issues of professional socialization, teacher-to-teacher collaboration, and the changing nature of the teachers' workplace. Finally, work in the third area—teacher research as a mode of inquiry—raises questions about the functions and strategies of teacher research in professional development and knowledge generation at various points across the life span.

The first group of studies explores the domain of language, learning, and literacy by looking at individual students, classroom interactions, and home-school connections. Focusing on the interplay of children's and teachers' questions and observations, Buchanan draws on one student's writing collected over the course of a year as she collaborated with different groups of teachers to analyze that work. She suggests that this dialectic altered her understanding of the child as a writer and as a language learner as well as her own constructs about inquiry as a mode of collegial learning. Like Buchanan, Starr looks at the language development of one child: a 10-year-old profoundly deaf since birth. She analyzes his writing strategies, demonstrating that writing development was a process of negotiating between the worlds of American Sign Language—his primary communicative language—and the English he encountered in print and books.

In addition to case studies of individual learners, the language, learning, and literacy pieces include several that take the classroom as the unit of analysis. Feldgus looks closely at how kindergarten children use environmental print when it is co-constructed by the teacher and children as an ongoing part of the curriculum. Drawing on observations of social interactions with peers, journal writing, and her own uses and demonstrations of print, she examines variations in how children used the genres, language, and world knowledge displayed in the classroom. Johnston explores the connections between the interpretive norms of eighth-grade readers and the social scenes of reading and response. She argues that understanding the social nature of response requires untangling the complex interactions of school practices, family, and community values. Baum-Brunner argues that high school students interact with one another and their teachers to create particular cultures of response and revision in writing classes. Close analysis of successive drafts and of classroom talk over a 15-week period allowed Baum-Brunner to see shifts in styles of writing and responding and prompted her to rethink the range of interaction patterns she regarded as effective. Also writing from the perspective of a high school English teacher, Farmbry describes how ethnicity and language differences may create barriers between students and teachers and between students and their own aspirations even when students and teacher share the same ethnic background. She traces her own deepening understanding of these issues by drawing on her early experiences as a beginning teacher and on her ongoing framing and reframing of these dilemmas over time. A teacher of adult learners in an urban literacy program, Belzer examines her own and her students' conflicting conceptions of learning and schooling. Drawing on critical teaching episodes from her journal, Belzer suggests that rather than functioning as barriers to learning, differences can become sites of inquiry for both adult learners and teachers of adults. Headman links classroom and home by co-investigating varying notions of literacy in and out of school with parents. Together, they observed, documented, and discussed children's experiences to create a new dialogue that enriched their interpretations of what contributed to children's development.

Although all of the pieces about language, literacy, and learning provide insights into how teachers and their students co-construct the curriculum, some pieces focus more explicitly on curriculum construction. Black et al., a group of 14 student teachers, reveal their struggle to raise questions about the traditional elementary school reading curriculum, particularly the widespread practices associated with basal reading materials and programs. Synthesizing data from their individual comparative analyses of basal reading lessons, they demonstrate how learning from learners in particular classrooms prompts unique rather than standard ways of using texts with children. A very experienced elementary school teacher, Strieb also explores how the curriculum in her first-grade classroom emerges from her ongoing language interactions with children. Documenting their collaborative observations of trees in detailed journal entries, Strieb reveals how she and her children jointly constructed knowledge of science, language, and social life.

The second group of studies explores the cultures of teaching by addressing issues in professional socialization, teacher-to-teacher collaboration, and the changing nature of the teacher's workplace. Joe explores professional socialization by focusing on her own experiences as a student teacher and then a beginning teacher in a large urban school system. Drawing on essays and discussions during and after student teaching, Joe identifies three broad issues in the literature that inform her work: power, evaluation of students and teachers, and teacher accountability. Wunner looks at the way that one school system constructs the professional socialization of teachers new to the system. Analyzing interviews with inductees, school system literature, and field notes that describe mentoring activities, Wunner argues that to "un-novice" teachers as quickly as possible, school systems seldom invite new teachers to question the assumptions and practices that are already in place. In a rare and intimate look at one teacher's work life over a 20-year period, Harris provides evocative detail about the changing nature of the urban high school as a workplace. Using excerpts from her journal as well as her current reflections on it, Harris presents a richly contextualized picture of teaching as part of the complex landscape of school cultures and communities, their histories, and the political and social climate of the times. Jumpp and Strieb extend our view of teacher culture by examining their use of journals as collaboration, curriculum, and assessment. Using excerpts from individual and dialogic journals with each other and with their students, they show how teachers from different worlds—grade levels, races, and professional experiences—can enrich each other's frames of reference for thinking about teaching, learning, and schooling. Fecho considers another dimension of the intellectual lives of teachers by raising questions about teachers as readers. He argues that teachers constitute a distinctive interpretive community with a unique perspective on educational theory and research and that acknowledging this perspective is integrally related to valuing teachers as professionals and as intellectuals. Brown describes the link between her emerging intellectual interest in feminist scholarship and the transformation that occurred in the texts she used in her classroom and in the invitations she offered students for making sense of those texts. She argues that using the "mother tongue" was critical to her own development as well as to the inquiries of her graduate equivalency degree classes of pregnant and parenting teens.

Finally, in the third domain, teachers explore teacher research itself as a mode of inquiry by raising questions about its role in their own professional development and about its function for knowledge generation and reform. Both Kanevsky and Colgan-Davis describe teachers' use of structured oral inquiries as ways of knowing about individual children on the one hand and about learning diversity on the other. Kanevsky provides a thick description of the "descriptive review" of a child, drawing on both the actual presentation and the author's retrospective analysis of the process and its underlying assumptions and values. Colgan-Davis chronicles the experiences of a group of K–12 teachers as they explore the meanings of diversity, their own experiences as learners, and their assumptions about school expectations and children's achievement. Sims traces the evolution of her questions about middle school students' literacy development by focusing on one student who had previously been essentially invisible in her classroom. Using as data her journal, interviews and protocols with the student, and colleagues' questions and recommendations, she demonstrates that teacher research is a social and distinctly nonlinear process. Brody et al., 11 student teachers who worked collaboratively, look at the way that they used essays to build understandings of teaching and learning and to raise questions about the relationship of the educational literature and their ongoing student teaching experiences in the classroom. Weaving together 33 essays written individually, Brody et al. reveal how they learned to pose questions, juxtapose theories and practices, and compare theoretical frameworks on related topics. Finally, Pincus analyzes the logic of her own evolution as a teacher and a teacher researcher by examining essays written over a period of 5 years for a variety of audiences and contexts. Following what she refers to as the "paper trail," Pincus reinterprets her work to explore her own personal change and its relationship to changes that took place as her high school underwent a process of radical restructuring.

We are suggesting, then, that one way to read the 21 pieces of teacher research gathered in this volume is in terms of their contributions to substantive domains in the study of teaching. The framework we constructed in Part 1 invited readers to raise several additional questions about teacher research as research on teaching, about types of teacher research, about its epistemology, and about the contexts in which it is created and used. We argued there that teachers' questions emerge from neither theory nor practice but from their critical intersections. The examples collected here allow us to elaborate this point: They demonstrate that when teachers do research, they pose neither the generic process-product question of "What works?" nor the broad interpretive question of "What's going on here and what does it mean?" Rather, teachers' research questions seem to take a different form, one that reflects their inescapable responsibility to the here and now as well as their ongoing need to construct and reconstruct intellectual perspectives for understanding their work. Hence, in a certain sense, teachers do ask, "What works?" but they mean, "What works in the complex contexts of particular classrooms?"—what works for whom, under what circumstances, and in what ways—as well as what "working" means for various participants in their classrooms, schools, and communities. Thus, a major contribution of teacher research is that it identifies and investigates a distinctive set of problems of practice that outside researchers cannot address because they do not stand in the same relationship to the practice of teaching. If we accept the premise that the function of research on teaching is interrogating, understanding, and ultimately improving the quality of teaching and learning for all students and moving toward more democratic and critical pedagogies, it is self-evident that teacher research, which by definition poses and explores problems of practice, has the potential to play an indispensable role. It can move this agenda forward partly by demonstrating that understanding the social and cultural practices of classrooms cannot be accomplished by university researchers alone.

From teachers' analyses of classroom and school data in these 21 pieces, we also learn—up close and in rich evocative detail—what it means for teachers to learn from teaching at various points across the professional life span. In Part 2 of this volume, very new teachers as well as very experienced teachers reveal how inquiry teaches. They show, for example, how teachers negotiate the terrain between following and leading the learner, how they integrate knowledge from a variety of sources, how they come to understand individual learners' constructions of knowledge, how they question the assumptions that underlie curriculum and schooling, how they make decisions to alter and evaluate routines and practices, and how they invent frameworks that allow them to understand their current work and also ask new questions about it. Other teachers as well as teacher educators and researchers may find teacher research—read as emic accounts of learning from teaching—particularly relevant to their own work.

6 | Journals

• • • • • • • • • • • •

Visiting and Revisiting the Trees

Lynne Yermanock Strieb

LYNNE YERMANOCK STRIEB *has taught kindergarten and first and second grade for 21 years in the School District of Philadelphia, most recently at the Albert M. Greenfield School. She is a member of the Philadelphia Teachers Learning Cooperative, the North Dakota Study Group on Evaluation, and summer institutes at the Prospect Center for Education and Research. A former Fulbright Exchange teacher in West Midlands, England, Strieb is a cooperating teacher in Project START, a teacher consultant for the Philadelphia Writing Project, and a consultant with the New York Literacy Summer Institute. Strieb's publications include: Trees: Excerpts From a Teacher's Journal (OUTLOOK, 1984), A Philadelphia Teacher's Journal, (1985), "Community and Collegiality" (with Traugh, Kanevsky, Martin, Seletsky, & Woolf in Speaking Out: Teachers on Teaching, 1986), and "When a Teacher's Values Clash With School Values" (NCREST, 1992).*

I am a teacher. I write about my work, about teaching, and about researching my teaching through my journal. I enjoy writing, but teaching must be at the center of any other work that I do; my research and writing must directly feed my teaching. Keeping a journal has been a realistic way for me to learn about, inquire into, collect data about, and enhance my practice as well as to learn about and plan for the children. Although writing in my journal each day takes time, it is economical and is the genre most compatible with my style of writing, my way of teaching, and my way of thinking.

I've always been a record keeper. I keep anecdotal records on my children; compose narrative biweekly summaries about them based on the anecdotes; write a monthly newsletter for parents; type all the stories that the children write, when there's time; and save the children's work.

I was studying with colleagues and with Patricia Carini, former director of the Prospect Archive and Center, North Bennington, Vermont, in 1974, when I began to inquire into my teaching. I did not begin by keeping a journal but rather by writing a profile of one child. Susannah interested me because she was a prolific artist and writer and because her work was very different from that of the other children. In 1975, I explored one area of my classroom: the clay area. I wondered what children were doing as they worked with this very popular choice time medium. I decided to think about the parameters of clay as a medium, to observe children at work in the clay area, and to describe the work of one child who stated that he enjoyed working with clay more than any other material in the classroom. During the summer of 1980, I formulated another question: Is feeling expressed in my classroom? If so, when does it happen? On the advice of Carini, I decided to keep a journal. Because I believed that I might find the children's feelings in the discussions that the children and I had about literature and real-life objects and events, I planned to collect those discussions and write about them in the journal.

For about 2 weeks in September 1980, my journal was a list of phrases—a list of the discussions and brief notes about what the children said—but few complete sentences or direct quotes. That was not at all satisfying to me, so I began to write in a more narrative style. I'd found my ideal mode of data collection. In the introduction to the published version of my journal, I wrote, "The more I wrote, the more I observed in my classroom, and the more I wanted to write. As I re-read my journal I got more ideas for teaching. . . . " (Strieb, 1985).

Since 1980, I have kept some kind of journal. During some years, the journal is more like a detailed outline, written in phrases rather than in sentences and paragraphs. During other years, it is the sort of narrative I wrote 10 years ago. Most important, I cannot teach without writing in my journal, and I am unhappy if I don't do it at the end of each day.

I continue to keep a journal for a variety of reasons. First and most important, it helps me with my teaching. When used in certain ways, the journal allows me to look closely at curriculum. As I teach, I wonder how my thinking and my students' thinking evolve over time. I wonder what I have valued and what the children are interested in and value. Lesson plans don't tell me this, but the journal does. My journal is a place for planning, for raising questions, for figuring things out, and for thinking. Did I stick to my plans? What did the children do with what I tried to teach? What did the children work on? What do they contribute to the life of the classroom each day? Did I do what I wanted to do that day? Have I accomplished what I wanted to accomplish over time? What are the possible extensions of what we are currently doing? I want to know these things—and many more—and the way I can discover them is by describing what happened each day and by reading and reflecting on it. The journal provides completion and closure at the end of the day. With it, it is possible for me to remember what I and the children have done. If I haven't noted at least briefly in my journal what happened during a day, I've lost that day in its freshest form.

A second reason I keep a journal is to share it with others. My journal has mostly been used as the basis for discussions with other teachers in seminars in, for example, Philadelphia and Ithaca, New York. At the seminars in Philadelphia, we benefited not only from reading about one teacher's practice in her journal but also from closely describing it. The format that we used to do this was a description of work, one of the reflective processes developed at Prospect by Carini and colleagues in which participants are encouraged to closely describe and analyze work such as a drawing, a piece of writing, or a block construction. In addition, through our journals, we teachers can also communicate to people outside of schools what we do in our classrooms—in our own words and not filtered through the eyes and words of other authors and researchers, no matter how sympathetic and accurate their work. Third, teachers' journals in general could be important documents for historians and other educational researchers. They are primary source material that has been gaining wider use. My journal may prove to be a useful contribution. Finally, the journal has been my way of telling my own children about my work and will do the same for my grandchildren.

Why have I chosen to "revisit trees"? Many aspects of science play a central role in my classroom. Although we also worked with animals, flowers, insects and spiders, shells, rocks, logic blocks, thermometers, microscopes, ramps and levers, and science books, the work on trees gave us one theme around which our interests were organized for 2 years. Trees are all around us and are important to our well-being and survival, but I knew from choosing, observing, and describing one tree during the summer of 1980 at Prospect that we adults rarely pay close attention to them. I believed that observing a tree with the children would be interesting not only to me but also to the children. I was right. Although many entries from the 1980–1981 journal, such as reading or writing, had been pulled out, printed separately, and used in seminars, those on trees seemed to be the most interesting and important to others. I have chosen to "revisit the trees" because the original study of trees continues to interest me and seem important, because I've never had a time to reflect on it, and because I plan to continue to do work on trees with children. I also wanted to use those entries to think not only about how my practice has remained the same and how it has changed during the past 10 years but also about why I did what I did then, how it related to other things that I did during that year and other years, and how I might do it now.

In this article, I use five entries to reflect on what happened when the children and I studied trees during the 1980–1981 school year. I include the entries as I wrote them in my journal. Then, under the heading "Reflection, 1991," I analyze each entry, trying to discover what I was thinking about when we did the activity and when I wrote about it. Occasionally, I realized that were I to do the same activity today, I would do parts of it differently, and I wanted to note that.

Interestingly, going back over my journal and rereading it and reflecting on it have never been as important to me as writing it. Perhaps that's because as long as I have the written record—because I have documented what happened—I know that there's always the *possibility* of going back to it at a later time, by myself or with colleagues, to learn what I can about my teaching from my teaching.

OCTOBER 22, 1980   Today Felicia answered my challenge to bring in a leaf larger than mine by bringing in an ENORMOUS leaf. We spent a long time talking about it. I got my leaf, which had dried and shrunk, and asked the children what they thought had happened to it. They talked about leaves drying in the fall and about how this happens when leaves get old. A few thought the leaf needed water. We'll watch what happens to the huge leaf, whose stem is now in water.

We talked about which leaf was bigger. After measuring the length of the leaf with Unifix cubes, which we grouped and counted in tens, we re-measured the drawing of yesterday's leaf. I asked if it would take more or fewer orange Cuisenaire rods (ten centimeters long) to measure the length and asked the children to guess how many before we measured. I'd still like to trace the leaves onto graph paper and do something with area.

I read aloud *Our Trees,* a library book, and talked about trees. We really do need to pick a tree to watch through the seasons, to explore under and around it, as they did in the book. Last summer, each participant in the Summer Institute at the Prospect School had a chance to choose a tree in North Bennington and observe it, and I learned a lot from that experience.

We must also go outside. So many of my memories of fall are associated with the suburban school I attended from fourth grade on. I feel bad that we must be closed into a gray room with NO view to the outside, with no sense of the seasons except what we bring in.

REFLECTION, 1991

In response to my bringing something to school and showing it to the children, a child, Felicia, followed my example. I wanted to show the children how much I valued her leaf, so we spent lots of time on it with the class.

The entry doesn't discuss everything we talked about when we got the leaves together, but we did compare the dry leaf with the fresh leaf and compared the sizes. This was one of many math lessons that involved using an object from nature and commercial objects. The experience is based on comparison. Comparison implies order. I want children to spend a lot of time comparing a great variety of things. The children first talked about which leaf was bigger. I wanted them to measure the leaves with two measuring units: Unifix and Cuisenaire. I posed two problems: whether it would take more or less Cuisenaire to measure the length than Unifix (which are smaller) and how many rods it would take to equal the leaf.

The rest of that paragraph and the other two paragraphs have to do with plans and why I think it's important to do the things I do or want to do:

- *To discuss area.* I like to push math lessons as materials as far as I can go with them. Leaves are a perfect material for beginning discussions of area.
- *To choose a tree.* I learned so much from observing and describing a tree by myself that I wanted the children to have a similar experience. I outline the activities I hope we will do, and I read a book as an introduction to the activity. I envision this as a long-term activity rather than as a one-time visit.
- *To go outside.* Again, my own experiences—my memories—influence some aspects of my teaching. I hate the gray classroom with no windows and I so loved the outdoors as a child that I want the children in my class to enjoy the outdoors as much as I did. Thus, we will get outside. But I also want to bring the outdoors inside, and that is one reason why I want the children to collect natural objects from outdoors and bring them into school. This is an aesthetic purpose buried in the academic purpose.

NOVEMBER 20, 1980   We went to look at our trees. (We call it "visiting the trees.") Henry's tree, the maple, has suddenly lost almost all its leaves. Lloyd said, "It's naked," and everyone dissolved into giggles. They noticed thicker and fewer branches on the bottom and thinner and more branches on the top.

The beech tree still has golden-brown leaves. It has lost about a quarter of its top leaves but there are still plenty on the bottom. The children noticed "white things" where leaves had fallen off. I asked what they thought these might be. Most thought they were seeds. Some called them balls. Only Atiya thought they were buds. I told the children I would not tell them, but that they should keep watching the tree and they would find out.

REFLECTION, 1991

It's important to me in my teaching to ensure that the children have a chance to return to activities, to experience the same thing again and again from a variety of perspectives and against different backgrounds, and to compare what is there now with what was there in the past. When I conceived of observing a tree and began the ongoing activity by focusing the children on parts of a tree (the leaves) and then by reading *Our Tree*, I knew we would not only observe it at regular intervals throughout the year but that we would do many activities related to trees.

I enjoy writing descriptions of the trees and do so in the journal. I did *not* describe the trees for the children. They described them. It was later in the year that I began to record these descriptions. I recorded most discussions that were held in the classroom. The children noticed buds but did not name them. I asked the children what the buds are called because I wanted to know if anyone knew what they were. I didn't respond to Atiya's correct naming in front of the other children, although I let her know she was correct. I did not tell them what they were because I don't always like to name things for the children, especially not at first. Naming often closes off discussion because, for some people, once you name something, there may be nothing more to say about it. At this time of year, I hadn't yet told the children what kinds of trees we were observing. Telling the children to keep watching the trees put the work of discovery on them. I assured the children that observing the trees carefully would yield important results. I let the children know that there would be time to get the answers and that all the answers didn't have to be given at the start of this ongoing activity. I value the question more than the answer—the observing more than the naming.

DECEMBER 1, 1980   We went to visit our trees. . . . I asked the children to notice the configuration of the trunk and the major branches of a magnolia tree we passed on the way to the front of the school. As we walked, I pointed out the tall, thick, straight trunk of the beeches in comparison. I've never really taken a long look at the form of a tree without its leaves. It's a powerful experience.

We walked close to and around our beech tree. It was the first time we've gone so close to it. The children noticed the circles on the bark, and roots of the tree (the "foot," they called it), and how much roots really do look like feet. They noticed the cracks. There is a nest in the tree. Each thing they noticed raised a question. Here are some of the questions: How did the circles get there? Look at the lines around the circles. How did they get there? What makes the cracks? Who or what lives in the nest? How do the birds and squirrels keep warm in the winter? Why do the leaves fall off the trees when the wind blows? How did this tree grow? Why do leaves change color? Where will the green leaves come from?

Always, I ask if anyone knows an answer to a question, and I let the children explain what they think the answer is. When I'm afraid of giving wrong information I say, "I don't know but we could find out if you want to."

Most of the things they noticed also evoked a memory and led to a little discussion: "My dad cut down a tree because it was leaning on our house." "Our tree at home has a nest, too." "I remember this tree sheltering the teachers from the rain during the strike. Would it keep us dry now if it started to rain?". . . .

I'll want to go closer to Henry's tree next week. I am not at all surprised that when we changed our perspective on the tree new questions and new excitement arose. The same thing had happened to me as I observed my tree at Prospect.

REFLECTION, 1991

Visiting the trees was not only a scientific experience. It was also an aesthetic experience as much for the children as it was for me.

I rarely did the describing, and when I did, it was to model for the children. I pointed out the color of the trunks because I myself was surprised that the trunks weren't really brown as they are depicted in most drawings of trees. Although I described the leaves in the entry, I'm sure the children did the describing when we were outside.

The children often likened parts of the tree to parts of the body.

I recorded the questions because questions both stated and implicit interest me. Knowing the children's questions helped me to know what to plan for and provide for in the classroom. Unstated in this entry is the way that I collected the answers from the children. I learned early in my teaching that if the first answer is a correct one, the other children don't have a chance to be correct and that praise for a single correct answer closes off the possibility of speculation from other children. By collecting answers, a teacher can learn a lot about how the children are thinking and about what they are thinking— correct or incorrect. I am ambivalent about giving information to the children. I know they need to have it, but I don't want to close off thinking by giving all the answers. I also sometimes gave information to the children, but I'm cautious about that because I'm afraid of giving incorrect information. I open up the possibility of our finding out information together, but I don't limit the ways we might do that. When is the correct time to supplement a lesson with a book? When is it okay to answer the children's questions with information? I know that when I wrote this, I was thinking about using books to get the information to answer the questions, and there are certainly other possibilities.

It was important to me to have the children see the tree from a variety of perspectives. I knew it would make them notice more, be able to make more comparisons, and raise some new issues for them. The change in perspective not only elicited more descriptive details and questions, but it also evoked memories for the children and me.

Today, I'd take more detailed notes, although it's hard to do outside in the winter. I now have the children either take their science journals outside with them and write and/or draw what they notice or have them do it immediately after they get back into the classroom. I've had each child choose a tree and observe it throughout the year, describing it in writing and drawing.

FEBRUARY 11, 1981   I've collected a variety of twigs from bushes and trees in the neighborhood. I had forsythia, honeysuckle bush and dogwood. There are a few I don't know. The warm weather makes me (and everyone) feel like spring. I dread the inevitable return of winter.

The first thing I did today was to pass one twig around the circle and ask the children to describe it: It has little flowers coming out. It is brown. It has bumps on it. I see seeds. It is smooth in some places with little bumps. On the bottom it's kind of straight. Branches are sticking up. It's big. There are little buds on it. One bud came off. The skinny branches stick up. It is pointing on top of the buds. Some branches are big, some are short. It is fat down on the bottom. It is half green and half brown. It comes from a tree. The little branches are skinny. Some branches have two buds at the top, some have one.

I asked the children to look closely at the tips of the twig and to describe what they were calling buds, as we passed it around again. . . .

I put the twigs in water in vases to force the buds open and I asked the children to watch them because the twigs would be changing. I'd had a little debate with myself about just letting the children see the trees and bushes bloom outside, without a classroom preview. But I need some color inside, and some life to overcome the drabness of this windowless classroom.

I'd like to do some sorting activities with the twigs before the buds open. I hope I can find the time.

REFLECTION, 1991

Teachers don't always write their lesson plans, but that doesn't mean they aren't thinking and planning ahead. I'd been collecting twigs or flowers and working like this with the children since I'd begun teaching 10 years earlier. In this instance, I didn't need to write objectives and plans. I realized that although I hadn't written my plans, what actually happened was exactly what I'd hoped would happen. Sometimes, as I reread my journal, an overview or a logic of which I was not consciously aware is revealed to me. Most of the materials and activities that I provide have involved planning, whether stated or unstated. Even when the children initiate their own activities at project time or choice time and I follow their lead, I have planned by providing materials and asking questions to extend their learning.

When children or adults describe what they see, they are doing some important scientific and language work. They must observe carefully and must use words that allow them to be as specific as possible so that they can accurately describe what they see. They compare objects with things they have seen before. I wanted to record their words because I wondered if this sort of group description would affect their spoken and written language.

Many times during class discussions, I asked the children: What has changed (in the classroom, with the mice, with pregnant parents, or with babies, for example). In this entry, I asked the children to observe the twigs. In telling them to observe and that what they would be observing would be changing, I was asking them to be ready to describe the changes they saw, to keep in mind what the twigs were like when we started that day, and to be able to describe what would be the same and what would be different at a later time. I recognize that bringing the twigs inside was another way of giving the children a different perspective (a close-up view of a small part of a tree)— something that comes through the journal as important to me—but I was unsure that it was right to separate the twigs from their surroundings. I was unsure because I knew the value of a close view. It's often difficult to see the detail because of the vastness of a tree in bloom. I believed that a classroom preview would help the children to know what was going on on a larger scale with the trees outside. I used the excuse that the room was so drab that the twigs would add the brightness and color so desperately needed.

This entry refers to other sorting activities that I initiated during the course of the year. Sorting and classifying are, along with observing and describing, important scientific endeavors, and many teachers use commercial materials such as logic blocks or attribute blocks to do them. Over the course of my teaching, I'd collected a variety of natural materials that I knew allowed the same possibilities for ordering, sorting, and classifying: rocks and stones, shells, feathers, nuts, bones, and seeds. The difference between these natural objects and the commercial materials is that the classifications are not so cut and dry: They are fuzzier, less definite, and less clear-cut.

Since 1980–1981—even during the following year of 1981–1982—I've had the children write about things they've observed. Sometimes, these journals have been associated with one activity such as planting or animals. More recently, the children have a science journal separate from their writing books in which they record observations—sometimes before we discuss them as a group. Recently, we described a mother and a baby who visited our classroom. I asked the children to write at least one thing they thought the mother would do and one thing they thought the baby would do. Each child had a chance to share their ideas with the group, and then they watched the mother and the baby and described what they saw. They then talked about whether their predictions were close to correct or not.

In these five journal entries, I have found some patterns in my teaching and, to a smaller extent, in the children's learning. Different entries would have yielded slightly different patterns, but many would have been the same.

Throughout the entries are examples of the things I do in the classroom, and sometimes I explain why I do them. For example, I value observing or taking a longer look as well as noticing. I encourage this by planning long-term activities—giving the children many chances to return to an object, to an idea, or to a thought. I realize that by observing an object from a variety of perspectives—from far away and close up, using the naked eye and a microscope (although that didn't figure into any of these entries)—the children see more. Changes in perspective, vantage points, and viewpoints cause the children to notice more. I value specificity of language and encourage it by having the children describe again and again what they see. I have observed that *their* observing leads them to ask questions about objects. I want the children to collect objects they have noticed—especially those from nature—and I ask them to bring them to school, where we use them for a variety of lessons. This not only values their contributions but also serves an aesthetic purpose for them and for me.

These entries of my journal show that I seem to be less focused on what the children learn. In them, I noticed that the children became more detailed and specific in their descriptions as they were given opportunities to describe. They learned by likening things to their own bodies. They referred to their memories, especially their implicit understanding that they can depend on the cycles of nature. They know, for example, that the leaves of the tree will return to green in the spring; they know that a nest must have an occupant.

I learned from my journal that I, too, depend on cycles: the cycles of nature and the cycles of teaching.

JUNE 22, 1981   This whole experience needs more review and thought with the kids. I hope there will be time during the next few days to make some plans with them about trees for next year, when they will return to my class for second grade. I have a few ideas: photographing the trees in all seasons; drawing the trees; each child keeps a tree journal; choose three different trees next year; don't be so formal (a hard one for me, since I feel that the group experience was a good one which I should continue); read poems about trees; write some tree poems; choose an evergreen tree.

That's one of the things I love about teaching. It never ends. Even as the children are saying goodbye, even as the year ends, I'm planning a beginning.

● ● ● ● ● ● ● ● ● ● ●

Looking Back: 20 Years of a Teacher's Journal

Mickey Harris

MICKEY HARRIS *has been a secondary school English teacher in the School District of Philadelphia since 1969. She received her bachelor's degree from Pennsylvania State University and her master's degree from the University of Pennsylvania where she is currently pursuing a doctorate. Throughout her career, her journals of classroom life have informed her work as they harbor questions, invite reflection, and pragmatically jolt her failing memory. They were a natu-*

ral extension of diary writing, begun when her mother gave her a Nancy Drew diary at age 6 with the hope that writing would moderate her talking.

I began writing for myself at a very early age—actually, as soon as I realized that it was more socially acceptable to write to oneself than to talk to oneself. In an earnest effort to sort out my thoughts and to dialogue with myself about my profession, I began a diary on my 1st day of teaching in 1969. I was an attentive diarist who kept almost daily entries for the 1st year. The regularity with which I chronicled the happenings in my classroom and environs gradually declined to a once-a-week glance at "the way we were." (It is much like the abundance of baby photographs we have of our firstborn. Regretfully, we capture fewer and fewer moments in time on film with each subsequent offspring.) Yet I did persist. In *A Philadelphia Teacher's Journal,* Strieb (1985) wrote:

> As I re-read my journal, I got more ideas for teaching. I expanded the journal to include other aspects of teaching—anecdotes, observations of children and their involvement in activities, interactions with parents both in and out of school, my plans, and descriptions of the pressures of public school interest. (p. 3)

Just as Strieb used her journal to mirror her life and the lives of her community of students and parents within and beyond the boundaries of the school yard, my teacher's tabloid has graphically revealed to me how my life and world affect my practice. Subsequently, I can trace with each reviewing of my "professional journal" how my journey of inquiry in the classroom has transacted with and shaped my life. Within my "Looking Back," I blushingly and with trepidation and exultation include excepts from journals that span 2 decades. My commentaries may change from time to time, but the vignettes of students' lives continue to inform and reform my vocation. Flannery O'Connor has wisely judged a story to be good when "you can continue to see more and more in it, and when it continues to escape you." I have found that my journal has helped me to focus. It reassures my faltering memory that these are the best of times and the worst of times.

LOVE AT FIRST BITE: BECOMING A TEACHER

I entered a classroom for the first time in my life on September 6, 1950, and have spent almost 40 years in front of, behind, atop, or around a teacher's desk. When Sister St. Cyr said, "Welcome to first grade," I knew that I had made it. With my Howdy Doody lunch box and my starched uniform, regulation blue and white oxfords, and Baltimore catechism, I felt that the apple on our diminutive instructor's desk was as tempting as any fruit tantalizingly proffered in the Garden of Eden. As Whyte introduced his *Street Corner Society* with a bit of personal background, I, too, find it necessary to offer—not as a disclaimer—my background and mind-set before continuing down the yellow brick road of ethnographic travel. I am a child of the 60s. I completed high school, college, and graduate studies in the decade of Camelot and flower power. I also began a new career, became politically aware, and became a "married lady." It was a frenetic 10 years!

During that time, my taste in lunch boxes and catechisms changed, but my interest in teaching did not dissipate. I had read *Good Morning, Miss Dove* and *Good-bye Mr. Chips.* I applauded the resonance of *Teacher* and the angst of *Up the Down Staircase.* I empathized with Kauffman's Miss Barrett on her first day in school facing a cacophony of confusion that eliminated the possibility of positive first impressions. In 18 continuous years of formal education, I had vociferously decided to become an actress, a writer, a dancer, a comedienne, a nun, a mother, a patroness of the arts, a policewoman, a politician, and a woman of independent means. In selecting teaching as a profession—although, in truth, I think it selected me—I felt that I could combine all of these vocational choices—except that of a woman of means—by becoming a teacher.

Through 20 years, 7 strikes, and over 3,000 students, I have "served my time" in one school, South Philadelphia High School, in the heart of a sprawling urban school system. My students and their parents have taught me cookery and tenacity, eurythmics and humility, heritage and humor. When I first began teaching at Southern, it was a huge, comprehensive high school of over 4,000 students. Because of the frequency of gang-related violence, mayhem in the cafeteria, overcrowded classrooms, and a neighborhood that cowered when students were dismissed en masse, the school district and the Naked City's police department decided to do away with study halls and lunch rooms by putting the entire student population on different shifts. Additionally, some core components of "special" programs would move out of the "Big House" and into makeshift annexes for a short time. In 1971, I moved with 14 equally beleaguered novices from South Philly's main building to a turn-of-the-century elementary school fortress, eight blocks and countless light years away.

This is where our temporarily moved enclave is still situated, on the top floor of an 1890's elementary school, with 300 9th- through 12th-grade students who must return to the main building daily to take the required physical education courses, varsity and junior varsity sports, orchestra, choir, or art.

The Motivation Annex is a program intended for students who fall into the middle range of the ominous classification umbrella of standardized test scores. These students are hoping to pursue a college degree and are therefore, with parental support, committed to a demanding array of academic course work, mandatory tutoring and cultural events, a closely monitored attendance policy, and a crazy-quilt community of learners. Although the Big House has lost 50% of its student population since 1968, our oasis remains constant. A full 90% of our students graduate and continue their education. We have an average daily attendance rate of 93%, which is 25% higher than our main building. We have a heating system that keeps our classrooms freezing every Monday and Tuesday, comfortable on Wednesday, and tropical by Thursday and Friday. We have water fountains that are a perfect height for second graders but give varsity basketball players a great deal of tribulation. Motivation runs out of paper by February, as teachers combine to purchase their own supplies or to call in citywide favors from supply-surfeited scholars. Most of our textbooks are from the 60s, as are most of our teachers. It is the last commodity that I think makes the difference.

DAY 1: SEPTEMBER 22, 1969   It's September 22, 1969, and I am a teacher! I have a roster, an attendance book, a homeroom (which I share with another teacher who has been teaching for *forty years),* a faculty lounge key, a ladies' room key, a coat locker, a parking sticker, lesson plan sheets, and a 3 x 5 hall pass which, I have been warned, is to be used in extreme emergencies only. Although I've never taken an education course, I think that I've found my niche. My own high school, dear old Cecilian Academy for Young Ladies, instructed one hundred and twenty giggling scholars while adhering to a lengthy code of conduct which included uniforms, mandatory chapel, Friday afternoon high tea, nuns, and no boys! South Philadelphia High School is teeming with mini-skirts, graffiti, football jerseys, a lunchroom that has a city-wide reputation for food fights, and no nuns, high tea, or chapel.

Because Southern is bursting at the seams with over four thousand students, we are on a split shift. I teach five tenth grade English classes from noon until 4:37. My department head, Mr. Ostrum, explained that my first and third period classes are slow, my second and fifth are average, and my fourth period is a star class. Each teacher's roster (and student's roster too) shows clearly in which designated class you are! I wonder what goes through a tenth grader's mind when he sees English 2 S on his report. What if someone in the Roster Room puts an Av. next to all of the * students and a * next to the Av. kids. . . .

DAY 8: SEPTEMBER 29, 1969   Well, they said I wouldn't last and here I am. I've been here one full week and I've been called "Yo, teach!" more times than I can count. I've had my hall pass stolen, my coat locker broken into, and my class lists keep changing from day to day. As soon as I memorize a name and connect that name with a face, both disappear. Where are all of these people coming from and where do they go when they leave me? Someone let the air out of my tires in the glass strewn parking lot but then wrote a note of apology, explaining that he thought it was Sy Ruben's car (the infamous social studies teacher). My students range from sweet to silent, somnolent to sarcastic. They don't seem to be sure of the fact that I'm going to stay. Although I arrived here on September 22, I was their fourth teacher. The guy who lasted for one looong day said that he'd rather flee to Canada than to get a deferment this way. There are sixteen new teachers at Southern this year. Six of the fellows in the group said that Vietnam had a lot to do with their career choice. Three of the sixteen are graduates of South Philly High and gave that as their reason for "coming home." We are to meet with Dr. Brancato once a week to air our questions, learn procedures, and "get to know the place." Dr. Brancato suggested that we walk around the neighborhood, visit the Ninth Street Market (where many of our students work), and judge for ourselves what makes this part of our city so unique. Our principal, vice-principal and twenty-five percent of the faculty are all from South Philadelphia. A Connecticut Yankee in King Arthur's Court might identify with me today.

P.S. I finally figured out why the elevator operator kept forcing me to get off her "express to the stars." She thought I was a student. Maybe some day I can accept that as a compliment.

Nancie Atwell (1987) assures us that teachers are ideally positioned to observe, describe, and learn from the behaviors of our students. Although we strive to create classrooms that are oases in deserts of unrest, we cannot dismiss the impact of the world at large on our microcosms of society.

APRIL 26, 1971   Today I am too tired to write. After two years of teaching and learning to trust my students as I would trust an extended family, I feel that I don't belong there anymore. The gang fighting, as you know, has been getting closer and closer to the school. Today it burst into my classroom with all the intensity and hatred of open warfare. And they were girls! I answered a knock at my class door and attempted to let one student in. Suddenly the door was thrown open and eight girls bounded across the room and dragged Lorraine, a tenth grader in my advisory, out of the classroom. I tried the emergency phone. It was dead. I asked for help, but my students seemed to have adapted a carnival personality and were applauding the frenetic brawl. When I futilely tried to unpile the eight-on-one confrontation, I was knocked unconscious. I awoke with a black eye, a cut lip, and a missing bicuspid. Lorraine is being treated at St. Agnes Hospital for cuts and bites. Tomorrow is my birthday. I am so much older than yesterday. I look and feel like a broken woman.

As researchers and as teachers and as human beings, we are in the business of learning by experiment. (Britton, 1987, p. 16)

Mr. Britton is much more comfortable with experimentation than I am. The ambivalence that I felt concerning the "go with the flow" theory of classroom discourse resurfaces throughout the pages of my journal. Spontaneity and pacing schedules do not happily coexist.

JANUARY 24, 1972

> Look how we can, or sad, or merrily
> Interpretation will misquote our looks
>
> William Shakespeare
> *King Henry IV*

This was the quote that opened our lesson today. I'm trying to get the kids from Rm. 415 to feel confident about reading some lines from Shakespeare and giving them meaning instead of viewing them as a foreign language. Sounded like a good idea to me. It worked when I was in high school six long years ago. I went out and bought little notebooks so that each student could copy a quote or borrow an idea for the day and write without worrying about the wicked pen of Ms. Harris— although I must confess that its bark is much worse than its bite. Well, those best laid plans of mice (Mickey) and men went "aft agley" again! After a relatively quiet time of responding in writing to the quote, Louie raised his hand and said that he could really "get into" the Bard's lines. The only problem was that Lou had misread the lines and had written "books" instead of "looks." He then artfully led the class in an animated discussion as to how books are open to a limitless variety of inter- pretations which means—you guessed it—all objective tests on literature should be abandoned at once. Even after I pointed out to the artful dodger that he had focused on a word which wasn't Shakespeare's, Louie was not deterred. What a fil- ibuster! Is South Philadelphia politics ready for him?

I keep trying to find a perfect formula for planning a lesson, a unit, a year. But I must confess that what I consider my most successful classes are often not at all what I had originally planned. A misquote, a fight in the hallway, a headline about the National Guard at Kent State, and we're off and running. My neat little lesson plan squares, full of my perfect Palmer Method handwriting, do not make my day memorable. It's the vitality and unpredictability of a room full of sixteen year olds that make my day. I have to accept that planning a class is not like writing a script. Everybody ad libs. . . .

MARCH 17, 1979 Happy Saint Patrick's Day! Today was indeed a great day for the Irish. My fifth period seniors turned in their final papers on *Tess of the D'Urbervilles*. I have thirty-one students and thirty-one papers. This is success! (Marisa was absent from school today but Gina, her ever loyal friend, brought her project in.) I don't know if my begging, my threatening, or my bribing encouraged the kids to meet my deadline. We celebrated the event by having scones and tea in honor of Tess, Angel Clare, and the bunch. At noon, we had early dismissal and took the bus to the Ritz Theatre to view Polanski's version of *Tess*. Everyone except Derrick attended the film. He had to re-paint the boys' room wall after writing something less than com- plimentary about Mr. Ridgeways's class over the sinks and across the mirrors!

Taking thirty seventeen and eighteen year olds to a theatre where they will sit in darkness for one hundred and seventy minutes is always a bit frightening, but—not to worry—they were great. They had never been to a movie theatre where, as Tanya exclaims, "Your feet don't stick to the floor!" When the ushers handed them the programs/study guides, they were suspicious. They were probably afraid a 50 minute test would follow. Everyone loved the film.

After the show we reassembled in the lobby. I'm still paranoid after all these years and count heads as well as check lists before and after each performance. Haven't lost a kid yet! While in the lobby, a debate spontaneously erupted between

David and Lisa on the subtle and not so subtle differences between rape and seduction with a wonderful comparison between the film and novel. When the manager of this "artsy" movie house joined us on the sidewalk, I was afraid that he would ask us to disperse immediately. Instead the man, a great judge of scholars, reported that the other theatregoers (many of whom were retired and enjoying a senior citizen's matinee) were delighted to hear the animated reactions of young people to a classic. Sure and begorrah, I'm so proud.

While selecting journal entries to be included in my walk/jog through time, I was struck (no puns intended) by Lynne Strieb's (1985) comment in the preface of her book—that she wrote this journal "before a long bitter teacher's strike; before a media attack on Philadelphia teachers. . . . It was written when I could concentrate on the children and what and how I teach them. 1980 seems long ago and far away" (p. 14).

SEPTEMBER 28, 1981   I haven't made an entry in my new school journal until today because I was hoping that I would be back in my classroom by now. This is my seventh strike since 1969. Each one seems to get more bitter, more frustrating. I leave my house at 6:30 each morning and "Walk the Line," as Johnny Cash used to warble, until 10:00. While we carry our signs, Ramona, Ed, Rosemarie, and I plan the year, schedule class trips, and watch substitute teachers go into a virtually empty building. I have spoken to most of the seniors who will be in my advisory. William and Denise meet me outside of school on Mondays and Fridays. They collect work and college applications from their fellow classmates. I write my comments, questions, and suggestions; then my super helpers distribute our bizarre communiqué. This class of seniors is concerned about a shortened year, college rejections, postponed graduation. Some have secured jobs that may lure them out of the classroom. Others are feeling as if no one really cares about them.

I worry about teacher morale too. Al and Buddy, two of the finest teachers in the district, are gone. They told me in June that one more strike would end their careers. Buddy was offered a job with Educational Testing Service in Princeton and Al is going to law school. Many parents are putting their children into private or parochial schools. The ultimate sorrow occurred when I finished picketing and returned home. The editorial in the *Inquirer* let me know that we are incompetent, greedy, overpaid drones who want to drain the coffers of a bankrupt city. . . .

The phone just rang and I'm joyful once again. A teacher from Council Rock High School has a nephew in my advisory. She has promised to lend me a set of *The Stranger* so that the seniors and I can meet at McDonald's (or as the kids say, Mickey D's) and "talk" the book. I have a set of copybooks—they are the old mustard yellow, wide-lined genre that the kids find aesthetically jarring, *but* they were free. We will be able to read, think, write, eat, and exchange on a semi-regular basis until the strike is over or until the McDonald's manager throws us out of his place of business. I am so homesick for room 308 that I'll never complain about asbestos chips, lack of heat, or missing wall phones again.

In *Reclaiming the Classroom* (Goswami & Stillman, 1987), Dixie Goswami interviews Ken Jones, who talks about teachers in the middle:

> I think teachers who are in the spot where I am—at middle age with 20 years teaching experience—are a forgotten group. Rural teachers, inner city teachers, minority teachers have stuff aimed toward them. And all we are—when there's an article about burnout or teachers leaving the profession, then we're mentioned, then we're included. But there are a lot of us who care about teaching. We stay in it not because it's a dead-end job; we stay in not because we can't do anything else; we stay in because we like it. (p. 61)

NOVEMBER 28, 1987   I should have known that it would eventually happen. Just as those silver hairs that persisted in springing forth to remind me that time and Clairol wait for no one, just as my middle age spread lets me know that its appearance is not premature, THE event has happened to announce me—and to the rest of a cheering and jeering faculty—that I had better start looking at the Pennsylvania Board Retirement Fund. Today I discovered that Lisa Howard, my homeroom assistant, is the daughter of Cindy Howard, my homeroom assistant of the class of 1969. Have I really been here that long? Who said "Education is hanging around long enough until you catch on"? Have I caught on?

When I started teaching I was five years older than most of my students. My relationship with my students has changed over the years—from big sister, to wacky aunt, to doting parent. When I first crossed the spray paint decorated threshold of South Philadelphia High School in 1969, I was one of the youngest teachers in the school. Almost two decades later I'm still one of the youngest faculty members. Southern once housed over four thousand students. Now we have half that number. City population shifts and alternative high schools have depleted our pool of students. Economic shifts and alternative career opportunities have depleted our pool of young teachers. If Barbara Walters were to ask me what I would do if I had to choose another profession, I wouldn't know what to say—I who never seem to be at a loss for words.

I have some wonderful students this year. They know how I feel about teaching. Will Michelle, Laquetta, or Louis consider entering the perfect profession for Peter Pan and Ms. Harris, Ms. Harris? I hope so—because when Lisa's daughter/Cindy's grand-daughter comes walking through the portals of room 308, "I'm outta here."

JUNE 24, 1988   Today is moving day. I'm packing boxes and emptying desk drawers and rusted file cabinets to make room for the new "tenant." Do I really want to take a sabbatical? It's only been twenty years. Sixteen of those years have been in this classroom. This is where I learned to trust my students and to share my thinking, my writing, my fears and hopes with these special people. In my first years of teaching I wanted my students to tell me all, to write and remember that I would be an appreciative audience of one, to take risks and be confident that risk-takers are applauded. Yet I didn't "tell all," nor did I share my writing, and risk taking was not on my agenda. Blame it on my youth? I certainly can't use that excuse anymore. I think that my wonderful children at home and my equally special students—

extended family—have taught me that showing by example is still an incredibly potent tool. Over the decades (Did I say that?) our classroom has evolved into a more democratic society. There are more choices, wider variety of activities, less teacher talk (just as many teacher puns, however), and more time for listening to the unpredictable, sometimes brilliant, frequently provocative inquiry process of a wonderfully engaging group of senior high school scholars.

My photos are in the trunk of my car. I've removed my name from the door. The greeting that proclaimed, "What test today!!" is on the floor next to my "This is turning out to be a C-kind of day" poster. I'll miss these four, soiled flamingo pink walls, and the mismatched desks, pigeon perches, and painted-shut closets. I'll miss the most wonderful faculty in the universe, but most of all, I'll miss the family of Room 308. But I know I'll be back in one short year. I offer you dear diary, dear journal, dear schizophrenic self, a reflection enclosed with my application for acceptance in the doctoral program this September.

> True ease in writing comes from art, not chance,
> As those move easiest who have learned to dance.
>
> Alexander Pope
> *Essays in Criticism, II*

When I turned twenty, I felt that I was "almost grown," that I had reached a point in my life when reflection and planning were profoundly scheduled. After honestly assessing that I had a paucity of plans or reflections, I, following the "law" of serendipity, decided to pursue a career in the teaching of English. The hedonist in me could fill the coffers with the beauty of great literature while the pragmatist in me (albeit a rather small segment) could repay student loans and surfeit my tab at the venerable Leary's Book Store.

As I approach another twenty year notch on my ever-expanding belt, I again find that it is time for plans and reflections. I have been teaching senior high school English and creative (whatever) writing for two decades, and as Mr. Pope suggests, I feel that "those move easiest who have learned to dance." I earnestly believe that my vocation/avocation is the best of all possible worlds, but I cannot quell an amorphous restlessness. I am not afflicted with middle age metamorphosis or baby boomer burn-out. I simply want to return to my students the riches which they have bestowed upon me. I wish to strengthen and combine practice with theory, philosophy with execution. I have, to date, totally reveled in teaching through "chance"—an instinctual crazy quilt—but I, Mr. Pope, yearn to learn to dance.

In *One Writer's Beginnings*, Eudora Welty divides her art and her life into "Listening," "Learning to See," and "Finding a Voice." The writer, the teacher, the dreamer all need to perfect each quality in order to grow. As the quintessential eavesdropper, have I really learned to listen? I delicately peruse the human condition, but do I profoundly see? I veritably love to be heard, but have I found my voice? The classroom has been my second home. Although I have not really left it in almost forty years, I feel the itch to return to it in a somewhat altered state so that I may find "that continuous thread of revelation" that Ms. Welty reverently defines. Look out sabbatical. It's my year to dance!

After 20 years in the classroom, I found my "year of living dangerously" in the rarified and strangely remote academic environment of university-based philosophy of education rather alien yet alluring. I welcomed the invitation to examine my practice in an orderly and conscious manner. No more sidelong glances and furtive peeks at the profound successes and equally provocative failures of Ms. Harris's home away from home!

During my sabbatical, the building that I had considered my other domicile—my second residence—was closed, and the students of Southwark Motivation Program were ushered to the Big House at Broad and Snyder. They lost their extra math and English classes, their core faculty, and their overwhelming sense of community. They retained, however, an unquenchable thirst for learning because they, as generations before them, see education as a key that embodies hope, success, and access to a better life. We missed our former location, the smaller scale of student population, and the more relaxed atmosphere of an autonomous alternative school.

OCTOBER 1, 1991   Today is my first anniversary, and I find myself caught in reverie—a dangerous state of mind for a woman who cries as she drives by a wedding at 55 m.p.h. or who mists mightily at the first strains of "Pomp and Circumstance." September 22, 1990, marked the end of twenty-one years at South Philadelphia High School, a term of office that exceeded my years (to date) of mother, that indeed outlasted my Toyota, my Seiko, and my marriage. On September 25th I was informed that I would be leaving my beloved post at South Philly and would be traveling north on Broad Street to Central High School, many miles and millenia away. Southern's population of 4,000 students in the psychedelic 60s had become an underutilized scaffold that claimed a student body of fewer than 1,400 young people. Central, the academic elitist on the hill, was bursting with a host of talented folks who needed one more English teacher. I spent four wrenching school days responding to students' journals, writing college recommendations, reminiscing with a few faculty members who tried to reassure me that I would find my new home an intellectually challenging and emotionally nurturing oasis. I was unable to tell my students, pack my belongings, or clear the classroom slate of my "Harris Clan Goals for 1990–91." On my last day I read to my classes. I read Sonia Sanchez's "Just Don't Never Give Up on Love," I gave everyone a copy of Maya Angelou's "Still I Rise" and tried to quell the surging tide of joy, gratitude, and unadulterated love that I felt for being part of so many people who nurtured me, who taught me how "to read the world" while I shared with them how "to read the word." Tony Bennett may have left his heart in San Francisco, but South Philadelphia will always own a part of mine.

CONCLUDING THOUGHTS

My colleagues were accurate when they predicted that I would find Central to be an oasis. It is an impressive edifice replete with young people whose creativity, intellectual prowess, integrity, and humanity seem to force the building to expand. I rejoice when I hear Brenda recite with such passion and clarity the words of Hester Prynne (with her pristine Reeboks jutting from beneath her austere Puritan garb). My heart sings (the only part of me that sings on key) when Xonqui volunteers to read his essay on *Native Son* or Sabina lets me know through the poignant pages of her journal how her culture affects her interpretation of literature.

Neither our vast school system nor I knew if a change of venue would result in a better world for Ms. Harris or her students. Yet I must admit that I did once again feel at home when I heard "Yo, teach!" from a smiling senior as I ambled toward my advisory this morning. When I was first told that I would be transferred although the school year had already begun, I called the Board of Education offices and charged, "You can't do that. I've been at Southern for 21 years!" The faceless response was, "Yes, we can. Now you can be at Central for the next 21!" Well, 1 down and 20 to go.

Zora Neale Hurston's mother issued her a challenge that serves teachers as effectively as writers:

Jump at the sun. You might not land on the sun,
but at least you'll get off the ground.

Has anyone seen my Air Jordans?

• • • • • • • • • • • •
Journals for Collaboration, Curriculum, and Assessment

Deborah Jumpp and Lynne Yermanock Strieb

DEBORAH JUMPP *has been a teacher in the School District of Philadelphia for 15 years at the middle and high school levels. Presently, she is a member of the Philadelphia Writing Project and writing coordinator of the Research Apprenticeship Program at West Philadelphia High School. She has also served as a leader of writing assessment seminars for the School District of Philadelphia and as an instructor in the Literacy Network for teachers in the Philadelphia area. Her work as teacher researcher includes serving as co-coordinator of the Philadelphia site of the Urban Sites Writing Network as well as delivering presentations at the Philadelphia Federation of Teachers Program on Education and the Keystone Chapter of the International Reading Association. In addi-*

tion, Jumpp coauthored a teachers' manual for the Philadelphia Inquirer enti-
tled "Using the Newspaper With the Pennsylvania Comprehensive Reading
Plan." LYNNE YERMANOCK STRIEB'S *biographical information appears with "Visit-*
ing and Revisiting the Trees" (this chapter).

We are urban teachers in Philadelphia. Jumpp has taught English in Philadelphia since 1975 and currently works with an ethnically diverse population at the
Jones Middle School. Strieb has been teaching first and second grade and
kindergarten since 1970. She currently teaches first grade at Greenfield Elementary. We met 3 years ago as participants in the Philadelphia Writing Project and
began soon after to work collaboratively, in part because we were intrigued by
our differences: one an elementary school teacher and the other a secondary
school teacher, and one a white woman and the other an African-American
woman who both worked primarily with an ethnically diverse group of African-
American, Latino, and white students. What brought us together, however, was
that both of us used journal writing as a critical way to construct the curriculum
and to learn more about our teaching by close observation of students.

In Jumpp's classroom, students had been using journals in a variety of
ways, among them daily free writing at the beginning of the period. In addition, Jumpp herself had been keeping an in-class journal written for her students, who were permitted to read it at any time during the class period if they
had completed their work or if they had finished their own journal writing. In
addition, Jumpp encouraged students to dialogue with her and with their peers
about particular entries in their own journals. At home, Jumpp kept a teacher
research journal, which served as a lens through which she could look at her
teaching practice, her students, and the environment of her classroom. Eventually, Jumpp began to plan lessons in her journal. Planning daily lessons in a
journal is quite different from an official lesson plan turned in to an administrator once or twice a month. The daily teacher journal was a place where
Jumpp recorded classroom observations and later, usually at home, mapped
out a lesson plan for individual students, including who would benefit from
group work or individual work, what the groups would be, and other decisions about how to manage the day.

Strieb had been keeping a journal and many other kinds of written records
about children's learning since she began teaching (see Chapters 2 and 4). Generally, she used her journal to record what happened in the classroom so that
she could go back and reflect on it in terms of curriculum, make observations
about children and other teachers, keep notes on books read and speakers
heard, plan for and think about her teaching, and share her work with others.

Over time, our individual uses of journals grew into a collaborative
research project in which they functioned as both subject and method. In other
words, we used journals to document our responses to each other's classrooms, to gain perspectives on the teaching and learning strategies of students,

and to compare and contrast our experiences in the Philadelphia schools. In this essay, we look at journals in three ways: as a way of observing a classroom during teacher-to-teacher collaboration, as a way of helping establish an interactive environment in which students can contribute to the creation of curriculum, and as an ongoing way of assessing students' learning.

JOURNALS AS TEACHER-TO-TEACHER COLLABORATION

At a teacher-research group meeting of the writing project, Jumpp asked if another teacher consultant would visit her classroom to give her a different perspective on what was going on. She had her own view of what the students were doing when they wrote in their journals, which she had written about in her own journal. She had also had formal observations written by administrators. However, she had never had another teacher observe and describe in writing what was happening in her classroom. On the other hand, as the following journal excerpt indicates, Strieb knew that she wanted to see Jumpp teach:

I was fascinated with the ideas about literacy, about non-dominant English, about young teenagers which Jumpp was expressing, but which were somewhat new to me. I knew that I wanted to see her in action in the classroom. . . . So when she asked for someone to come and observe their journal time, I jumped at the chance. . . . .

Strieb had always taught young children from 4 to 8 years old and had been fearful of working with older kids. She was mostly afraid that, as she put it, they would laugh at her. Observing a teacher who not only wasn't afraid of working with these students but actually enjoyed it seemed like a good, nonthreatening way for Strieb to break down the fear.

Strieb visited two classes of eighth-grade students, each with 33 students. The students were classified as Chapter I because their reading levels were below the 25th percentile on citywide tests. Her journal included first impressions of the school:

Jones Junior High was built in the 1930s. Its halls are lined with marble and granite, and it gives a clean, grand appearance. The school population is mixed white (German, Irish, Polish), Hispanic, and African-American. It is truly a desegregated school. Deborah has told me that the children with whom she works are all "at risk" for failure and dropping out of school altogether. They are, in some cases, older than they should be for their grades, having been retained two or more times in lower grades.

In one class she visited, Strieb wrote a detailed description of Jumpp's interactions about an ongoing project, which involved both the gathering of oral histories and extensive writing about families. The students were talking about customs, traditions, and recipes that had been passed on from generation to generation. Strieb also wrote about the contrasts she noticed when the second class entered:

This group of students seems much older, more settled yet louder to me. They walk in in a noisier way than the last group. Some children sit and do nothing—just sit. Others get immediately to work on their journals. The tension is great. A boy to my right sits, one hand on chin, writing nothing. He has removed neither his journal nor his pencil from his bag.

Deborah says, "Okay, everyone should have a journal out." A female student says loudly, "I lost mine. (Pause) I lost mine."

Deborah responds, "Okay, take out a piece of paper. You know the procedure."

The young man finally takes out his journal. He looks around, not writing. He stares off into space. The girl who lost her journal takes a long time finding a piece of paper. She noisily shuffles through her book bag until she finds one and settles down to work.

The boy (M.T.—it is written on his journal cover) flips through the pages. He sits with his hand on his mouth. (Three minutes have passed.) Deborah passes out the students' papers, quietly talking to them. "Bring your writing to some kind of closure." Many of the children continue to write. "Before I ask you to move with your study partner for revision and editing. . . I told you to bring your journal writing to closure. . . . Sit up, Julia. I want to see your pretty face." Eight minutes had passed and M.T. had not really begun to write.

Strieb showed Jumpp her observation entry for the day of the visit, and Jumpp responded in her own journal:

Lynne came yesterday. She stayed for two classes. It was quite a delight to have her in the classroom. She was there for sections 805 and 803. Section 805 responded very well to what she had to say. So she will be a mentor to Ann, Alicia, Dora, Chloe, and Jasmin. Out of this group all are probably going to stick it out except Jasmin. Lynne brought in her rough drafts of her manuscript. The kids got a chance to see how a real author writes. They even asked some questions. I mean they asked GREAT questions. They asked if she made any money from writing the book and about how long it took her to write it. What fascinated the students was the number of rewrites that Lynne had to do. She did them all on the typewriter, she explained to the students.

Lynne said she could tell that the kids were rough. She wrote about how they came into the room very reluctantly, and their resistance to writing. I guess I must be so accustomed to these kinds of behaviors, I thought they were being real good today, and I mean, REAL good. The class Lynne saw was a different one from the one I had been seeing. I never viewed the kids as rough. I didn't notice those students having difficulty writing in the journal. My afternoon classes wanted to know why they didn't meet Lynne.

Lynne detailed more information about my classroom than the official observations I had experienced. She wrote about the periodicals and books that I was using. She talked more about the classroom climate and the students. Lynne wrote descriptions of what I actually did in the classroom. It was good to hear my voice because in the description she included direct quotes. It was almost like looking at a movie or a video.

Lynne also learned a lot from that visit:

I saw two groups of children, children who were traditionally considered difficult, working calmly, quickly and with purpose at writing. I got some ideas about curriculum—the oral history project—and I saw materials which I did not have in my classroom, but from which I knew my young children would benefit. I saw a wonderful teacher at work. She turned my visit into an effective lesson—a lesson to which the children listened attentively. I saw a teacher who skillfully got the children to work together quietly and seriously. And I did have some contact with these eighth grade students. I actually did a lesson with them, and they didn't even laugh, as I had feared they would.

Visiting across grade levels and schools was new for both of us. Our journals gave us a way to see what another teacher saw and found significant. From these observations, we raised some new questions: about literacy, about labels that children carry, about authorship in writing, and about the school and classroom climate. In short, the journals gave us a new way to collaborate across the different worlds of our practice.

JOURNALS AS CURRICULUM

Jumpp's own in-class journal was used to encourage students to write about classroom concerns, to practice self-expression, and to solve problems. In most cases, her in-class journal encouraged students to express their personal opinions honestly. Jumpp responded to every student who took the time to write. Her responses were intended to encourage the students to write more, to elicit more thought and writing on an issue already generated by the students, and to stimulate student inquiry into topics. The following is a brief excerpt from Jumpp's in-class journal:

NOVEMBER 13   Today is a beautiful day. It is sunny and pleasant outside, and it is Friday. I have to work tomorrow, but after work I can have fun. My sons have cup day tomorrow, and I will have to miss part of it because I have to work. Last night I got no studying done. I must concentrate and set aside time to do my studying. I have a paper due in November which is just two weeks away, and I really need to get busy. I don't feel like it, but I must do it.

As this journal entry conveys, Jumpp used her in-class journal to let students have a window on her life. She wanted the students to see her own struggles as a writer and a learner and wanted to use the class journal to invite students into the world of writing and learning. The journal was a way of demystifying learning and showing that everyone struggles with language.

Strieb's journal also became a part of the curriculum in Jumpp's classroom. Jumpp asked Strieb to show her students several drafts of her journal and to talk about her struggles to have it published. The students saw Strieb working with writing, language, and learning and saw that the struggles were the same in their own journals, in Jumpp's journal, and in Strieb's journal. Strieb described the use of her journal as part of Jumpp's curriculum:

I read a portion of my journal from December 1980 to the students, telling them that I chose that day because, since they are writing about their family Christmas traditions, I wanted to read to them about a Christmas tradition in my classroom that involved a recipe. It was about making the gingerbread house.

I told them how I wrote the entries, where I worked and how. I showed them my rough draft of the journal, which I handwrote on loose-leaf pages and are now in a binder. I showed them pages that had many mistakes crossed out, and told them that I don't care what my writing looks like when I first write it. I also told them that things had changed so much now because in 1980 no one had personal computers and now I mostly write on my computer. I asked them if there were any questions and they asked me how long it took me to write it and if I earned any money from writing it. I told them about the many rejections. I asked them how they come to closure when Ms. Jumpp asks them to stop writing. "Exactly what do you do?" Several students answered.

(Then Deborah held up the Sunday Magazine section of the *Philadelphia Inquirer*. She showed them an article about Fishtown, the neighborhood in Philadelphia in which they live. The article was originally journal entries, and she urged the children to read it. She told them a little about it, and suggested that they might try to use it as a model for writing about their families. She suggested, as was done in this article, that the students take photographs and include them in their writing. She says, "I have a camera, and you can borrow it from me if you want to include pictures. It's just an idea.")

It's interesting to think of the many layers of journal writing that occur here. There were descriptions of what happened in two of Jumpp's classes written in Strieb's journal and shared with Jumpp. There was Jumpp's reaction to Strieb's journal, written in her journal. There were the children's journals, in which they wrote every day and which, with permission, Jumpp read and responded to. There was Jumpp's public journal, which she kept on her desk for the children to read. Jumpp planned a lesson about Strieb, who lived in the school neighborhood until she was 9 years old. In addition, Strieb read from her published journal and showed the children the handwritten first drafts of that journal. Finally, there was the article in the Sunday magazine section written by a resident of the school neighborhood, which had started out as a series of journal entries. Holding it all together was Jumpp's vision that children need to know that their writing is legitimate and important. This lengthy entry shows two of the ways we used journals as curriculum: to help students learn about their own learning and to help them learn about journals as a versatile genre.

JOURNALS AS ASSESSMENT

For both of us, journals also function as part of the ongoing assessment of students' learning. In Jumpp's classroom, having a place for students to write down ideas also provided them with a way to reflect on, summarize, and synthesize information. At first, the students used journals for personal writing, but later, they began to see them as tools for problem solving and reflection. Eventually, students began to generate topics for their own learning and to raise questions. The journals also gave Jumpp a way to learn more about her students: She could see their interests and their developing abilities as writers. That students began to see that they could write to Jumpp and that she responded with meaningful comments were of great importance. As Amy wrote in her journal:

I was reading a book about the Negro in the Civil War. I was truly surprised because a lot of things that were very important was [sic] not mentioned in the movie, "Glory."

It was only through the journal that Jumpp knew that Amy had seen the movie "Glory" and was reading a book on African-Americans in the Civil War. Jumpp got a look at Amy's learning: that she remembered details from the movie and could compare and contrast those details with a historical reference. Amy went on to write in her journal:

When I'm done I'm going to write all the important things the movie just so happened to didn't think it was important.

Jumpp wrote to Amy in her journal:

I, too, did some research after looking at "Glory" and found many falsehoods, some major and some minor.

Amy and Jumpp became coinvestigators on a topic initiated by a student—
a kind of role reversal. Amy was questioning, seeking answers, and taking the
initiative to research without prodding from the teacher. She was free to write,
learn, and move toward her own conclusions. Amy wrote back to Jumpp in
her journal:

I like the way you take time to write what we say and think down on paper. It makes
us or at least me feel that you do care about what we feel and how we think.

This journal entry shows a student and teacher dialoguing and in doing so
validates the student's thoughts and interests.

Another exchange on quite a different topic also reveals the power of a
journal to let the teacher know what her students are thinking:

RAY: What's the world coming to? Yesterday I heard and read about a man being
     beat to death by two police officers. If we are not safe from the police then who
     are we safe from?
DEBORAH: Yes, this was very traumatic. The news media said he died from a cocaine
     overdose. What do you think?
RAY: MRS. JUMPP READ THIS. So if he did have drug in his body that don't give them
     a reason to kill him!!!!!!!!!!!!!!
DEBORAH: The police are saying that they didn't kill him. They are saying that he died
     of a drug overdose or complications from using crack. For example, if you take
     crack and run, for some people, they have a massive heart attack because of
     what crack does to the heart and respiratory system. What do you think?
RAY: Well what about the eyewitnesses. They said they saw the police beating on
     the man. If he had crack in his system beating and wrestling with the man still
     brought his heart to a racing beat. That would bring anybody's heart to a faster
     heart beat. Right or wrong?
DEBORAH: Dear Ray, you're absolutely right. We will have to see what the investiga-
     tors/courts will say.

In this exchange, Ray started out with something that really interested him.
Jumpp prompted Ray to write more by asking a question at the end of her first
comment. Ray did the same thing to Jumpp. By deliberately taking another
position, another side of the argument, she got him to think more about it.
Ray's text was becoming a persuasive piece of writing.

Strieb also used her journal for assessment of children's progress, sometimes by describing conversations with other teachers about how children
learn:

Last Sunday the Philadelphia Teachers Learning Cooperative met with Pat Carini.
Rhoda brought a tape recording of a child and we listened to and described her
reading. We had a wonderful discussion about children pretending to read, about

the natural order a child brings to reading, and about how this might contrast with the conventions of reading itself. That seminar has had a wonderful effect on me.

Strieb wrote observations of individual children in her journal. The following excerpts from Strieb's published journal (1985) were written over several months. They focus on two children about whose progress in reading Strieb was concerned:

JANUARY 27   Sally's been having a really hard time with reading. She gets so nervous when asked to read. She forgets, she makes wild guesses, she shakes and moves around. I'd vowed to keep away from her rather than ruin things completely for her. (p. 37)

As for Foster, last week I learned that he has *Little Black, A Pony* at home, and that he memorized quite a bit of it. He volunteered this information. (p. 37)

MARCH 17   Nina is so much fun to watch at Sustained Reading Time. She wants to learn to read so badly but is still not remembering words. She loves the "Breakthrough" books and makes up stories that are not only coherent but also close to the text. (p. 63)

In these instances, the information that Strieb gained from attending a teacher group meeting, taking notes on classroom observations, and writing and reading her journal came together to change the way she was teaching:

JANUARY 27   I got a Breakthrough Book, *I Fell Down,* and asked Sally to read it to me. I told her it would be all right if she couldn't read the words. She could pretend to read it. So she started by describing the picture: "He fell down, she fell on top of him, his mother came out," etc. The story is written in the first person and I was concerned about what to do about that. After she read it, I read it to her twice. Then I asked her to read it to me again, then I read it to her. Then, before I asked her to read it one more time, I told her that the boy is telling the story, so every time she thinks she should say "he" she should say "I—I fell down" not "He fell down." She understood that and the final time she read it to me, the words she read were very close to the text. She said, "I can read this now" and she left me happier than I'd seen her all year. . . . At the end of the book, the song "Happy Birthday to You" appears. We sang it while Sally pointed to each word at my request. Although she knows the word "to" she never hit it corresponding to when we sang it.

JANUARY 27   I think for [Foster] as well as for [Sally] memorizing and pointing will get them to understand at least a part of reading. It will bring the spoken word and the text together.

MARCH 6   Today [Nina] told me a book called *I Go Shopping.* As she told it, she took on the manner and speech of a beginning reader—word by word. She told it to me again, then I asked her if she wanted me to read it. When I finished reading the first page, Nina said, in a surprised tone, "I read it wrong?" She was so sure that what she'd done was reading. I said, "You read it fine. I was just reading the words."

In these entries, Strieb traced very specific details about the ways that first graders handled books. She noted their pretend-reading talk and their comments as they looked at familiar books. From her own notes and observations, Strieb pieced together an understanding of what was happening with individual children as they grappled with early reading, and she also made a plan for how to continue to support them. Both of us, then, found that our journals helped us to deepen what we knew about how our students learn.

Although journals have in a sense become a common part of many elementary and secondary classrooms, what we have done is make journals pivotal to our work in classrooms. What we have tried to show here are some of the many ways that we both use them: for recording our own reflections, for sharing perceptions with each other, for learning from and about our students, and for creating curriculum. Journals have linked our separate inquiries as teacher researchers and have connected us in new ways with our students' inquiries as well. We have used journals to guide our decision making, and they have helped us to expand the lines of communities between teachers in very different settings and between teachers and diverse students in important but unexpected directions. Taken together, these examples suggest the potential of journals as a research process that crosses classrooms, grade levels, and school communities.

7

Oral Inquiries

• • • • • • • • • • • •

Descriptive Review of a Child: A Way of Knowing About Teaching and Learning

Rhoda Drucker Kanevsky

RHODA DRUCKER KANEVSKY *has taught in the School District of Philadelphia for 20 years. She is presently at the Powel School, where she teaches first grade. She is a founding member of the Philadelphia Teachers Learning Cooperative and has had a long association with the Prospect Center, North Bennington, Vermont. With others, she contributed to Speaking Out, Teachers Talk About Teaching (Traugh et al., 1985), and she is the author of Descriptive Review: Values and Assumptions (NCREST, 1992). Kanevsky was also a collaborating teacher in the Educational Testing Service reading study, which resulted in Inquiry Into Meaning (Bussis, Chittenden, Amarel, & Klausner, 1985). Currently, Kanevsky is an associate director of the Philadelphia Writing Project, a cooperating teacher in Project START, and a member of the Philadelphia team of Project 2061.*

I have always been fascinated by how persons think and learn. When I began to teach in a Philadelphia public school in 1961, I was delighted to discover that I could explore my interests in the classroom by observing children over time. Through the years, I have found other teachers who shared my excitement about the classroom. Using the documentary reflective processes developed by Patricia Carini and others, my colleagues and I have been discussing teaching and learning for the past 17 years. And since 1978, we have met every Thursday afternoon as the Philadelphia Teachers Learning Cooperative (TLC) to use these processes to explore our work (Philadelphia Teachers Learning Cooperative, 1984).

After our TLC meetings, each of us returns to the classroom with new insights into our work. What we do is so much a part of our teaching lives that we never thought of calling it research. Thursday afternoons feel like extensions of our teaching. Each meeting arises out of a question from our classrooms and results in a shift in awareness, new knowledge, questions, and ideas about how to be responsive and reflective practitioners. Our lives as thinkers and teachers become integrated.

What makes our meetings work? The reflective processes, procedures that are both open-ended and systematic, enable us to have productive conversations week after week. They allow us to hear our individual voices as we pursue collaborative inquiry. By using these procedures, we have developed a sense of ourselves as a community of learners, raising issues, solving problems, and thinking and planning on behalf of the students we teach. In this paper, I discuss the descriptive review of a child (Carini, 1986) as a way of knowing. This is the central process we use to find out what is important to a child, how a child thinks and learns, and what can support the child's education.

We take notes at all our meetings and even audiotape occasionally, but everyone agrees that the recorded documentation of the meetings does not reflect the complexity of the learning that happens during a descriptive review. Engaging in reviews of children over time deepens our understanding of children and teaching and changes our practice. I try to convey how the participants in a descriptive review build on each other's insights as they question the presenting teacher about the child and then make recommendations. I demonstrate how the descriptive review is a way of knowing not about just one child but about children in general as well as about classrooms and schools.

THE DESCRIPTIVE REVIEW PROCESS

When Janean was in first grade, I presented a descriptive review of her at a TLC meeting because I had serious concerns about her progress. My focusing question was, "How can I support her learning and help her grow academically?" I hoped that this focus would give me a better understanding of her approach to learning and offer ways to help her to gain academic competence. Eventually, Janean was retained in first grade, following one of the recommendations that she needed more time. After her 2nd year in first grade, Janean had made great strides in reading and writing and was ready to go to second grade. I wanted to review her work over 2 years. The focus of the second descriptive review was, "What recommendations can I make to Janean's new teacher and to the school community about how to support her academic growth?" In this paper, I use excerpts from the second review and include reflections on what I learned from both reviews.

The focusing questions in both of Janean's reviews are examples of the kind of questions that teachers choose for this process. They focus the participants on what the presenting teacher wants to learn from the review. Other focusing questions have been, "How can I help the child to get along with other children?" "How can I help the child to become more independent?" "How can I help the child to get more involved in school life?" or "How can the child bridge the gap between school requirements and his own interests?" The teacher may be puzzled by discrepancies in the child's work or behavior. However, reviews do not always focus on problems. Special abilities or talents may also draw a teacher to a particular child, and the teacher may want to present a review that has an exploratory focus to learn more about the child's experiences in the classroom. Sometimes, a teacher chooses to focus on a child who seems to be "invisible" in the classroom because the teacher needs to make the child visible again.

Before each presentation, I discussed the focus for Janean's review with the designated chairperson. To give a full portrayal of the child in all areas of the classroom, I prepared a description of her according to the five headings of the descriptive review: physical presence and gesture, disposition, relationships with children and adults, activities and interests, and formal learning. Based on my classroom observations, I wrote down everything I could think of under each heading and I collected her work, including drawing/writing books and journals, drawings, and paintings. The headings are not discrete categories. They overlap and interrelate, giving coherence to the description. During the presentation, information from one heading may lead into another heading. I can gather anecdotes together as I speak and connect the portrayal by circling back to earlier statements. Through the portrayal, the child emerges as a unique person with integrity and wholeness, trying in her own way to create meaning in the world:

> An underlying assumption of the Process is that each child is active in seeking to make sense of her or his experiences. By describing the child as fully, and in as balanced a way as possible, we begin to gain access to the child's modes of thinking and learning and to see their world from their point of view: what catches their attention, what arouses their wonder and curiosity, what sustains their interest and purpose. . . . (Prospect Center documentary processes, June 1986)

Because this is a collaborative process, I feel confident that if I have omitted something in the portrayal, it will be drawn out in the questioning period. The listeners' roles are vitally important. They must listen carefully and attempt to construct actively a picture of this child from my description. When they do not have a clear picture of the child, they must ask me specific questions. The questions bring out new information that contributes both to their own efforts to see the child through their own eyes and to my efforts to understand the child better. When the Janean I describe begins to resonate with other children they know, they begin to grasp the child and see her through their own perspectives. Their questions make me begin to see other sides of her as well and can make me shift my focusing question and the expectations I have for the review. The first descriptive review I did on Janean did, in fact, do just that. It made me shift my way of looking at her so that I began to understand her in a new way. I changed some practices in the classroom as a result of my colleagues' questions and recommendations. Their questions balanced my portrayal and kept me from being limited by my own biases.

It is important that participants keep questions separate from recommendations and avoid making recommendations until everyone has a more complete picture of the child. This process takes time and patience. The picture of the child emerges slowly as questions prompt the presenting teacher to add more description. Before the group can make recommendations that are consistent with the child and the classroom, the group also needs information about what the teacher has already tried, how the classroom works, and what resources and supports are available in the school. As participants wonder out loud about one particular child, they are reminded of children in their own rooms. Their questions reflect their own assumptions and expectations. They think about strategies they have used for supporting other children they know. Drawing on their own experiences, they bring depth to the questions and recommendations.

When everyone is satisfied that the description is full enough or when time runs out, the participants suggest recommendations. The teacher writes down the recommendations without responding or indicating her willingness or unwillingness to use them. The recommendations help the presenting teacher with her questions and concerns, but everyone benefits from hearing them. In the process of asking questions and making recommendations, teachers create knowledge about teaching and learning. New ideas and insights are generated about children and classrooms. Each person builds on another's ideas. As participants think of strategies for supporting Janean, they envision many children they have taught or will teach in the future. The recommendations are intended to help the teacher to create opportunities in the classroom for building on the child's strengths. At the same time, the recommendations support the strengths of the teacher and the realities of the classroom.

The descriptive review is a way of knowing that starts with a description of a particular child and ends with insights and theories not only about the child being described but about children in general. Through each review, the participants create a rich body of knowledge and open up new questions and possibilities for understanding and educating the children we teach.

LOOKING AT JANEAN THROUGH A DESCRIPTIVE REVIEW

In this section, I present the steps involved in the descriptive review process, including both information that I shared at the actual review and comments in retrospect. My commentary reveals some of what I learned from preparing the portrayal and presenting the review. In the far left column are excerpts from my descriptive review of Janean as I presented it step by step. On the right are my reflections about the presentation: preparation of the review, teaching of the child after the review, and new questions and thoughts about children in general that grew out of looking closely at Janean. Questions and recommendations come from my TLC collegues who were present that day.

Step One: Convening the Session

The chairperson convenes the session, giving the name and age of the child to be reviewed, the ages of any brothers or sisters, and the focusing question. [The teacher uses a pseudonym for the child to protect the privacy of the child. When the teacher's setting is unfamiliar to all the participants, the teacher begins the review by first showing the group her room plan and schedule.]

PRESENTATION: Janean was 7-1/2 at the end of the 2nd year in my room as a first grader. She was 5-1/2 when she began first grade. Her birthday is the end of December.

J. was among the youngest children in my class when she entered first grade. I was worried about her. At the end of her 2nd year in first grade, when I did the second review of her, I realized how much progress she had made.

PRESENTATION: She has a brother, 6 years old, who is about to enter kindergarten next year. Her two cousins and their mother also live with her. One cousin, Y., is 6 months older and was in my room the first year. R., the other cousin, was in the other first grade.

Because she couldn't stay in kindergarten another year, her kindergarten teacher made sure that she went into my room. She was worried about her from the beginning. I talked to her mother about the other children in her home.

PRESENTATION: How can the school community and Janean's new teacher continue to support Janean's learning? What specific recommendations can I make to Janean's new teacher about how to support her strengths and help her continue to develop as a reader and writer?

Often for children who are struggling, the choice is retention or Special Education. After the first review, I thought she needed another year in a language-rich classroom before considering any other intervention. J. made a lot of progress since then, but she may have difficulty making herself visible at first.

Step Two: Describing the Child

The teacher presents the child according to the five headings. The portrayal is usually uninterrupted.

Heading One: Physical Presence and Gesture

- Characteristic gestures and expressions: How are these visible in the child's face, hands, and body attitudes? How do these vary and in response to what circumstances (e.g., inside and outdoors)?
- Characteristic level of energy: How would you describe the child's rhythm and pace? How does it vary?
- How would you describe the child's voice (rhythm, expressiveness, and inflection)?

PRESENTATION: Janean, an African-American child, has a tiny oval face with a pointy chin, braided hair with barrettes; she is one of the smallest children in the classroom. Although she seems slight and birdlike, her tough wiry body stiffens if she is angry. She was timid, quiet, and watchful when she first entered my room, but I often noticed her asking other kids questions. Most of the time, it is very hard to get her to talk. When she does talk, her voice is husky and hesitant and it is hard to understand what she means or even to hear what she is saying. Often she doesn't finish her thought and she gropes for words. She often repeats words. In group discussions, I make a special point of telling the other children to wait and be patient, because it takes her a long time to make a comment. Frequently late and absent the first year, especially on Mondays and Fridays. I tried to find mittens and boots for her in bad weather, and I gave her extra snacks when she was tired and hungry. She becomes extremely focused at journal time, leaning her whole body over her work with one arm covering it. She is persistent, working for long periods of time on writing or drawing.

When I observed her to prepare this description, I got a better sense of her in the classroom. Although drawn to her because of the poetic language in her dictated stories, I didn't realize how much she watched and tried to make sense of school. As I presented her, I had a vivid picture of her working on her journal and moving through the room. I was impressed by how she persisted. Her ability to physically focus her whole body for long periods of time is unusual for a child this young. Her ability to become absorbed in her work is a terrific strength I can build on. By the end of the 2nd year, she had made a lot of progress.

- The timidity, watchfulness, toughness, and resistance all interest me.
- How can I get her to talk more?
- Is she afraid, uncomfortable, ill at ease?
- Is she unsure of her thoughts? Does this happen at home or is she unsure about how school works?

- I think she is "priming the pump" when she repeats words—keeping herself going until the thoughts come to her.
- I wonder if she gets teased by the children in her household? Is she slow to express herself at home as well as in school?

Heading Two: Disposition
- *How would you describe the child's characteristic temperament and its range (e.g., intense, even, lots of ups and downs)? How are feelings expressed? Fully? Rarely? How do you "read" the child's feelings? Where and how are they visible? What is the child's emotional tone or "color" (e.g., vivid, bright, serene)?*

PRESENTATION: She is mostly serious, perhaps even moody, intense, and engaged. A little shy. She doesn't laugh freely, but she seems happy when she is writing, drawing, cutting, or painting. Then she can be steadily engaged for long periods of time. She hates to be pulled away from her work. Sometimes she is animated when in the block corner.

She strikes me as subdued, unless she has a conflict with someone. At times this year she has been very rebellious and angry. She looked like she was saying, "You can't make me." She can act tough. Sometimes she hits, swaggers, postures, and grabs what she wants and won't let go of her anger. There have been changes from year 1 to year 2: She could get very upset with me in the 2nd year. She would freeze up and glare at me if I had to reprimand her. I sometimes tried to tickle her to get her to smile again.

I realize why I felt conflicted about her this past year. In the 1st year, when she had trouble with other kids, I tried to find ways to help her feel stronger academically to help her become more secure socially. I kept showing how much she was learning.

- Her persistence often turns into stubbornness.
- She needs opportunities to talk things out without sulking and posturing.
- What would help her use talk more effectively?
- J. doesn't like me to interrupt her.
- Does she get upset with all adults when they try to interfere with her own personal agenda?
- How can I help her be more public without embarrassing her? She needs opportunities to feel strong within the classroom community.
- Whatever the "reasons" for her behavior, I had to make the limits clear during her 2 years with me, but I also had to keep supporting her.
- I want her interest in learning to give her a sense of her own power and of possibilities in the world.

Heading Three: Relationships With Children and Adults
- *Does the child have friends? How would you characterize these attachments? Are they consistent? Changeable? Is the child recognized within the group? How is that expressed by others? Is the child comfortable in the group? How*

would you describe the child's casual, day-to-day contact with others? How does that vary? When there are tensions, how do they get resolved? How would you describe the child's relationship to you? To other adults?

During the 1st year, she was part of a consistent group of friends that included her cousin. They often played at recess and worked together at project time. She also chose to do many things alone. At journal time, she often asked other children questions about her writing, and they always seemed glad to help her. I also saw her helping other children, too, but at choice times she often was in the role of baby in the blocks or in plays. When she was the baby, she stayed perfectly still and pretended to be asleep.

In the 2nd year, she knew the routines and this gave her confidence; she loved showing others around. There were 20 boys and only 10 girls in the class and none were from her neighborhood; she seemed on the edge of the group. A few girls who "lorded it over her" in skills sometimes teased her at journal time. I saw more provocative comments, posturing, bravado in her interactions with others, especially in lines. She wouldn't easily give up her anger. Sometimes she was surly and glared at other kids. But she could be lively and cheerful at other times. She loved dramatic play and in both years planned plays. Most of the time she was pleasantly engaged with others at the sand table, blocks, paint, and science activities. She was accepted by kids at discussion time. They waited and never teased her for taking so long to say something. In the 1st year, when we were telling ghost stories at Halloween, she needed lots of encouragement but then ended her story with a poem, and the whole class joined in.

She was appealing to adults. She was persistent and tried hard. She used adults as resources. "Want to give me a little hint?" she asked a researcher who was observing in the classroom. The assistant took dictation from her at journal time. When she needed something, she would follow me around until I helped her. Her kindergarten teacher, who was fond of her, felt that she was young and needed more time. The librarian did special things to help her when she was working on independent library projects.

Heading Four: Activities and Interests
- *What are the child's preferred activities? Do these reflect underlying interests that are visible to you? For example, does drawing or story writing center on recurrent and related motifs such as superhuman figures, danger and rescue, volcanoes, and other large-scale events?*
- *How would you describe the range of the child's interests? Which interests are intense, passionate?*
- *How would you characterize the child's engagement with projects (e.g., quick, methodical, slapdash, thorough)? Is the product important to the child? What is the response to mishaps, frustrations?*
- *Are there media that have a strong appeal for the child (e.g., paint, blocks, books, woodworking)?*

Janean is interested in words and letters. She copies whatever is displayed in the room: charts, schedules, poems, and songs. She loves drawing and writing in her journal and works on it for long periods of time.

Motifs in her work include castles, stars, rainbows, animals of all kinds, flowers, trees, and hearts. She was very interested in nature and science—the life cycles of butterflies and moths—kaleidoscopes and mirrors. She became very involved with whatever we were studying in class: dinosaurs, African animals, silkworms, etc.

Activities she did a lot were cutting, book making, pasting, drawing, painting, clay, puzzles, construction and Lego, sand table, and blocks of all kinds, especially pattern blocks. Lots of pictures of constructions that look like pattern blocks are in her journals. She often sat and looked at books and used tapes at the listening center.

Heading Five: Formal Learning

- *What is the characteristic approach to a new subject or process or direction? In learning, what does the child rely on (e.g., observation, memory, trial and error, steps and sequence, in getting the whole picture, context)? How does that learning approach vary from subject to subject? What is the child's characteristic attitude toward learning?*
- *How would you characterize the child as a thinker? What ideas and content have appeal? Is there a speculative streak? A problem-solving one? A gift for analogy and metaphor? For image? For reason and logic? For insight? For intuition? For the imaginative leap? For fantasy?*
- *What are the child's preferred subjects? What conventions and skills come easily? Which are hard?*

One strategy was her copying of all kinds of things from around the room. In her journals, she copied and recopied the dictated stories the teachers wrote for her. She copied the publication information that was on the back of the book, *Brown Bear,* when she made her own stories. She read and reread easy books. She skipped words she didn't know and told the story from the pictures. She used predictable books. She was very responsive to books on tapes, especially Bill Martin books with music. By the end of first grade, she could read *People Read,* the second preprimer in the Bank Street Readers, and was wobbly in the primer. Her mother agreed to let me hold her over in first grade to strengthen her reading. She went to summer school and didn't pass. Now at the end of the 2nd year, she can read books like *Frog and Toad.*

The stories she dictated were poetic, like: "Rainbow color hearts took me away and shot me with green and orange hearts" and "I am dying because I am trapped in the rainbow flower, and can't get out, and I can't breathe." She played with words and letters, making Os into hearts, decorating some words and outlining others.

- *The teacher shows selected drawings from both the early and later journals and passes Janean's journals around the group so they can see her work across the 2 years.*

The 2nd year, she remembered the word "proboscis" when we were talking about the butterfly. She compared the births of the silkworms to the chicks.

In her 1st year, her number sense was very weak—she couldn't do addition and subtraction and got mixed up with numbers over 4. They didn't seem to stay still for her. By the end of the 2nd year, she was able to do pages of algorithms. She could play the Powers of Ten game.

She did a lot of experimentation in spelling. The letters and sounds were often inconsistent in her invented spelling.

She was persistent and kept at things for a long time. Her journals show that she was very productive.

- *Summing up. The presenter characterizes the child's strengths and vulnerabilities.*

Her strengths are that she is open to learning; she draws on whatever is available in the school environment. She can focus and be very persistent.

Her vulnerabilities are that I am afraid she will have trouble keeping up and meeting the expectations of school in the required time frame. Although it is easier now, it is still hard to understand the meaning of what she is saying. She can be timid and embarrassed. Her tough, defensive attitude gets her into trouble sometimes. There is little parental support for both academic and social development.

Step Three: Restating the Themes

- *The chairperson makes a short restatement of the portrayal, calling attention to the dominant themes running through the picture presented.*

Janean is small and young. It is hard to get her to speak. She has working relationships with other children. Sometimes she is on the edge of the group. She can be very persistent in arguments and when she needs help from adults, as well as in her work, dramatic play, and writing. Adults are drawn to her because of her efforts to learn. Her activities and interests include drama, drawing, writing, nature, and all areas of study; frequent motifs of color, hearts, rainbows, castles, stars, and constructions occur in her journal. She has a deep interest in copying.

Janean is focused, persistent, persevering, and resourceful. She seeks out things on her own. She loves repeating things like songs, poems, stories, and constructions. There are contrasts and inconsistencies. Although there is not much eye contact, she seeks out adults for help. Although she is often resistant and belligerent, she is described as timid but is continually connecting with others in the classroom, including them in stories and dramatic play.

Her strengths are her openness, persistence, and desire to learn. Her vulnerabilities are her academic inconsistencies, timidity, and defensiveness.

The teacher did several things to support her strengths. She told other children to wait and give her time. She encouraged invented spelling. She conferenced with her mother and got her to agree to give her another year in first grade. She let her copy and recopy. She noticed her interest in songs and repetition and had her use predictable books at the listening center.

Step Four: Other Descriptions

- *If appropriate, there may be descriptions from other staff who have had the opportunity to work with the child or who have made observations specifically for the purposes of the review.*

   The chairperson gives a brief account of the child's previous school experience, any important medical data, and any relevant information supported by the family for the use of the school. (Unless the parent is a copresenter with the teacher, family data are used sparingly to avoid hearsay.)

Step Five: Questions About Janean

- *The chairperson opens the review for the questions and comments of the teachers participating in the review.*

What kind of a classroom will Janean go to next year?
Describe more about how you talked with her about her reading.
Can you describe the progress of her stories in her journal from the 1st year on?
Was Janean physically active?
Did you notice any patterns in her writing?
How would she approach an unfamiliar book?
What other language experiences did she have outside the school?
How much is her mother able to help her?
What did she say during group discussion times?
What strategies did she use to solve social problems?
Did she ever take a leadership role in the classroom?

Step Six: Recommendations

- *At the close of the discussion, the chairperson briefly restates new information gained from the questions, restates the focusing question, and asks for recommendations.*

Recommendations: How can the new teacher and the whole school community support Janean's growth as a reader and a writer?

1. Arrange to have a conference with her next teacher to discuss J.'s learning approach, using selected pieces of work to show how she works with whole ideas, whole images, and geometric patterns. Describe her reading strategies and the experiences that helped her to be successful. Emphasize the growth and change in the 2 years. Show how much she absorbed language by copying, reworking, and making things her own.
2. Involve her parent in the routines of school in a positive way.
3. The theme of time was important. She needs to be given time to articulate, to think, to repeat, and to imprint as she learns.
4. Don't make assumptions and underestimate her ability to understand things.
5. Have her read to the kindergarten children on a regular basis.
6. Have her write letters to people she knows and likes and who like her.

*   *The chairperson groups the recommendations as a way of "pulling together" a final statement about the review, plans for a follow-up on the child, and asks for a critique of the process.*

CONCLUSIONS

The descriptive review is a way of knowing that embodies a particular set of values and assumptions about children, learning, teaching, and schooling.

The descriptive review is a way to know a child and her values and to make recommendations based on the questions and concerns that a teacher brings us. We are looking at strengths, struggles, and finally the connections that the child is making. Through the descriptive review, we discover the standards she holds for herself, what is important to her, and what she cares about and chooses on a daily basis. In addition, we want to understand the contexts of meaning she draws on for her continuing growth. Thus, we are also concerned about the values and standards within the classroom and the expectations that school holds for the child. Teachers who have participated in many descriptive reviews feel that the process has assumptions with wide implications for teachers and for schools. Following are some of those that I have drawn from conversations in TLC (Kanevsky, 1992):

1. Teachers have knowledge about children and classrooms.
2. Through descriptions of particular children, teachers can share knowledge. Every person is active in seeking meaning in the world.
3. Every person has strengths and the potential for growth and change.
4. The teacher's question is important.
5. The procedure provides a framework for an inquiry process, but what happens through the process is not predetermined.

6. We use the same headings to describe many children, but each child emerges as a unique person.
7. The process implies interpretation, which is mediated by the multiple perspectives of the participants. This creates balance.
8. We assume that the group will not attack the presenter or judge what he or she has or has not done.

These assumptions reveal certain values:

1. We value the teacher's role as the observer in the classroom.
2. We value description and context. We describe a child's experiences in the classroom setting at the present time. We use specific details grounded in everyday classroom activities.
3. We value plain, nonjudgmental language. We try not to use jargon.
4. We value collaboration—active and attentive collaboration.
5. We value the child's point of view. We ask what arouses a child's wonder and curiosity, what sustains interest. We try to see the child's world.
6. We value what a child and a teacher can already do and build from the strengths we see.
7. We value the teacher's judgment to choose recommendations that he or she thinks are useful.
8. We value what we do. One of the participants takes notes, and we save the notes in three-ring notebooks.

How then is the descriptive review a way of knowing? Teachers say that it expands their vision and that it becomes another way of looking. This has to do with the power of descriptive knowledge: knowledge and vision becoming one. Descriptive knowledge is different from abstract knowledge that is external to the person. Himley (1991) calls the talk that is based on description "deep talk" and says, "deep talk is a constructing of knowledge that values many ways of knowing—spirit, will, imagination, intellect, emotion. . . . Description becomes a habit of mind, a genre, an art of seeing" (p. 68).

Carini (1979) suggests, "To abide with something, is to make visible its dwelling place—that is, all of the object's multiple points or relatedness to other things and to the passage of time. Therefore, observing locates the thing in the vicinity of other things and makes visible both its continuities and transformations through time" (p. 18).

Because we base our conversations on knowledge that is descriptive, out of our observations, experiences, and reflections, we see things in new ways. By looking at a particular child, we avoid having the issues become abstract. We start with the child and then think about children in general and finally the larger issues and educational purposes.

• • • • • • • • • • •
Learning About Learning Diversity

Penny Colgan-Davis

PENNY COLGAN-DAVIS *is the director of Friends Select Lower School. She has taught all elementary grades in the School District of Philadelphia and in two area independent schools. She has a BA from Guilford College and a master's from the University of Pennsylvania and is currently working on her dissertation at the Graduate School of Education at the University of Pennsylvania. Colgan-Davis was a cooperating teacher in Project START for many years and is currently involved in the Philadelphia Yearly Meeting's Nonviolence and Children Project.*

In 1989, Friends Select School, a private Quaker prekindergarten through 12th-grade school in downtown Philadelphia, began a new approach to the professional development of its faculty, administrators, and staff members by instituting a series of study groups. The groups, which were organized around topics of interest, were clerked by members of the faculty and administration and were an opportunity for the school community to come together to pursue in depth questions about their practice. Topics included the diversity of class, culture, and race; Quakerism; the development of character, math, and writing; the school's urban location; and the different ways that children learn. The work of the study groups, which were to meet once a month for 2 years, would be defined by the members of the group, including any decisions about presentations or final products. The expectation was that through systematic, reflective study of a topic of interest, each member of the school community would deepen his or her understanding of that topic and would enhance his or her practice. An additional expectation focused on achieving continuity in a school with three divisions: lower (prekindergarten to 4th), middle (5th to 8th), and upper (9th to 12th). Learning about the school's prekindergarten through 12th-grade program and developing a deeper understanding of the values and philosophy that guide the school would nurture a more coherent understanding of the whole school.

THE GROUP BEGINS

As clerk of the study group on learning diversity, I kept minutes and distributed summaries of our discussions and helped the group to clarify its initial questions and planned activities as the work went on. Periodically, I completed summaries of where we were in our work and led the group in setting new goals. I was also a liaison with the inter-school curriculum committee, the group that oversees professional development within the school. Although there had been a tradition in our school of teachers working together across divisions, the idea of different study groups was a new one, as was the idea that no final outcome was expected except increased understanding of and reflection on one's practice.

Learning diversity was selected as a topic for the study groups because of a long-standing concern among the faculty that the school was accepting more and more children whose learning styles were different and that the faculty was not trained in how to teach to such a wide range of learning styles. The school expected that if teachers could come together and look closely at how individual children learned and at what was successful with different kinds of learners, the teaching skills of the faculty would be expanded, and more and more students' needs would be met.

The membership of the study group on learning diversity was a diverse one. Over the course of the 2 years, we had as members two upper school chemistry teachers, a gym teacher, a middle school art teacher, two kindergarten teachers, a first- and second-grade teacher, a third- and fourth-grade teacher, the director of admissions, the school receptionist, the director of the Lower School, and the secretary to the headmaster of the school. This was a wonderful cross-section of the school, especially when one considers that of that group, members were parents of recent graduates of the school and of current middle and lower school students. The majority of the membership stayed constant, with a few changes when teachers left the school and new faculty and staff joined the community. Each monthly meeting was 1 hour and 45 minutes long.

Members joined the group for a variety of reasons. The questions that members posed focused around the following central issues:

- How to work with children who learn differently
- How to help the school to clarify its mission and decide what kinds of students it can educate and which students would be more successful in another setting
- How to better understand learning, which is essentially a hidden act
- How members, as parents of children who learn differently, can help the school to understand better their children

Throughout the 2 years, the group used a variety of discussion formats, data, and activities, including looking closely at one child's work from first through sixth grade (including reports written by teachers), describing our own learning histories, reading articles, interviewing current and former students about their experiences as learners at Friends Select, and looking closely at one child or one class currently having difficulty to help the teacher find ways to support the child's or the class's success. In each meeting, there was time for careful consideration of a question or a child, time to help one another to improve practice, and time to talk in more general terms about teaching and learning.

FOCUS ON INDIVIDUAL CHILDREN

A significant series of meetings in the 1st year centered on the difficulty that teachers have in separating behavior issues from learning issues. When asked to describe a student who was presenting challenges to us as teachers because of the way he or she learned, teachers often mentioned the child's behavior as part of the problem. This generated much discussion about whose responsibility it is when a child is having academic difficulties and about where the locus of change ought to be. Teachers of younger children saw the responsibility as theirs: The program needed to be altered to support the child's strengths. Misbehavior was seen by these teachers as a result of an environment that was not appropriate for the child, as opposed to intentional misbehavior by a child in control of the choices that he or she was making.

At one meeting, each member described a student who presented a challenge to the teacher because of the way that the student learned. Teachers of younger children could keep their focus on the learning style of the children and on why it was a challenge to them as a teacher. Teachers of older students tended to describe their students' behavior or misbehavior rather than their learning style. What follows is the description of a third grader, Ted:

[Ted] was a third grade student of mine who was a strong member of the class, happy, an organizer of activities and a good reader. In math he worked very slowly and made frequent errors. He did not seem to understand one to one correspondence and could not count beyond thirteen. He could not do any multi-step problems. I worked with him on simple counting, using counters, chips, whatever made sense to him. We went back to the very basic ideas of number in school and for homework. At the same time, Ted organized a videotape broadcast of a news show, following many steps, all in the correct order. I learned, through this, that he could put meaningful things into a sequence. (Description of a student by a member of the study group, January 16, 1990)

It is clear in this description that Ted needed extra help in identifying sequences and that math had become confusing for him because of this difficulty. His teacher understood the difficulty and went back to very beginning mathematical concepts and activities with him and gave him other opportunities to learn about sequences, such as the videotape broadcast.

Teachers of older children tended to shift responsibility to the child. Students who were experiencing difficulty were expected to come to the teacher for extra help and to try harder and not give up. Altering teaching practice to fit the child's needs was not a possibility that many teachers of older students embraced. When an older student was misbehaving, the behavior was not seen as the result of academic difficulties but of a *choice* that the student was making. Yet when teachers were later asked to describe the choices they felt they as adults had in their own lives, they had great difficulty. In the following description, Jake is a student who has difficulty taking notes from the board and taking tests that are not theoretical in focus. There is a wide range in his performance, a frequent clue that there may be learning problems. This range in performance is not picked up on; rather, Jake's behavior is called to task:

[Jake] is too cool to take notes. He is, by all appearances, quite bright and able to grasp new ideas easily. But he won't take notes, and he won't participate in class work that is concerned with the solving of problems. Jake flunked the first test. He was totally unable to solve problems that we had gone over many times on the board. He barely passed the second test, which was also about solving problems, and got a 100% on the third test, which was more about theory.

I suppose to take notes is to give in to the "system" for Jake. He is a very alert classroom student when he is given a chance to speak in class about ideas instead of answers to problems. Jake has said some rather nasty things to me when he gets behind and asks for extra help and I will not give it to him if he has not tried the problems on his own.

The positive side of not taking notes and doing all the work entirely on your own is that you would have a real sense of ownership of the material you learned. You would feel that you did all the work yourself, that stupid teacher didn't teach you a thing. I find this attitude better than a totally passive one, but the nasty comments might backfire.

I am not trying to change Jake. He is old enough to see the advantages of being the traditional note taking type of student, and he has chosen to be cool. His grades will be lower, but he might feel cool. A tough choice in high school. (Description of a child by an upper school teacher, January 16, 1990)

In these two examples of students experiencing academic difficulty at school, it becomes clear that older students were being given more agency in their academic lives than younger children and that younger children's misbehavior was understood by teachers as a function of their learning struggles rather than as a choice they were consciously making. Teachers of younger students felt more responsibility to change the learning environment and their teaching practice to meet their students' academic needs than did teachers of older students.

Uncovering the underlying assumptions that each teacher made when discussing learning difficulties was extremely helpful to the group and to each participant. It meant that we could each rethink the assumptions we were making about agency and responsibility and about how best to support a child who was having difficulty. It was only in the 2nd year that the group could rethink its practice and approach with a different eye children who were having difficulty. Two members from the upper school left the school and were replaced in the study group with a teacher new to the school. This teacher was better able to understand that when students are not succeeding, they often misbehave, but that the problem was academic, not completely behavioral.

The 2nd year began with a few new members and the task of reforming the group. Each member took time to describe his or her learning history, focusing on what had gone well in school, what had been difficult, and what had been helpful. The summary was illuminating because of the number of teachers who could remember real struggles in school and teachers who had recognized their struggles and had helped them, and teachers who had been completely unaware or unsympathetic. The group was also amazed at the diversity of experiences in and responses to school; we had not all had a smooth, successful school history!

While there is a huge range of interest and success in school among group members, each of us can remember struggles with particular teachers or subjects. Math anxiety, a few of dissection in biology, gym teachers who terrorized me, being lost in a crowd of students or being put in charge with inadequate training and no authority were all examples of painful memories for us.

We also could identify teachers and events that were significant turning points for us. There were teachers who valued us and taught us how to pursue our own questions and do research on our own. There were teachers who exhibited an authentic enthusiasm for their subject that was transferred onto us. There were the graduate-level programs that were flexible enough so that we could pursue topics of personal interest and plan the ways we would gather information and communicate it. There were events, such as an eclipse, that instilled great wonder in us and impelled us to learn more about the world and solar system.

Each of us also seems to want to "right" some wrongs in education. We all bring to our teaching a commitment to supporting all kinds of learners. Our own stories reinforce the commitment to seeing each child as an individual (rather than just one of many), to meeting each child at an area of strength (rather than focusing on the areas of deficit), to seeing parents as important advocates of their children (rather than complainers) and to reflecting upon one's teaching practice to see how it can be broadened to include more children successfully. Remembering our own experiences underlines for us the significant part school plays in the developing of self-image and the special responsibility we have as teachers to support and protect children from failure. (Summary of group discussion by clerk, November 13, 1990)

At the end of this series of meetings, the group began to ask how successful Friends Select School was in supporting diverse learners. Members knew all too well the current "failures" of their own teaching practice. What they wanted to know now was, from the students' perspective, how successful the school had been in supporting their academic development. Each person committed to conducting a lengthy interview with a current middle or upper school student or a recent graduate. Summaries of each interview were shared at study group meetings as they were conducted. After all of the summaries, the group then described the strengths of the school vis-à-vis learning diversity and areas that needed attention: The data collected from our interviews of students were extremely helpful to the group. They pointed the way to new discussions that can be followed up on in the future—discussions that could focus on the different needs of middle school and upper school students, on how to expand the social and educational territories for students who find the school confining, and on how to vary one's teaching practice to accommodate all kinds of learners (something that lower school teachers seemed to understand but that teachers of older students are not yet skilled in).

Our final meeting centered on what each member had learned from the 2-year experience in the study group. One member expressed appreciation for learning how teachers wrestle with issues of diversity and for hearing the compelling stories about their practice in a more "neutral" arena so that everyone could be open and supportive of one another. One teacher shared that she had learned greater tolerance and patience and had become more open:

Each time I learn more openness, that openness is "squared"; it's always exciting! I also have a stronger sense of where my bottom line is and feel more justified now in calling kids on rudeness, for example. (Study group meeting, April 23, 1991)

An upper school teacher commented:

The assignments meant I had to reexamine the way I had been doing things, if I had been effective and whether I had been doing it wrong. It took me a while to realize that we weren't looking for clear-cut recommendations for the school, that our job was more to bring the three schools together and to reexamine ourselves. (Study group meeting, April 23, 1991)

Probably the most compelling of the responses came from a lower school teacher:

I began last year with a very difficult group [her class] and felt very supported by the study group. This was more like group therapy; I could vent, be heard, hear other people's "war" stories and hear from other experienced teachers who also were having trouble. Our work opened my eyes to how deeply I care about my work. It also helped me see that, at times, I have to step back and not get what I want and forgive myself for what has felt like failure. I now look back and see that I did the best I could. It may not have been enough, but it was what I could do. There should be excellence, but having nothing ever be good enough is poisonous.

This year my class is very different; they come from very different places. This study group has helped me think about how I'm going to describe what the differences are in how each child approaches learning. This is especially helpful to next year's receiving teachers, knowing the strengths and not just what isn't there. That way a student's new teacher will not judge him by what he isn't. The storytelling we did was especially important to me. (Study group meeting notes by clerk, April 23, 1991)

From getting help and support from colleagues for a difficult class to expanding her awareness of the children in her class to deepening her understanding of what she needs to let the next year's teacher know, this teacher grew in varied and important ways. The fact that this was "almost like group therapy" testifies to the trust and sense of community that were created. No "handbook on how to teach diverse learners" came out of the group's work. Rather, increased understanding of the complexity of learning and a deeper appreciation for the importance of what we do were two of its most important results.

Teachers usually teach in extremely isolated situations. Rarely are there opportunities for teachers to learn from each other, get and give support to each other, or talk over time about large and important questions of teaching and learning. Rarer still is time to reflect, sit back and think over one's practice, critique it, and grow. The study groups at Friends Select gave teachers, administrators, and staff members in the community that time to reflect and to give and receive support as well as an opportunity to deepen their understanding of large educational questions. The study groups also created an important community of educators who have come to know and respect one another and to cherish a school that cares so much about their own professional development.

The account of one particular study group in one school will hopefully encourage administrators to create time for teachers to work together to pursue large questions about teaching practice. Through these meetings, one group of teachers was able to expand its definition of a "problem" in teaching—children who learn differently—and found strategies that could support themselves and others. In addition, it is hoped that the reader will recognize the importance of uncovering educators' unexamined assumptions about children and learning in order to begin to look critically at the environments they create. Finally, it is hoped that the reader will see the value in educators talking to each other directly and honestly about what concerns them as a way to limit their isolation. Teachers have much to offer one another when they can meet as colleagues instead of as competitors for scarce resources. Giving teachers time to talk creates a climate in which each educator gives and receives affirmation and help.

8 | Classroom and School Studies

Walking to the Words

Eileen Glickman Feldgus

EILEEN GLICKMAN FELDGUS *teaches kindergarten at the Disston School in the School District of Philadelphia. In addition to her 19 years of kindergarten teaching, she has also taught nursery school and first grade. Eileen's professional activities include the Philadelphia Writing Project and the International Reading Association. She is also a cooperating teacher in Project START. She frequently makes presentations at conferences and conducts staff-development sessions in the areas of emergent literacy, children's literature, and teacher research. Feldgus is a doctoral candidate at the Graduate School of Education at the University of Pennsylvania, where she teaches courses in children's literature.*

I watched the unfolding scene through tears in my eyes:

Bobby rushed into class at nine o'clock on "Mixed-up Monday," the mid-year day on which he changed from the afternoon to the morning kindergarten session. Quickly getting a magic marker, he crossed out the title "afternoon" which headed the daily list of children scheduled to play a special learning game, replacing it with the word "morning" which he carefully copied from a container which held the children's name tags. Lauren immediately drew a line under the *ing* in morning as I often do when I write with the class.

I had been charmed and challenged by Harste, Woodward, and Burke's (1984) suggestion that the most valuable gift to give young language users is to "litter their environment with enticing language opportunities and guarantee them the freedom to experiment with them" (p. 27).

Bobby and Lauren had been immersed in a classroom environment that was rich with environmental print—print that was created with the children as we lived together in the classroom. This environmental print included functional signs such as "Stop" and "Go" on the bathroom door and "Limit—four people in the Play House." It also included large-chart teacher writing that recorded class-directed information, songs, children's personal news, a time line for recording events, writing on large murals, and any other print created either independently by the children using invented spelling or created by me in a teacher demonstration mode.

How had Bobby and Lauren, two 5-1/2-year-olds, become empowered to act on the print in their environment? This question haunted me. Although I had been reading much in the early childhood professional literature that advocated the creation of a literate environment (DeFord, 1980; Mavrogenes, 1986), I wanted to know more about how children actually use environmental print in their own development as writers. By environmental print, I mean any printed materials present in the child's environment. These may be child generated, teacher generated, or commercially available materials and include but are not limited to signs, large-chart writing, and books.

Informal observation of my children as they wrote indicated an awareness and excitement as they often incorporated elements of the print from their environment into their own writing. This was a new phenomenon in my classroom that began the previous year, when I began to find ways for children to use the writing on large charts as part of the ongoing activity of the classroom.

As I surveyed the literature, I began to make connections to my own classroom. Research in early writing has revealed the importance of the environment: physical, social, and emotional. Hall, Moritz, and Statom (1976) found that children who were in a home environment where writing was used in meaningful ways attempted to write at an early age. This environment, like that of children who pretend read, was emulative—not instructional (Cochran-Smith, 1984; Galda, 1984). Like the "bedtime story" environment in reading acquisition and the supportive rewarding of approximations in oral language acquisition, the environment of early writers is often one in which children's productions are responded to with pleasure and their questions are answered when asked (Galda, 1984).

Not only were the children using the surrounding print in meaningful ways, but they also seemed to be increasingly aware of the mechanics of the creation of that print. Donaldson (1984) notes that although many children are surrounded by print in their home environments, they may never see print being produced. Except in unusual cases in which the reader watches the moving hand and interprets the words as they reach the page, written language is separated from its author in both time and space. I was demonstrating the heretofore invisible bridge between the writer and the written word. My thinking kept coming back to Halliday's (1975) theme that children do not first learn language and then apply it to various uses. Children learn language as they learn of its uses (Halliday, 1975). I thought of Ferreiro's (1978) suggestion, "In order to understand the writing system that society had forged for them, children must reinvent writing and thereby make it their own."

I was trying very hard to help the children to simultaneously orchestrate the complex message-creating and message-encoding process of writing (Dyson, 1987b). In addition to creating a nurturing and exciting print-rich environment that would allow children the freedom to find and test their own hypotheses, I was attempting to demonstrate multiple strategies, including using the print in their environment, to enable my emergent writers to convey their messages independently and permanently through writing and to help them develop the belief that they were, indeed, "members of the club" (Smith, 1984) who could successfully use these strategies, as Lauren and Bobby had done.

In addition to writing in a center called the Writing Is Exciting Workshop! children were also encouraged to write in all of the other learning centers. Children were expected to compose through speech, gesture, drawing, and writing using invented spelling. Children wrote however they could, rather than have adults take dictation from them. They were encouraged to use a horizontal line as a place holder to represent any sound or word they didn't know. This "magic line" was a strategy that freed them to continue composing when they got stuck. Early in the year, several children who had not yet made sound-letter connections were writing exclusively using magic lines to represent their thoughts. I believe such teacher acceptance and expectation send the message to children that they *can* write. Adults then underwrote the children's writing, using conventional spelling and praising the children's approximations. This process permeated all of the children's writing in journals, class books, and independent projects. Children were encouraged to help one another whenever they wrote.

At the beginning of the school year, I used only a few commercial materials in the classroom environment: alphabet, number, and color charts. As the year progressed, virtually every other available space was filled with writing that emerged from our curriculum-related projects. These included a time line with children's observations of the life cycle of silkworms; a large mural that depicted scenes from the book *Over in the Meadow,* on which number words were written; and charts that followed the format "What we know," "What we want to know," and "What we learned" about topics being explored.

LOOKING MORE CLOSELY

Although I had a sense of the children's excitement and interactions around environmental print, I needed to look more closely to understand more fully what was happening in the contexts—physical, pedagogical, temporal, and social—of my own classroom.

The study was conducted at the end of February in my half-day kindergarten class in a working-class urban neighborhood. My student teacher, classroom assistant, parent-scholar, and I kept journals for 2 weeks, noting writing behaviors of target children and interactions of all children in proximity to them. So that the research would reflect the natural contexts of the classroom, we observed these children during the usual 1/2-hour daily journal-writing time. Additionally, I interviewed the target children at the end of the study to gain insights into their understanding of teacher demonstration writing and of their own ways of writing. Children's journals and field notes and all classroom environmental print were collected.

I was an "observant participant" (Florio-Ruane, 1986) of six target children whom I selected to represent varying levels of accomplishment in the approximations of the conventions of writing. Christopher and Elizabeth represented the least accomplished, Billy and Alison the most accomplished, and George and Amy a mid-level of accomplishment. I investigated three areas:

Genre. How were the children using the genres evident in classroom print?
Language. How were they incorporating the actual words used in environmental print?
World knowledge. How were the children using the topics and information that were in the classroom environment?

Additionally, social interactions were analyzed to see how the children were helping one another through talk and action. Journal data was also analyzed to see whether children "knew" words in the classroom environment; spontaneously sought them out independently; found the words only after the prompting question, "Where can you find that word in our room?"; or were unaware of the presence of needed words even after the prompting question. Teacher demonstration writing was also analyzed for genre, world knowledge, and language in an attempt to find relationships, with the understanding that these were not necessarily causal relationships.

As I analyzed the data, I noted the varying ways that individual children seemed to respond to classroom print. I analyzed six children's writing behaviors to discover patterns of usage of classroom environmental print and to discover the meaning that children constructed for themselves of this print-rich environment.

GENRE

The most consistent findings across ability levels appeared in the genre analysis. The following transcriptions of children's writing illustrate this phenomenon. From George's <u>mydogpedonter g</u> (My dog peed on the rug) to Amy's <u>my ncl Has Lots Of fish</u> (My uncle has lots of fish), the target children overwhelmingly preferred to write in the personal/family news genre. Forty-eight out of 65 entries fell into this category. This small sampling seemed to reflect the preferences of the class as a whole.

Other genres represented were inventories of letters, numbers, and names. In addition to the usual inventories, Alison experimented with constructing lists of rhyming words, referring to the alphabet chart as she wrote, <u>At, BAt, CAt</u> and <u>BAg, TAg, Hag.</u> She initially called them "bug, tug, hug" until the student teacher read them aloud to her.

Elizabeth showed the most genre flexibility, writing many ideas and concepts such as <u>girs gtrb w trw rwtbc srwtbc</u> (Girls are teenagers because they're wild). She also wrote in the fantasy genre: <u>I havtwocatzand RPL ingWthRtB</u> (I have two cats and they are playing with heart balloons).

Billy was the only child who wrote a song in his journal. He wrote, I MAD UPASOG 6324 _____ ShAVANEW, 6324 _____ ShAVNeW (I made up a song—6324 Longshore Avenue).

The children's genre choices for their journal writing were very narrow when compared with the wide range of genres that had been created in teacher demonstration writing.

LANGUAGE

The most revealing information came out of the analysis of how children were incorporating the words that appeared in the environmental print into their own writing. Not only were they using whole words (sometimes by rote and sometimes by finding them in the classroom), but they were also creatively extracting and transferring word elements such as digraphs, suffixes, and roots in the creation of words they needed.

Children used their phonics skills to locate words and word segments; in turn, this usage strengthened those very same skills. George found the <u>ch</u> digraph in <u>chocolate</u> and correctly applied it to <u>Bch</u>/beach. Billy combined phonics with environmental print when he wrote <u>playd</u>/played, locating <u>play</u> in Play House and adding the final <u>d.</u> In one humorous instance, Nicole directed George to the "Over in the Meadow" mural to find the word <u>bee.</u> George, focusing only on the beginning sound, copied the word <u>buzz</u> instead. After much giggling, Nicole gave George a phonics lesson on attending to the ends of words as well as the beginnings.

The ways that the children interacted with the words in their environment were related to their abilities to approximate conventional writing. The least accomplished writers, Christopher and Elizabeth, were the least aware of the words surrounding them. They rarely sought out words on their own. After a reminder that they could find a word they needed somewhere in the classroom, they could sometimes find it independently. Sometimes, classmates or adults helped them to locate these words.

The most accomplished writers, Amy, Alison, and Billy, were the most active users of classroom print. (Although Amy had originally been selected as a mid-level writer, closer reflection showed that Amy was also advanced. It should be noted that most of my children were writing quite well by mid-year, when the study was undertaken.) All three children used the print in their environment very independently. They were very aware of its existence and location. They often spontaneously "walked to the words" on their own, and when prompted with the question, "Where can you find that word in our room?" they were consistently able to find it independently. George, a mid-level writer, actively used the words surrounding him, although he often needed prompting to remind him that they were available.

WORLD KNOWLEDGE

All of the children seemed to accurately "know their own knowledge" of the words in the classroom environment. Although there was much interaction with children "walking each other to the words," there was clear-cut evidence that those who "knew" were the ones who spontaneously and happily helped those who needed help. Those who needed help often remembered the original source of words when they needed them on subsequent days. This interaction was a reminder that children's achievements may be influenced by their relationships with each other and may not be based solely on teacher-child interactions (Dyson, 1987b).

Children used a very wide range of sources to find the words and word elements they needed. The functional signs, on/off, the time line, and the classroom murals were among the most frequently referred to. Perhaps the stability of these items in the classroom invited familiarity with them. This was in contrast to other writing, which changed over time to reflect the changing curriculum.

The final area that I explored was how the children were using the topics and information that were available in the classroom environment. I found that the children's journal writing was rarely related to the environmental print surrounding them. When they did use topics suggested by the environment, the children were likely to adapt them for their own fantasy purposes. When George wrote, "I WNt to stheinDins the TEEPEE GTBRK" (I went to see the Indians, the teepee got broken). George referred to the time line for the word "teepee," which reflected our earlier study of Indians in which we had constructed a teepee. He did not write about any of our actual explorations related to Indians.

At the end of the study I conducted interviews in an attempt to find the children's understandings about writing. I specifically wanted to see if writing was perceived to be a meaning-centered activity in the classroom in which children were encouraged to use environmental print to produce their own print. When I asked the children, "How do you know how to write the words you need?" every child indicated multiple strategies for encoding. Use of classroom print was consistently mentioned. "Lots of things happen. I sound them out; look at the words in our classroom if we have them." It would appear that children were, indeed, looking at writing as a meaning-making endeavor. They used the environment to help them create their personal meanings.

LOOKING BACK

As I reflect back on what I learned and the impact that this learning has had on my practice, I realize that I have never stopped studying my children's use of their print-rich environment. Once one looks so closely, it's almost impossible to stop seeing! This continued study was especially important given the limited scope of the initial study. My conclusions are influenced by this continuous "seeing."

When I think back on the children's overwhelming genre preference for writing personal news, I ask myself if I had somehow conveyed the misperception that this was the preferred genre for journal writing. Children wrote in many other genres at other times during the day. What message had I unconsciously sent to them that seemed to restrict their choices? This study took place last year. In quest of providing expanded choices for children this year, I seem to have narrowed the choices equally well. This year's children overwhelmingly prefer the fantasy genre. Is this a response to my cue, "Tell me the story about your picture?" Possibly/probably. Teacher language is so important! I'm planning to have a class discussion about the many possibilities of journal entries in the hope that this will encourage the children to experiment with various genres.

The children's differential use of the actual print in the classroom was very revealing. When the study ended at the beginning of March, the most accomplished writers were the most active users of the words in the environment. However, by the end of the year, the more accomplished writers had "learned" many of the words available and no longer had to find them to write them conventionally. The availability of words in meaningful environments in the classroom (as opposed to the lists of preprimer words often posted in kindergartens) seems to have served as an important scaffold in helping these children to become increasingly independent writers. The children who had been mid-level writers in March were the most active users by the end of the year.

Many children went through a process of finding a word in the environment and referring back to that word in their own journals when they needed it at a later time. Harris (1986) notes that one of the major goals of providing print in the classroom environment is to attract children's attention so that they have increased opportunities to construct knowledge of the forms and functions of print. I would add that by creating this environmental print together with the children, they also gain an understanding of the process of writing.

The notion of collaboratively creating the print is an important one. Children referred to the number words we had created on our mural and to our progressively sized numerals rather than commercially prepared materials. Stability of the print is also important. If I want children to access the language in print, they need time to develop a relationship with that language. Rapidly changing bulletin boards would seem to be counterproductive!

The social context of the classroom in which children were encouraged to both give and receive help as they explored what our classroom offered seemed to be a crucial factor in helping these children to become successful, independent writers. I am aware that the way that they approach writing is consistent with the way that our classroom works in all areas. It is a discovery-based, collaborative classroom in which children are encouraged to use a variety of resources for learning. Environmental print was one resource among many that helped these children in their literacy learning.

Another personal belief that has been strengthened is that children should be allowed time in the school program to choose their own topics for writing. These children wrote for 1/2 hour each day about what was important in their personal lives, affirming the importance of their individuality as they became more skillful writers. This is in contrast to the practice of teacher-assigned topics, which is prevalent in many classrooms.

Looking closely at six children's uses of print in their classroom environment has strengthened my conviction that emergent readers and writers need to be immersed in an environment rich in print. However, immersion is not enough. Children must be given appropriate opportunities and encouragement to most fully utilize a print-rich environment in their own literacy development.

Parallels have been drawn between a literate home environment and a literate classroom environment. A significant difference lies, I believe, in the greater potential that the classroom environment offers for direct teaching that incorporates that environment. Teachers can consciously maximize children's interactions with their print environment in ways directed toward the accomplishment of school-related literacy tasks.

As the children were told to "mark under the word *five*" during citywide testing, Lauren turned her chair completely around backwards to face the number words on the "Over in the Meadow" mural. A mother who was assisting in the administration of the test was flustered at Lauren's antics.

I was delighted!

• • • • • • • • • • • •

Lessons From the Road:
What I Learned Through Teacher Research

Patricia Johnston

PATRICIA JOHNSON *is supervisor of curriculum and instruction for the Centennial School District in Warminster, Pennsylvania. She has taught reading to students in the middle and senior levels for the past 18 years. Her publications include "Coming Full Circle: As Teachers Become Researchers So Goes the Curriculum" (Students Teaching, Teachers Learning, 1992) and "The Ethics of Our Work in Teacher Research" (Workshop 4).*

After 18 years in the classroom in the middle and senior grades and only recently in a larger field working with teachers to examine and develop curriculum and instruction, I bring a particular perspective to what it means to be a teacher and a researcher. At the same time that I have managed hall passes and Sony Walkmen, I have read student journals that have revealed more about the sorrow of youth than I wished to know. Much like embarking on a journey toward making sense of classroom practice, I found that the doing and the being of teacher research are at once second nature to me and somehow touching on foreign soil.

In the winter and spring of 1987, I took a close look at the reading practices of six eighth-graders. The students agreed to participate in a book discussion program called Best Books, and they agreed to take part in a study that questioned the nature of response. Reading as a social activity was my terrain. I argued that students could create an interpretive community when given an opportunity to do so within the school framework. What I did not understand were the particular threads that wove a response community together. I could not articulate the interpretive norms of an eighth-grade reading group. How do one student's individual reading style and critical orientation to text influence the meaning constructed in group discussion? Furthermore, what is the relationship between an individual's response and the collective's response? I questioned the roles that students create within a group and the ways that those roles are negotiated—if, in fact, they change—over time. What do students consider significant topics for discussion, and who determines what gets said when the teacher is no longer an instructor but is a participant-observer? This adventure through uncharted territory revealed much about student response, the development of community, and the structures within schools that must be rethought.

SETTING THE COURSE:
QUESTIONS, METHOD, AND STUDENT RESEARCHERS

My normal teaching schedule at this time included regularly scheduled reading classes and, for several periods each day, classes of small groups of young readers who gathered for book discussions. Loosely based on the Great Books structure, this book discussion program enables volunteer readers to meet about every 10 days to discuss books that all have commonly read. Here, I noticed a string of differences that prompted me to think about reading and response. As facilitator of small book groups, I heard students contribute differently than when I stood in front of rows of desks. Students enjoyed a freedom to develop answers over time without the worry of being right. The seating arrangement—a circle of desks—enabled collaboration. Best Books was both voluntary and ungraded; students had a say in what they learned and were freed from the constraints of evaluation. Students chose the books they read from a canon of 18, each selected for their appeal to young adult readers; self-selection mattered. In each book, the protagonist faced a moment of confrontation with a reality about life and living and had to make a decision. There were no easy answers—no clear-cut, definitive choices about right and wrong. The framework for my study emerged from these observations of difference.

My questions narrowed as I listened to the group discussions. I focused on what students knew about individual texts and textuality as they came to the group after having read alone. Locating my questions among the existing literature, I borrowed from the work of Stanley Fish (1980) and wanted to know how an interpretive community could develop in an eighth-grade classroom. Fish argues that language is perceived within a structure of social norms and that interpretation is thereby a product of social relationship. Attention is drawn to the readership and what they, as readers together, do: "It is not that the presence of poetic qualities compels a certain kind of attention but that the paying of a certain kind of attention results in the emergence of poetic qualities" (p. 326). The interpretive community, the social group of readers, responds from the set of norms and standards that they, themselves, have created. I wanted to know what the interpretive norms of eighth-grade readers would be. What do they pay attention to when they meet to talk about books? What poetic qualities would emerge from their discussions? I wanted to know more about the relationship between individual response and group book discussions. What do individual readers say about books, how do individual readers respond to text, and what is that in relationship to their group response?

The group that became the student researchers of my study was composed of 13-year-olds: five females and one male. For six 55-minute periods, we sat in a circle with the tape recorder turned to "record" and with books on our desks, and students discussed their views and ideas about books, about reading, and about life. Discussions were constructed around *House of Stairs* (Sleator, 1974), *Z for Zachariah* (O'Brien, 1974), *Little, Little* (Kerr, 1981), *Cracker Jackson* (Byars, 1985), *Journey to an 800 Number* (Konigsburg, 1984), and *Gentlehands* (Kerr, 1984). Although I wanted to question and to know more, I learned how to be still.

We met often during that winter and spring for studies of independent reading, group interviews, individual interviews, family meetings, and group meetings to analyze what we had done together. Students kept journals of their responses to their readings and answered specific questions.

Borrowing from Lytle's (1982) strategies for comprehending texts, students and I met individually in reading think-aloud sessions before and after reading each text. Twelve think-aloud procedures for each student researcher helped determine a particular comprehension style for a student's independent reading. Through interview questions and others designed for students to focus on parts of the text that were significant for them, I saw that students were, in fact, literary critics; each could be characterized by a specific literary theory. Although not the academic adult readers of Stanley Fish's interpretive community, the eighth-grade readers of *House of Stairs* and *Cracker Jackson* did have particular views of textuality that influenced their response.

To make the connection between the interpretive norms of the eighth-graders and the social scenes of reading and response (Johnston, 1987), I met with other teachers, the librarian, the principal, and the Best Books program developer. Their perspectives remained school based and schoolbound, although I knew that students came to classrooms with messages about literacy that are constructed around dinner tables and playing fields. So, that winter I journeyed to the kitchens and living rooms of my students and their families. With cups of coffee in hand, we talked about reading practices at home and literacy values in the family. My sense as a teacher—and now as a researcher—suggested that response to reading was constructed differently.

Side Trips: Beyond the Classroom

The discussions helped me to understand the construction of meaning over time. Protocols, interviews, and journals caused me to see students as readers in very specific and interesting ways. Teachers and families offered other perspectives that I could not have imagined. The students themselves, however, understood the journey with enviable clarity.

I think that the reason the author wrote it was just to have a good story and that, yes, because there's something about a good story that if you tell it well [and then] drag it out too long, you would just destroy it.

Furnifold Simmons

An appraisal of Furnifold Simmons' reading protocols—that is, the texts of his personal reading as he reads silently and thinks aloud while reading—suggests that Furnifold is seeking a story logic. He questions, probes, and conjectures as he reads. In the early readings of texts, particularly, Furnifold's think-alouds are characterized by "I wonder." Later, he often pauses, says "hmm," and reports a hypothesis or a supposition about the book. Clearly, Furnifold is attempting to put together a sense of what he has read. He remains open to possibilities as he begins his private reading. His posture is not so much uncertainty as a willingness to play. He seems at times like a detective, putting the pieces of the story puzzle together as he reasons his way through a passage. The detective has fun while reading; in this passage from the text of Furnifold's 11th protocol prior to his first reading of *Gentlehands,* his hypotheses set up a sort of dialectic:

Who's they? And why do they have particular tones and accents? And what was his mother right about? Ah, I was right. My suspicions were confirmed. He likes her and is dating her. Taking her out. And why does this kid have the name Streaker? It's probably a nickname like Goat or something, one of those cutesie names. What does daddy mean, what does any of this mean? That's what you do when they say something you don't like. "Well, what do you mean anyway? That doesn't have anything to do with what I'm doing." Again, the same thing. What does that even mean? It's just a rhetorical question. He knew. He knew what he meant. An explanation of meaning. Oh, well.

It became apparent from a look at the book discussions that this manner of making sense of text was carried over into the group talk for Furnifold. Furnifold, for instance, was the participant who felt that most was gained from discussion when the group was "argumentative." He said, "Debate in a group is great. I think if everybody had the same idea about a book there wouldn't be much discussion. . . . This sounds strange, I know, but lately I've come to realize that I like to argue. I don't mean a free-for-all or a brawl, but a loud discussion about a book. I'll fight things out." His independent reading style provided a foundation for the ways in which he, like his counterparts, introduced and sustained discussion of topics in the more public arena of classroom talk.

Sitting in the Simmons' family room one icy February evening, his family and I discussed common definitions and understandings of what reading is and what it is not. Mrs. Simmons maintains that someone who is a reader is "somebody who can read things and digest them and be able to discuss them." She reports that Furnifold's 7-year-old sister loves to read, but it is Furnifold who is set apart from the rest of the family: "I mean, Furnifold will read anything. There couldn't be a printed thing that went by that he didn't read." She admits that she, however, would do most anything rather than read. Mr. Simmons, on the other hand, finds that he reads constantly at work, where he often has to skim material to pass on or file for company records. This kind of reading is like a "survival skill that you have to pick up when you're faced with a large amount of documentation. . . . You either learn how to do it or you don't survive."

Mrs. Simmons is admittedly not a reader, although she has great admiration and respect for those who are. Both she and Mr. Simmons come from families of readers, and she speaks wistfully about particular family members' abilities to sit down in the evening, open a novel, and continue reading until the early hours of the morning. What Furnifold appears to have learned from his mother and from her attitudes toward books and reading is a tolerance for difference. In his enjoyment of argumentation in discussion, Furnifold admits that he likes differences of opinion, attitude, and outlook. He demonstrates an appreciation for the comments and analyses of his fellow group discussants and encourages their contributions. The attitudes modeled in Furnifold's home are those that he brings to his response group:

No one has ever experienced a nuclear war so it's sort of hard to get into the book because you couldn't put yourself in her place. If that was me, in the second week I would either go totally insane or kill myself. It was also a survival book. Just one girl trying to survive in a civilization where there is no civilization.

Robert Smith

Sensory imagery predominates Robert's attempts to construct meaning. She says, for example, in *Z for Zachariah*, "I'm thinking of the fire burning the trees and the rain putting it out"; in *House of Stairs*, "I'm getting a picture of a house with just stairs, no walls or ceiling"; and in *Journey to an 800 Number*, "I'm picturing what the tablecloths look like." With few exceptions, virtually every sentence from a collection of 12 protocols begins in a like manner. Clearly, Robert relies on visual imagery to create meaning from text. One statement that warrants special mention occurs in her initial protocol for *House of Stairs*. For a reader who relies so heavily on sensory impression, an interesting dilemma is raised in her think-aloud: "I'm getting a picture of nothing."

The topics that Robert finds either interesting or at least worthy of examination are similar to the topics that interest the adult readers in Elizabeth Long's (1985) study of the popular novel in the United States. Long analyzes the American best-seller over 3 decades and finds that the reading public, like Robert, prefers novels that examine relationships and that encourage self-reflection. Robert's choices of passages also focus on human and humane concerns. In contrast to what gets foregrounded, when Robert chooses or prefers not to read a passage, she is notably uninterested. The task, if done at all, is performed grudgingly. She constantly shrugs as a response. Brevity is another way that Robert rejects an assignment. She often states, "I don't know," when asked to elaborate an answer. She is not really registering doubt so much as she is taking a position.

"I don't know," brevity, and nonparticipation are for Robert all about one thing—resistance. Consistent with what she writes in her journal and says about school, Robert tends to dismiss what does not hold her interest. She gets very involved in what she likes, and it is apparent that she enjoys the group of six readers very much. Her participation in the group, however, is consistent with her individual reading style: She reports that although she can learn from the others in the group, she is not about to be influenced by them. She makes it clear that there is an important distinction; they may confirm an idea she has, but they are not about to change her mind.

Robert is accustomed to a hands-off approach toward reading in her home. By allowing her daughter to come to an appreciation of reading in her own time and on her own terms, Mrs. Smith encourages the somewhat critical reader. Robert knows that she is permitted to express herself openly: Her feelings are significant to her mother, and Robert knows the freedom to experience literature in a way that is comfortable for her. As the resistant reader, she both expresses her identity and makes sense of a text; what is encouraged at home is practiced at school.

WHAT MY TRAVELS REVEALED

It became apparent over time that the group of six readers formed their own interpretive group in very specific ways. There were markers of community. First, the role of questions within each book talk changed. Students spent time at the beginning of each discussion organizing the facts of the story; questions and answers were used as a kind of place-saving device in which the readers oriented themselves to one another before engaging in a topical discussion of the book. In the later discussions, however, this need for negotiation through questions was dismissed. Questions were instead used as rhetorical devices for students to assert their own opinions and to make a point. This shift suggests movement toward bonding: familiarity with a variety of reading styles, comfort with alternative interpretations, and involvement with a group-defined task.

A second indicator of community was a shift in the role of students within the group discussions. In time, a leader emerged. Furnifold and Amber were consistently leaders in introducing and sustaining topics in the first book talk sessions. Early discussions indicated that Asheley scarcely contributed, made only a few assertions of opinions, seldom questioned, and made only occasional comments. Her leadership role emerged gradually over the six discussions. She became a major contributor in discussion 5, not only in her introduction of topics but in the way she was able to change the direction of the book talk. Furthermore, by the sixth discussion, she was the first to speak, she readily constructed meaning with other students, and she claimed the largest portion of the talk time.

It is difficult to unravel the influences on student response and to know the ways that the threads are interwoven. What is certain, however, is that all have to do with what people value. Evaluation is the fiber that interconnects all of the strands of this particular "web of meaning" (Geertz, 1973): It is a social fiber that connects a comment made by Furnifold during a reading protocol to a comment made later by Amber in the group talk. What is valued by this community of readers is a reflection of other classrooms and other contexts in which readers use text. When the layers of context that inform student response are untangled and the relationship between response and context is examined, this community of readers is better understood in terms other than their mere knowledge of literary conventions or historical literary perspectives. What must be revealed are the realities of the students' lives and the social relations that unite and fragment the group of readers. The responses of the six are organized by norms that suggest that the group is more appropriately named an evaluative rather than an interpretive community.

THIS PART OF THE JOURNEY ENDS

Casting myself as a teacher researcher has led to professional change. As in any worthwhile and meaningful learning, the struggle has resulted in small personal transformations as well. Furnifold, Asheley, and Melissa Ann helped me to slow my pace in an attempt to see the world as someone else might see it. It was Robert Smith and Dusty Bottoms, for example, who helped me to see that distinctions in response are not between the subjective and the objective, as I had always understood, but that response is always subjective. Differences have to do with public and private ways of reading. I would have missed this had I not learned how to travel with my six eighth-graders. They showed me what to explore and pointed out vistas that would have been overlooked had I trusted only in myself.

Because I have learned so much from my students and their families, I seem to have a growing sense of what collaboration means. I have helped students in other classrooms and other contexts to see that the "text" of the classroom is not always what they think (Johnston, 1992). I learn from other teachers who care about inquiry, who formulate questions, who meet in classrooms after normal school hours, and who wonder what works and why it works.

• • • • • • • • • • • •

Finding Our Way: A Deaf Writer's Journey

Penny A. Starr

PENNY A. STARR *is a teacher at the Pennsylvania School for the Deaf in Philadelphia. She has taught 9- and 10-year-olds for the past 5 years. Along with her involvement in a schoolwide language and literacy research group, she was a discussion leader at the Ninth Annual Language Coordinator's Workshop, and she presented a paper on poetry with deaf students and second language learners at the 1991 New York State Whole Language Conference.*

My students and I write, and then I catch myself looking away. My students are deaf. How do they fit in? How are they different? How are they the same? My students are confronted with two different languages: American Sign Language, their primary communicative language, and English in print and books. English is a second language for my students and is so very different from American Sign Language (ASL), which is their native visual language. Children in my classroom tell stories with vivid signs and body and facial expressions and then are faced with a blank page and words that do not match a visual sign. The words seem motionless and inert compared with the fire and intensity of signing.

What happens when my students compose in ASL and then try to transfer it to standard written English? What strategies and processes do they use? What have we learned together in our years together that has helped with their transition? So many questions arise from our daily interactions. Both they and I are challenged, frustrated, and sometimes ill at ease with writing in this different language of English.

DEAFNESS AS CULTURE

I am a teacher at the Pennsylvania School for the Deaf in Philadelphia (PSD), Pennsylvania. PSD is a private, state-chartered city school that serves approximately 170 deaf students aged 2 through 15. At PSD, ASL is used when teaching in the classroom and is an essential part of the school's education and communication philosophy. One of our key goals is to encompass all cultures and languages to enhance learning. The teachers at PSD immerse children in a language-filled environment, and ASL is recognized and supported throughout the school. Everyone at PSD can sign, with varying degrees of ASL fluency.

Language is the heart of every community, and ASL is the foundation of the deaf community. It is the primary language of thousands of the deaf in America and carries with it the culture and values of generations of the deaf. It serves as a primary identifying characteristic of members of deaf culture. ASL *is not* based on or derived from English. ASL evolved separately from English and possesses its own grammar and syntax. It is strictly rule governed. The use of spatial relations, direction, orientation, movement, and hand shape as well as facial expression and body language all constitute the grammar of ASL. It is a beautiful, visual-gestural language with its own vocabulary and lexical features. The rules, vocabulary, idioms, and lexicon differ from those of English, just as they would from any other language. Signs in ASL are units that can have both concrete and abstract meanings. Constructions that combine two or more signs express meanings more completely and complexly than can simple signs or single words. These constructions are also rule governed. The syntax of ASL tends to be relational and spatial and can sometimes follow a structure of subject-object-verb. Anything expressed in English can be expressed in ASL.

ASL is not a written language. No newspapers, books, or texts are written in ASL. The use of English to represent ASL is simply a convention that has been adopted until a written system for ASL is developed. As ASL does not have a written form, an English "gloss" of ASL, the closest we can come to translating the meaning of the ASL expression using English words, is used.

These glosses are not English sentences, nor should they be expected to be. For example, an English sentence, "I went to play," would be "Play me go finish," when glossed in ASL. "Play me go finish" is a perfect ASL construction. It is also possible for a translation in ASL to be parallel to English. "I have a blue car" in English is "Have blue car" in ASL. It is more likely, however, that a person will find the translation to be quite different. For example, the sign "look" can mean literally "look," the English word. The same hand shape for "look" with different direction, motion, and force can mean "glance," "stare," or "scan." The same hand shape is used, but in a different visual way. Two or three English words may constitute one sign. The signs for "wake up" and "look for" are each one sign, although they are pairs of words. The sign in ASL and the spoken word in English do not always match. Yet there is no way to write the little nuances, the facial expressions, and the body movements.

Difficulties are raised with glossing ASL using English words. ASL in the written glossed form may appear to be "bad" English or "broken" English because the grammar and order appear in ASL. People believe that ASL is ungrammatical or has no syntactical rules because they have compared written ASL with written English. Seen instead as a whole system and as a language in its own right, ASL is quite like any other language. Its elements contrast and complement each other, but the contrast and complement are visible, not audible.

THE WRITER IN MICHAEL

I teach a classroom of six 10-year-old students at PSD. I have them for a period of 2 years, as is typical in the elementary department. I have them for all subjects. My students are all profoundly deaf. They have various mixtures of communication styles. Deaf children have different styles, just like no two hearing children communicate in exactly the same way. Some use strictly ASL, some use signed English (signs in English word order), some mix ASL and signed English, and some function with voice and sign simultaneously. When I work one to one with a student, I suit my sign to their mode, which may or may not include voice. When I am with a group of three or more students, I invariably do not use my voice and only sign conceptual ASL.

For 2 years, our classroom community has been reading, writing, talking, and learning. We are nearing the end of our 2 years together. Are the children really that different from hearing writers and how? Have they adapted different processes, changed them, or perhaps revised a little to better suit their needs as deaf writers? Does their lack of fluency in English impede their process as writers? How do they compensate, and how do they overcome? Most of all, how are they faring right now? If together we are builders of knowledge and makers of meaning in writing, how can I continue to encourage them to build bridges?

These questions have always been with me since I began teaching at PSD. It was not until these 2 years that I began to search deeper for some answers. To explore these questions, I began to look closely at one student's strategies, process, and progress in our community of writers. I chose to look closely at one writer's progress over 2 years with me, in the hopes that understanding one child more fully would increase my understanding of them all.

Michael is a 10-year-old deaf boy in my class. He has been profoundly deaf since birth and has been at PSD since approximately 3 years of age. A strict ASL user, Michael is very comfortable in his communication style and has an innate sense of the language and structure of ASL. This was one of the primary reasons I chose to look at Michael and his progress in writing English.

Many strong connections have been made that the knowledge of a first language provides the building blocks for the acquisition of a second language. Edelsky (1982) has often pointed out that the first language forms the basis for acquiring the second language rather than interferes with it. I believe that Michael's ASL is a basis for his skill in acquiring English. He is well above his deaf classmates in written English skills and seems to have a real feel for the language and knowledge of rules that others in the class do not. His reading skills are approximately that of a first grader, which is a little below that of his deaf peers, most of whom at age 10 are reading at a second- to third-grade level. Michael consistently uses print in his environment for both reading and writing. His development as a writer has grown from his early starts of drawing to presently writing books and poetry. I believe that his print-rich classroom, a whole language environment, and his high level ASL have all contributed to his success as a writer in the class.

INNER VOICE: MICHAEL COMPOSES

When Michael first sat down to write, I was a bit baffled. As he looked at the blank page, he began to sign to himself. He sat, shook his head, wrote something, and then went back and signed it. Sometimes he was happy with it, and sometimes he wasn't. I wondered just exactly what he was doing. A few times, I sat down beside him, perhaps hoping to catch a glimpse of understanding. Then, as I was writing 1 day, I reread out loud to myself what I had written. The words didn't sound right together, so I changed them. It hit me. Was this what Michael was doing, only in sign? If the practice for hearing people is the sound, is the practice for deaf people the visual? Had Michael adapted the sound of words to the look of his signs? Was he checking how his writing "sounded" by signing it?

Hearing people compose and prewrite before the pen is to the paper. We listen to the words in our head, our own inner speech, to hear how the words sound together. Once we commit to paper, we may say it again to ourselves to see if it really does "sound" right. When the deaf compose, is this inner speech an outer visible sign? Do they invent, compose, and build meaning in the primary language of ASL? Michael sits, signs to himself, writes some, and then goes back to sign and revise what he has written. As he signs to himself, he does not really watch his hands but rather gets a feeling for the signs flowing together. For Michael, the writing and constant rewriting that we as hearing people do in our heads seem to be accomplished by the visible rehearsal of signs in his inner speech of ASL. In observing Michael compose and write, I believe this is what he is doing. I also have many questions. Is his whole inner speech an outer visible speech or does he have both an inner speech *and* an outer visible speech? Have they been blended into one or are they two distinct processes for Michael?

As Michael first began to use print in his writing, he looked for a complete word to match with every sign as he composed and thought of what he wanted to write. Many times he did not recognize the printed word for the sign. We were struggling. What did Michael do? Two years ago, I would actually find pictures of movement or of the shape of the sign itself. This seems to be a common practice with young deaf writers. For example, the sign for "cookie" is a C hand shape made in the palm of the other hand two or three times. Michael would write C C C on the paper to indicate the word cookie. He denoted the spelling of the word by the hand shape and the movement of the sign. Later, as Michael's print-to-sign abilities strengthened, I saw the beginning of invented spelling due to his exposure to spellings in print. Michael has most recently been an avid user of classroom print to help with his writing. He knows where to find words he needs, along with having a "bank" in the room that we have developed since the class started together. Now, Michael relies on the look of the printed word. He recognizes the words as having a particular sign. He continues to struggle when two or more signs can be translated into one English word or when one sign equals two or more English words.

Michael later used techniques created in class to aide him with bridging the gap between signs and words. It was clear we were joining two worlds and two languages when we wrote. Many times, a sign was represented by two or more English words. I saw Michael wanting to write "wake up," which is two words but only one sign in ASL. He found the words "wake up," copied them, and then put a "bridge" between them. He indicated this was one sign by using the bridge. This was later a classwide technique, but Michael began using it so early in his writing of words that I think it was a real need of Michael's to make connections between his two languages. He repeatedly uses bridges today, often independently in his daily journal. Are these bridges also a conscious consideration of his audience, who are mostly deaf and know ASL? The reader, in Michael's view, will most likely be deaf. Did Michael begin to take his audience into consideration with this development?

BUILDING NEW BEGINNINGS

While Michael learns to write, he seems to be learning his second language at the same time. Writing instruction for my students seems to occur at the same time as language instruction. They learn to write in the second language while still learning the language itself. Michael does not sign English. Writing, however, for him is in transcriptions of English words. In our classroom and throughout Michael's development, the ASL-like writing is accepted as writing in his primary language. If I allow Michael to be fluent in using his nativelike ASL grammar when writing, will it encourage him to take some risks in English? Will he acquire the second language if he is confident enough with his first?

The first stories Michael wrote were written in glossed ASL. Michael's story, "Time. Finish. Bed wake up." was an early writing. At that time, it meant "When time was finished, I went to bed and then I woke up" in English. The glossed ASL writing was a valid story for Michael. The ASL-like writings should, I feel, continue to be legitimized as bridges to building English and gaining confidence to take risks and experiment. The ASL-like writing enables Michael to show what he knows rather than what he doesn't know. Creating meaning in his primary language allowed for ideas and concepts to be brought to the second language learning. By giving him freedom and acceptance in his ASL, he is acquiring English with some ease. Michael, however, may be the exception in my class. He has a strong internalized ASL to learn from, whereas the others do not have that building block. Will my other students go through the same stages Michael is moving through, only later?

As soon as Michael entered the class, he was an authentic author. He wrote, rewrote, and published, all in glossed ASL, which is typical of the younger children at PSD. *Michael is an author* and is treated as such. He uses his own texts to learn to read. His texts are valued. They are his language and his work. In class, I also rewrite some texts into an ASL-type grammar for my class, which legitimizes their ASL. Many stories in class are dictated to me at first. I transcribe their signs so that the writing is very close to their talk. This may be one way that I began to connect ASL and English for Michael and others. I had to begin somewhere, showing connections, bridges, and ways into writing. The language that my students are most comfortable with, tied to a meaningful context, provides a way for us to make meaning with our writing. The language that I documented in dictated stories did not need to be explicit because we assumed our audience would be our class and others who knew us well. There was first the transcription in print and then the risk in discovering sign to print connections in English. The center of Michael's learning began with strength and confidence in his native language.

As Michael continued to write, how was English grammar influencing his writing? Did his increased awareness of a grammar different from his own impede, encourage, or have any impact on his process? Perhaps Michael was making meaning more easily with a limited awareness of the patterns and "restrictions" of English. He did not know enough of the grammar rules in English to let them block his meaning making. If Michael had been as aware of the grammar of English as the grammar of his own native ASL, would that have benefited him even more?

Two years ago, when Michael began to join words in sentencelike structures (groups of two or more words), I saw appearances of early English-like grammar. Michael used phrases such as "go movie Superman" and "go home." In ASL, these phrases would most likely be "movie Superman go" and "home go." Funny he should use English grammar—or was it? I still saw Michael adhere to the topical aspects of stories, which is strongly ASL. I was struck again and again by Michael's English-type sentences. I didn't see it until I reread his pieces. Some of my previous questions surfaced again: Did he change to English in his inner voice prewriting? Is he aware of this grammar? I began to think he used what he knew of English at that time to make meaning.

After half a year with me, Michael continued to experiment with English structure throughout his writings. In February 1989 in his 1st year with me, he began to use "to go" and "to come." In ASL, one does not say "to go"; instead, "go" is used. Why did it seem important for Michael to use this structure? Perhaps it clarified for the reader, who would know the tense of the action. Also, these phrases might have occurred in Michael's surroundings and texts during that time. I saw Michael move on independently to more complex sentences in his personal journal in October 1989, the beginning of his second year with me. Michael wrote, "Yesterday was Happy Birthday party." This comes very close to a formal English sentence. The ASL equivalent might have been something like "Birthday party yesterday."

In February 1990, I saw complex structures for Michael again: "Day go to Mom and Dod houes paly toy and paly Nintenodo." This sentence structure was never taught as a set of rules. When we looked at the sentence together later, I told him I noticed the "go to" usage in his sentence. I noted that it was a very English phrase. His own writing and risk taking became the catalyst for teaching about structure in a different language. I felt we trusted each other enough that I could comment on the structures he used without making it seem that English was "right" or "better." I would not have done this with him nearly 2 years ago. We had to trust each other. He knew there would be no formal criticisms or corrections of his piece into "better" English. Instead, there was discussion, support, and encouragement to take chances, experiment, and see what happened. We could discuss his writing, and he could risk; I could ask, and he could become a part of his own process.

A MOMENT OF DISCOVERY

Near the end of our 2 years together, Michael composed a story entitled "Zorro." When he presented the full page of his piece to me, it was already self-edited. He had already moved through the piece. For example, "I good" became "I is good." I noticed the movement of a sentence in the story. He had changed "Zorro I like" to "I like Zorro." I asked why. He replied that "I like Zorro" was better and that the other was "boring," so he changed it. We talked about his other revisions and possible publishing. He decided to publish it, so off he went to type on the computer.

After printing, Michael wanted to recheck and add more ideas, so he revised again. The title changed; some spelling was circled; and numbers 1, 2, and 3 now denoted the order of new sentences within the piece. We talked about the last sentence of his story: "Zorro. Michael V. happy." I questioned him about exactly *who* was happy because it wasn't clear to me. He said that both were. My objective was now to encourage him to clarify this meaning and to guide him toward structures he had used previously. I wrote each of his words in the sentence on a separate card and then added two of my own words, "and" and "are." Would this make sense to Michael? Could he fit in these two extra words and create the meaning that both were happy? The following is what happened:

P.: Can you make a new sentence that you can understand? Try and move the cards until it says what you told me about both being happy. Tell me when you are finished.
M.: *Zorro and happy are Michael V.*
(hands still on cards, thinking; picks up *and are Zorro*)
Michael V. are happy and Zorro
(picks up *Michael V. Zorro*)
happy and are
(rearranges cards)

Michael V. are happy and Zorro
(leaves cards, goes and gets two pieces of paper, and writes two words: *are happy*)
(rearranges cards)
Michael V. are happy and Zorro are happy
"Finished."

P.: "Can you read it for me?"
M.: "Michael V. are happy and Zorro are happy."
P.: "What does that mean? Who is happy?"
M.: "Both happy, better now, boring before, same."
P.: "Do you want to use this new sentence in your story?"
M.: "Yes, better."

Michael really thought about creating this new meaning. He clarified his intended meaning, which he knew before he revised again. By giving him examples using his own text, I feel that I nudged him toward English-type grammar. I also feel that I may have intruded on his writing and made it mine when it is not, and that bothers me. For whom am I changing his writing— myself? Did it need to be changed? The reader probably would have understood. I want Michael to have ownership and control of his writing. Does this kind of activity defeat or encourage that? He had a decision to use the final sentence or not, but the extra word cards were *my* words, not Michael's. Am I "nudging," as Graves might say, or am I intruding?

Revision plays a crucial role in composing for hearing writers, and for deaf writers like Michael, it plays a similar role. How is revision changed for deaf writers, though? Deaf students have less knowledge about the structure of English, having never heard it. Their exposure to English occurs through literature and those who use signed English. For deaf children, the visual printed word must play a larger role. They write words to match their signs, and the words are there to leave or change depending on one's making of meaning. Yet when one simple word is changed, signs are changed and meaning is again altered.

Michael goes through a process of internal revision, discovering and developing what he has to say. He edits and revises his own work, signs the text to himself, adapts the signs, and then changes the print. He revises for meaning the first time through his writing. Does he need to "hear his own voice" at first to the exclusion of others? If I look at a text that Michael has revised for his own personal satisfaction, I see carats making inserts, crossed out lines, and writing in the margins. I see him moving, changing, and discovering his own meaning. Does this need to revise come from a strong inner voice, a need to be heard, and a need to make meaning?

What Michael does to communicate to his audience after he has read the text himself seems to be external revision. He looks outward to his audience.

Michael now reads the text as an outsider to a certain extent. But it also makes me wonder if this external reading is any different from his internal reading. I've noticed Michael is much more comfortable when he is doing his "internal" revision.

In a story late in our 2nd year together, "Nintendo," I asked Michael exactly what he meant by a list of books he had written down for his story. Did he have these books, want these books, or like these books? I discussed with him that if someone read this list, they really wouldn't know what he meant. I gave examples of people "guessing" at his meaning. He laughed. It seemed that he knew what he had to do, yet as he walked away from our talk, he had a look of slight concern on his face. I wondered exactly what he was thinking, and most of all, what he was going to do with his story. Two days later, he brought me the piece with insertions of "I have" and "I have not" before each book on the list. We talked about what he had done and the process of doing it. Michael increasingly revised his texts with these types of comments and rethinking. My hopes are that Michael will slowly learn to question himself about his texts. I look to my other students when I see Michael do revision of this type, and they seem to let structure and "correctness" get in the way of their meaning when they write. I hope I can encourage the others to risk, to let ideas come, to put them down, and not to be afraid to change their words, because they may just hit on what they have wanted to say all along.

DISCOVERIES AND ENDINGS

Deaf writers modify their processes of writing to meet their specific needs as users of a visual language and as users of English as a second language. I would like to see further study into the implications that ASL has on the development of written English skills, especially that of internal revision. We need more exploration into how younger deaf children learn to write. When ASL instruction begins early to establish a strong language base, does second language acquisition come easier? How can we take advantage of what the students already know of ASL as a tool with which to teach English skills? Does simultaneously teaching ASL and English structure to deaf students empower them in their English? The real benefits of future research lie in the focus on the bilingual potential of the young deaf child and how to capitalize on it.

Michael's journey as a writer of his world has shown the adaptation and change of one child's process to suit certain needs. It also shows his determination to be a writer with something to say. His development supports a language-filled environment that allows for risk, diversity, and acceptance of who a child is. It emphasizes that valuing a native language in all aspects encourages deaf learners to take risks in acquiring a second language.

We have come to the end of our 2 years together. It has been a struggle, a joy, a discovery, and most of all, a rich learning experience for both of us. By looking closely at one of my students, I have gained a better understanding of how we learn together and how we write. It took time, it took risk, and it took a willingness to become involved in the search for meaning. Sometimes we felt like we were diving into unknown waters, and sometimes we were. It was worth it. For Michael and myself, it allowed us to look around at all we have done together and how much we have gained. Learning to write and communicate has been a journey. We do not speak the same language, but I come away with the sense that we have built a bridge, one that has brought us closer together.

• • • • • • • • • • •

Leaving the Script Behind

Leslie Black, Howard Bousel, Leah Beth Byer, Linda Cimakasky, Deborah Coy, Pamela Freilich, Barbara Hartman, Dimitrios Hilton, Samona Joe, David Lawrence, Maureen Mahoney Hanley, Jeni Snyder, Jan Swenson, and Bruce Winklestein

The coauthors of this article are 1991 graduates of Project START at the Graduate School of Education, University of Pennsylvania. LESLIE BLACK *is a substitute teacher and volunteer in science and other curricular areas in a variety of Philadelphia area schools.* HOWARD BOUSEL *teaches second grade in Camden, New Jersey.* LEAH BETH BYER *teaches a combined second- and third-grade class at the Jewish Primary Day School in Washington, D.C.* LINDA CIMAKASKY *teaches fourth grade in the School District of Philadelphia.* DEBORAH COY *teaches third grade at the Mann School in the School District of Philadelphia.* PAMELA FREILICH *teaches first grade at the Caln School in the Coatesville Area School District, Pennsylvania.* BARBARA HARTMAN *teaches kindergarten and a third-grade enrichment program at the Ross School in Ross, California.* DIMITRIOS HILTON *teaches third grade at the Barkley Elementary School in Phoenixville, Pennsylvania.* SAMONA JOE *teaches sixth-grade math and science at the Barratt Middle School in the School District of Philadelphia.* DAVID LAWRENCE *teaches sixth-grade mathematics and social studies at Cabot School, a public elementary school in Newton, Massachusetts.* MAUREEN MAHONEY HANLEY *teaches elementary school in Hanover, New Hampshire.* JENI SNYDER *teaches elementary classes at the North Shore Country Day School in suburban Chicago.* JAN SWENSON *teaches fourth grade at Merion Elementary School in the Lower Merion School District, Pennsylvania.* BRUCE WINKELSTEIN *teaches third grade at Longfellow School in Teaneck, New Jersey.*

Dick and Jane were having one of their many fights.
Dick said, "Grades reflect intelligence."

Jane replied, "The question is do grades reflect intelligence or task performance."

Dick replied, "But grades are the only sure way to rate students."

Jane replied, "The question is whether students need to be rated."

Finally, Dick got exasperated, and said, "You think you have all of the right answers."

Jane smiled and replied, "No, just the right questions."

What does it mean to ask the right questions? As student teachers, we are challenged to think about such issues as cultural diversity, student assessment, the teacher's role in the classroom, and how our personal educational experiences affect our teaching styles. We continually wrestle with our emerging perspectives concerning our roles as teachers by asking questions such as: Who are we? Why are we in the classroom? Who are our students? What are their cultures? What are their individual needs? How can we best serve them? and How can we deal with the incredible diversity inherent in any group of children? It is these kinds of questions that we as student-teacher researchers must ask to best meet the needs of our children and to continually reassess our roles as teachers.

LOOKING AT BASAL LESSONS AS STUDENT-TEACHER RESEARCH

Our experiences with teacher research include journals and essay writing, child observations, studies of lessons as well as discussions and reflections on various issues. One set of issues we examined both as a class and individually centered around the use of basal readers in teaching reading and language arts.

During the first term of our program, we read and discussed various and opposing viewpoints on the use of commercially prepared readers that we felt valued mastery of isolated skills (vocabulary, spelling, phonics, and so on) above all else, particularly understanding of the literature as a whole. Reading instruction using preplanned, publisher-imposed methods seemed to us to strip the teacher of any meaningful decision making in his or her own classroom. Following the step-by-step format of a teacher's manual relegates professionals to mere script-reading technicians.

Generally, our sentiments were more closely aligned with the current "whole language" movement, which emphasizes an active, sense-making, literature-based approach to language learning and deemphasizes the passive, isolated skill exercises so dominant in basal instruction. We had come to feel that literacy development must be about the reader's ability to make sense of print. Children learn to read by reading and are motivated to read by reading interesting, relevant text, that is, literature of whatever kind that is meaningful in their lives.

On the other hand, we are wary of the "whole language" movement becoming yet another fad in educational reform. The notion of holistic, literature-based instruction is not a packageable commodity or a set of how-to instructions to be distributed during one or two in-service workshops. Rather, it seems to us that whole language represents an attitude toward and about literacy development. It is about making decisions regarding how children go about learning and making sense out of print and language, and it is about who is important in the learning process: the learner, the teacher, or the instructional program.

During October and November of our fall term, one of our projects was to prepare and teach two language arts lessons using basal readers and focusing on teacher-researcher questions of our choice that we wanted to explore. These questions, which sometimes changed during the course of our assignment depending on a lesson's outcome, were designed to guide us in our inquiry and to help us think critically about what we were doing. Our instructions for this basal assignment were to teach the first lesson strictly according to the teachers manual (i.e., using the various pre- and postreading exercises as outlined in the basal instructions to the teacher) and to modify the second lesson according to our many readings in pedagogy and language as well as our own emerging theories of reading instruction. Basically, we could teach the second lesson as we saw fit—using a story in the basal and crafting questions and activities that we thought would be engaging and stimulating for the children. Then each of us wrote a paper comparing the two lessons. We reflected on our data and teacher-research questions, came to tentative conclusions about basals, and more often than not, raised new questions for further reflection and examination.

This basal project had three functions for us. First, it gave us an active teaching experience in our student-teacher classrooms (for many of us, it was our first experience in teaching and learning how to teach). Second, it was an opportunity for us to construct curriculum as well as to experience the traditional basal methodology. Finally, this project was perhaps our first chance to actually "do" teacher research—that is, question, plan, and collect data to reflect on what we and our students were accomplishing in the classroom.

Late in January, about 6 months into the START program, 14 of us collaborated on this group paper, giving us the opportunity not only to share and learn from one another's research from the fall but also to see how our 14 experiences, as reflected in our research papers (our data), could be combined and synthesized into a larger, more inclusive, thematic piece of research. More specifically, we each read and analyzed our own and one another's papers; categorized them; and came up with recurring questions, themes, and patterns. We took notes and discussed at length one another's ideas, questions, reflections, and tentative conclusions. We were again interested in making sense of some of the inquiry methods we were learning as student-teacher researchers. This collaborative effort forced us to think even more deeply and critically about our individual basal lessons and about how we were learning to teach.

A central purpose of this paper is to share voices not often heard in the area of teacher research, those of the student teacher. For most of us, the basal lessons we taught in the fall allowed us to experience for ourselves the difference between scripted lessons performed in the basal mode and the more thoughtful teacher-created lesson planning created within the context of a holistic approach.

STUDENT TEACHER INQUIRIES AND LESSON PLANNING

Each of our basal research papers centered around a focusing or guiding question, and each of us asked different questions depending on our own level of student teaching placements. As every class had its own personality and culture, our research reflected that uniqueness. Some of us initiated our basal projects to test theories and assumptions about the value of basals as a means of language arts instruction. Pamela wrote:

[M]y initial objective was to see how differently the children would react to my own original lesson and that of the basal text book, a resource written specifically by "professionals" for fourth graders in order for them to achieve specific skills and understandings.

Others took advantage of the activity as a way to explore and evaluate different methods of instruction. Jeni expressed:

I wanted experience [in order] to support my assertions with self-generated understanding and passion.

In another example, while planning his modified lesson, Howard reflected on the problems he found in his strict basal lesson. He felt that by engaging his students in a sculpting activity, they would be able to make the basal story about the artist Alexander Calder more meaningful for themselves. Howard said:

I would never have discovered the way of tying art and writing together with the modified lesson unless I had undertaken the research and thought things through carefully; the process allowed for creation.

Our exploration resulted in new avenues for student-teacher research through the development of questions. At the end of his paper, Bruce noted:

Based on this set of lessons, my next step would be to explore basal readers as a collection of stories for reading and writing. Some of the questions I would explore or continue to explore are:

> How do the "best and worst" readers do with this collection? Are they challenged or are they limited?
>
> How does the basal reader as a textbook affect individual enthusiasm towards reading?

Some of us also examined the impact of the follow-up exercises on the lessons. Many undertook research with mixed feelings about basal texts but came out with strong questions about the value of the basal materials that were used. When Leslie asked the children what they thought of the basal story, she observed:

> [T]hey shrugged and gave halfhearted responses: "No I don't like reading anyway."
>
> "No, it was boring."
>
> [T]he basals in fact do little to encourage reading. The story seemed to take forever and I shared my students' sense of restlessness; they and I were anxious to return to our discussion.

Leah Beth reported that her students were annoyed at having to use the basal text and accompanying work sheets:

The following week, my cooperating teacher announced that teacher Leah Beth needed more volunteers to help her complete a second reading lesson assignment for Penn. Although lots of children had volunteered for Basal Lesson#1, no one seemed interested now. "Ah, shucks," sneered Ryan, "I'm not doing that again!" Not until I explained that [the second lesson] would be very different from the [first] did anyone volunteer.

Leah Beth recognized that to interest her students in the lesson, she would have to involve the students more actively than the basal script allowed.

Our basal lesson research projects provided one vehicle to explore our theories and to enrich our development of individual teaching styles and philosophies. Having read articles that discussed the positive and negative aspects of basal programs, we questioned various perspectives on reading instruction. For example, Maureen wrote:

I was tossed from one viewpoint to another and began to wonder if there is a place for basal readers or not. Do they breed mediocrity among teachers and illiteracy in children, or are they a mere target of yet another "progressive" move in education?

As we have mentioned, we are constantly questioning ourselves, and these questions shaped our basal research papers. For example, Samona (after reading Edelsky and Smith, 1984) grappled with what constitutes valuable reading experiences for the children in a reading group:

How can I make reading/writing more authentic while using what I perceive as inauthentic text?

Jan chose a different line of inquiry focusing on Rogers, Green, and Nussbaum's (1988) concept of "pseudo questions," which are kinds of questions used when the teacher already has a specific answer in mind. She asked:

[H]ow much authority and control should the teacher have, and whose "voice" is valued, or even heard, in the classroom?

As we taught our respective basal lessons, we observed our students' reactions and performances as well as our own personal feelings and responses to the basal experience. As Barbara noted:

In hindsight, what I should have done to foster a more active student-centered perspective is have the children make up their own story. While this may utilize the framework of that lesson the method is different. What is crucial about this experience is that the children draw ideas and words from a meaningful source: their lexicon.

To explore our individual questions, we used various forms of classroom data that included but were not limited to children's work like writings, drawings, work sheets, and projects. We also used our journals, tape recordings of the lessons, conferences with students, and our observations. No two people's methods were alike.

We learned that if we want our lessons to be a part of our students' lives, we need to plan them in accordance with the students' interests. Not only do we need to respond to what they enjoyed but also to listen to how they viewed the world. The students in David's classroom give us a child's-eye view of city life. Following the teacher's manual, David asked his group what they thought of when they heard the word "city." The teacher's manual instructed David to wait until the class had offered the words *busy, big, buildings, stores, cars, people, streets, New York, Chicago,* and *Los Angeles.*

I got the distinct feeling from the instructions that I was not supposed to continue until my kids came up with these particular ideas (or until I force-fed them).

The children were not yet trained to know that I needed to hear canned, "correct" answers. They shouted out, "Drugs! . . . Crime! . . . St. Louis! . . .

Baseball! . . . Rape! . . . Murder! . . . Pollution! I somehow managed to coax the "correct" answers out of them, at least enough to satisfy the constraints of the manual. Again, an uneasy feeling stirred in my gut. This wasn't going to be much fun.

The script of the traditional basal lesson did not match the children's perceptions of city life. In fact, the prepared answers of the basal instruction manual discounted or ignored many of the personal lived experiences of the children in David's classroom.

We also learned that beyond getting to know our children in terms of how their personal experiences and views inform our lesson planning, it is important to us as student-teacher researchers to get to know our children as individual people. We realize that if nothing else, teaching and learning are social activities. They are about interactions—with texts, concepts, theories, and above all, people. Therefore, we believe it is crucial to be constantly involved in better knowing our children as well as ourselves so that we may maximize and enrich those interactions.

When we wrote our basal papers, we used our data (children's work and responses and our observations) as the basis for comparison of our lessons. We also drew from our knowledge and assumptions about life, education, and prescribed and modified lesson plans as well as teacher and student reactions to and reflections on the process. Deborah explained both her and her students' reactions as she reflected on her basal assignment:

[W]as there really so little for them to attend to in this piece that it only took 15 minutes for us to "cover" the points? Possibly it was the structure, or lack of it; also, it may not have been a topic in which they were really interested.

All of our questions and reflections on our basal experiences, like Deborah's, enriched our developing perspectives on children's literacy.

FOUNDATIONS FOR MORE PENETRATING QUESTIONS

We have found that the purposes and processes of our student-teacher research have profound implications for us in a variety of ways, both as student-teacher researchers now and as classroom teachers in the future. Our inquiry process makes us constantly reflect on what we are doing and thinking in the classroom and forces us to question carefully, to evaluate our assumptions, and to synthesize knowledge of theory with actual practice. David stated:

Though I am still far from expert on the subject of reading instruction, the concrete demonstrations of these lessons provided me with a firm grounding to base future inquiry and teacher research.

David's research gave him a foundation on which he may form more penetrating questions.

Feeling frustrated over management issues that arose during her modified basal lesson, Jan offered another reflection:

My sense of having lost control made me unable to hear the myriad possibilities for further meaningful discussion. I fell back on the old familiar teacher-imposed power base that I grew up with. So, my practice does not always dovetail with my theory, but it is fascinating (and frustrating) to be aware of my own limitations and to consciously work at breaking some of these internal barriers.

Our student-teacher research transforms our role from that of script follower into that of questioner. We look to research to open us up to further inquiry, a process that never ends. We hope that being researchers will make us more likely to question our observations and thereby look more closely at the children we teach.

Many of us began our basal research with a narrow focus and expanded it to include a broader view and more comprehensive questions. Linda reformulated her focusing question after her initial basal experience:

My initial focusing question was: what would student response be to a traditional lesson in terms of participation, quality of responses, and subjective reactions. However, after teaching the traditional lesson and observing my students' positive reactions I realized that the issue of whether children "like" or "dislike" basals was somewhat irrelevant . . . the more important question was what kind of message does a basal program give to students about reading.

It is clear to us that in finding our voices as teacher researchers, the quest is not for definitive answers but for appropriate questions. Examples of such questions are: Will strict basal lessons hinder the children's learning processes? and What types of literary experiences are an impetus to "authentic" reading and writing? It is by asking these types of questions that we are able to continually observe and rethink our previously held notions of education.

The notion of continual inquiry implies that our conclusions are tentative and subject to further reflection and revision. For instance, Samona stated in her premise that she was wary of "falling into the trap" of wanting to abandon basals altogether:

Although there are problems with the [basals] . . . I didn't want to judge the entire idea of basal reading programs unfairly.

Perhaps the message for us as student-teacher researchers is that we must constantly explore and decide what pedagogical methods work best for us depending on the contexts and cultures of our students and schools.

Our research on basal instruction is just one example of how we are making sense of what we think are appropriate methodologies in language arts. We are concerned with the way that children make meaning out of their lives and out of what goes on in their classrooms. We are equally concerned with the impact that our teaching has on their learning. Some of us question those who control learning, those whose authority counts, and those whose voices are valued in the classroom. Struck by her observation that it was the teacher's voice and not the students' voices that dominated strict basal lesson discussions, Leslie asked:

I wonder why it is that so much reading instruction . . . seems to foster reactive learning and passivity on the part of the students. . . . Given the beauty of their voices, why aren't students' voices being heard?

While exploring the notion of students' choices and its positive effect on his modified basal poetry lesson, Dimitrios remarked:

I think teachers should be asking children more questions about what the children are interested in.

One of our roles as researchers and learners is to keep our teaching dynamic. Dimitrios also addressed this idea when he wrote:

I like this duality of operating as a teacher/learner, and I hope it becomes my safeguard against professional boredom.

So, by its very nature, research is a continuous process of thinking, learning, and self-awareness; seeking new ways of looking at things revitalizes us and keeps our teaching fresh.

As we learn how children struggle to find their voices in the classroom and in their lives, so we, too, will learn to find ours. One of the most exciting ways of beginning to discover our voices is through the experience of instruction and lesson planning. We're not just reading and writing about theories and methods; we're creating our own methods.

Another part of finding and strengthening our own voices is discovering attitudes in ourselves, some of which we do not like. Some of us found that even though we were aware of some of the disadvantages of following strict basal instruction, a degree of comfort was provided by its structure. Samona wrote:

I was actually comfortable in an uncomfortable sort of way during the lesson. That is to say, I felt I had a safety net in the book. No matter what happened, I could just stick to the script and go from question to question, page to page.

CONCLUSIONS

Our research teaches us how our profession is one of extreme diversity and individuality. As no two learners are alike, no two teaching styles are alike. Although the parameters for our basal assignment were set fairly uniformly, each of us approached our assignment differently, and no two experiences were identical. What we all learned, however, were the human variables that make each of us, students and teachers, unique and inherently interesting. This is apparent when Leslie noted the lack of personal input permitted when teaching a by-the-book basal lesson:

The students and I were acting out a script. I was the star, the director, and the stage manager, and my students were mere supporting actors and actresses with one- and two-word lines.

Leslie's experience demonstrates the need for student-teacher research to be a personal process; the results and implications will vary from student to student, teacher to teacher, classroom to classroom, school to school, and year to year. As we reflected on our basal research, we found that for many of us, the focus of our inquiry shifted. At the beginning of our projects, we tended to focus on ourselves as beginning teachers and as creators of curriculum. However, during the course of teaching our basal lessons, we were forced to pay close attention to the effects we were having on our students. By the end of our research, culminating in the comparison papers we wrote, many of us ended up with questions that focused on the children and how they were learning. We were and are becoming child-centered educators.

As we prepare to enter our chosen profession this fall, we will be emerging from the security and theoretical support that we found in our student teaching experiences. On our own, it will be up to us to decide and to create the environment for the children we will be teaching in our classrooms. So, in a real yet also a figurative sense, we will be leaving behind the scripts and guides of our cooperating teachers, professors, and predecessors as we begin our own journeys into teaching.

• • • • • • • • • • • •

Stepping In and Stepping Out: The Making of Hindsight

Shelley Baum-Brunner

SHELLEY BAUM-BRUNNER *holds her doctorate in reading, writing, and literacy from the Graduate School of Education at the University of Pennsylvania, where she teaches courses in composition and short fiction in undergraduate*

English. She also teaches education as well as reading, writing, and literacy courses at Beaver College and La Salle University. A former English department head, director of the Writing Center, and teacher of students in grades 6 to 12, Baum-Brunner uses her teaching experiences and her own teacher training to continually rethink and reflect on how best to teach.

Current research in composition indicates that conferences, peer groups, and workshopping are productive, collaborative activities that enable students to get responses to their written work "in process"—before final drafts are due (Bruffee, 1984). These pedagogical activities for response are grounded in theories that intersect social and cognitive processes. Specifically, they build on Vygotsky's (1962) finding that learning is mediated and transformed by social interaction and speech. Important to the pedagogy of collaborative response, these views of social interactions or complex conversations are, however, too often missing in the designs of research on response. Instead, the research shows most often only "strips of dialogue about texts or isolated instructional conversation" (Florio-Ruane, 1986). Because of this fragmentation, we too often see composition research on products *or* processes or on writers *or* their texts (Stallard, 1974). Or we see the comparative effectiveness of conferences (Harris, 1986) versus peer groups (Gere & Stevens, 1985) versus whole group workshopping (Graner, 1987). From these studies, we understand the overall effectiveness of each of these collaborative groups without understanding the nature of response that occurs in each (Reither & Vipond, 1989). Furthermore, because we see little about how writers talk to and negotiate with one another or about how that interaction affects response to and revision of texts, we see taxonomies of response along broad, dualistic, and fairly static lines. "Interventionist" versus "maturationist" (Kroll, 1980), "text-based" versus "evaluative" (Newkirk, 1984), or "specific" versus "ideal" response (Gere & Stevens, 1985; Sommers, 1982) indicate broad ways that readers read others' texts. However, as dichotomous distinctions, they give us little information about the intersection of what gets said to whom, by whom, when and under what circumstances, and what kinds of response are effective or how or why they work. Furthermore, there is little in the taxonomies to indicate the impact of students being influenced by *and* influencing others in a process over time.

To address these limitations in the research on response, I designed a qualitative study to get more information about the changing, interactive nature of response. In this study, I pay particular attention to my concerns about *the individual* and the individual's impact on his or her own and the group's response. My research can therefore be seen as merging the work on individual variations in the making of response (as Anson did; Onore, 1989) *with* individual variations in the receiving of responses (as Onore, 1989, did). By focusing on the interrelationships between the making and receiving of response and the resultant changes in texts as well, I investigate the ways that language and meaning are mediated and transformed by the day-to-day *interactions of individuals* and their talk in a particular context over time. To do so, this research draws on Vygotsky's (1962, 1978) theory of speech and learning and Bakhtin's (1986) theory of speech genres for both individuals and groups.

STEPPING INSIDE THE CONTEXT OF SCHOOLS: DESIGNING THE STUDY

To see the ways that individuals interact with one another in shaping both response to and revision of texts, I analyzed the ways a group of writers individually and collectively came to understand the demands of a writing task that was new to them: the writing of the college application essay.

The senior students whom I taught and studied attended a private, selective school, which I call the Solomon School. The school served approximately 300 Jewish day students, all of whom were college bound. As a result of both external and internal pressures to get into the most selective schools, the seniors were focused more on their freshman year in college than on their current senior year in high school. Aware that this college admission pressure often distracted them from their "normal " studies, I designed an elective course in writing—Writers' Workshop—in which I attempted to capitalize on the students' interest in college admissions and simultaneously teach them what they needed about how to write. In Writers' Workshop, the college application essay was the primary genre of writing assigned. Workshopping, or whole group response, was the main method for responding to these college application essays and for teaching students how to write. In workshopping, the entire group of students and teacher talked as one group about the "strengths" and "suggestions" of each student's read-aloud college essay draft in order for each student to then revise.

The study was conducted in my own section of Writers' Workshop. I had 10 students over the course of one semester for 15 weeks. As a teacher researcher with an ethnographic perspective, I looked at these 12th-grade students in each of four periods a week for between 40 and 50 minutes 2 days a week and in one double period for 90 minutes on a third day. I tape-recorded all the class workshopping sessions from early September to late December. I collected the drafts and revisions of each student's essays and dated them to correspond to the tapes of the class sessions held. These two data sources were the primary focus of my study. From these data sources, themes or codes were constructed inductively and tested against each other and the published literature on revision and response.

As a teacher researcher, I gathered the data over 15 weeks as I taught the class and, for the most part, analyzed the data retrospectively. The original study focused on the entire group of students and on four individual cases.

STEPPING OUTSIDE: LESSONS OF HINDSIGHT AND WHAT I LEARNED

The following discussion of individuals' responses in interaction with others focuses primarily on Chaim, one of the weaker writers in the group. Using him as an example, I first show his unique style of talk. Furthermore, I show that his style of response to others was bound as much by his individual identity— the way that he acted around others (Brooke, 1988) and that others acted around him—as by concerns for others' texts. Then I show that his style of talk has an impact on others *and* is reflected back on himself. Although I show that I initially judged this student's style to have been counterproductive, I later saw that, in fact, it was not. Had I been able to step outside at the time that I taught, rather than only retrospectively, I would have better understood the impact that his style had on others and how that ultimately reflected back on him. With the insight/hindsight that teacher research provided, I would have been a different and, I believe, better teacher to Chaim. With the knowledge gained from having conducted teacher research, I would have changed my responses to him and encouraged, not discouraged, the "imitative" style of responses that he gave.

PROFILE OF CHAIM, THE IMITATOR

Chaim, a fast-paced talker and wiry-haired blond, was the school's basketball star, who hoped for an athletic scholarship to a major state university. Unique in his responses, Chaim quite often merely repeated what others had already said. Seen as a me-too type, Chaim usually used imitation in his response to the group. In the following example, during workshops, Chaim responded imitatively to my response to Jay's draft about a summer job. I said to Jay, "[You need to] first tell us about your experiences in the computer center." Six turns later, Chaim repeated almost precisely what I had said: "I think you could mention the kind of job you'd had [in the computer center]." For roughly the first third of the term, Chaim continued the imitation talk. When I studied the transcripts, I was embarrassed to see that in one way or another, I had conveyed to him the displeasure and concern that his imitative style evoked in me. In response to almost each episode when he spoke in an imitative mode, the data showed that I either laughed ("We're laughing because *we* said that a few minutes ago"), was annoyed ("Shhhhhh . . . CHAIM!"), or was sarcastic ("Good suggestion!?!"). What I found so problematic about Chaim's imitative style was that it seemed to flout basic conversational rules. Rather than repeating someone else's idea and then acknowledging that the idea belonged to someone else, he repeated ideas as if they were his own. I wondered, perhaps, if in flouting the rules, he was mocking me or the class. I wondered if he was just trying to get attention, as that behavior frequently produced a laugh. Perhaps he just didn't know what was going on. Either way, I felt he was getting little out of workshopping class. I believed that if he were only repeating others' remarks, he was not thinking for himself. If he wasn't thinking for himself, how would he ever be able to critique or revise? And perhaps even worse, if he didn't critique or revise, would he distract the others from their serious participation in workshopping class? It seemed like a game or charade that he consciously played.

RECIPROCITY AND CHAIM'S IMITATIVE STYLE OF RESPONSE

At the time that I taught Chaim, I was concerned that Chaim's style of response was not particularly helpful to him. I believed that he was getting little out of workshopping class. Yet when I analyzed the transcripts of the classroom discourse, I found his style was more helpful to his development in writing and in response than I had originally assumed it to be. Furthermore, when I completed a retrospective analysis of the classroom tapes, I learned that Chaim's style of response was more significant than I'd originally assumed it to be, for it affected not only Chaim but also the other students in the room. It impacted on the way that Chaim spoke to others and the way that others spoke back to him! Having expressed himself so openly to others in an imitative style, he was spoken to in an imitative style in return. In other words, Chaim's style of response was reciprocated or mirrored back to him.

This mirrorlike or reciprocal relationship between the imitative style he gave to others and the style of the responses he received in turn is demonstrated in the following summary of response from Chaim's workshop session. It reveals how Chaim's imitative style helped to shape the responses he received. In Chaim's workshop session, Sharon, one of Chaim's peers, tried to tell him that the second half of the essay he read on basketball should be cut, but she had trouble finishing her thought. Chaim interrupted at least five different times over the course of only 10 conversational turns. In response to his interjections, everyone kept repeating or in a sense imitating Sharon's initial point: to cut after the tryouts part. Through restatements, summaries, clarification, and repetition of Sharon's point, Liz, then I, then Gaye, and then Sharon continued to repeat the same idea for Chaim over and over again. In slight variations on Sharon's initial idea, we said:

Cut that [other than the tryouts part] ; keep this [tryouts] part; I was bored here [after the tryouts part]; this [the tryout part] was interesting; you have 12 ideas, so pick one [the tryout part].

Thus, rather than avoiding more repetition, Chaim received a round of repetitious responses not unlike those that he had given to the group.

As a researcher, I learned that Chaim's imitative style had an impact on his revisions as much as on the group's response. Anxious to please, he copied or imitated suggestions, incorporating them into his writing exactly as told to him. For example, in his first essay on basketball, he began by saying: "I have all these ideas, but I don't know how to get it into a paper."

In response, he was told to write down his ideas, just pell-mell. He did that and had a second draft with, not surprisingly, too many disparate ideas. His second paper had paragraphs on the value of sports to life, the value of team-work, friendship, family, social activities, competition, meeting interesting people, how basketball is good for business, the basketball tryouts, and the coach—to name just a few. In response to that pell-mell draft, he was then told to focus on the best part of his draft. As he was told, he focused on the team-work part. In response to that next more focused draft, he was directed to add a few more details to flesh out the paper's unsupported views. In the fourth draft, as with the others, Chaim did exactly as he was told. In the final draft, he added detail and even borrowed some of the precise language given to him by the workshop group. Chaim followed suggestions well but so literally that he made only one major change per draft. Moving one step at a time, he revised, incorporating an imitation of what he'd been told.

OVER TIME: MOVING FROM IMITATION TO INITIATION

As much as I was concerned about Chaim's imitative style, I learned in retro-spect that this style had in fact worked well for him. From systematically ana-lyzing the classroom conversations, I discovered that Chaim had developed over time and response from an imitator to more of an initiator in his style of writing. I demonstrate first his change from imitator to initiator; then I account for the change.

At the time I taught, I had a vague sense that Chaim had improved a bit over the course of the term. However, an analysis of the data indicated more specific information about the nature of that change. What I learned was that after the first 5 weeks, Chaim rarely imitated what others said. Instead, Chaim initiated ideas more often over the rest of the term. A bit bolder later in the term than he'd been earlier, he disagreed with other students and even inter-rupted me once to say, "I'm not done." Obviously much more assertive than in his role of imitator, he corrected me for accepting suggestions during the wrong part of workshopping time ("We're on strengths *now*"). On another occasion, he told me to perform *my* appropriate role by "get[ting *my*] piece of paper out" during workshopping time. To a student who was stating an idea that he had had, he shrieked, "[Stop!] You're taking *my* comments." Showing a new willingness to talk about his own ideas, he initiated much more often.

He began not only to initiate but to make quite sophisticated and adept remarks. He pointed out logical inconsistencies or identified important themes that had only been implied. He could more easily imagine future drafts. He initiated remarks directly linked to the intended theme. For example, he said in response to Tammy's draft about an episode in which she appeased an irate customer, "He sounded like trouble. Tell more about why. Use his tone of voice. Then tell how he changed."

Understanding that it was important for Tammy to support her claims, he asked her in effect to show more and not just tell. Furthermore, he understood that the crux of her essay rested on the fact that this customer had changed in response to her. Unless she could convey this change subtly through the customer's actions and tone of voice, she had little hope of portraying all that she hoped she might.

Although this is indicative of only one of the insightful remarks Chaim made on a regular basis in the latter part of the term, he clearly changed roles in the room. Chaim became an initiator in response to classroom behavior, class rules, and other students' writing, but he also became an initiator in his writing as well. In fact, after writing a delightfully refreshing essay about the problems of keeping kosher at a fancy, pretentious restaurant, he elicited a round of essays—from even the best writers in the room—about food fads, food fetishes, and food fears. One wrote about how tomatoes spoil salads, and another wrote about the perils of eating at restaurants that serve fast foods. Chaim now generated a round of imitation *of* him rather than imitation *by* him, with the students in effect acknowledging his original ideas and his new initiator role.

STEPPING OUTSIDE TO UNDERSTAND CHAIM'S CHANGES OVER TIME

What accounts for Chaim's shift from imitator to initiator? Did he change because I discouraged his early imitation role? Or is it possible that the weeks playing the imitator role had laid the groundwork for his change to the initiator role?

When I was teaching, I had not really understood what in retrospect became so clear. I had lost sight of the importance of imitation as a learning style (Brooke, 1988). I had assumed that imitation was a form of resistance rather than accommodation to what was being taught. As teacher, I did not recognize the extent to which imitation was a beginner's way of interacting and being a member of the group. Like young children who imitate adults to learn how to talk and behave, Chaim's imitation was, I saw later, useful, productive, and possibly even necessary for him to succeed.

Analyzing the class's interactions enabled me to view Chaim's initial imitative style differently and to value rather than diminish his earlier role. Only by analyzing both the content of the talk and the number of conversational turns each topic took did I see that the style of talk he received could be considered strong. Like good writing, the imitative style of talk was to him focused on only one or two major points, was elaborated on in various ways by various speakers, and was summarized or repeated over and over again. With each imitative variation, he heard abstract ideas supported by concrete examples and modeled words. With all this repetition, he had opportunities for reinforcement of ideas as he listened and rehearsals for these ideas as he talked. The repetition gave Chaim numerous occasions to listen to and understand others and to talk and be understood himself. Thus, the imitation, mirrored by and for Chaim, was not an interference but was an opportunity for him to rehearse in aural, oral, and written form. These rehearsals served as a foundation for learning a new kind of conversation he had never experienced before.

Chaim's speech style engaged him in more social interactive speech. According to Vygotsky (1978), the strong relationship between speech and learning means that Chaim's style gave him more opportunities to master his own surroundings through the help of speech. Similar to Vygotsky in his view of speech, Bakhtin (1986) believed that "the more interactions with [others], the better the command of speech genres, [and] the more freely [they were] employed" (p. 80), the more speakers could move on to another role. Thus, the additional speech opportunities that repetition encouraged gave Chaim the models he needed to rehearse for his later role. These rehearsals, like those for any kind of performer, gave Chaim confidence to act the part of the writer and respondent and to move him from his imitator to his initiator role. Imitation, serving as both a rehearsal for and a link to the initiator role, was found to be more productive for Chaim than I had assumed at the time I taught.

STEPPING IN *AND* OUT: IMPLICATIONS FOR COMPOSITION AND TEACHER RESEARCH

In this study, I identified Chaim's unique style of response. I further identified the impact that his style of response had on his own revisions and on the responses that others made to him. Attending to the complex social interactions of individuals responding in groups, I designed the research to reflect more consistently the theories that lay the foundation for collaborative response. In other words, this study's interactive notion of response more accurately reflects sociolinguistic principles: that the variety of responses is complexly shaped by various particular individuals in various contexts and various points in time. Thus, the more we understand the ways that teachers and students read each other as well as their texts, the more we understand what kinds of responses are most helpful or what combinations of individuals constitute effective groups. The more we understand about respondents' individual styles of response, the more responses can be consistent with and effective for particular responding and revising needs. In these ways, this study moves toward an understanding of individuals' roles in the pedagogy of revision and response. It further argues for paying more attention to the individual as a key ingredient in defining effective response.

As teacher, I taught this class and consciously shaped it through my training, beliefs, and knowledge of the field. I also shaped it through my understanding of the students I taught and the genre of college application writing I assigned. I even believed I understood consciously or intuitively most of what was occurring as I taught. Yet by audiotaping the classes and systematically analyzing the tapes, I realized I had *not,* in fact, accurately interpreted the interactions that had occurred. From a researcher's perspective, I saw that I had originally viewed Chaim's imitation as counterproductive. Later, after retrospective and systematic analysis, I saw that his imitative style helped him to rehearse a kind of talk he didn't originally know how to make. Had I to do it over again, I would not have discouraged his imitative talk. Instead, I would have accepted the imitation—and perhaps even encouraged him to imitate more.

This insight was born out of *my* hindsight: my misjudgments and erroneous assumptions placed beside *my* view of the facts from another point in time. Because of that, an outside researcher would have gotten a different view. Trained as both teacher and qualitative researcher, I was not interested in Myers' (1985) suggestion that teacher researchers merely duplicate other quantitative educational research. Nor did I find, as Berthoff (1987) suggests, that I already had the data I needed to "REsearch" or reexamine what had occurred. In fact, I would argue that unless I had made and transcribed audiotapes using well-accepted methods for qualitative research, I would never have realized that I had made erroneous assumptions about Chaim as well as two other students in the group. Only with formal research came the hindsight that I had misperceived a total of three cases out of four! The making of hindsight came from overlapping and intersecting roles: From my experience as a teacher, I was familiar with the students and the day-to-day operations of the class; from my experience as a researcher, I was familiar with the literature and with ways to analyze data in my field. From the intersection of the two, I gained insights, made hindsights, and came to understand deeply what I had falsely presumed I knew.

Had I been provided with this information at the time that I taught, I would have been able to perceive some individuals differently. I would also have been able to develop more effective responses for those particular students in the group. I would have been a more helpful teacher to many students than I now realize I was. From this experience, I argue that including teacher research as part of regular classroom practice (with released time or other practical compensations provided) helps turn after-the-fact hindsights into insights beneficial to the students being studied or taught at the time.

If we rely on researchers to seek answers to only the particular questions that they may have, the researchers may miss out on the information that sits in the seams of disparity between what a teacher believes is occurring and what really is occurring. If we rely on teachers to only teach, without stepping out to reflect on and analyze what is going on, they may believe one thing is occurring when in fact it is not. Thus, without formal procedures to gain a teacher researcher's unique perspective, reams of data may sit uncollected. Without those data, many critical concomitant conclusions will be nearly impossible to reach. Therefore, change in the schools may depend on a merger between teacher and researcher. Yet unless the teacher and researcher are one and the same, important insights may remain hidden or elusive—out of grasp or reach.

• • • • • • • • • • •

Listening to the Voices

Judy Buchanan

JUDY BUCHANAN *has been a fourth-grade classroom teacher in the School District of Philadelphia for 17 years, most recently at the Samuel J. Powel School. A member of the Philadelphia Teachers Learning Cooperative since 1978, she was also the first Philadelphia Writing Project Scholar (1986–1987) and is now a director of the Philadelphia Writing Project. In addition, Buchanan has served for many years as a cooperating teacher for Project START. Her publications include articles in The Voice and Work in Progress (both Philadelphia Writing Project publications) as well as Teacher As Learner: Working in a Community of Teachers (NCRE, in press).*

I have always thought of myself as a teacher who listens carefully to the voices of my students as well as other teachers. This article tells the story of how one fourth-grade student, Anwar, helped me to learn in a new way about the importance of questions and reflections in my classroom. This learning took place as I observed Anwar in the classroom, raised questions about his work, and met with groups of teachers to share. Many strands of questions and reflections—Anwar's, my own, and other teachers—were woven together throughout the school year. Having time for thoughtful conversation and reflection significantly altered my understanding of Anwar as a student and my perspective on teacher inquiry as a model for staff development.

THE CONTEXT

I have been a third- to fourth-grade classroom teacher in Philadelphia for 17 years. As a young white woman new to the area, I had beginning years of teaching that were shaped and supported by experienced teachers asking questions, offering advice, and talking about their students. This talk occurred in after-school meetings of the Philadelphia Teachers Learning Cooperative, in lunchtime conversations, in rushing past each other in hallways, and on the playground during recess duty. As my own teaching matured and developed, the dialogue continued. Reflecting on my work as a teacher with other teachers became a steady companion to the active life of a classroom teacher with sometimes as many as 37 students to teach. Five years ago, I took a sabbatical year at the University of Pennsylvania Graduate School of Education to try to change the balance of action and reflection in my life. For 1 year, as the first Philadelphia Writing Project Scholar, I thought I would read and think about, reflect on, and try to make sense of my life as an elementary classroom teacher. The sabbatical year, although wonderful, was for a variety of reasons just as frenetic as my teaching years had been, but I did return to my classroom the following September with new ideas to talk about with my colleagues and new questions to reflect on within the four walls of my school.

I returned to my small elementary school and to the third- to fourth-grade team-taught classroom that I had shared before my sabbatical year. The class had 57 students, and Katie Zimring, my coteacher, and I divided the students into small working groups for various subjects, thematic research projects, and hands-on activities. The class was a high-energy group with many demanding students who covered the full range of academic abilities as well as being racially and culturally diverse. Although we worked together for most of the school day, we divided the children into grade groups for math instruction.

THE BEGINNING: ANWAR'S INITIAL QUESTION AND MY INITIAL INQUIRY WITH TEACHERS

On the 2nd day of school, Anwar, a fourth-grader, asked a question during math class that I noted, answered, and filed away to think more about later. *"There's just one thing. What exactly does p. mean?"* I had written an assignment on the board after a math lesson using the abbreviation for page, and Anwar was uncertain as to what to do. The question surprised me. Had I forgotten what most fourth-graders knew after being away from the classroom for a year? Why didn't anyone else speak up? Anwar was able to complete the math assignment without difficulty. His question intrigued me. So, when I was asked to conduct a staff development meeting for a group of elementary teachers on "expressive" writing at the end of October, I thought immediately of Anwar and decided to focus on his writing.

I hoped that through studying one student's writing, teachers would be able to ask questions about both the writing and the writer, an opportunity that often seemed to be missing from teachers' professional lives. I had been uncomfortable for some time with staff development that dealt with writing but did not look at the larger context of the student and the classroom. Through a dialogue with teachers, I also hoped to learn how others viewed Anwar's work and what questions seemed important to him.

I began with a brief description of Anwar and my classroom, noting that he was a tall, handsome African-American boy who loved sports and asked lots and lots of questions during the school day. Anwar had repeated first grade at our school because he had a slow start in learning to read. He was a good math student and was well liked by his classmates, although he didn't seem to have any special friend in the room.

Then the group shifted its focus from listening to my brief comments to looking at Anwar's writing, which had been produced in three contexts: a literature response log, a writing folder of free-writing pieces, and a learning log of observations and questions.

The piece that Anwar wrote in his learning log on the 1st day of school is reproduced as follows exactly as he wrote it. As we read this piece closely, we noticed Anwar's honesty and his willingness to write even when he was not sure of the correct spelling for some words:

SEPTEMBER 11, 1987
The First Day of School
I felt very narvise.
I had to met new teacher and new stutents.
When I met new chids we had fun.
at the end I had a nice day.

We also looked at several pieces of free writing about his neighborhood football team and the monarch butterfly in the classroom and at his observations of the moon as written in his learning log. The final piece that we studied, reproduced below with my response, was Anwar's first literature log entry and was written as a response to an assignment to read a "chapter book" and write to me about the story.

OCTOBER 10, 1987/*LITERATURE LOG*
Herny Aaron
Dear T. Judy I read about a famas baseball player but I stared in the middle of the book because the middle was butter then the frist page. When I was reading I saw a intresting part about the book it said that there were a part about a left fielder hit a dirve to center fiedl he ran so fast that when he slide into the base he never got back up he boak three places in his leg the next day the manger of the braves said to Hank that is up to him. When hank hit the ball he would hit con of funny because when he hit left haned his right would be at the bottom and the left hand would be on the top. One day when the braves play a tem Hank had a hard time hitting in a

ining Hank hit a drive lke bobby thompson did now Hid boak his ankle manger of the braves said that he didn't no what do do because both of his men where gone so manger of the braves had a hard time playing and wining because he didn't a good left fielder by the season the could have bobby and Henry Aaron. The End

Dear Anwar,
Thanks for telling me so much about the book you read about Hank Aaron. I sometimes start in the middle of books, too.
    I want to be sure that I understand the interesting part you told me about. Were Hank Aaron and Bobby Thompson injured in the same way?
    What book are you reading now? There are some good sports books by Matt Christopher in the IMC if you are looking for a good book.
    From Teacher Judy

Dear T. Judy,
no Hank did not get injured in his leg he got injured in his ankle but his friend Bobby Tompson his got and three diffrent places but hank boak his leg in one places

These excerpts from Anwar's learning and literature logs gave us a starting point as we worked to see who Anwar was as a student. They provided the focus for a rich discussion about classroom structures that might foster student writing and about what to do about the mechanics of Anwar's pieces. The teachers were surprised by the increase in the length of his writing and noted his willingness to take risks, both on the 1st day of school and when he started in the middle of the book. They also noted his perseverance with what appeared to be a difficult text. Most of their questions were about my practice: What was I doing in the classroom? What kind of lessons was I giving? What had caused this development in Anwar's writing?

REFLECTIONS

This opportunity to look collectively at Anwar's writing excited me. His work raised important questions for me and for the other teachers who studied it. How much time did he spend writing each day? How did he approach each assignment? Did he always take risks as a learner? How much revision and editing should he be doing?

    I realized that I had been developing for several years a rationale for my classroom practice with fourth-graders and their writing. I had decided that I would help students to revise, edit, and publish specific pieces of teacher-assigned writing but that I would leave their free-writing selections in draft form unless they requested to work on them further. I developed this approach after many unsuccessful attempts to conference with my students about the free-writing pieces they produced. I wondered whether free writing was a kind of play that students engaged in with written language. Adult interventions seemed unwelcome, and although the students enjoyed sharing their work with their peers, they were not particularly interested in changing their stories. However, I did not have this same struggle with teacher-assigned writing. It did not seem to be only a question of my skill in conducting writing conferences, but also a question of audience and purpose. "Their" writing did not need "fixing," but they were willing to revise and edit specific assignments.

MID-YEAR DISCOVERIES: HEARING ANWAR'S VOICE

In January, I had the opportunity to explore Anwar's work with a different group of teachers. This helped me once again to view his development through others' eyes. This time we looked closely at his writing about Native Americans: both at a piece that was not revised and at his notes and two drafts comparing two Native American folktales.

The unrevised piece, written in December, let us see how much Anwar had learned about a particular tribe of Native Americans:

Back in the old days there where Indians. the men indians didn't do as much except killing buffalo and the womens would do everything else. When it would be time to move the women could take the tipi down in about 5 minutes and they could set it back up in the same time. the skin was made out of buffalo hides to cover the tipi and the womens was in charge and they could take down anytime they want and the floor were made out of Bare earth the buffalo hides was so ston [strong]

The teachers noted his strong beginnings, evident in much of his writing. His spelling, even in unedited writing, was improving. He seemed to write in one breath, and periods along with some capital letters were often missing. Yet he had a clear sense of introduction and often a clear structure to his pieces. Together, we explored some of the same issues about my teaching and his writing that the first group had raised. How did he have so much to say about particular topics? In what ways was I helping him to develop the needed mechanics in his writing?

Anwar's brainstorming notes, written as the first step of an assignment to compare two Native American folktales, provided us with a record of his thinking:

Arrow to the Sun	*Gift of the SacredDog*
same	same
It is a quest	It is a quest
father	buffalo

It has it in the End	It has it in the End
father	horses-buffalo
<u>Diffrent</u>	<u>Diffrent</u>
Diffrent tribes	Diffrent tribes
Pueblo	Sioux
It doesn't have horses	But it does
no Dog	a dog

The notes show how Anwar worked to find similarities and differences in these texts. *The Gift of the Sacred Dog* is not about dogs at all, but there is a dog in the illustration on the cover. Although Anwar listed a dog as one of the differences in his initial comparison, he deleted it from the short paragraph he wrote about the two stories. His final draft of the comparison of the two folktales was sparse but clear and accurate:

I read *Arrow to the Sun* and *Gift of the Sacred Dog*. They are both folktales. They both are a quest. The boy in *Arrow to the Sun* looks for his father and the boy in *gift of the sacred dog* looks for buffalo herds. They both are diffrent. They both come from diffrent tribes. *Arrow to the Sun* comes from Peublo and *Gift of the sacred dog* comes from sioux.

Even after conferencing, revising, and editing this piece, Anwar made errors in copying over his final draft. However, several teachers thought that this piece was a turning point in Anwar's writing because he structured it so tightly.

When reading aloud a free-writing piece at the January workshop, I was struck again by the differences in Anwar's formal writing assignments and the pieces he seemed to "write in one breath." I read aloud only the beginning of a piece that went on for five pages:

PlayOff NFC wild card
Last week the Vikings won over the saints in hearthbreaker they played metradome thats the home town of the saints but the saints scored first so the score was 7 to nothing but the vikings scored 3 points with a field goal so the score was 7 to 3 so the saints had the ball for a whole but they didn't score another T.D. . . .

In this piece, Anwar described the sports event play by play, without a period but with exacting and accurate detail, until the game ends. In this piece, as in "Back in the old says," we could hear his voice and the powerful and folksy introductions he used in his work. The teachers were surprised by the range of his writing, and they wanted to know how I found time for the students to do so much writing. I wanted to know more about how Anwar was learning to express himself clearly in so many different genres.

REFLECTIONS

Anwar clearly knew how to change styles when writing a report for a teacher and when writing for himself or his peers. What had he learned about public and private discourse? Was writing in all of these various contexts what was strengthening him as a writer? How was he incorporating the feedback he received from his peers and his teachers? I wondered about the connection between Anwar's strong voice in free writing and his constant questioning in the classroom. How was he able to move from speech to writing in his free-writing pieces and still maintain his voice? Did he ask many questions outside of the classroom?

My observations revealed that Anwar was also using writing time to share his stories with his peers. He developed a friendship with another boy in the classroom, who had also repeated first grade, loved sports and reading, needed help in math, and wrote long adventure stories in his free-writing folder. One result of this friendship was that Anwar asked fewer questions of his teachers and began to find support from students as well as adults in the classroom.

Classroom projects during the winter included biographies and autobiographies. Pursuing his interest in sports stars, Anwar chose to read about Jackie Robinson, Willie Mays, and Jim Thorpe. He often seemed to have an urgent question about the texts he was reading. After finishing the biographies of Robinson and Mays, for example, Anwar asked, "Did they ever play against each other?"

I was beginning to see connections between Anwar's ability to observe the world around him (as revealed in his writings about the monarch butterfly and the moon), his constant questioning, and his ability to reveal his thoughts and voice in his written work. When I shared his work with other teachers, they were always interested in the interrelationships of his growth as a writer and my practice as a teacher. I found it difficult, however, to convey to others my growing understanding of how important my short, often hurried conversations seemed to be in supporting Anwar as a student. I was also becoming more convinced that working with a student on a few pieces of assigned writing over time was a powerful tool for improving the student's overall writing and that writing freely in many genres made the work on particular pieces more effective.

END OF THE YEAR: LOOKING BACK AT ANWAR'S WRITING

The final thematic unit of the year was a schoolwide study of Chinese history, folklore, and art, part of a whole-school focus on the literature of different cultures. My fourth-graders had studied the literature and culture of Greece, Africa, and China in first grade; Native American and Greek literature again in second grade; and African-American and African literature and culture in third grade.

As with other units in the classroom, the students had writing assignments with many topic choices about Chinese literature and culture. I structured the classroom writing assignments so that students wrote in several genres and also did library research on topics related to China (e.g., the Great Wall, ancient China, the giant panda, symbols in Chinese art, and characters in Chinese folktales). Anwar wrote a fable that follows, as well as a report about pandas. He chose to do his final library project on Chinese folktales, writing his own version of a story about Monkey, an important character in Chinese folklore.

The Story of Panda and Rabbit
Once there was a smart rabbit and he liked running and when he was running a mean panda came up and they bumped into each other. Panda said, "watch where you're going" and rabbit said, panda, you watch where you are going." Panda said, "OK tough guy challenge me to a race." Rabbit said, "you're on." Peacock and every other chinese animal came. Peacock was the judge. Peacock said, "On your mark, get set, go."

Rabbit had the lead and panda got very mad and his face got red and panda jumped into a tree and jumped out of the tree on rabbit. He threw rabbit 4 feet and rabbit started to run but now panda was in the lead. But then rabbit said to himself "I'm smart. Maybe I can do a trick." Rabbit stopped and disguised his voice as panda and said, "come get me snake." And snake started to slither to panda and panda climbed a tree and that slowed panda down and rabbit caught up with panda and won the race. Panda got down from the tree as snake left and said, "OK you win but I hate losing."

Moral: Don't be mean. If you try to trick others, they'll try to trick you.

A third group of teachers looked with me at the body of Anwar's work for the year. They viewed the panda and rabbit folktale as one of his best because it brought together many of his strengths as a writer. His voice, his use of dialogue and colorful language, and his clear sequencing of events were described as evidence of his growth. Several teachers recognized the influence of trickster stories from other cultures and wanted to know more about the connection between reading and writing in my classroom.

REFLECTIONS

As I shared Anwar's work for the final time during the school year, I was intrigued by my colleagues' perspectives on a student I had now come to know so well. Different pieces of his work stood out for different teachers, but for all of them, the overall body of his work was a compelling testimony to a student's willingness to persevere and to experiment, to explore new genres, and to share with different audiences. Just as I had first noticed Anwar because of his questions in the classroom, other teachers felt they had come to know him through his voice in his writing.

School success was not easy for Anwar. Through looking closely at his work and reflecting with others, I found some new ways to support his learning in the classroom. I was left with more questions to think about after a year of looking at Anwar's writing with different groups of teachers. How did all of Anwar's questions help him as a student? How could I develop more structures to support students' questions and to create opportunities for dialogue in the midst of the often rushed and fragmented school day? Would Anwar be able to hold onto the gains he had made in reading and writing when he went to middle school? (After several years, the answer seems to be yes. He has been a steady learner, an average to above-average student, well liked by his classmates, and elected to a class office.)

Looking back, I see that I learned as much from teachers' questions about the writing program in my classroom as I did from Anwar's questions. Focusing on one student's work with groups of teachers made staff development sessions into opportunities for teacher inquiry about students as well as the larger contexts of classrooms and schools. The opportunity to ask questions and to reflect on one's work is essential to learning regardless of the age of the learner. Sharing my questions with my colleagues and in turn listening to more voices enlarged and deepened the conversation about teaching.

• • • • • • • • • • • •

Parents and Teachers as Co-Investigators

Robin Headman

ROBIN HEADMAN *is a fourth-grade teacher at Marshall Street School in the Norristown Area School District, Norristown, Pennsylvania. She has taught for 24 years in grades four through seven and has participated in numerous curriculum committees in her school district. She presented her research during the teacher researcher segment of the Ethnography and Education Forum in 1991.*

To begin to understand the complexity of children's literacy in and out of school from the perspectives of parents, teachers, and children, parents of students in my fourth-grade classroom joined me in a coinvestigation. We observed and documented the children's literacy experiences and met together weekly to analyze and interpret, from our diverse perspectives, the experiences of their children. We were creating a new relationship as researchers together.

The study had two phases with two groups of parents. This text describes and discusses only the first phase. It sets the study within the literature that analyzes home and school literacy models, identifies the purposes or questions that each participant had at the outset, describes the methodology, analyzes the dialogue with one family, and suggests implications for my own as well as others' theory and practice.

HOME-SCHOOL LITERACY MODELS

As a classroom teacher but not a parent, I wonder about the usefulness to parents of the information that schools impart to them. Frequently, parents receive and ask for suggestions of ways they can help their children at home with reading and writing. These suggestions may come from a teacher's experiences with her own children, from the practices that the teacher has deemed successful in her classroom, or from the literature that correlates home characteristics and student success in school. The agenda often appears to be a reproduction in the home of literacy at school with suggestions for parents to duplicate the school's dimensions of literacy. Auerbach (1989) labels this a "transmission model" that "starts with the needs, problems, and practices that educators identify, and then transfers skills or practices to parents in order to inform their interactions with children" (p. 169). The transmission model is a deficit model: It assumes that the home is not providing the appropriate literate experience for the child.

Many studies that connect family literacy with school literacy report that the quality of a family's interactions around reading and writing has an impact on the children's literacy learning in school (Anderson, Wilson, & Fielding, 1988; Heath, 1983; Teale, 1981). In response, some of the interventions for reading in particular attempt to bring the home and the school together by instructing parents in how to participate in specified literacy tasks (Tizard, Schofields, & Hewison, 1982; Topping, 1987). They attempt to remedy a deficit in the home or in the child rather than to increase home-school communication and create a shared knowledge base of the student's literacy development in different contexts.

The problem is that many of the current interactions between parents and teachers *assume a transmission model* and may place limitations in terms of what is possible. There needs to be a transactional relationship between school and home that is clearly missing in practice and in the literature. Auerbach (1989) suggests a "social-contextual model of family literacy that asks, How can we draw on parents' knowledge and experience to inform instruction? rather than, How can we transfer school practices into home contexts?" (p. 177). The school needs to know how families use literacy and how parents interact with their children around literacy tasks. Literacy acquisition and development are processes that are negotiated through interpersonal relationships in the home, in the school, and between the home and the school. These processes are far more complex than a correlation of certain teaching or parenting behaviors with student outcomes at school.

We know that learning in and out of school is not identical (Resnick, 1987) and that families construct different relationships with their children's schools, based on their perceptions of schooling and learning, that have an impact on the children's school achievement (Clark, 1983; Connell, Ashenden, Kessler, & Dowsett, 1982). We know about the literacy practices of some school-aged children in the home (Heath, 1983; Taylor, 1983; Taylor & Dorsey-Gaines, 1988). What we need to know is more about how children, families, and schools make connections between literacy learning in and out of school. We need to know more about ways in which home-school interactions around literacy learning can be more collaborative, drawing on the knowledge and experience of the home as well as the school (Auerbach, 1989).

OUR QUESTIONS OR GOALS

My interest in this study grows out of my belief that schools often inappropriately assume that parents, especially those of children who are having difficulty in school, are not providing adequate literacy experiences for their children and that the school ought to help them accordingly. Many times in parent-teacher conferences, however, parents have shared with me brief anecdotes of their personal literate interactions with their children that would seem to disconfirm this assumption. I wanted to know more about parents' beliefs about literacy and learning, about how they interact with their children in relation to literacy and learning, and about the nature of the children's literacy experiences out of school. Furthermore, I expected that if parents and I spent more time discussing our various perspectives on literacy and learning, our observations of the children's literacy experiences, and our critical reflections on our interactions with the children, we would generate a new knowledge base from which we could help each other to provide appropriate experiences for the children at school as well as at home.

Each of the parents who joined in our study had unique purposes for participating. One mother wanted to find a way to get her son interested in reading:

I mean, that's my biggest hope, to spark an interest, to get him, what is it they say, turned on to books, turned on to reading. And if you read, you're gonna write.

Her husband acknowledged a similar purpose. Another mother noticed a big difference between her daughter's reading at home and in school and wanted to better understand it:

I notice a big difference in I know that she has a problem with reading, but there is a difference with her reading in school than when she reads at home. . . . This is the only way I can, I myself can see what's going on and try to understand what this is all about.

The third mother noticed how her son had improved in reading and thought that what he did at home might be interesting to my research:

I think I said yes because I thought it would help you mostly and that because I think [my son] went up a lot in reading because of these crazy things that he does at home.

Our questions or goals for participating in this research were not alike. Each was important and had an impact on the research design. Initially, my questions structured a format for observation, but the parent's goals helped to direct our observations, reflection, and analysis.

METHODS

This first phase of the study took place during the spring semester in my fourth-grade classroom. The school, which was in the greater Philadelphia area, housed approximately 600 students in grades one through five, a population that was in diverse ethnic and socioeconomic neighborhoods. The reading and writing levels of the students in the fourth grade ranged from grades two to four, levels that were primarily determined by district reading and writing assessments. This diversity of background and reported literacy ability was reflected in my classroom as well as in the families that participated in the study. In this first phase, I extended an invitation to all parents in my classroom to participate. Six families responded affirmatively, and three completed the study.

Once a week for 7 weeks, the parents and I met together. Two of those meetings, one in the middle and one at the conclusion, were combined meetings with all participating parents. At our initial meetings, we agreed to use first names to help us move away from any authority we might attribute, by title, to each other's role. During this first phase, the children were not required to attend. It was left to the discretion of each parent. For the most part, the children did not come to our meetings.

Between meetings, the parents and I each kept a diary of the children's literacy experiences that we noticed that week. The format was open with three columns: "Dates/Times," "Literacy Experiences," and "Comments." What was written was up to each participant rather than prescribed. During this time, I had a student teacher, which freed me to take notes while I observed the children.

Initially, the parents expressed concern about whether they were writing the right things and guilt that their notes weren't as detailed as mine. Over the time of the study, these feelings seemed to diminish. I always tried to affirm in our conversation that the parents should record what was significant to them. In fact, they identified a distinct difference between their diaries and mine.

In addition to the shared copies of our literacy diaries, data consisted of the transcripts of our conversations at each of our meetings. In this dialogue, much more about the children's literacy experiences at home emerged than parents had recorded in the diaries.

AN ANALYTICAL FRAMEWORK

One framework for analysis of these transcripts comes from Lytle's (1991) research on the assessment of adult literacy. She identifies four dimensions of literacy learning: plans, practices, beliefs, and processes. Each of her dimensions also characterizes many of the statements that the parents in our study made about their children's literacy.

DIMENSION 1: *Plans* are the adults' short and long term goals and the nature of their involvement in decisions that affect the attainment of these goals.

PARENTS' RESPONSES: Maybe I can get him [her son] to read Poe, *Murders of the Rue Morgue*, or O'Henry.

I did some thinking about what we could be doing in the home. I think that would be, well to encourage the writing more.

DIMENSION 2: *Practices* are the range and variation of literacy and literacy-related activities adults engage in in their day-to-day lives.

PARENTS' RESPONSES: She [her daughter] buys little pads all shapes and sizes and she also gets the pads that the waitresses use when they take your order. And she'll write down each person's menu and calculate how much each thing costs and total it up.

DIMENSION 3: Beliefs are adults' theories or concepts of language, literacy, learning and teaching.

PARENTS' RESPONSES: I feel that with some of the Nintendo games, some of the strategy that you have to use, it really leads you to think.

We [at an earlier combined parents' meeting] were wondering if you [teacher] would have more one on one with students and things like that. I don't, I didn't really agree with that myself. . . . It's not you and one person. It's you and the whole rotten world. And so you have to be able to compete and catch up.

DIMENSION 4: *Processes* are the adult learner's repertoire of moves and strategies for managing practices considered purposeful in their lives.

PARENTS' RESPONSES: He [her son] wanted me to tell you [teacher] that he doesn't need a dictionary when he doesn't know how to spell a word. He can find it somewhere. He can read it. He might not be able to spell, but he can find it somewhere else and then he can copy it from there.

To understand parents' perspectives on their children's literacy, it is essential to identify the beliefs that frame them. As the teacher, I did not want to impose a belief system. Instead, I wanted to uncover the beliefs that were important to each parent. Throughout our discussions, I consciously guarded against initiating statements about beliefs and waited until such statements emerged from the parents before asking for an explanation or elaboration of them. The parents explicitly stated beliefs about literacy and implicitly assumed beliefs in their plans, practices, and processes of literate interactions with their children.

Auerbach (1990) notes the importance of uncovering themes that are significant to the participants of family literacy programs and notes that these themes often emerge spontaneously. So it was in our coinvestigation. Our focus was the literacy of the children in and out of school, but as the parents talked about school, literacy, and their children's experiences, their own beliefs became salient features in the decisions they made for their children's literacy learning, in their expectations of their children and their children's school, and in their description or definitions of language, literacy, learning, and teaching.

I will focus in the remainder of this text on the beliefs that emerged from one set of parents, whom I'll call Joe and Doris Preston. Before this study, I had not met either parent, although I had spoken to Doris a number of times over the phone, usually in relation to some homework that her son, whom I'll call Eugene, did not complete. Neither of the parents attended parent-teacher conferences or other programs, such as Open House, that the school sponsored. Doris ran a small child-care service in her home, and Joe specialized in tree care. Earlier in their lives, Doris wrote cartoons for a local newspaper, and Joe earned a degree in German literature. Doris describes herself as an "avid reader," especially of science fiction, and Joe states that he is a regular reader of the newspaper. These factors had an impact on the Prestons' definitions of reading and writing and on their beliefs about teaching and learning.

DEFINITIONS OF WRITING AND READING

Joe defines good writing as coherent, cogent, and grammatically correct, a characteristic he finds infrequent in many students' writing. He equates good writing with good speaking:

To write is to me like speaking. I mean you're not going to use bad grammar and incomplete sentences.

He distinguishes between writing that is copying as "mechanical" and writing that is composing as "cognitive." Furthermore, he gives writing with a word processor a different name and description: "wordsmithing," a process in which the writer uses the computer to "delete or add at will," to "craft . . . without having to erase and crumple paper," and to "finely hone" a text.

Doris defines writing as "making words." In particular, she did not describe Eugene's pictures or cartoons in the notes he sends her as writing until he added word balloons. She questions Joe's focus on the correctness of writing: "Let 'em go. Let 'em write." She would first have children write something down and then teach them how to improve it. She describes her own early experience with writing when her father gave her a word or a sentence, telling her to write a story around it. "I started by writing, but not by writing well."

Joe confirms a tension between creativity and correctness: "But don't stifle creativity." In fact, in other contexts, Joe refers to Eugene's writing as a means of expression. Examples include his using check marks to give a "feeling of authority" and saying, "Writing a book was a chance for Eugene to express himself."

Eugene's parents' disagreement about writing is not unlike the process/product perspectives in writing research (Delpit, 1986; Freedman et al., 1987). Doris challenged Joe's emphasis on writing well. To her, there was a difference between "writing" and "writing well." Similarly, writing research in the 1970s focused on the process of writing as a response to limitations in previous research that focused primarily on the product. Joe acknowledged the dilemma by attempting to integrate form and creativity.

Doris defines reading comprehension as being able to tell what you read. It is more than reading with an expressive voice sounding as if the text has meaning. "Looking at" a text may or may not be "reading" in Doris's definition. Some texts, like a cereal box, can be read by looking at them, but others, like a fishing book, demand more than looking at. In addition, when she asks Eugene, "Well, are you reading it?" she differentiates between Eugene reading the text, someone reading the text to him, or the whole class reading the text. The latter two cases are, according to Doris, *"reading in a structured environment . . . because it's part of the curriculum."*

Although Doris did not elaborate, it would seem that she distinguishes between how one reads based on the purpose for reading. Reading a cereal box by looking at it may simply be a way to pass the time at the breakfast table, but looking at a fishing book would not be sufficient to understand a detailed explanation of fishing. Also, reading for someone else's purpose, including the school's, is not the same as reading for oneself.

Doris's beliefs about reading comprehension are consistent with descriptions in *Becoming a Nation of Readers* (Anderson, Hiebert, Scott, & Wilkinson, 1985). First, reading is more than identifying letters, words, and sentences (p. 8). It is more than knowing the tone or inflection of syntax. Doris made this distinction when she described her older daughter as having a learning difficulty: *"a loose wire . . . she can read anything. . . . But it's not—She can't tell you what she read. The comprehension is gone. . . . She just reads words."* Second, how skilled readers read depends partly on the complexity of the text and their purpose for reading (p. 13). Looking at the cereal box suited the text's complexity and reader's purpose. Third, independent silent reading correlates with improved reading (p. 76). Doris placed a higher significance on reading silently for oneself than she did on reading as a class or the teacher reading to the class.

Doris also believes in a reading/writing connection:

If you read you'll write.
Reading and writing go hand in hand. Somebody that reads well writes well.

However, both Doris and Joe hold more importance for reading:

By not reading Eugene will end up far behind.
You have to read to do anything . . . to get anywhere.
If you read you can go anywhere, imagine you're anything, be anyone, do anything.
Reading is the key to other subjects.

Doris and Joe make no statements like these in regard to writing.

Doris and Joe seem to hold a linear model of reading and writing development (Chall, 1983; Emig, 1985). When Joe said that writing was like speaking, he assumed that speaking with correct grammar and sentence construction preceded good writing. When Doris said that people who read well write well, she assumed that good reading preceded good writing, a belief consistent with research that correlates writing with reading development (Flood & Lapp, 1987).

BELIEFS ABOUT TEACHING AND LEARNING

Doris and Joe share several examples of the ways that they and peers affect their children's literacy learning. Joe gives the example of how the grammar of his oldest daughter is deteriorating because she is learning bad grammar from her peers that is not being corrected in school. Although not giving a specific instance in their family, he generically describes how children imitate their parents: "Kids when they're little are like dad. You know, daddy's got the newspaper." Doris shares that Eugene copies the cartoon character that she had published in a local newspaper. He maintains an interest in cartooning as the comics are the one section of the newspaper that his parents have observed him reading, as he cartoons notes to his mother, and as he creates cartoons for school newspapers.

Neither Doris nor Joe believes that you can force a child to read or that a favorable environment is all that is necessary. Joe says that it is necessary to "cultivate a special interest." That process of cultivating may be in what Vygotsky (1978) labels the zone of proximal development, the distance between the child's actual developmental level and his or her potential level of development.

At church, Eugene's parents help him to follow the order of service. To keep track of the sequence of events in the church service, Eugene tears corners off his program and marks each place in his hymn book. Doris describes how she taught Eugene instead to mark two ahead by folding the program in half. This was a more socially acceptable practice to Eugene's parents, who described his program as looking like a rat had gotten to it. In addition, Doris whispers to Eugene during the service to help him when he loses his place in a hymn, a text she describes as hard to follow because of its recursive format in print. She is guiding his learning within the "zone of proximal development" (Vygotsky, 1978).

CHANGE

During our 7-week coinvestigation, the Prestons changed some of their beliefs and raised questions about others. Joe, for example, broadened his definition of literacy:

> Interacting with text whether being read to, reading alone, or reading with a partner.
> You don't think of things being literacy when they are.

Doris commented on how she didn't think of the times when she answered Eugene's many questions as being instances of learning. The process was an unconscious one. Our discussions, however, enabled her to bring to the forefront the value of this process.

She began to question the images of reading that she was expressing to Eugene. Although she finds reading to be a form of relaxation, she wonders whether she is really communicating that message to Eugene. Saying that reading is fun is not enough:

> [It] may be a bad thing to associate reading and homework. . . . If it's in Eugene's mind that when I'm telling him to read it's work, it's not fun.

Probably the most significant change was in the beliefs that Eugene's parents had about his reading. During our first meeting, they described the voracity and interests of an older brother's and sister's reading. They gave no examples of Eugene's reading. Instead, they made statements such as:

I'm a very avid pusher of reading. It hasn't rubbed off on Eugene.

If I thought standing on my head would do it, I'd do it; but I don't think that would. Poor Eugene.

I guess somewhere you have to find that spark that will get them. I just don't know what it is with Eugene.

I'm trying to think if he even reads the cereal box, but I can't even—He doesn't even read the funnies.

At our final meeting, however, Doris and Joe made the following statements:

I never realized how much he did read. He's my closet reader.

Eugene's more aware now of making certain connections between reading and writing. And also the fact that we were interested that he feels more free to talk to us now maybe than he could before.

There was a distinct change in my belief about the relationship of Doris and Joe with Eugene and the school, a change that is not recorded in the dialogue of the transcripts. Before this study, I wondered about the sincerity of Eugene's parents about his education. They did not come for conferences, and Eugene frequently did not hand in his homework. In the conversation that we shared, however, it emerged that Doris did not have a driver's license and refused to be "stood up" by the local cab service anymore. In addition, she ran a small child-care service in her home. She did not come to conferences due to transportation and other responsibilities, not because she was not interested in her child's learning. In fact, she described in our meetings many cases of activities that she created within their family for her children to learn new things, particularly scientific. I began this study surprised at the Prestons' interest in participating, thinking that they probably wouldn't come. However, in fact, they committed to the study and engaged in a continual reflective analysis of their son's literacy at home.

PARENTS AND TEACHERS TOGETHER

This has been an analysis of just one segment of our coinvestigation. Had we not taken the time to investigate together, I might not have known of the ways that the Prestons contributed to their son's literacy learning, and they might not have realized the variety of literacy experiences that their son practiced.

The parents and I had entered into a new relationship in an attempt to create a new dialogue to understand children's literacy in and out of school. Our purpose was to learn together, not to change each other. What the parents shared enriched my analysis of observations at school and vice versa. We began to see the children's literacy through new lenses—lenses that we ground into a sharper focus or a wider angle.

Through our coinvestigation, we were generating a "social-contextual model" (Auerbach, 1989) of home-school literacy that has implications for decisions that parents and teachers might make about their children's literacy experiences. Together, parents and teacher might see strengths of interactions in the home or school context, ways that they might mesh, and ways that they might be distinct. Together, parents and teachers might find new ways to talk about children's literacy, new ways to interact with children, new relationships between the home and the school, or new questions to ask about children's literacy in and out of school. We will need coinvestigations to add to our understanding of the complex relationship of home-school literacy. Alternatives to traditional parent-teacher conferences might be explored to provide structures for a transactional and more substantive dialogue between parents and teachers.

We as educators should not assume that *we* need to tell parents what to do to help their children learn. Nor should parents assume that *they* don't know what the school thinks they should do. Rather, by dialoguing together, parents and teachers can *both* gain a richer understanding of children's literacy. Of course, we will each need to have eyes that see through one another's lenses and ears that hear one another's voices. That may, for a time, place us in problematic, uncertain, or unconventional situations; however, as we continue to dialogue and respect one another's contributions to the conversation, we will together create a new lens and voice to observe, discuss, and plan for children's literacy in and out of school.

● ● ● ● ● ● ● ● ● ● ●

Great Expectations

Kathleen E. Wunner

KATHLEEN E. WUNNER *prepared to be a teacher in Glasgow, Scotland, where she taught for 6 years before coming to this country in 1976. For the next 16 years, she was a classroom teacher in the Tredyffrin Easttown School District, where she taught first grade and was involved in staff development. She described and analyzed the induction experience of new teachers in this school district for her doctoral dissertation completed at the Graduate School of Education at the University of Pennsylvania in 1991. Wunner is currently the head of the Lower School at the Haverford School, an independent college preparatory school for boys in Haverford, Pennsylvania, where she and her colleagues are actively pursuing their interest in teacher research.*

The 1st year of teaching has always had a particular interest for me. From my own anxious 1st year to the second "1st" year 6 years later when I immigrated to the United States from Scotland, through 20 years of supporting ex-student teachers who would call for help from their new assignments in Florida or Ohio, the 1st year of teaching has held an enduring fascination. As a teacher researcher, my area of interest lay not only in my classroom but in the broader arena of the school district and other teachers' classrooms. I studied the induction of new teachers in five elementary schools in one district.

INDUCTION

By 1986, 31 states in this country had mandated that school districts provide specific programs for new teachers in their 1st year of teaching. These programs are now generally known as induction programs. In the pages that follow, I present an interpretation of the process of the induction of new teachers in one suburban school district. Ryan (1970) states that "the beginning teacher must live by the expectations of others" (p. 185). I suggest that it is not only the new teacher who approaches the 1st year of teaching with great expectations of induction but also the school district and the profession in general.

The study was carried out over the course of 1 full academic year, with data gathered before the opening of school and collected finally in the last weeks of the school year. As a classroom teacher turned researcher, I solved the problem of time for data gathering by taking a one-semester sabbatical. The data were collected through participant observation at workshops and meetings, extensive interviewing, and collection of all documents pertaining to the program.

THE EXPERIENCE OF DISEQUILIBRIUM

It is well recognized that professionals at the beginning of their careers or in new appointments live through a period of what I call *professional disequilibrium* while they come to grips with new tasks and a new culture of work. This disequilibrium means coping with change, experiencing a lack of certainty, and having to struggle to achieve personal and professional balance and security of identity in a new situation. Disequilibrium describes a time of questioning, seeking, and reevaluating. The process of working through this phase of professional development is similar to what M. Scott Peck (1978) discusses when, talking of life in general, he describes a "map of reality" that a person mentally draws to allow him- or herself to "negotiate the terrain of life." During this period, which I describe as professional disequilibrium, teachers have to adjust and redraw their "reality map," a process that Peck characterizes as "frightening, almost overwhelming" (p. 44).

In the next few years, our schools will face far more professional disequilibrium than they have had to address in the past. We should not be surprised to find that more programs and policies aimed specifically at this stage of staff development are being initiated all over the country. However, the situation is not quite as simple as hiring new teachers and then providing them with some in-service support. Other factors impinge on these programs, not the least being that these programs are being formulated and implemented in a climate of reform. In this climate, the problem of large numbers of inexperienced teachers entering the schools is compounded by recent concern for quality in education. School districts now have to face a growing number of new teachers at the same time that they are responding to a decade of criticism and demand for reform. The traditional response to a labor shortage in education has been to sacrifice quality for quantity. Historically, a teacher shortage has been met by lowering standards of entry into the profession. As Goodlad (1990) notes, "Throughout the history of our public educational system, making sure that we had enough teachers has taken precedence over making sure we had good ones" (p. xi). This course of action has, however, been fiercely criticized and rejected as a response to the current teacher shortage (Carnegie Forum, 1986).

On one hand, then, school districts have to find ways to attract and keep new teachers. On the other hand, they are under pressure to quickly transform novices into skilled teachers. The pressure to be excellent while coping with a huge increase in professional disequilibrium is a critical problem for those in school districts who are concerned with staff development. The question they face, in its simplest terms, is how to teach new teachers to teach as *well* as possible and as *soon* as possible. States and school districts have responded to this challenge in a variety of ways. Beginning salaries have been improved, and opportunities for career development, such as financial aid and incentives for graduate work, have been increased. However, the most notable and prominent change has been the development of programs especially designed to support new teachers.

Such programs have come to be known as induction programs, and the states that mandate them propose that they are one effective response to the problem of dealing with an influx of new teachers while maintaining educational standards. However, at the moment, more questions than answers exist concerning the effectiveness of these programs. My analysis of the literature on induction leads me to suggest that what is expected of these programs by the profession in general is the facilitation of what I term instant professionalism. At the root of all induction programs is the idea of getting the novice "unnoviced" as soon as possible.

UNNOVICING THE NOVICES

My data, collected over the course of 1 year of induction, revealed this process of unnovicing as a time of great expectations. Interviews and documents showed that the school district had expectations that the program would maintain its standards, and of course, the new teachers came to the 1st year of teaching and the induction experience with many expectations, not the least of which was that induction would be a help and support in their time of disequilibrium.

In early March, a new teacher came into my room just to talk, as she had often done since September. As a 1st-year teacher, she had spent the morning at an induction workshop. It had been a good workshop, but she had not been able to get her heart into it. Bright, pleasant, and seemingly confident, she described herself on that afternoon as "sort of falling apart." She couldn't understand why she was feeling so bad, she said. She knew it was her 1st year, and considering that, things were going pretty well, so why was she so anxious all the time? Why did she end up in tears when she got home some nights? Why did that parent conference bother her so much? She remembered how she had felt in September, and she wondered what had gone wrong. These were her words:

I felt really, really lucky, I mean, I couldn't believe it, that I got hired *here—in this district!* I thought it was going to be great—I thought, "I *must* be good to get hired here!" I mean, it was like a dream come true.

But now I feel terrible, like I can barely survive till the next day. I'm just, oh, I don't know, like overwhelmed. Will it always be like this? Will I ever feel on top of things?

But, I mean, there are days, well, I told you how I thought my actual teaching was coming along great right now. My kids have really made progress, they *really* have.

It's just—oh, I don't know, I just don't know what's wrong with me. I can't figure it out. I can't deal with it. I should be planning for next year, but I can't deal with anything right now. I have to kind of ignore it. Well, that's how I deal with it. I go home, and I try to put it all out of my mind and just get caught up in my wedding. I think I'm going crazy. Or—I don't know.

I told her she was not going crazy, that her feelings were completely normal, and that everybody felt like this in February of the 1st year. I told her that she was doing a great job, was handling things really well, and was very good with the parent who only this week said to her, "I know this is *only* your 1st year." However, I did not tell the new teacher that she was suffering from the burden of what I call instant professionalism: that for 9 months she had been trying to blend newness with expected excellence and that she was probably tired and worn out.

This new teacher was very aware of the expectations of the school district because they are clearly spelled out in district goals of induction and they are articulated by district personnel at all levels of the organization. Most induction programs are written and centered around the needs of new teachers as described in the literature (Griffin, 1986; Huling-Austin, Odell, Ishler, Kay, & Edelfelt, 1989), but this program differs in emphasis and focuses primarily on the needs of the district. The needs of the new teachers are not ignored, but central to the induction program is the belief that the most important need of new teachers in this school district is to know what the district expects of them. And district officials expect of the new teachers exactly what the community expects of the district. High academic success has always been the major goal, and the school district's first goal in induction is to ensure that new teachers understand this and that they maintain the acceptable standard of academic program delivery. The school district wants to make certain that the disequilibrium of the 1st-year teaching does not, in the words of one supervisor, translate into any students "paying a penalty for having a new teacher."

At the beginning of the school year, the district supervisor was able to articulate in an interview what the district meant by expectations:

First off, it [induction] directed the focus of the inductee to understanding what the expectations of this district were for them.

Let's start with the understanding of curriculum. I would say first and foremost in this school district is the expectation that teachers know what the curriculum is, that they deliver the curriculum to students in an understandable, clear way. It is very academically oriented. A teacher who comes into our school district and determines that they want to establish their favorite subject as top priority or browse around through a textbook without understanding that there are district objectives that run concurrently with that textbook—they do a disservice to themselves, the teachers in this district, but they also fail the students in this district. So, that's an example of number one. Teachers coming in know that: Look at the district curriculum, follow the district curriculum. We talk about that on orientation day, the support teacher talks about that, and the principals talk about that.

Another clear example of how this is going to fit in has to do with behavioral expectations. Expectations for how they deal with parent conferences. Expectations for grading. These are all covered in the workshops. These expectations and district standards . . . are pretty much set by the community. The district has set the standards. They are based on community expectation. And we are able in a clear, concise way to deliver these expectations to the new teachers so that there's no question in their mind that they have to uphold the standards of the district and the policies we have in place for them.

The administration was very clear about what the major goal of induction was: to communicate district expectations and standards. The nature of those expectations was also clear: New teachers should know the curriculum, and they should be aware that there are standards in the delivery of the curriculum and standards in many other areas to which new teachers are expected to conform.

THE EXPERIENCE OF INSTANT PROFESSIONALISM

Pressure arose, however, from the district expectation as stated by a district supervisor that no student "pay a penalty for having a new teacher." Inductees were very aware that no allowance for newness would be made with regard to standards for student achievement and that they were expected to cover the same material as well as other experienced teachers do. They were expected not only to know the curriculum but to be outstanding teachers from the 1st day. One administrator explained that:

The biggest problem new teachers have here is that they don't have more than 5 minutes to get settled. There is no time to get used to things. It's here you are, now be a fantastic teacher.

Barb Pollock, one of the two novice inductees in the program, stated that although she knew it was her job to know and deliver the curriculum, she felt a great deal of pressure in that she believed that to achieve district standards was a very tall order for a novice:

My job as a teacher is to know the curriculum and be able to follow through and all that. In your 1st year, it's just impossible to manage all of that—what's when, where, and how.

However, knowing and delivering the curriculum were not enough. The supervisor for staff development reported that the major goal of induction was the maintenance of high academic standards, but for Julie this meant, "it's creating this feeling that these kids can't leave here being below average." Inductees felt immediately that doing an average job as a teacher would not be enough. They felt that their teaching performance had to be excellent despite their newness. Novice teachers felt—perhaps more because of the team structure—that they were being compared with their much more experienced peers and were expected to produce the same results as more experienced teachers. They voiced some frustration at the unfairness of these expectations. Barb commented:

I put a lot of pressure on myself because I'm thinking, okay, here I am as a teacher and Polly Stoughton is a teacher. Why don't I have that kind of rapport, why don't I have that kind of discipline? Why don't I have that skill? And I was comparing myself to teachers like yourself [with] years and years of experience. I expected myself to be like that, but then I thought I was only a 1st-year teacher but I should still be like that. That's no excuse.

Liz Joseph was not a novice inductee but a mature and experienced teacher returning to the classroom after 12 years. Even she found herself making comparisons between her own expertise and that of her colleagues. For her, however, working with other successful teachers was an opportunity for growth.

I've grown and I'm learning all the time. These people that I'm teaching with are very capable, and there are different styles all around me and lots of ideas, and I'm trying to get myself organized and holding on to some of these ideas and filing them away for future use.

For novice Julie, however, the pressure of instant professionalism outweighed the opportunities for growth. Julie talked about the kind of teacher she thought she should be and remarked that on occasion she achieved that vision but that she struggled with the fear that she couldn't be excellent every day. She felt that Strathclyde expected everyday excellence, but she questioned whether this was realistic not only for her but in general. Of all the inductees, Julie dealt most thoughtfully with this issue. She constantly weighed the pressure to perform to a high standard against the fact that she was inexperienced. It was as if she, at least, had to make a point of forgiving herself for her newness although the district might not. In her view, the district expectation of instant professionalism might serve district needs but was not practical in reality:

If I had to pinpoint the teacher that the district would love, it would be someone who comes in like that 1 day I had when I thought about every kind of learner. I think they would like a teacher who does that every single minute of every day and that kind of thing. But I don't think they can really expect that. So, maybe that's what they're trying to get, that's this district, you know. It's so well known for being such an excellent school district, and everybody who works in Strathclyde is an excellent teacher, and it's not realistic because my view of an excellent teacher is not your view of an excellent teacher.

The struggle to become a teacher in the 1st year intensified by a perceived pressure to be an excellent teacher is in some ways made more difficult by the team structure of the district elementary schools, where new teachers could not conceal their inexpertise in autonomous work in their classrooms. The culture of the team demanded that new teachers participate in group discussion and decision making on matters of curriculum, standards, methods, and practices. In this, the novice found herself or himself at a disadvantage. It is well documented that when teachers talk, experience is the factor that holds most weight—and this is what the novice did not have. Teachers new to a district may in fact be able to contribute to the group some substantial, recently acquired theoretical knowledge, but in the culture of schools, this type of knowledge is rarely held in high esteem. As Hargreaves (in Little, 1989) states, "Experience counts, theory doesn't" (p. 24). When teams of teachers in the school district involved themselves in the group process, new teachers found that their theoretical knowledge base was not as respected as the experience base of their colleagues, and they were again left trying to measure up with the professionals, with whose years of service they cannot compete. Little (1989) suggests that this problem is central to teaching groups and is not unique to these inductees, but the situation clearly adds to the district novices' burden of instant professionalism:

> Even when teachers have access to a broader base of knowledge (gained through reading, university study, in-service education, talk with colleagues or observation) there is some evidence that such "outside" knowledge is selectively discounted when decision making groups come together. A conservative bias is introduced when the most powerful warrant for action is personalized and localized in classroom history. (p. 24)

An example of this can be seen in a recent discussion in my own team meeting on the issue of grouping the lowest-achieving students into one class. They are already grouped together in one room during part of the day for reading and language arts. I opposed this practice and was horrified at a suggestion that this grouping be extended to all day. The teacher involved said she could do so much more with these kids if she had them all day for all subjects. I stated all the reasons I felt such a move would be wrong, and the teacher replied:

But, Kate, you don't see the progress these kids have made in my room in reading. They would do so much better with the consistency if they could just stay for math and all the other things. It would be so much better for them—splitting them all up like we do in the other groups is not helping them.

When I replied to this that nearly all the research on tracking showed that keeping low-achieving students together did *not* help them, the teacher replied angrily:

I don't care what the research says. I know what I see in my room! I can see the results, the progress. Most of that research is written by people who haven't been in a classroom for 10 years or have never been in a classroom! It doesn't apply to my kids. I know how they are doing. And can you imagine if you were trying to teach them to read, mixed in with your group? What chance would they have, with all those readers?

Consider the position of a new teacher in this same discussion: Upon the dismissal of her theoretical knowledge of the problems of tracking, she would not have been able to weigh in with her 20 years of experience. She would have been efficiently routed from the discussion by the other teacher's reference to the wisdom of experience. Although a novice may indeed have a much broader and more informed view of the whole issue of tracking, in the real world of teacher talk, that does not count for much. In this example, the burden of instant professionalism felt by Strathclyde inductees is brought into sharp relief. Achieving a vision of oneself as equal to one's colleagues is difficult when knowledge, status, and expertise are measured by experience in the organization and when recently acquired academic, theoretical knowledge counts for little. New teachers perceived that administrators, parents, and colleagues expected them to perform to the standards of their peers, but they had few resources to enable them to live up this expectation.

A NEW APPROACH TO INDUCTION: EXCEEDING OUR EXPECTATIONS

For so many decades, the conditions of the 1st year of teaching were ignored. The concept of induction has indeed changed our professional thinking on this period of teacher growth. It has filled a void and is infinitely better than what we had before, which was some recognition of but little initiative in the problems of the 1st year of teaching. Induction does afford significant benefits to the profession. When induction works well, it support new teachers, benefits school districts, and increases retention (Odell, 1989). However, I ask here whether the process of induction may in fact be able to accomplish a lot more than we presently expect. Should our expectations of induction be greater for the 1990s? My data show that our present view of induction is limited by our inherent assumptions about teaching, learning, and the role of new teachers (Cochran-Smith, 1991). I believe we should expect effective induction to go far beyond the mere transmission of instant professionalism.

Present expectations of induction are not only limited in what they assume about induction but they are limiting to the process as it develops. My data show that the instant but unquestioned professionalization of new teachers means that induction at this time, even when it works well, maintains and reinforces the status quo. It does not challenge or disturb long-established theory or practice. It does not demand a reinterpretation of the role of the new teacher or of our beliefs about teaching and learning.

One example of this is Huling-Austin's (in Hirsch, 1990) statement that effective induction can make good teachers out of novice teachers in one year:

"The first purpose is to improve teacher effectiveness. The assistance and support provided through these programs can help ensure that well-prepared students become good teachers during their first year" (p. 2). Central to this expectation is the assumption held within induction programs concerning the nature of a good teacher. What does Huling-Austin mean by the term "good teacher"? As a result of my analysis of the literature on induction, especially when it blends with the literature on staff development, and from the data collected in my school district's induction plan, I conclude that when the term "good teacher" is used in induction, it means a teacher whose skills are equal to the best teachers in the system at the moment. In other words, we mean as good as the best we have. The same is true of most of the components of induction: "Good mentoring" means the best of what we have; "good inservice" is the best of what we currently do. Neither at the level of discourse nor at the level of implementation do we question, through induction, our assumptions about the dominant institutionalized norms of schooling.

The literature on induction does not say, How can we induct a new breed of teachers for the new century fast approaching? Rather, it clings to models and assumptions about teaching that were developed at the beginning of this century. The induction of teachers into teaching still accepts basic premises about the nature of teaching and learning, the work of teachers, and the organization of children—adopted in a different time to meet the needs of a different age. Models of teaching and learning from even 20 years ago are rendered inadequate now by the advancement of technology and changes in society. However, induction does not question or challenge these long-held, timeworn assumptions about what teaching and learning should look like, feel like, or sound like in the future. Goodlad (1990) categorizes some of these as "the bizarre assumption" made about the uniformity of readiness for instruction; ingrained beliefs about mastery learning; and theories concerning grade level, promotion, what constitutes failure, and grouping and tracking. He suggests that many of these assumptions go "in and out of fashion" from year to year (pp. 23–24).

The authors of descriptions of induction do not call for programs that critically examine the norms described here by Goodlad. Inductees are generally not expected to question school district practices in grouping, promoting, retaining, or grading. They are expected to find out what is usually done and then to conform to regular practice. I ask here, however, if our expectations of induction are inherently limiting—even when induction is carefully implemented and "succeeds," as in my own school district—because we do not demand fundamental change in the profound ways demanded by those who look to the future of education (Carnegie Forum, 1986; Eisner, 1985; Goodlad, 1984). Our expectations do not demand the emergence of a new breed of educator who will challenge the institutionalized norms and underlying assumptions of teaching and learning. If novice teachers continue to be inducted into current practice and if there is continuing resistance to allowing new teachers to develop new practice, induction cannot meet the challenge of the new decade in reforming or even improving education. Goodlad (1990) warns what this will mean:

> It means changing our schools in profound ways; the schools of tomorrow must be highly deviant from the school of today. The required change will not occur if we continue to prepare teachers for the school circumstances now prevailing. (p. 27)

Drastic as this call for change may seem, it is actually an echo of the findings of the Carnegie Forum (1986), which totally rejected the notion that reform meant a return to older standards or maintenance of present ones. It stated:

> Our view is very different. We do not believe the educational system needs repairing; we believe it must be rebuilt to match the drastic change needed in our economy if we are to prepare our children for productive lives in the 21st century. (p. 14)

Goodlad argues that teacher education must play a substantial role in rebuilding the educational system. My study asks whether the same argument can or should be made for new-teacher induction.

9 | Essays

• • • • • • • • • • •
Lighting Fires

Shirley P. Brown

SHIRLEY P. BROWN *has been a GED teacher at Comprehensive Services for School Age Parents, School District of Philadelphia, for the past 20 years. In that capacity, she has modified her curriculum to feature the literature and history of women, particularly African-American women. A teacher consultant in the Philadelphia Writing Project, she is also a discussion leader for the Pennsylvania Humanities Council's women's studies book and discussion series, as well as a coleader in two ongoing colloquia on women's studies. In addition to serving on the executive board of Community Women's Education Project, an agency that serves low-income women, she is pursuing a Ph.D. in reading/writing/literacy at the Graduate School of Education, University of Pennsylvania.*

Teachers are always tinkering with the curriculum, adding a short story here and there, eliminating a novel, and so on. But when I recently took a careful look at my classroom, I realized I had done more than tinker. The transformation on one level seemed so logical and commonplace that I hesitated to claim, on another level, that a major change had taken place: a change in both my intellectual understanding and my classroom practice. In fact, I began to wonder whether anything really "important" had occurred. Weren't changes in the literary canon likely in all classrooms in light of the recent growth of feminist scholarship? Wasn't everyone incorporating multicultural approaches into their teaching? Could I claim that by altering the visible curriculum of classroom texts I was also affecting the hidden curriculum of male hegemony in litera-

241

ture? My personal interest in feminist scholarship had made me uneasy with the curriculum and prompted me to raise questions about my intellectual life as a teacher and my daily work in the classroom.

I teach pregnant and parenting teens in a graduate equivalency degree (GED) class. Looking back, I see the irony of ignoring the absence of women in the curriculum while pursuing an intellectual interest in feminist work. In both cases, I was dealing with the needs of women, yet I did not connect feminist pedagogy with the needs of an all-female class. Furthermore, when I tried to write about the new curriculum that I was constructing, I asked myself why my work didn't sound important, academic, and serious. Why did it sound natural, plain, and minor?

In part, I think the answer lies in Ursula K. LeGuin's (1989) insightful analysis of the dialects of our common language. She sees a language of power— social power—that she calls the father tongue. This is the dialect that many people see as "the highest form of language, the true language, of which all other uses of words are primitive vestiges." It is expository and scientific discourse. However, there is another dialect: the mother tongue. As LeGuin expresses it, "It is a language always on the verge of song. It is the language stories are told in. It is the language spoken by all children and most women. And so I call it the mother tongue, for we learn it from our mothers and speak it to our kids."

The dialect of the mother tongue honors the personal, the subjective, and the different, and it was through my immersion in women's studies that I began to understand the power of language, the meaning of feminism, and the hidden agenda of the curriculum. Simply put, although feminism is not monolithic and embraces varied goals of political and economic equity—from separatism to androgyny—the common link is placing women and their concerns and issues at the center. As my life as a teacher for the past 20 years has been spent with poor, young women who are expectant or parenting mothers, I realized that my work, my journey, and my transformation as a teacher and as a woman could only be described through the mother tongue. The father tongue of power was not a useful discourse in my classroom or in a description of my journey. Objectivity, universals, and anonymity were not a part of my students' world and, I belatedly realized, not really a part of mine either. My students didn't use the father tongue, and they rejected my attempts to make it the *lingua franca* of the classroom. Once I realized that dialect and not my journey was the issue both in the classroom and in my portrayal of it, I knew that describing women's studies as a source of classroom transformation could only be presented one way. It is in the dialect of the mother tongue— with apologies to LeGuin, for I lack her lyricism—that I can best describe and make sense of how my continuing journey in women's studies has influenced my classroom and my view of teaching.

A BRIEF HISTORY

About 5 years ago, I became keenly aware of a lack of fire in my classroom. Lessons were going forward; youngsters were learning, passing tests, and so on. But where was the engagement—the sense that there was meaning in the classroom and that students could use what school had to offer in their everyday life? The short stories, novels, and history we read and discussed seemed like mere exercises to get students ready for the GED examination. There was little sense that Poe's "The Tell-Tale Heart," for example, had meaning for the class outside of the school. Seldom was there pressure or desire to continue a discussion past an allotted time. It wasn't that there was no room for Poe's stories in my classroom, but that there was a greater need for a different kind of curriculum—one that encouraged engagement and started fires.

My students range in age from 16 to 21 years old and are preparing to take the GED examination. Theoretically, the GED examination covers math, composition, and reading in social science, literature and the arts, and science; however, in fact it is largely a test of reading skills. The workbooks designed to prepare students for the tests are dull, mechanical, and disconnected. In their place, I had for years substituted short stories, poetry, and essays. I had reserved the workbooks for occasional practice with the GED test form. My choice of shorter pieces was also deliberate. As these young women often find regular school attendance to be an ongoing problem for a variety of reasons (e.g., illness, both their own and their child's; unreliable child care; financial problems; family problems), I wanted literature that could be read, discussed, and written about in shorter, more self-contained time periods that would correspond to the class time of 2-1/2 hours a day, 5 days a week.

Like many other teachers, I wanted to share my enthusiasm for what I loved in "literature," which is itself a father tongue appellation. (After all, who decides what gets elevated from just plain writing to literature? What qualifies as literature as opposed to ordinary prose?) I rhapsodized over Shelley and Wordsworth. We read O. Henry, Poe, and de Maupassant. Students were mildly interested. But I was most aware of the dissonance between students' lives and much of the material we were using in class. I justified my choices by relying on the claims made for the universality of the canon.

I knew that the curriculum wasn't directly related to their lives at the same time that I knew, in an abstract way, that connections should be made between students' lives and the curriculum. Clearly, bridges were not being built. I could see that assignments that were personal and that allowed students to draw on their own experiences were successful, while more abstract ones were tortured. But how could the lives of students be important in academic work? What connection could there be between their personal lives and important themes in literature? Caught in the dialect of the father tongue, I couldn't see or hear that it was the language of the patriarchy that supports separating the objective from the subjective and that honors universality over particularity. The language of schools and academia supported the notion that there was a general norm that all people aspired to, and at the time I didn't question the classist, racist, gendered biases of such assumptions. Because I felt responsible for preparing students for academic discourse, I, too, maintained the schism between the lives of students at home and in school.

Other questions were beginning to form. Didn't an all-female class require an acknowledgment of some sort? Were there curriculum changes that might turn adequate lessons into interesting, engaging sessions? Yet I was puzzled by what the nature of the change should be and was reluctant to give up the father tongue.

Serendipitously, I began to find some answers to my questions. I became aware of a National Endowment for the Humanities (NEH) summer seminar on the works of four Southern women short story writers: Kate Chopin, Flannery O'Connor, Eudora Welty, and Alice Walker. The seminar focused on the discontinuities that they represented, and of course, I realized that my classroom was a further example of discontinuity in schooling. Generally, novels written by white men from the Northeast define what is important and of consequence in the literary world. The form (the short story), the region (the South), and the authors (all women) represented seemingly fragmented, nonmainstream breaks with the American current of literature, just as a class for poor, African-American, pregnant girls represents a rupture with the mainstream, middle-class, white world of adolescence and high schools.

It was in that seminar that the world of women's studies opened up for me and made clear the importance of the personal in the classroom, the power of curriculum and language, and the gaps in my education. By the time I finished the seminar, I was transformed. I was reading through a different lens, envisioning a different classroom dynamic, and looking for nonconventional sources of information. This seminar was not an academic exercise, but a way to view the world very differently. Women's studies articulated the nature of the dissonance in the classroom and laid bare the politics of critical judgment.

I returned to my classroom that fall and immediately made room for Alice Walker, Eudora Welty, Anne Petry, and other noncanonical writers by enlisting the support of my administrator in ordering new books. Some old favorites remained, particularly de Maupassant, but I knew that I needed to know more. Local universities were, however, unlikely to provide a neat fit between my hunger and their offerings. Fortunately, two significant connections soon became available that further whet my appetite for women's studies.

About a year after the NEH seminar, I became a participant in a local gender studies seminar that was led and facilitated by teachers themselves. At the same time, I was a member of a community college English department where I was able to organize a colloquium in women's studies through funding by a local, public education support group: the Philadelphia Partnership for Education. We hoped and expected that our colloquium on black women writers would foster a network of teachers at all levels who were interested in educating themselves so that they could modify their curricula.

MULTICULTURAL GROWTH

The colloquium was highly successful in promoting such a network and in stimulating further individual study. Participants shared titles and sources, and guest presenters sparked more intense interest and work in specific topics. In fact, I was one of those who began to develop some very specific questions. I became interested in Caribbean women writers vis-à-vis African-American writers. Some of these writers were in both camps, such as Paule Marshall, but others were firmly rooted in the landscape, history, and folklore of the Caribbean, such as Erna Brodber. I realized that I really knew very little about the literary tradition of Caribbean women writers and that, like women and minority groups in this country, the Caribbean was not taken seriously.

Intending to compare the literature of African-American women writers with that of Caribbean women writers, I embarked on an independent study project funded by the Council on Basic Education and spent a marvelous summer reading and studying the subject of my choice. I discovered the wonderful worlds of Merle Hodge, Beryl Gilroy, Sylvia Wynter, and Michelle Cliff, and I reread Jamaica Kincaid and Jean Rhys. I struggled to understand the effect of enslavement in the Caribbean and how and if the history of enslavement in the Caribbean differed from the history of enslavement in the United States. I read to understand gender, race, and class in a different culture.

To provide a check on my reading, I relied on the process of research that I had been schooled in. I looked to critical essays, books, and reviews, but they were almost nonexistent. Thinking that my research was inadequate, I reached out to academics who were doing similar research and was able to confirm that, indeed, little critical work was available. One scholar from the University of the West Indies advised me that the critical materials, letters, and diaries I was interested in were mainly available at her institution and that they would remain there, an oblique but cogent reminder of resistance to imperialism. However, at least I was able to test my understanding of terms such as "Creole" and my understanding of the impact of present-day racism in a situation where slavery was outlawed earlier than in the United States and where the majority of the population is black. Although my research focused on issues of gender, race, and class, a glance at my journal for the project revealed how primitive my conceptual framework was at the time. Instead of understanding how interconnected race, class, and gender were and continue to be, I persisted in viewing them separately. On the other hand, I also learned about the power of culture when I read materials that were baffling because I wasn't familiar with the cultural references in them.

The independent study project meant more resources in the classroom, however. Jamaica Kincaid, Michelle Cliff, and Merle Hodge made their appearance there, and students became engaged with Kincaid's memory of her mother, Cliff's angry portraits of colonialism, and Hodge's portrayal of class differences. In particular, Kincaid's "Girl" elicited writing about the students' own mother-daughter connections and their projections about their own children. Predictably, many of the cautions they had for their children were the same ones they had heard from their own mothers. Additionally, a few students from the Caribbean added to our understanding of expressions such as *benna,* and the smiles on their faces as they enlightened us about the Caribbean were proof of the connectedness between the literature and their lives.

As for my own classroom, the curriculum continued to become more inclusive. Through the availability of other grants, my colleagues and I were able to supplement and supplant the literature that was centrally available through the school district with feminist and multicultural choices, buy videotapes, and have programs that served to raise the consciousness and sensitivity of both staff and students. Yet the question that continued to nag was how to change methodology to fit the goals of a feminist pedagogy. Here my participation in the Philadelphia Writing Project (PhilWP) played a key role. Through PhilWP's emphasis on student-centered classrooms and on using writing to learn and valuing the personal, a real commingling of practice and theory could be achieved and an appreciation of the mother tongue could occur. Not only did PhilWP provide the theory for many otherwise intuitive observations, but as a teacher collaborative it sanctioned the right of teachers to experiment, with the knowledge that changes in the classroom sometimes succeed and sometimes fail. I welcomed the idea of building on and extending student agendas.

Working with other project teachers, I saw that reading is no longer a game of invoking abstruse commentary and looking for "great themes." Reading can begin to empower readers by divesting the author and text of absolute authority. Discussions value multiple viewpoints, and there is no search for the "right" answer. Students support their views and willingly translate their opinions into brief essays.

The combination of women's studies and the culturally responsive pedagogy of PhilWP was moving my classroom further in the desired direction. I was no longer asking students to write about plot and theme and girding myself for the anticipated mumblings of "I don't know what to write." Instead, I was asking students to make connections with ideas, issues, and echoes in the literature and in their lives, and students had no trouble finding subjects to write about. Moreover, I saw that writing was important in itself and not just as something preparatory to traditional expository writing. This is not to say that students wrote extended essays effortlessly, but they didn't dread writing. They willingly responded to literature and shared their writing.

Students used their journals to make connections between Jamaica Kinkaid's "Girl" piece and their own mothers and/or between "Girl" and how their own children would see them as parents. They wrote about courage and determination after reading Maya Angelou's "And Still I Rise," about injustice in J. W. Houston's *A Farewell to Manzanar,* about civil disobedience in Richard Rive's "The Bench," about difficult choices in Langston Hughes' "Professor," about desperation and suicide in old age in Arna Bontemps' "A Summer Tragedy," about jealousy and mothering in Cynthia Ozick's "The Shawl," about domestic violence in Ann Petry's "The Winding Sheet," and about the will to live in Alice Walker's "To Hell With Dying." I could feel the fire in the room.

In response to Richard Rive's "The Bench," students wrote with passion and intensity:

The story, "The Bench," written by Richard Rive, is about a black South African man named Karlie who took a stand for what he believed to be wrong. One day he purposely sat on a bench that was marked *Europeans Only.* He knew what that meant, but he sat there anyway. Just sitting there was action on his behalf to protest the statement written on the bench. He felt as though anyone should be able to sit there if it was available. He was scared on the inside, but he felt he was doing the right thing. In some sense it made a difference, and it didn't make a difference. Karlie knew what was going to be the outcome in his situation, but in his own personal way he felt good about himself for just taking a stand. If others decided to act on their feelings, maybe the message would get across to people and encourage them to get involved and maybe then it would make a big difference like Dr. Martin Luther did.

Students were also willingly doing what Wolf (1988) calls "criss-crossing the landscape of literature," as in the following student piece, also a first draft:

I compared "Like a Winding Sheet" to *Kaffir Boy.* Like "The Winding Sheet," *Kaffir Boy* has prejudice and violence. Johnson had hate in him every time someone said something to him, and when he finally hit someone, he enjoyed it. He couldn't control it just like the white Africans of South Africa.

Not content with an array of literature that conveyed a sense of the multicultural nature of the world, I also sought out and incorporated essays and short stories on homosexuality. Audre Lorde's "Transformation of Silence Into Language" and Anne Schockley's "A Birthday Remembered" became a part of the curriculum. I was determined to have everyone in the room represented, and I was reading furiously to fill in the gaps. Ultimately, two colleagues and I compiled a set of readings to correspond to their work in job readiness and parenting education and distributed it to the students in the class. Working around themes such as self-awareness, responsibility, and relationships, we developed units that included such pieces as Alice Walker's "Beauty: When the Other Dancer Is the Self," Toni Cade Bambara's "Raymond's Run," and Alice Walker's "Everyday Use" together with related material in the areas of job readiness and parenting education. Our idea was to build bridges between literature and practical concerns to make the students think more deeply about issues.

In many ways, the compilation became the capstone in my intellectual journey at that time. Not only was the collection of readings noncanonical, multicultural, and women centered, but it also invited students to include their own journal writing so that they could quite literally enter into conversation with the materials.

The issue of language, however, continued to be a source of conflict, and I asked the students to engage in the struggle between the mother tongue and the father tongue. As a product of a patriarchal education, I wavered on the issue of how important it was for students to master both. I first asked them to distinguish between the two. I asked them to describe the kind of writing they did in their journals, the mother tongue, and the kind of writing used for formal assignments, the father tongue. Some of their responses are telling:

If I write in my journal, I write about my thoughts about something. It's sort of personal, but I don't mind sharing it. If I'm writing an essay about birds, I would just write about birds and their nature and not my thoughts about it.

When writing in my journal, I write about my feelings and how I react to them. When writing an assignment, I have to think hard about what I say, how I say it. It must have right grammar, and it must be punctuated. When in a journal, you don't have to worry about how you say it, but it should be punctuated. An assignment must have facts, examples. You get graded on it, and it must be specifically about that subject.

How sad that students feel that their thoughts and feelings have no place in academic subjects and that they must reserve any expressions of personal reactions to private, not public, papers. Here is evidence that students see the difference between the dialect of power and the dialect of disempowerment very early.

Women's studies prompted me to question a curriculum that was unrepresentative of American culture. For others, there may be a different route through African-American, Asian-American, or Latino studies, but once I became aware of the political implications of the curriculum, there was no turning back. Even today, as I continue my independent study of multicultural literature, I do so with an added emphasis on the gender component.

A colleague of mine frequently questions whether a teacher's pursuit of knowledge is selfish or is a genuine part of a teacher's professional life. There is no doubt in my mind that as a teacher grows intellectually, there are many rippling effects in the classroom and among staff and colleagues. Learning is part of teaching, and teaching tests learning. As Lorde (1989) says, "We teach our students what we need to know ourselves."

I would contend that it is the teacher—the one who is closest to her class— who is in the best position to analyze the politics and the power structure of the classroom. Who is being empowered by the curriculum? Who is being disempowered? What is to be done? And who will do it? Teachers have the power to transform a disempowering curriculum through their own research, but it should be done in the everyday language of women. Weiler (1988) argues that the social reality of women needs to be made public:

> This entails the creation of a new "naming" of women's experience. Feminist theorists argue that this cannot be achieved through the present abstract language of male theory. Instead, women must create a new language based on women's actual lived experience. (p. 61)

For me, this meant dismantling my curriculum and pursuing one that raised issues of gender, race, and class and struggling to value the language of the young women in the class. It meant that what I was finding empowering through my own study had direct implications for the classroom. Finally, it meant that what some people refer to as women's intuition is really no more and no less than close observation and that women teachers in particular should trust what they see as sparks in the classroom.

My own research continues as I wonder about the implications of a feminist classroom. I still struggle with the idea of cultural relevance in conjunction with cultural broadening. I vacillate about the need to know the various dialects of language: the mother tongue and the father tongue. I am concerned about the ways that a teacher can encourage language versatility without privileging one dialect over another. And ultimately, I have a strong hunch that there is a positive correlation between a multicultural and gender-balanced curriculum and student and teacher empowerment when the curriculum is expressed in the mother tongue.

• • • • • • • • • • • •

Following the Paper Trail

Marsha Rosenzweig Pincus

MARSHA ROSENZWEIG PINCUS *teaches English and playwriting at Simon Gratz High School in the School District of Philadelphia. Her essays about teaching have been published in* Works in Progress *and* The Voice, *both publications of the Philadelphia Writing Project. A Rose Lendenbaum Teacher of the Year in 1988, she is also the recipient of the first George Bartol Arts in Education Fel-*

lowship for her work in teaching playwriting. Two of her students have been winners of the National Young Playwrights Festival, with their plays read professionally at the Playwrights Horizon Theater in New York.

In "The Teacher As Researcher," Berthoff (1987) argues that teachers "do not need new information. We need to think about the information that we have. We need to interpret that information and in turn interpret our interpretations" (p. 30). Through our looking and relooking and our interpretations and reinterpretations, we can discover our knowledge about teaching. Through systematic and intentional inquiry, we teachers can prompt a powerful intellectual critique of strategies, assumptions, and goals, both in and out of the classroom.

Over the past 5 years, I have written a number of essays about my teaching practices for a variety of audiences in a variety of contexts. Each individual essay represents a small piece of teacher research in that it emanated from some dissonance I felt about some aspect of my classroom practice, which in turn led to questions. These questions sent me in search of answers, which then caused me to develop a new concept of the issue in question, which then brought about a change in my classroom practice. The new change in practice inevitably created a new dissonance, which began the process anew.

These essays, taken as a body of work, constitute data: data about my growth and transformation as a teacher as I have engaged and continue to engage in inquiry about my teaching. In keeping with the spirit of Berthoff, in this paper, I offer no new information. Instead, I follow the paper trail that I left behind from the very first essay I wrote about teaching in 1986 to the present essay. This is my attempt to reinterpret my work in an effort to understand how it is that I have changed over these years and how my personal change relates to the systematic change now occurring as we in the comprehensive neighborhood high schools in Philadelphia undergo restructuring.

The first essay I wrote about teaching, "Will the Real Marsha Please Stand Up?" written as a final piece to be shared with the other participants in the first Summer Institute of the Philadelphia Writing Project (PhilWP), was inspired by a powerful memory of my own schooling, which the institute evoked. This incident occurred when I was in the seventh grade. I had written a book and sent the manuscript to a publishing company. Although the book was rejected, the editors sent me an encouraging letter, which I immediately brought to my English teacher, Mr. Spitzer. He looked at me in a strange way, handed back my letter, and said quietly, "Very nice, Marsha." I write:

It wasn't until I participated in this institute and began to explore my own feelings about writing and my personal history as a writer that I realized what he didn't say. HE NEVER ASKED TO SEE MY BOOK! This singular event shaped my feelings about writing for the rest of my education and in my classroom. I learned you wrote one way for school . . . you wrote another way for yourself . . . so much of what I became as a teacher, what I viewed as my obligation to my students was defined by my own education. . . . Because of my encounter with the people of this institute, I am re-visioning writing in the classroom and I am re-visioning myself.

It seems very significant to me that the entire process of change that this discovery set in motion originated from an understanding of the connection between my own experiences as a learner and the experiences I offer my students as their teacher. It is also significant that it is within a community of other teachers that I gain the courage and confidence to try to make a change. As my teaching moved from a teacher-centered to a student-centered stance and as I moved from being product minded to being process minded, I began to experience a lot of dissonance around the issue of control. While writing this paper, I discovered that one reason I had used my previous strategies was that I could better keep my students under control. I documented my uncertainty as I relinquished some of that control and handed it back to my students.

During this year, I began to venture out of my classroom for the first time and began to collaborate with teachers in my building as a teacher consultant. Such collaborations brought up issues of control, power, and trust as we teachers found ourselves in different relationships with each other. For the first time in our careers, we entered one another's classrooms, exposing our vulnerabilities as well as sharing our expertise.

I raised further questions about this issue in "Power, Voice and Necessary Loss," written at the conclusion of my participation in the second Summer Institute of the PhilWP in 1987:

What is it that teachers must give up in order to empower our students? One consequence of empowering our students is the possibility that we might not agree with what it is they have to say. Are we ready to listen and respect their differences? Who will the audience be for the student's voice when it is critical of the teacher, the administration, the curriculum or the system?

I also speculated that only empowered teachers can empower students but that teacher empowerment, too, comes with its necessary losses for us, the teachers:

As we become empowered, we lose the luxury of complacency. We can no longer remain silent and uncommitted about the future of our profession. If we no longer see ourselves as powerless victims of the system, but as vocal integral components whose voices can be heard, we can and must share in the responsibility for policies which affect curriculum and instruction.

At this point, I was still unsure of how teachers would gain the confidence and knowledge to enable us to assume these new responsibilities; however, in

"Teacher As Researcher: Conversion of a Skeptic" (1988), I wrote about my discovery of inquiry as a powerful tool for coming to understand the meaning of my own work. Written for the Ethnography Forum, this paper revisited my experiences from the previous year and reinterpreted my conversion to the process approach to teaching and writing:

In the spirit of a true believer, I became a born again teacher, ready to proselytize and awaken my unenlightened colleagues. My conversion to the process approach to the teaching of writing is swift and complete marked by a few questions. My euphoria was too great to be contained within the walls of my own classroom. . . . I had a lot of energy that year. What I didn't have was a critical perspective on what I was doing.

I went on to recount my moment of discovery. During the second Summer Institute of PhilWP, I read an article by two college English teachers who engaged in a collaborative research project about their composition classes. I had what Emig (1987) calls an "AhA!" experience as I came to realize the role that teacher research can play in offering teachers a necessary critical perspective on our own practices. After reading this article, I came to understand how teacher research is beneficial not only to the participants but to all others who read about their work. I wrote:

On one level the Rorschach and Whitney article offers real insights into how certain assumptions about authority and voice translate into specific behaviors in the classroom which either support or negate a teacher's stated objectives. But, on another level, I also learned a process for engaging inquiry in my classroom—the type of inquiry which could give me that critical perspective on my own work which I desperately lacked last year.

I concluded this paper with a promise:

I will now begin to examine what is happening in all of my classes through careful documentation. I am poised on the brink of diving in and immersing myself in the murky waters of inquiry.

Once I adopted this critical stance, no aspect of my work was immune from scrutiny. And once I began to document what was happening in my classroom and to question myself about my assumptions, strategies, and goals, no issue escaped investigation. Suddenly, nothing was a "given" any longer. The texts I taught, the way I taught them, the way I tested my students, the way I thought about my students, the way I thought about myself as a teacher—once familiar and immutable—now appear strange and elusive.

During this time, I kept a journal on a fairly regular basis, logging my reactions to the daily life of my classroom. I also responded to readings from a seminar on teaching and learning that dealt with issues such as tracking, race, multicultural diversity, and assessment as they related to my classroom practices. I wrote long explanations for myself along with my weekly lesson plans, turning each lesson into an opportunity for discovery about teaching.

This "quiet form of research," as Britton (1987) calls it, inspired my next three essays, each of which dealt with a specific issue that bubbled up for me through my reflections on my teaching. Emblematic of my writing from this period is "Assessment in the Urban Classroom" (1990). Originally written as a speech delivered to a panel of assessment experts convened by the Philadelphia Schools Collaborative, this essay made a case against standardized tests and in favor of alternative indicators of student performance. As one of two teachers invited to participate in this discussion of assessment, I pleaded for more teacher involvement. Using a story from my classroom experience as the basis for my argument against the efficacy of the citywide English test, I wrote:

My students had learned about drama from the inside out. They had collaborated with one another in improvisational workshops. They had written and rewritten scenes. They had produced, directed and acted in each other's plays. In addition they had attended five plays at the Annenberg Theater, seen at least six professional productions at our school, and read at least five plays including the work of Sophocles, William Shakespeare, Arthur Miller, Charles Fuller and August Wilson, and Nto Zake Shange.

When the city-wide standardized final exam came along, I certainly wasn't worried that I hadn't covered the drama part of the curriculum. But what my students encountered on that test was 25 lines from a turn of the century British play, followed by multiple choice questions about the vocabulary in the dialogue. My class did poorly on the drama portion of the exam.

Rather than conclude that there was something wrong with my students or there was something wrong with me, the teacher, I suggested that maybe—just maybe—there was something wrong with the test. I began to question the relationship between instruction and assessment and educational goals:

Surely I will teach drama in one way if my goal is to have my students see drama as a living breathing art form with a history and a tradition—an art form they too have the ability to create. I will teach it another way if my goal is to have my students see drama as just another text to explicate. We cannot look at assessment without considering the content of our curriculum and we cannot consider curriculum without examining our purpose as educators.

I concluded with a question:

If the test determines how and what teachers teach, shouldn't we teachers help determine what and how we test?

Clearly at this point, I was gaining confidence in my ability to speak about teaching. Through my careful examination of my students' performance on the drama portion of that test, my analysis of the types of questions, and my comparison of those questions with the strategies I employed in teaching drama, I discovered fundamental differences between my goals and the goals of those who developed the test. Rather than conclude, as I might have in the past, that I needed to change my practices to bring myself more in line with the test, I suggested that knowledge about assessment can flow from inside the classroom out to the testing experts as I and other teachers begin to engage in a serious study of alternative means of assessment and their relationships to the delivery of instruction, the content of the curriculum, and our overall educational goals.

Once initiated, my inquiry became self-perpetuating, impelling me to do some deep thinking about substantive issues. Changes in curriculum, instruction, assessment, and grouping practices represented *real* reform. Implementation of these changes, I believe, would prevent the restructuring effort from becoming a meaningless exercise in reshuffling.

The teacher's role in the process of restructuring was the subject of my next paper, "High School Restructuring: A Teacher's Perspective." Written at the request of the Philadelphia Schools Collaborative, this paper was delivered as part of a panel discussion on restructuring. Also on this panel were a high school principal and the superintendent of the School District of Philadelphia. This represented a coming out of sorts for me—a very public statement of my feelings about teachers and our relationship to reform. And I realized that I was a very far cry from the "real Marsha" who lacked the confidence to teach in any way other than how she had been taught. The focus of the paper was, not surprisingly, teacher empowerment. I wrote:

Teacher empowerment becomes a paradox when it comes as a directive from the administration. For administrators cannot empower teachers; we must empower ourselves. Empowerment comes from confidence and confidence comes from knowledge.

I then drew connections among teacher knowledge, school reform, and the teaching and learning seminar:

It is in seminars such as these that leaders of reform will come. It is in seminars such as these where teachers will form partnerships to design the academies of the restructured high school. It is in seminars such as these in which teachers will gain the confidence needed to question the inconsistencies and contradictions we see between where we are and where we'd like to be. And realize that we have the power to participate in meaningful change.

That was written in spring 1990. Today, I am no longer as optimistic as I was then. The realities that accompany the establishment of a charter school within a school have tempered my enthusiasm. The issues of power and control that I discerned 5 years ago still linger, only now they are reframed in the context of school-based management. The contradictions of reform and the resistance to change remain.

The process of writing this paper has brought me to the present. Although many of my past concerns linger, the dissonance that sent me back to examine my paper trail has also raised new questions for me about individual teachers and our relationship to school and systemwide reform.

From the deeply personal "Real Marsha" piece, to the very public paper on high school restructuring, I have been documenting my transformation as a teacher. What I have rediscovered about myself is that the *inquiry feeds the reform*. The questions gave the reform direction; the search for answers to those questions gave the reform substance. Through the course of this journey, I have noted my shifting relationships with students, colleagues, administration, and the wider community of educators. These relationships will undoubtedly shift again as we in Philadelphia attempt to move toward school-based management. The administration has urged schools to establish governance councils comprising faculty, administration, and community members to assume control of school reform.

And here is where my skepticism returns. For what happens when the individuals entrusted with the power to make these decisions are not inclined toward the systematic and intentional inquiry that engenders the best reform?

How can it be ensured that the individuals who serve on these councils are brought into the process of inquiry? We who are already committed to such inquiry must make the mandate to reform spark the process of inquiry in others to bring about useful and positive change.

• • • • • • • • • • • •

Faith, Love, and Polka Music

Dara Brody, Elizabeth Cornman, Madeleine Rawley Crouse, Larry Greenspun, Janet Klavens, Teresa Donato Miller, Keith Patton, Elizabeth Powers, Marjorie Callahan Ritchie, Pamela Rogers, and Debra Miller Schefer

The coauthors of this article are 1990 graduates of Project START at the Graduate School of Education, University of Pennsylvania. DARA BRODY *develops and teaches physician education programs for newly licensed pharmaceutical products throughout Europe.* ELIZABETH CORNMAN *teaches fourth grade at the Coolbaugh Elementary Center in the Pocono Mountain School District, Pennsylvania.* MADELEINE RAWLEY CROUSE *teaches third grade at the Barkley Elementary School in Phoenixville, Pennsylvania.* LARRY GREENSPUN *teaches first grade at Merion Elementary School in Merion, Pennsylvania, and is principal of the Har Zion Temple Hebrew High School.* JANET KLAVENS *teaches elementary school in Vermont.* TERESA DONATO MILLER *teaches kindergarten at William Rowen Elementary School in the Philadelphia School District.* KEITH PATTON *teaches in the School District of Philadelpia.* ELIZABETH POWERS *teaches reading and art at Middle Years Alternative, an alternative public middle school in West Philadelphia in the School District of Philadelphia.* MARJORIE CALLAHAN RITCHIE *taught kindergarten at St. Mary's Hall/Doane Academy in Burlington, New Jersey, and coauthored two papers at the Ethnography and Education Forum in 1992.* PAMELA ROGERS *teaches second grade at Reynolds Elementary School in the School District of Philadelphia.* DEBRA MILLER SCHEFER *teaches the middle school at the Columbia Grammar and Preparatory School in New York City.*

Although a great deal has been written by educational researchers about student teachers and their experiences in preservice training programs, very little has been written by student teachers themselves. This paper was written collaboratively by 11 student teachers in Project START (Project Student Teachers As Researching Teachers).

While we were taking a required course entitled "Language, Learning and Looking," we were frequently asked, "What do you *think* you think about . . . ?" In considering this question, we were challenged to examine carefully our course readings and the educational theories they presented, as well as our student teaching experiences, and to react to them in writing. Rather than accept theories and practices at face value, we were encouraged to look closely at each one, especially at unclear arguments and inherent contradictions, and to analyze them in light of our preexisting notions and experiences in education. We found that what we thought about particular issues or situations changed or was not what we had originally thought after taking the time to sit down and think about it. The focusing question, "What do you *think* you think about . . . ?" provided the framework for each of us to write three reaction essays in which we examined theory and practice to begin building our own understandings of teaching and learning. We could choose any issue or situation to react to and write about from the assigned readings (a collection of articles and excerpts pertaining to various aspects and issues of current educational thought) and from our ongoing experiences in our student teaching classrooms. These essays were intended to foster in us a different way of thinking—not only about educational issues but also about the process of *thinking* about them. This kind of thinking is evolutionary because it initiates a process of constant evaluation and reevaluation of the theories and practices that we encounter daily in the field of education.

After the course was finished, 11 of us were invited to look back and examine in depth 33 pieces we had written as we redefined our thinking processes. In essence, we researched our own research as student teachers to define and understand the role that essay writing had played in the early months of our teacher-education program. We thought that in doing so, we would be able to understand better the contribution that essay writing could make to our research as classroom teachers. We discovered that essay writing had functioned for us in three different ways: finding questions, comparing theory and practice, and comparing theories. Those of us who used the essay as a form of internal dialogue to find questions were attempting to make sense of our ideas about teaching and learning by putting our internal confusion down on paper. When comparing theory and practice, we evaluated specific experiences that occurred in or out of our classrooms in light of the current theory and research we had read. Last, we used essays to compare one theory with another theory, analyzing, synthesizing, and uncovering subtleties. Each kind of essay writing functioned not only to clarify our thoughts but also to raise questions about the nature of teaching and learning. As evidenced in our essays, these questions have become important stepping stones in the formulation of the educational philosophies we take with us to the classroom as 1st-year teachers.

To illustrate the different ways that we used essay writing to define and structure our thinking, we have presented in this paper excerpts from each of our essays. Taken together, our essays make a collective statement enriched by our individual voices. These essays reveal the great potential that essay writing holds for both experienced and beginning teacher researchers in their efforts to build theoretical and practical understandings of the processes of teaching and learning. Essay writing serves as one lifelong tool that can inform teaching practice.

FINDING QUESTIONS

The following four excerpts are from essays we wrote at the beginning of our year-long student teaching experiences. In these early essays, we examined our new student teaching experiences in relation to our preconceived notions about education. These essays took the form of an internal dialogue in which we wrote our way into questions by writing about our own confusion. For Maggie, for example, it was important that she work out for herself what it means to be a teacher researcher. She wrote:

Notes accumulate in my journal throughout the school day. Page after page is filled with records of small incidents with the children, specific techniques, ideas to try out at a later time, and questions regarding my own philosophy of education, as well as that of my cooperating teacher. Some days it seems as if the volume of what is noteworthy is far too much to record properly. It is so very difficult to discern that which is important from that which is less vital. It is unclear if I am able to make that distinction at this time, or if I should even try to do so. Am I doing research? Or is my compulsive note gathering simply an exercise in being a thorough student?

What and how children were learning were important issues for Dara in her kindergarten student teaching placement. In one essay, she wrote:

I was a skeptic—well, more than that, I had fears that my students were going to end up being what I call "creative dunces." It seemed to me that what I did each day in kindergarten was exactly what each article in my bulk pack [assigned readings] and stack of books recommended, but I wasn't seeing any results. It's mid-December and most of my students still don't know their ABC's! I thought this "anything goes" atmosphere was marvelous in theory, but a disaster in my classroom.

While Dara was dealing with pragmatic issues, Pamela was wrestling with ideological ones. She wondered how she could preserve her own vision of teaching in the face of the often overwhelming daily logistics of the classroom:

Theory-based learning equips a student teacher with ideals. It gives a prospective teacher a sense of how things should be but not of how they are. It leaves the student teacher with a burning desire to change things without a full awareness of what she might be up against. Without a clear sense of the obstacles to overcome and without a clear sense of how to go about it. How can someone go along with a system and fight it at the same time? When I walk into the school where I'm student teaching, theories lose their vibrance and fall like ashes around my ears. My vision has been dulled and I haven't even made it out of grad school yet. How will I stand against people who are willing to hurt me for the sake of tradition? How will I stand when I am no longer supported by a teacher education program full of caring people?

Keith addressed yet another side of education, the practical issues of the classroom. In his first essay, he wondered how to set up and structure a classroom to enhance learning:

As I began to share with my journal my initial, anxious thoughts upon entering Mrs. Marshall's fifth grade classroom at Edwin Forrest Elementary School, my mind could conclude just one word, "What a Mess!" As we sorted, arranged, and rearranged her "stuff," I could see that her room contained everything but the proverbial "kitchen sink," and in fact, a part of a faucet was under some rubble. Her colleagues, who would periodically peek into her classroom, simply shook their heads in disbelief. I couldn't recall clearly my past elementary school classroom environments, so I was faced afresh with a question of dubious importance—"Is there an ideal learning environment?" or more accurately, "What type of learning environment do I wish to provide for my pupils as I take the wheel of my first classroom?"

Our year was a whirlwind of intense study and deeply involved student teaching. The process of writing these essays was, for us, a way to respond on a personal level to what we were experiencing in our teacher training program. Putting words down on a page allowed us to sort through a myriad of thoughts, emotions, and fears that grew in response to our teaching, as well as the theories that we were exposed to in our courses. Within these essays, our thoughts were not merely listed; they were harnessed, organized, and confronted. They acted as catalysts for internal dialogue and debate and helped formulate questions. These particular essays gave us the opportunity to reflect on our evolving thoughts and theories. They were never a simple statement of our beliefs but were instead an attempt to bring order to what was often internal chaos. Perhaps for those of us who wrote this type of essay, an internal dialogue had always been a natural way to process information, learn, and come to grips with ourselves and our experiences.

THEORY AND PRACTICE

A second way that we used essays was as a lens for examining both theory and practice in education. In our courses and student teaching classrooms, we were confronted with ideas that at times coincided, at times contradicted, and at times affirmed our experiences both as student teachers and as learners in life. For some, writing essays helped us to integrate learning and teaching experiences with educational theory. For others, writing essays mediated conflicts found between the two. In both cases, we used essay writing as a starting point for formulating our own theories to bring to our classrooms.

In her essay, Teresa wrote about an incident involving her own child's education. She wrote:

Since my 6-year-old daughter has been writing, we have encouraged her to spell in any way she wishes so that she might avoid frustration when attempting to get her thoughts down on paper. As a result, Valerie writes reams of paper: books, lists, stories, poems and a local newsletter that she publishes and sends to our neighbors.

To my dismay last term, I found a checkmark beside "improvement needed" on my daughter's report card under "ability to express ideas on paper." During a conference with her teacher, I discovered that Valerie used only two words, "faith" and "love," in every essay [she wrote for religion class] that report card period. I was quite puzzled by this problem and explained that I knew Valerie to be a prolific writer, a child who enthusiastically expresses herself through many writing activities. As we continued to discuss this problem, I began to realize that Valerie's teacher was not an advocate of invented spelling and, in fact, was unfamiliar with this developmental writing stage. As I struggled with this dilemma, I began to suspect that Valerie's reluctance to write emanated from the discrepancy between her teacher's view and my view on invented spelling. While at home I was encouraging her to write for meaning and disregard spelling, as many theorists advocate, at school, her teacher was insisting all words be correctly spelled. I was able to confirm my suspicions when I questioned my daughter, and she impatiently stated, "Mommy, those are the only words I'm sure I can spell, and we HAVE to spell them right!"

Through the process of essay writing, Teresa was forced to examine the above experience, define it more clearly through reflection and analysis, and take from it meaning for herself. Putting her thoughts down on paper enabled her to tie together her personal sense of how children learn, her daughter's experience at school, and the educational theory she was learning at the University of Pennsylvania. The resulting essay became for Teresa a starting point—a way of sifting through theories; linking them to practice; and developing her own position on language, writing, and spelling.

In his essay, Larry used academic theory to make sense of an episode from his own school experience. He wrote:

Dr. O'Breza, my high school English teacher, was returning our first written assignments ("What does the 'Means' Mean in 'Cadbury Means Good Chocolate'"). He explained that it was his custom to listen to music while grading our writing, the selection determined by the quality of the essay. A good solid effort was accompanied by Bach or Mozart, and for a truly inspirational piece he would break out the Beethoven. My composition was returned with this comment scrawled on the cover: "Heard any good Polka Music lately?"

I had written my composition the way I thought Dr. O'Breza wanted it to sound. I thought writing was an exercise in putting words on paper your teacher wanted to hear. Whatever writing was, I, apparently, was not too good at it, like someone trying to play "Fur Elise" on an accordion, according to Dr. O'Breza.

When preparing to write his essay and thinking about Donald Graves' (1983) methods for helping children to develop a sense of voice and audience in their writing, the preceding anecdote was jarred in Larry's memory. He was able to identify Dr. O'Breza's critique as the catalyst that had forced him to recognize the generic nature of his own writing. Larry concluded that this incident was the point at which he began to develop his masterful sense of voice and well-defined understanding of audience.

Writing about the anecdote allowed Larry to make the connection between

Graves' theory and his own experiences with writing. While composing his essay, Larry discovered a point of great personal growth. Dr. O'Breza's comment encouraged Larry to look at his own writing, evaluate its strengths and weaknesses, and determine to establish a voice. Understanding Graves' theory in light of his own experiences gave Larry a framework and the terminology that enabled him to pass on his understanding to his own students and help them with their own writing.

There are a number of examples from our student teaching experiences in which theory and practice seemed to collide. In these situations, essay writing served as a way to work through and make sense of these conflicts. Often, writing essays helped us to develop a fuller picture of the relationship between theory and practice by forcing us to find a theoretical basis for events that occur in the classroom. In the first of Libby's essays, she contrasted the research on power and culture with an incident in her student teaching classroom. She and her cooperating teacher had caught one of their students lying about a writing assignment. Her cooperating teacher felt that the student's actions were allowable because he was not only a child from a minority culture but also new to the school. For Libby, this situation made apparent the complexity of the problems that can arise because of cultural differences. She wrote in her essay:

I must admit that I feel at a loss in the problems of culture conflict. Is the only solution to have teachers who are culturally related to the students in their classrooms? Of course, realistically, this in not possible . . . especially where there is a cross-section of different cultures.

This brings up another question. When there are a great variety of cultures within one classroom, can one teacher be expected to be able to cross all the cultural boundaries? Delpit does offer some theories for breaking down the barriers of culture such as working to put one's own beliefs on hold in order to allow another's to emerge. I wonder if a teacher can both follow her own values and beliefs and also be able to withhold them in order for her students' beliefs to emerge. If this does happen, will it really help to break down the cultural barriers?

Debra also explored theory that collides with practice in attempting to answer the question, "If Whole Language Is 'Whole,' Then Why Does Phonics Instruction Work in My Classroom?" She wrote:

Originally, I thought that it was an either/or situation—you either "did" Whole Language or you "did" Phonics—but that the two were mutually exclusive. A situation in my classroom made me realize that the two could work together. I asked a six-year-old child how she was able to read the word "People." She replied, "Well, it starts with a "P" and "p" sounds like "[p]" and the "E" sounds like "[e]," and there are lots of people in the picture on this page.

To write her essay, Debra pulled out pieces from the theory that made sense to her intellectually and considered them in relation to pieces from experiences in her classroom. In the process, it became clear that the child was using a combination of phonics and contextual clues to decode words. Writing her essay helped Debra to realize that whole language is not a method of teaching reading—one that emphasizes context clues—but rather a philosophy that could support many strategies, including phonics, for reaching the greater goal of learning to read by reading. Thus, Debra began in her essay to construct her own theory of emerging literacy. This theory, in turn, continues to develop as she is influenced both by other thinkers and by future classroom experiences.

THEORY VERSUS THEORY

In essays of this type, we juxtaposed one educational or philosophical theory against another. Our goal was to reconcile our own ideas on education, teaching, and learning with the latest research and methodology. Some of us challenged certain theories directly by disagreeing with the theories and working out our reasons on paper. Others of us attempted to find a balance between seemingly contrasting theories. And still others synthesized related theories to forge a deeper understanding of their intricacies. In all cases, we were attempting to develop a greater sense of the theoretical issues and to find direction for our own practice as teachers.

Many of our essays dealt with the conflicts between whole language learning theory and the reading subskills approach that is traditionally used. In her essay entitled "Phonics: The Great Debate," Tiz wrestled with these often contrasted theories on teaching reading and writing. After reading both *Becoming a Nation of Readers* (Anderson, 1985) and *Counterpoint and Beyond* (Davidson, 1988), she felt bogged down in the theoretical debate between whole language and phonics. Tiz knew it was an important debate, but it didn't make sense to her. Finally, she realized that she didn't need to concentrate on the issue but to broaden it. Working out her thoughts in her essay, Tiz wrote:

I wish discussions of whole language would move far beyond the phonics issue because I think whole language as a theory applied to reading instruction has so much to offer that isn't seen when whole language theory is compared with the phonics approach. I also think that discussing language learning in terms of focusing on instructional methods is ineffectual because there are so many other issues to be considered.

Janet used whole language theory also as a critical lens in examining particular aspects of children's reading in her essay *Sam I Am, Green Eggs and Ham*. She wrote:

I understood that readers use the four language systems of graphophonics, syntax, semantics, and pragmatics to make sense of what they are reading. What I couldn't see was how a child could make sense of stories that appeared to lack these language cues.

I had been grappling with this question ever since our professor told the class that "he heats meat" is a terrible sentence for a child to make sense of. Apparently, creating a sentence for vowel sounds rather than for meaning generates an artificial type of communication that can often confuse children (i.e., how does he heat it, what type of meat, why didn't they say steak?). Why then, is "Sam I am, green eggs and ham" any more coherent? (Is green eggs and ham his last name?)

Within her essay, Janet attempted to find some evidence of the four language systems in a variety of Dr. Seuss stories. Her initial question guided her through an investigation of the language used in his books as well as the benefits of reading them. By writing this essay, Janet was able to reevaluate what these four systems meant to her. In turn, she was able to find those systems in Dr. Seuss. As a result, her views on his books have entirely changed. Although "he heats meat" is a terrible sentence because it is isolated from context, "Sam I am, green eggs and ham" is not. The child, using the story's context clues, sing song rhythms, and four systems of language, may see that there is a point to these words and that green eggs and ham are what Sam is trying to feed his friend.

Others essays dealt with the larger issues of the relationship of culture and society to educational practices. In her essay entitled "Mirror on Society: Issues of Power, Equity and Entitlement in Education," Madeline attempted to make sense of the complicated interrelatedness of the ideas presented in a series of articles on the culture of power that she had read at the University of Pennsylvania. To make sense of the articles, she paraphrased each one and pulled out their explicit and implicit arguments. Then she attempted to synthesize these arguments into one. In her essay, she wrote:

The articles seem to share a common concern to create a more equitable system of education, within a newly defined pluralistic society. Each author explicitly desires to give all children, regardless of race, religion or sex, the opportunity to participate fully in this new society. To accomplish this, they propose establishing learning environments in the schools that foster individual growth and aid in developing one's relationship with the society at large. They are for expanding traditional notions of teachers, students and the classrooms they operate in.

Integral to this synthesis process was wrestling with the complex issue of diversity and what it meant to her. She continued:

The problems encountered in creating a new societal vision stem from . . . what is basic in human nature: the need to identify with others. As Perrone said, "The outsider, the person who is different, is typically viewed with suspicion, not just in America, but in most parts of the world. What is needed is a re-education on what we know about being decent human beings." And I now add that what is also needed is a re-education on what we know about how it is that we are different and how it is that we are similar.

By causing her to reflect on the nature of education, its participants, its methods, and its overall role in society, essay writing began for Madeline the necessary process of developing a personal philosophy of education, which was critical to her future work as a teacher researcher.

CONCLUSION

As student teachers working to be researchers, we used essays as different ways of exploring educational theory to produce our own understandings. Our exploration involved questioning—of the theories themselves, of practice, and of experience. We found that in our essays, the process of questioning theories and the ways in which we applied them were more helpful than refuting them. Maggie utilized this process of questioning when she asked in one of her essays: "Or perhaps does the very act of my embracing this single philosophy transform me into a sort of technician, a whole language technician?" When we raised questions, individual theories were broadened to capture issues and circumstances beyond their original scope. The result was sometimes a deepened understanding or an enhanced definition of a particular topic. Most often, however, questioning a theory caused us to reevaluate our own thinking and practice. In doing so, new issues were addressed, and still more questions were raised. Questioning in essay writing was and is an ongoing process through which we are continually defining issues, challenging accepted theory, and creating meaning for ourselves.

We began this project as student teachers. The final revisions for this chapter were completed midway through our 1st year of teaching, and our audience has changed. We no longer write for our professor or our classmates and only rarely have the opportunity to exchange ideas with one another because of the logistical difficulties involved (e.g., time constraints and geography). However, the process of examining our practice through writing continues to be an integral part of our teaching experience and serves as a vehicle for further investigations of the teaching and learning process.

Rather than a required assignment, essay writing now functions as a tool with which we are able to build the theoretical and practical foundations necessary to establish our own classrooms. As 1st-year teachers, we have found ourselves formulating increasing numbers of questions. We are at times inundated and challenged by these questions—so much so that we are compelled to write. We write to structure, examine, and resolve some of the issues that arise, which in turn generates even more questions.

In practicing essay writing as a part of our student-teacher training, we learned not a technique, but a system of inquiry that will continue to serve us as classroom teachers. As we confront ongoing issues, we are able to utilize essay writing to inform our practice and mold our understanding of learning and teaching. In sum, we have come to see ourselves not as technicians who follow the results of others' research but as reflective professionals who build our own theories of children's learning to create the most successful classrooms for the children we teach.

• • • • • • • • • • •

Reading as a Teacher

Robert Fecho

ROBERT FECHO *has been teaching secondary English since 1974 in the School District of Philadelphia, where he is currently on the staff of Crossroads, a school within a school at Simon Gratz High School that was conceived by himself and two colleagues. A teacher consultant with the Philadelphia Writing Project since its inception, Fecho is a member of the group's steering committee and the founder of two of its publications, The Update and The Voice. Supported by a 1988 National Council of Teachers of English teacher researcher grant, Fecho studied writing conferences in his classroom and continues to research his classroom as a member of the Urban Sites Writing Network. His publications include "Meeting Strangers in Familiar Places: Teacher Collaboration by Cross-Visitation" (with Susan L. Lytle, English Education, 1991).*

As a teacher, the list of verbs that describe what I do is long. I support, question, mediate, lecture, monitor, encourage, admonish, explain, allow, disallow, value, elicit, invoke, involve, challenge, admire, and try any number of additional actions that might advance learning in my classroom. And of late, it seems that, more and more, I read.

This should come as no surprise. Reading is the first of the three Rs, and it would be natural to assume that someone whose charge it is to teach reading would also be a reader. By itself, this is not a problem. Indeed, it is my love of reading—and its counterpart, writing—that is largely responsible for my having become a teacher in the first place. Books are like worlds to me, and time after time they collide with my own world and, having done so, change it. I wanted that experience for others. I became a teacher.

My peers are English teachers who do not think twice about inhaling a good piece of fiction over a winter weekend. I certainly don't mind doing the same. But recently, much of my reading time is spent rummaging through theory and research related to reading, writing, and learning in general. I trade my Updike, my Walker, and my Wideman for a Rosenblatt, a Rose, and an Ogbu. I do this most willingly, for my need to learn has always fueled my teaching. Yet I have noticed that I read these works differently than other audiences do and that academics, would-be academics, and administrators read these works from different perspectives and with different purposes than mine. They read in manners that fit their needs and objectives. And so do I. In my estimation, I read as a teacher.

What does it mean to read as a teacher? It is my belief that teachers constitute a distinctive interpretive community and that this community—particularly as it relates to the reading of educational research and theory—has clear values and standards that dominate the ways that teachers approach and ultimately interpret readings. I further believe that acknowledgement and acceptance of this interpretive community—by those both within and without its borders— are integral if teachers are to be valued as professionals and seen, as Giroux (1985) suggests, as intellectuals. What I want to argue here is that unless teachers seriously consider what it means to read educational theory and to research as teachers, we will continue to replicate the administrative and research communities that exist already. Consequently, our voice will not be heard except as an echo. This chapter argues that as teachers, we have a unique and necessary perspective in relationship to theory and research and that our conceptualizing of what that perspective is and what it can mean will create for us a niche that will give our collective voices both authenticity and resonance.

Before I can argue for teachers as an interpretive community, I need to clarify the concept of interpretive community in general, several conceptions of which exist among reader response literary theorists. Broadly, the concept attempts to mitigate the transaction between culture and individual readers as individuals attempt to make meaning of text. For Fish (1980), who is commonly credited with inventing the concept, this transaction is predominantly culture to individual, with the former supplying the latter with interpretive heuristics and conventions. Others such as Michaels (1980; reported by Thompkins) argue that a concept of the self is created through its close association with the surrounding culture. It is Bleich (1975), occupying a middle ground between Fish and Michaels, who avers that the individual negotiates a consensus of agreement as part of a larger interpretive community.

In addition to these descriptions by literary theorists, J. Harris (1989), working from a composition perspective, delineates what he calls a "discourse community," a concept that has much in common with the notion of an interpretive community. Drawing on the idea of community as a group with common interests and goals, he suggests that such groups describe and limit the modes of discourse valued by the community. What seems to be in concert among the various descriptions of community is the belief that there exists a group of shared interests at large that alternately exert influence on and are influenced by the individual. What remains constant is that in each conception, the individual and the community enact a transaction; what fluctuates is the degree of interaction between the two.

When using the lens provided by an interpretive community, any text is interpreted and ultimately valued through strategies, needs, and expectations apparent within both the individual and the interpretive communities to which he or she belongs. Such a community can be as large in space and time as an ethnic or national culture. However, as Bleich would certainly agree, subsets of this larger community—some as small as a classroom—exist and exert influence. For our purposes here, it is important to conceive of the interpretive community as any group of readers and writers held together by common purpose and by a consensus of values. An interpretive community is a work in progress with members coming and going as needs arise and with common values reinterpreted by each new incarnation of the group.

As readers, we can belong to several interpretive communities simultaneously. A female African-American medical student with a working-class background, for example, reads with the experience of her race, her class, her gender, her current status as a student, and her future status as a doctor all acting on her transaction with the text. In my own life, I have often seen how defining myself as a member of an interpretive community has altered the way I ultimately read texts. Most recently, when I took a sabbatical from teaching to labor full-time as a graduate student, I read as a graduate student. With my classroom seeming as distant as Aleppo, I was able to detach, get distance, and read an article looking for how it might expand my ever-growing conception of literacy education. When I looked for connections in response to a certain article, I did so at a level that considered the field, the body of existing literature, and implications for the profession. Freed from the necessity of having to immediately translate theory into practice, I was able to read, consider strengths and weaknesses, ruminate, and catalog without having to put into use—at least not any time soon. In short, I had time to wonder.

However, once again, I am both teaching full-time and attending school. Again, there is an immediacy that stalks my reading as a teacher that never emerges if I am reading as an academic. I can best illustrate this shift in approach by relating my experience with Heath's *Ways With Words: Language, Life, and Work in Communities and Classrooms* (1983). I first encountered this book during my sabbatical year. I remember being fascinated by Heath's research methods. She had painstakingly recorded the lives and thoughts of three distinct communities and, with equal deliberation, had described these communities in the pages of her book. It was also quickly apparent that what Heath had done was present a convincing picture of how culture, literacy, and education all interact with an individual's ability to function in the classroom. As a grad student, I viewed her book as a seminal piece—a touchstone of sorts—with which all other literature in related subjects could be placed in juxtaposition. Heath's work also served as a working example of how extensive a true ethnographic narrative needs to be to adequately capture the site of study. And if I was irked that much of the narrative seemed drained of political import despite it subject matter, I could not deny that Heath had broken precedent and had forced readers to consider ways that schools do not take advantage of the diversity at their disposal.

A year later when I was again teaching in the classroom, I returned to Heath, but this time I found a different book. I could still admire all that I had discovered there earlier; however, now I found myself looking for connections to my immediate classroom as opposed to the broader field. If Heath's findings implied that the culture of a community has a direct impact on literacy learning, it was important for me to investigate the culture of my own students. Knowing how to make this happen became paramount. I found myself more drawn to the parts of Heath's book in which she detailed how she transformed both students and teachers into ethnographers and less drawn to her wonderfully detailed descriptions of home life. As a teacher, I needed to understand Heath's book in terms of what it meant for the wider field of literacy education, but more immediately, I needed to read Heath for insight into the practice of my own classroom.

Thus, reading as a teacher means, most of all, reading to translate theory into practice. Let me rush to add that by "translate" we do not mean the wholesale consumption of ideas created by so-called experts from outside the classroom. Instead, the person who merits the title teacher is constantly making meaning of the range of theories that exist and using them as mirrors to hold up to current practice. I was motivated to examine my own practice by the criticism of teacher and student writing conferences by Michaels, Ulichney, and Watson-Gegeo (1986) and Florio-Ruane (1986). It was not as if I read their remarks and suddenly began to follow steps 1 to 4 to better teaching. Instead, using their critique as a guide, I set out to tape my own conferences, examine my own data, and adjust my practice as I felt necessary.

The key to remember is that very little concerns most teachers about theory and research unless practice is also considered. It is not that teachers are incapable of critique or abstraction—they must, in fact, do both before theory can become practice; however, they cannot allow themselves the luxury of time that lingering in critique or abstraction demands. By playing the role of consumers of theory and practice, teachers make possible the dialectic between theory and practice, without which "theory is lifeless" (Crusius, 1989). As teachers continuously adapt theory for use in classrooms, they sustain the process that allows theory to be studied, rethought, and recreated. But to play this role, teachers to date have needed to sacrifice their intentional voice in the discussion. Rather than actively engage in data collection and in subsequent writing about their practice, teachers have until recently been content to allow university researchers to be the sole documenters of the classroom. Although their actions provide a link for theory to inform practice and for practice to inform theory, teachers are often too involved in keeping the cycle going to be little more than silent partners in the process. In short, teachers are so busy putting theory into practice that they have little time to write about how they do what they do.

This returns us to the concept of an interpretive community and the recognition of teachers as just such a distinct group. This belief in teaching as an interpretive community with its own standards and conventions is important because teacher roles are currently in an immense state of flux. In an educational climate, where the wind often blows two directions at once, what does it mean for a teacher to be a reader? On one hand, school districts are churning out standardized curriculums and prescriptive teaching formulas faster than they can be bound in plastic. On the other hand, there is a growing movement afoot that would have teachers reading current theory, conducting our own research, and sharing our practices in an ever-widening professional dialogue. Although I laud these latter trends, which seem to support the professionalism of teachers, I worry that the new roles will be merely added on to already overloaded shoulders. Hargreaves and Dawe (1989) suggest that teachers are being asked to be more collaborative precisely when they have less to be collaborative about. I would take that one step further: Teachers are being asked to be professionally responsible although at the same time little is being done to alter the conditions that lead to five classes of 33 students per day.

When I write to this length, one heuristic that I use is selecting a word that captures the idea of what I wish to discuss and setting it below the current text as a reminder for me to address the issue. While writing this paper, I chose the word *schizophrenic* as a place marker for myself. How else can I feel? As a professional, I need to be aware of current theory, to interact with current theory, and to adapt current theory in order to construct even more current theory. Yet little is being done to alter my teaching load or the institutional structures that would enable me to do what the preceding sentence has described. I am both a professional and a clock-punching worker in an assembly-line education factory.

As teachers, we also contribute to a concept of teacher work that begins and ends at the classroom door. I know of many teachers who want to write more, who want to do teacher research, who want to collaborate with colleagues, but who say the students must come first. And they are right. I know by my own experience that if I had time to read student papers or write in my research journal—but not time for both—I would choose the student projects. First and foremost, facilitating the education of students is what teachers do. Yet researching, writing, and collaborating are also important to our profession and to the students we teach. It is not enough to say that these activities would be nice if we had the time. Instead, we must continue to lobby administrations, school boards, and the general public to broaden their concept of what constitutes teacher work.

For this to happen, teachers must begin to see themselves as a community that is unique and valued for its particular potential. Most important, teachers must recognize in a conscious and deliberate manner their own worth as a interpretive community. In addition, the academic and administration communities must come to accept what it means to read as a teacher. Universities tend to want teachers to become academic researchers and thus to read like university researchers. Administrators, too, frequently want teachers to be consumers of information as opposed to consumers of theory—the former being passive while the latter is active in nature. Very often, teachers themselves seek only to learn the narrow lesson plan rather than the supportive framework, and thus they unwittingly conform to others' theoretical concept of what a teacher is. It is important that teachers instead consider themselves a separate interpretive community, one responsible for its own standards. Only then can empowerment—the power that comes from self-identification of worth—occur.

In the current and important trend toward teacher as researcher, much has been made of the nature of such research and of whether it conforms to the paradigm of more traditional inquiry. More and more often, I hear the answer that teacher research does not necessarily conform, nor should it. It is suggested that such writings as teacher journals and essays, which are not normally considered by academic researchers, should be taken as data for classroom research. This is as it should be. If teachers are to contribute as researchers, it should be on the strengths that their unique perspectives can bring. If research data can be considered a text, teachers have an angle on that text that differs from those of university researchers and school district administrators.

It is this same unique perspective that teachers bring to the reading of research and theory. Although I am leery of capitalistic metaphors, the one that I offer here seems to fit: Teachers are consumers of theory and are therefore the marketplace. If a teacher hasn't been either totally turned off by the aloofness of educational theory or discouraged by the proliferation of teacher-proof curriculum, he or he will continue to read theory in terms of what it means for the classroom. No one else who reads theory does that consistently. A researcher or administrator can attempt to imagine what a theory might look like once adapted for the classroom, but only teachers can, day in and day out, interpret theory for praxis.

I can liken this to an experience I recently had in Chicago. While touring the Art Institute, I came upon six grain stack paintings by Monet. Each presented essentially the same subject—a grain stack or two—but seen in varying perspective, light, and season. By giving the viewer a variety of impressions, Monet acted much like a university researcher who from several vantages attempts to describe working classrooms. However, as diverse as these views are, Monet could never give us the viewpoint of the grain stack even if he were to stand directly inside one. He was not a grain stack. He was an artist and thus saw with the eyes and the experience of the artist—not of the grain stack. So, too, the researcher, no matter how caring and empathetic, cannot see the classroom from the eyes of a teacher.

If I had not taken the time to visit the Art Institute, I would never have transacted with those paintings, and my life would have been devoid of that learning and experience. I would have been a culturally poorer person and probably been ignorant of that fact. In like manner, if teachers do not take it upon themselves to engage in reading of research and theory and in active reflection on their own practice, they are ignoring an opportunity that would give them a voice equal to that of the academy and the administration. Worse yet, they would probably not be aware of the power that could have been theirs.

As members of an interpretive community, teachers, having dispensed with the unacceptable, read with the intent of adapting, juxtaposing, and integrating what is left so that another possibility is added to the repertoire of practice. By interacting with theory, teachers transform that theory and thus continue the dialectic between theory and practice. So, too, as more descriptive research is generated, teachers read the research, adapt ideas for the classroom, and generate new descriptions. This role has been played tacitly by teachers for years. Just as we have closed our doors and achieved our surreptitious autonomy, we have turned our back on our dialoguing about research and theory and have allowed others to describe and interpret what we do. Similarly, as we must open our classroom doors, we must also agree to write about what we read, how we interpret it, how we employ it, and what it means to us.

What has been offered here is one view of the teacher as a reader, admittedly a very subjective one. It may not be the only view of that interpretive community. As Fish explains, "Interpretive communities are no more stable than texts because interpretive strategies are not natural or universal, but learned" (Michaels, 1980, p. 183). Particularly in education, this instability is extremely evident and is precisely why teachers must seize the moment to define themselves in these terms. By seeing themselves as readers of research and theory with a unique relationship to those texts, teachers will continue to create a better understanding of the role of teacher, both for themselves and the world at large.

When Fish (1980) discusses the acceptability of theory, he suggests that total consensus is not required. It is enough that those who do not agree with a certain theory feel compelled to argue against it. By not dismissing it outright, the detractors give life to the very thing that they wish to discredit. Whether or not the reader can accept my perspective of the teacher as a reader, the time has come when the overall importance of the concept cannot be denied. It matters little to me that anyone accept my theory of what it means to be a teacher who reads theory. Instead, it is enough that the concept of a teaching interpretive community be acknowledged, even if that acknowledgement appears negative in nature. It is my hope that all who read this will consider what I have written, take from it what they will, and put those selected thoughts into practice in their own lives. This would be tantamount to reading as a teacher.

● ● ● ● ● ● ● ● ● ● ● ●

The Warriors, the Worrier, and the Word

Deidré R. Farmbry

DEIDRÉ R. FARMBRY *is special assistant to the superintendent of schools in the School District of Philadelphia. For 14 years, she was an English teacher and department head at Simon Gratz, a comprehensive high school in Philadelphia. Farmbry presented a keynote address, "Language and the Affirmation of Identity," at the Conference on Literacy Among Black Youth sponsored by the Literacy Research Center of the Graduate School of Education, University of Pennsylvania, and at a training session for participants of the STEP Program in Scotsdale, Arizona, where she has also served as a curriculum consultant. Farmbry also serves as a consultant for the College Board's Educational Equality Program and is a member of the Philadelphia Chapter of Black Women's Educational Alliance, the Philadelphia Writing Project, and Women in Education.*

"Hey, what are you?"
comes before, "Hello."
(As if my face is strange, you know.)
"Are you Indian, Puerto Rican, or plain old 'us'?"
(Seems to be their major fuss.)
Now,
while you'll see in my face a lingering trace of several ethnic binds,
just who I am cannot be shaped by someone else's mind!
So while deep within the shades of my skin are tones of brown and red,
I proclaim very loudly for all to hear
of the beauty of BLACK instead!

This brief ditty, which I wrote in the early 1970s during my 1st year of teaching, reflects a major theme in this essay: the potential of ethnicity to be a barrier between students and teachers and between students and their expectations for themselves. The sentiment in the verse flowed effortlessly from my pen in response to my students' numerous inquiries regarding my ethnicity. Their questions stemmed from several factors: For convenience sake, I wore my dark brown hair parted down the middle and pulled back in a bun (East Indian style, they informed me), and I had an affinity for silver and beaded jewelry (American Indian style, they informed me). My students attempted to use such information as clues to my identity and erroneously labeled me East Indian, Puerto Rican, or Native American depending on the external variable of the day. However, it was another assumption, based on a feature more permanent than my coiffure or adornment, that presented me with a jolting introduction to the complexities of ethnicity and self-identity and to their impact on school achievement and expectations.

As a young, black teacher assigned to a high school with an all-black student population, I had the luxury of enhancing the rapport with my students through the special bond created by our ethnicity (once I apprised them of the ethnic group I called kin) and, at that time, proximity in age. I shared with all of my students the bond of pigmentation. I shared with some of them the bond of having been raised in a somewhat disjointed, occasionally tumultuous household. I shared with some of them the bond of early parenthood. Despite these similarities, my students pointed out on several occasions a major difference that, according to them, created a chasm between our worlds. They made it clear that my use of language, which contrasted with theirs, deemed me not truly one of them.

Needless to say, as a black teacher, I was disturbed by this revelation by my students that language style could invalidate membership in a particular ethnic group. I felt that if I bought my students' theory, I would be forced to bear the weight of a burden more oppressive than racism or sexism: the burden of in-group alienation, a burden totally unfamiliar to me yet one that I soon learned was at the very heart of my students' attitudes toward achievement. As one who was new to the ranks of "the professional class," I wondered if others like me who were proud of their ethnicity and who attributed the ability to overcome certain odds to their affiliation with that ethnic group had ever had to wrestle with uncertainties about language. I thought of great black teachers through the ages and wondered if they had ever been accused of being other than who they were.

All through childhood, I had been taught that education, especially verbal proficiency, was the great equalizer. But my students viewed my speech patterns, word choices, inflection, and intonation as "different," "foreign," "correct," "proper," and most disturbing of all, "white." Although my students respected me, my accomplishments, and my earnest desire to help them to do well, they persisted in denying me full claim to being black because I did not talk the way they did. This was my first encounter with a theme that is now prevalent in the literacy research: the relationship among language, self-image, and school achievement.

Ferdman (1990) offers a social/psychological perspective on the relationship between literacy and the individual. He asserts that a person's identity as a member of a group is intertwined with the meaning and consequences of becoming literate. The consequences of becoming literate for me related primarily to career prospects, but the consequences for my students seemed directly related to group affiliation. I understood this better when I later read Ferdman's work on literacy and cultural identity. Ferdman's theories, particularly the idea that "emblematic indicators" serve an identity function by marking boundaries between groups, helped me to see that the real obstacle to my students' success was not their lack of ability. I realized that the acquisition of verbal skill could potentially erode their perceptions of themselves and that the fear of that loss was indeed the culprit. My task in the classroom then was to shift emphasis from the skill to the will. Convinced that my students could learn the skills related to literacy and verbal proficiency, I decided to put the emphasis in my teaching on generating in my students the will to let language fluency open additional doors of opportunity. I sought to do this by building bridges between my students' way of speaking and my own way of speaking to make my students consciously aware of the rich variety of speech among people who are black.

I used several strategies to build bridges between their way of speaking and mine. I began by revealing that my identity as the teacher was one reason I felt compelled to speak a certain way in their presence but that my other identities—mother, wife, daughter, and friend—elicited variations, some more subtle than others. I acknowledged before my students the presence of certain emblematic indicators that I relied on to enable me to "fit in" when necessary. I proceeded in this vein, based on my emerging sense that affiliation and identity were two separate factors, with ethnicity associated with identity and language associated with affiliation. Once convinced of this relationship, I tried to get my students to see that ethnicity was impervious to theft by language because ethnicity was a given but affiliation was a variable that influenced language in use.

One resource I used in class was an article in *Newsweek* written by Rachel Jones, who was at the time a sophomore at Southern Illinois University. Jones wrote about her personal agony of growing up speaking standard English and the number of times she had been forced to defend her speech habits. She, too, had been accused of "talking white." I shared the article with my students and used it as the basis for classroom discussion. What made the article so effective and created the greatest impact was the author's observation that none of the black leaders held in high esteem had become famous by using nonstandard English. The people whom Jones mentioned in her article—Martin Luther King, Jr., Malcolm X, Toni Morrison, Alice Walker, James Baldwin, Andrew Young, Tom Bradley, and Barbara Jordan—were all recognized and accepted by my students as heroes and role models—black heroes and role model—who spoke with eloquence, passion, and conviction on issues affiliated with blackness.

"Black English: So Good It's 'Bad,'" an article in *Essence* magazine written by Geneva Smitherman, a professor of speech communications, presents a stark contrast to the article by Jones. Smitherman valued the verbal nuances labeled black English and noted their use by a few of the same black leaders mentioned by Jones. Smitherman claimed that the ability or inability to shift to other forms of English when necessary is what separates black people along economic lines. Smitherman's reference to economic class helped me to gain another perspective that reinforced the point that race was a given but affiliation was the variable. It also opened up a possibility for exploring with my students relationships between language use and economic potential.

Regardless of the current economic status of my students, all of them had dreams of one day being employed and self-sufficient. We talked about the various costs of self-sufficiency. Although my students accepted the fact that job entry might necessitate casting off faded jeans, few realized the impact that language would have in determining the parameters of their occupational mobility. I vowed to generate classroom activities that would let my students see that neither my speaking patterns nor theirs were issues of racial identification but were, once again, issues of affiliation, audience, and purpose. Just as my students understood that toddler babble gains approval from an audience of adoring relatives and that teenage slang guarantees approval with the audience known as the peer group, they began to realize that standard English was most likely to be the language of the work force and most readily accepted at the job interview. My students began to see the relationship between language and livelihood.

I began to develop a unit called "Acceptability/Flexibility." Using various literary works and writing exercises, I was able to explain the concept of audience and the need for bilingualism if the language acquired from the initial affiliation group, the family, is different from that of the business world. My aim was to identify items in the language that remained constant as well as those that were most subject to transformation as audiences changed. Students discovered that the bulk of their language was acceptable for multiple audiences, including work-related audiences, and that their use of audience-appropriate language made them no less black. Although some found the flexibility exercises fun and beneficial, others who had been raised primarily speaking standard English found that their writing and speaking did not alter drastically as they converted their work to make it suitable for one audience or another. In essence, my students were encouraged to build on the strengths they possessed while accepting personal responsibility to increase their options in life by being verbally flexible.

Since my early initiation into the complexities of language and identity, I have continued to read the works of various scholars who chose this area for the focus of their inquiries. Paulo Freire and Donaldo Macedo (1987), two prolific writers on literacy, helped me to understand the hunches I felt as a 1st-year teacher. From their perspective, language projects different world views. In essence, my students' verbal codes transmitted their world views. In their codes, I heard the world view of the southern experience because many of my students were perhaps only the second generation to have been born in the North. In their codes, I heard street culture, with its signifying and slang. I heard the culture of the adolescent with its quick-fire transformation and its roller-coaster ride to obsolescence. All that I heard, I saw in their writing, and I understood what they said and what they wrote. The difference, however, was that although I validated what they relayed through their writing and speaking, I also let them know that they were capable of learning another dialect, what I called the "dialect of options." I borrowed from Freire's philosophy that educators in the United States need to use their students' cultural universe as a point of departure, which enables students to recognize their own cultural identities.

The challenge for students is to attain fluency in language to increase their options in the world. As literacy education is a form of socialization, students need to know that being literate implies knowing which literate behaviors are appropriate for a given situation. The challenge for teachers is to assist students in their progression toward this understanding. It is critical, however, that in guiding students, teachers do not denigrate the social relationships in which students learned their present patterns of speech. In other words, teachers must beware of trespassing on speech patterns shared by members of the students' nurturing base, for those patterns will most likely remain a key component of self-identity.

Over the years, I have seen evidence that students' abilities to expand their verbal repertoires do indeed develop. Most students whom I have encountered years later have made the transition to verbal variety and proficiency and seem to have done so with their sense of identity intact. I hear familiar voices from classrooms of the past with confident cadence and melodious metaphors. I hear former students introducing me to their children and correcting their grammar in my presence. They are my students—black, beautiful, and proud—traveling life's road with confidence and self-determination.

• • • • • • • • • • •
Doing School Differently

Alisa Belzer

ALISA BELZER *has tutored individuals, taught classes, and coordinated programs at the Center for Literacy, a large citywide adult literacy program in Philadelphia, for the past 4 years. In addition to providing direct services, she has developed special peer-tutor training, collaborative learning orientation for adult learners and their tutors, and has done program evaluation and research in the areas of alternative reading and writing assessment, curriculum, and program retention. Belzer is currently cofacilitating a teacher-research group of adult literacy teachers and program administrators and is also a doctoral student at the Graduate School of Education at the University of Pennsylvania.*

When I think back over my experiences as an adult literacy teacher, I am struck by the evidence that both the learners and I come to the experience of teaching and learning together with a well-formed set of beliefs about what our class ought to be like. We come with conscious and unconscious definitions of reading and writing, teaching and learning, and their subtle and complex interrelationships. These expectations are shaped for all of us by our personal learning histories. When we think about instruction and assessment for adult learners, it is especially important to understand what those beliefs are— by explicitly seeking evidence of them and exploring their meanings individually and collectively as well as examining the ways that they change over time. It is with an eye toward revealing some of these complexities that I share some stories from my teaching.

In this essay, I explore three episodes from the two classes I worked with during my 1st year of teaching. Drawn from my teaching journal, these vignettes are used to demonstrate some of the ways that the beliefs a teacher and learners bring to a classroom shape expectations of what should be taught and how. As I discuss them, I point out both the difficulties as well as the opportunities that a variety of beliefs coming together in one classroom offer the teacher and, hopefully, the learners. Trained as an elementary teacher, I chose not to enter the classroom after graduation. I did administrative work and one-to-one tutoring in an adult literacy program for about a year and a half. When I did finally enter the classroom, it was as an adult literacy teacher.

IS LEARNING "LEARNING" IF IT'S NOT LIKE LEARNING IN SCHOOL?

The settings for adult literacy programs range from public libraries to church basements, from public schools to storefronts. Each site conveys implicit messages about reading and writing, teaching and learning. During the year of teaching that I discuss in this essay, my classes took place in two sites: an elementary school and a city recreation center. Both classes were aimed at parents of school-age children. The fact that one class was held in a school, a building most symbolic of traditional learning, foregrounded for me the contrast between my way of teaching and the way that many learners expect teaching and learning to be.

Each fall, the school's reading specialist hosts a workshop for parents to explain the reading/language arts curriculum and its grading procedures. Meeting at this school site, I began to recognize all the powerful albeit subtle messages that adult learners in our culture continue to receive long after they leave school—messages about what school and the relationships between teachers and learners and between readers, writers, and texts should be like. For 2 years, the people in my class and I attended the workshop for parents. The focus of instruction was on getting kids through basal readers, workbooks, word lists, and curriculum-mandated writing assignments. Parents were advised to drill their children on word lists and to create other schoollike reading and writing tasks at home. My students as well as the other parents at the meeting sat quietly. They asked very few questions. They appeared rather bored.

This workshop illustrates the overwhelming and powerful messages that adult learners often continue to receive long after they leave school—messages about reading and writing as a group of subskills and about teaching and learning as a process wherein a teacher deposits knowledge in a learner much as a banker deposits money. When I chose to do things differently in my classroom, I was bucking a very prevalent and thus very powerful model of the way reading is frequently taught in schools. Certainly, I taught differently from the teachers with whom my student's children spent their days learning. But who was I to decide to teach differently? Why should learners operating with a traditional model of reading, which is congruent in approach with that of the expert teacher of reading in their children's school, feel comfortable with my approach, which is holistic and learner centered? Ideally, I can make an alternative approach so engaging, so motivating, so interesting, and so successful that learners come to see that learning can be different and still worth the time and effort. I hoped that they would come to see that learning in school does not always have to be school-like to count as learning.

However, no matter how effectively I taught according to my beliefs, this "conversion" was not a foregone conclusion. What happened instead was that learners asked me, in a variety of ways, why our school wasn't more like their children's school and, indeed, more like their own past experiences with school. After all, here we were teaching and learning in a school. It is certainly not surprising that these same learners asked me when I was going to bring them workbooks, questioned me on whether I was planning to test them, and stated flatly that I wasn't doing my job if their homework involved composing word problems for each other rather than preparing commercially produced worksheets for drill and practice.

There were many ways in which I tried to do school differently from how it is done in traditional schooling. As a result, sometimes the learners looked at me strangely, sometimes they complained, and frequently they resisted. I found myself with a complicated dilemma on my hands. On one hand, I believed learning is not only more interesting but also more effective, both individually and socially, when I teach "my way." On the other hand, embedded in "my way" is the belief that teachers must have a deep respect for what learners know and bring with them to the learning situation and must find ways to make that knowledge a part of what gets shared as we work together.

DOING SCHOOL DIFFERENTLY: WHAT SHALL WE READ TOGETHER?

Here, I demonstrate some of the ways I did school differently from what most learners came to school expecting. The first example, although complex and difficult to understand, is in some ways not atypical of the dilemmas I faced as I tried to choose materials to use in a class.

In keeping with my beliefs about reading and writing as well as teaching and learning, I feel it is important and worthwhile to provide reading materials that are interesting, are relevant, and relate to the learners' plans and goals. I also believe that it is often easier to comprehend and certainly more motivating to read materials that cover topics about which the reader has some background knowledge. For example, because my class is made up of African-American women, I try often to include texts written by African-American authors about themes from the African-American experience. I read widely to find materials that fit the bill—not only topically but also in terms of language complexity.

At one point, I came across an article on teenage pregnancy, a mini-ethnography of sorts about a counseling/support program for teen mothers that was held in a recreation center in the Bronx. For the most part, the author let the mothers speak for themselves. In fact, it was specifically to learn directly from the young women about their experiences that the author went to spend time with them. I liked the piece because it privileged the expertise of the participants and questioned the wisdom of the "experts." I decided to use it as a way of looking at and talking about point of view and journalistic bias. As almost all of the women in my classes were then or had been teen mothers, some of them were mothers of teen mothers, and one student was teenaged and pregnant at the time, the piece certainly seemed relevant.

Although it was unusual for this to happen, both classes began the article at the same time with a great deal of enthusiasm and interest. Only one class chose to finish it. The discussion generated over the first days was some of the best we had all year. Everybody had something to say, to contribute, or to add. I also found amid this positive energy a willingness to deal with the text in an exploratory, interactive way that had been rare up until that time. I felt confirmed that materials can make all the difference and that in this case I had struck gold.

I looked forward to getting back into the article at our next meetings. While one group continued to plow through the article over the course of the next two or three class meetings, the other group did an abrupt about-face the very next time we met. We began reading together, but right away I noticed that people were quieter, were less willing to read, and were exchanging glances with one another. After not very long, one student said something that opened up a tirade. Amid a great deal of hostility, I was accused of being a racist for bringing in material that was so biased—biased, one student explained, because the majority of the girls in the article were black. One student wondered aloud what had possessed me to think that this was appropriate material to use in the classroom. The students made it clear that they did not want me, a white teacher, to use materials about black people—especially if the images they portrayed could in any way be construed as negative. They told me that they felt that an article about black teen mothers was doing just that by portraying a negative image of blacks and that it was therefore biased and racist and so, by association, was I. They added—and this made the whole thing more confusing—that they didn't need to read about black teen motherhood because they had lived it. I wondered whether the article wasn't so much biased as it was true and hitting too close to home.

I left class that day confused and shook up. On one hand, I felt that much of what I believed about materials of instruction had been challenged by the group, whom I believed should have a strong voice in choosing those materials. Although I had offered students the responsibility of making those choices directly, no one had ever taken me up on that offer. Alternatively, I believed that I was using what they had taught me about their interests, experiences, and concerns to inform my choices. I didn't pick this article in a vacuum. In this case, however, my beliefs about what makes for a good class text was coming into direct conflict with those of the learners. I wondered about the whole concept of relevance.

I wanted to try to understand this episode a little better, so shortly after the event, I decided to ask each of the two groups of learners why they thought the other had responded so differently to the materials. Although the two groups appeared to be demographically very similar, the angry group told me that the other group was too ignorant, unsophisticated, or Uncle Tomish to voice their resentment or perhaps to even feel their anger in the first place (it remained unconscious). The unangry group was similarly denigrating, telling me that the others were too ashamed of who they were to enjoy reading about their own culture.

Certainly, this vignette covers many very complex questions about the role that race and class play in learning situations when students and teachers come from different worlds. Class and race are inevitably tied in with the beliefs and expectations that we all bring to learning situations. Still, I haven't and may never come to understand all the implications of this story. I think, however, that in spite of the conflicts and discomfort that the experience caused, some very important learning also occurred. For one, learners were responding to texts in new ways: They were actively expressing preferences, arguing for and against specific positions, and in one case were empowered enough to choose to stop reading. Inadvertently, I had created a new context for responding to texts. There was an excitement about reading and an acknowledgement of the power of a text that I had never seen before in this group. I also saw the readers in that room taking control of the text and their learning in a whole new way.

As a teacher, I learned about the power of a text to excite response. I learned about the complexity of those responses. Most important, I learned that there are no easy, pat answers about the relevance or appropriateness of texts for learning situations in which the teacher—despite an interest in sharing power and decision-making roles—still chooses and initiates the reading of specific texts. I have not yet figured out a way to get learners to want to participate in making these choices. The bigger question here is what beliefs drive a teacher and learners to see a text as appropriate for teaching reading. For me, the fact that the article was about experiences that I knew the learners had had, led me to believe it was appropriate. For some of the learners, this very same logic made the article inappropriate. In a class in which the opinions of learners are valued, there is an obvious tension. In retrospect, it seems that the only way to deal with that tension is to bring it out in the open as part of the learning process. In another way, however, I believe that school reading has to be done differently.

DOING SCHOOL DIFFERENTLY: HOW SHALL WE WRITE TOGETHER?

I believe that growth occurs when writers treat composing more and more as a process that benefits from rereading, revising, and choosing to take or not to take suggestions from colleagues. With this belief as a guide, over a period of time I had worked hard at getting people in the class to be willing to share their writing as well as to feel comfortable with and competent at giving and taking feedback. This process came hard to many of the learners, so I was pleased one day that Donna, a learner who had just joined the class, offered to share with the group her very first piece. Although there had been productive give and take between the learners on other days, when Donna shared, the first or second person to respond to her piece surprised me by breaking all the ground rules of the class. Without responding to what Donna said in her writing or even saying anything at all positive, she very strongly stated that Donna had a major flaw: She was connecting every sentence with the word "and." Donna went from looking proud and pleased about not only writing her first piece but also sharing it, to looking hurt. She had tears in her eyes. Although it was clear at the time that this experience was a blow for Donna, it was only later that I came to realize how deeply stung she had felt. Two things happened in Donna's writing that clued me in to the significance of the episode. The first was that she stopped using the word "and" in her writing.

Instead, she simply substituted the word "in." For example, she wrote, "Lavonia in her two girls came home to visit family in friends." At first forgetting the earlier episode, I assumed she was simply confusing homonyms ("in" is a near homonym for "and" for many of my students). When we discussed it, however, she told me she was using "in" because she had been told not to use "and." She was trying to avoid further criticism. After spending a little more time in the class, Donna used an open-ended homework writing assignment to write a letter to me that she chose to deliver by reading aloud to me and the class during writing time. In that letter, she wrote that as a result of my always asking the group for feedback on everyone's writing, she had lost her self-confidence as a writer. She concluded her letter by telling me that this approach had left her feeling that nothing she wrote was ever good enough.

On one hand, I felt terrible that my intentions and expectations of encouraging the group to write collaboratively and to learn from one another had been so misunderstood or poorly communicated. On the other hand, my own feeling as a teacher was that this was the most powerful, self-assured piece that Donna had ever written. Donna had found her writer's voice and learned about the power of the written word. I realized that in trying to treat writing as an ever-evolving process, I was coming off as an ever-critical nag and was encouraging the learners to do the same.

We were coming from different places, but we were learning. I saw Donna become a better writer in spite of her lack of self-confidence. I was learning that my beliefs about writing and the teaching I did to support those beliefs were not always shared or even well understood by the learners. I knew that in the case of teaching writing, a particular belief implied particular teaching activities. However, I was learning that depending on one's beliefs, those activities could be interpreted as having more than one meaning. Donna and perhaps others in the class did not share my beliefs and thus understood the writing activities as having completely different meanings. Although her writing still improved, her beliefs remained unchanged. I wonder in what ways a change of beliefs would have benefited her writing growth even more.

LEARNING FROM THE DIFFERENCES

As a teacher researcher, I see with growing clarity the inherent contradictions in my visions of teaching and learning. Everything I am as a teacher suggests the importance and value of making the knowledge and beliefs that learners bring to a class a part of the content of learning. But two things happen as a result. Learners are offered and often take the opportunity to express those beliefs, *and* those beliefs often carry with them expectations that are in opposition to a class that offers them control and voice. I view learning as a collaboration with my students—a coinvestigation, if you will—but it is bound to be complicated if learners don't share with me a belief in coinvestigation. They are often neither prepared nor expecting to be coparticipants in my vision. Rather, they bring with them their own set of beliefs about reading and writing as well as teaching and learning—beliefs that are well formed and reinforced through years of experience and that are often very different from mine.

As I have gained confidence in my teaching and in the ability and strength of the learners with whom I work, I have become more comfortable in embracing our differences and less fearful in confronting them within myself and publicly with groups of learners. On my good days, I have learned to believe that it is okay to use differences as opportunities for more teaching and learning—as a way in fact to further the case that we are involved codependently with one another. I see the opportunity to make our beliefs explicit as a way to assess learners initially and over time. After all, if beliefs become part of the stuff of the curriculum, presumably they change and grow richer over time. We are never all going to agree on the best way to teach and learn, to assess, and to relate to each other. But what I am coming to understand is that the point is not simply to convey a set of beliefs via a set of learning activities, to hope that the reasons why I choose to teach a certain way are clear to learners, or even to wish that by some magic tricks or fast talking learners will see things the way I do. Rather, I have come to treat the differences not as simple conflicts that can and should be resolved—not as disagreements in which if I do the "right thing" we will all agree—but as opportunities for us to learn and grow together—to do school differently.

• • • • • • • • • • •

How My Question Keeps Evolving

Michele Sims

MICHELE SIMS *taught in New York City for 10 years before joining the School District of Philadelphia 6 years ago. An active member of the Philadelphia Writing Project, Sims has participated in the Pennsylvania Assessment System Writing Sample Field Test and the Pennsylvania Department of Education Chapter V Learning Outcomes for the Arts and Humanities. With colleagues, she recently received a PATHS grant for exploring portfolios/performance-based assessment and joined the Urban Sites Writing Network, a national network of teacher researchers. Sims has presented her classroom research at various local and regional conferences, and her article "Inquiry Through the Lens of Urban Classrooms: An African-American Female in Search of Truth" will appear in Theory Into Practice.*

This essay tells about my journey into inquiry and how it led to a dramatic shift in the way I view teaching as a professional and the way I think about my classroom. In the essay, I draw on journal entries, protocols, and field notes.

Gathering data in the classroom was interwoven with working with students as coinvestigators, consulting with colleagues individually and collectively, and dialoguing with university faculty. My journey was neither linear, solitary, nor sequential but was instead a messy process of coming to know myself, my questions, and my work. Over the course of a year, my research questions kept evolving as I developed new perspectives for exploring students' needs, classroom environments, teaching strategies, and teacher collegiality. Throughout this piece, my questions appear in italics as a way of showing their evolution over time.

GETTING STARTED

I am an African-American teacher who has taught primarily African-American students for the past 12 years. I think of reading as a lifeline that stretches across and encompasses the intellectual, social, and emotional aspects of our lives as we struggle to do what Freire (1971) calls "reading the word" and "reading the world." The students with whom I work have been designated Chapter I eligible in both reading and mathematics. For a number of years, I have been perplexed about these students: *Why do middle school students with average intelligence struggle with comprehension?* My underlying assumption had been that these students can become "successful" readers and that it is teachers who have been unsuccessful in finding ways to help them to make the connections needed for greater comprehension.

Without knowing it, this question was one that I brought with me to a Philadelphia Writing Project Summer Institute, where I was introduced to the notion of teacher as researcher and to the processes of think-aloud protocols. I was excited at the prospect of trying a strategy that would allow me insights into what happens when students initially interact with print. It wasn't until almost a year later, during a second Summer Institute, that I framed a researchable question about my curiosity: *For students for whom decoding is not an issue, what kind of meaning do they make of written texts?* I wanted to know what I could learn regarding students' comprehension by examining their thinking aloud about print read silently. At that point, my question was: *What's involved when students transact with informational text? What allows students to interpret a character's motives? How do students formulate theme and main idea?*

I wanted to coinvestigate these questions with students, but I was unsure about whether one student would be more suitable than another as coinvestigator. Writing in the journal helped me realize how many questions I had about the ways that students make sense of texts. But I was still unclear about whom to select as a collaborator. I asked my colleagues in our teacher-research group to think with me about who should participate. For many in the group, this issue of selecting a student was problematic. As the discussion progressed, the following suggestions were made: Consider someone you are curious about, invite students who are likely to be agreeable to a collaborative working relationship, or approach students who have a stable school history and a consistent attendance record. Ricardo seemed to stand out for many reasons: He had an above average attendance record but was a student who didn't make the expected gains in the previous year. He wasn't someone that I felt particularly close to. He often seemed puzzled when many other students seemed to be clear. He had supportive parents who came to school whenever we requested. And he was someone whom I wanted to know and felt I should know better. Here was a student whose mother's voice cracked with emotion as she told of how "grateful" she was that Ricardo was in the program again. It was then that I began to realize that perhaps I was shortchanging students like Ricardo who didn't make overt demands on me. When I invited him to participate, I was struck by his eagerness to become a part of this journey and felt that I had made a sound choice.

MAKING PROGRESS

Having embarked on this journey as a teacher researcher, I discovered my first frustration was finding a way to take a closer look at Ricardo while meeting the demands of the class. This became another question as I worried: *How can I meet the needs of my more quiet students while productively channeling the energy of my more aggressive students?* My journal entry at that time gives insight into the complexity of conducting teacher research:

I'm making a conscious effort to collect as much of Ricardo's work as possible. It's difficult. I think this shift in the kind of attention I'm paying to him has him somewhat rattled. I sense he has mixed feelings about this. He seems to enjoy the conversations we have, but when it comes to collecting his work, he may feel that he's being put under a microscope. Maybe he's become quite accustomed to a type of invisibility. Is it safe to be unnoticed?

Before having Ricardo participate in the protocols, I was curious about his attitude toward reading. I developed an oral interview and a written reading survey that explored his history as a reader.

The following is a sampling of Ricardo's responses. By examining his responses to similar questions in different modes of inquiry, I gained greater insight into how Ricardo viewed himself as a reader. In his responses to a written reading survey given first, Ricardo commented, "I am [a] good [reader] but not grait because it is hard to consomtate [concentrate] whith the diffent group." He felt that a "better reader" was one who could "consomtate ezaly." His earliest memory of reading was of "contests" in the first grade called "read out," in which making "a mastke" [mistake] in reading orally eliminated you from the game. In contrast, when I interviewed him about a week later, I learned that Ricardo didn't consider himself to be a good reader at all "cause I read slow." He thought of Khadijah as a good reader because she not only concentrates but "looks at the word before she reads it." Once again, time and speed were critical connections made in his earliest and current notions of being a good reader.

WRITTEN READING SURVEY: OCTOBER 19, 1990
Do you consider yourself a good reader?
I am good but not grait because it is hard to consochate whith the diffent group.

What do you think would make you a better reader?
If we just had one big old grop because peopl be talking and some don't. A better reader to me is a person who can consomtate ezaly.

What is your earliest memory of you as a reader?
It was in my first school called berny in the fist [grade] We use to have contes of wo can read an if you made a mastke [mistake] you where out it was called read out

What types of reading do you enjoy and do?
I like to read advchor [adventure] storeis and sports stories.

ORAL READING INTERVIEW: OCTOBER 27, 1990
If you were to describe yourself as a reader, what might you say?
I'm not a really good reader, but I can read.

What makes you say you're not a really good reader?
Cause I read slow.

Is there anyone in the class you consider a good reader?
Khadijah.

Why Khadijah?
Cause she concentrates . . . she looks at the word before she reads it. And she picks it up real quickly.

I want to go back to your earliest memory of learning to read. When was it and what was it like?
It was fun because we was like in the first grade . . . and . . . uh . . . we used to . . . like my teachers . . . they used to let us play games . . . with reading and uh . . . we used to time ourselves, who could read the fastest.

Do you think of yourself as a good reader now?
Uh . . . I'm not a very good reader . . . because I read . . . slow.

Later that month, Ricardo and I made our first think-aloud protocol, which was not very productive and in fact ended with Ricardo's comment, "I don't wanna do this anymore. This don't make sense. None of this make sense." Nonetheless, I learned some important information about Ricardo. He was a reader who had the explicit need to derive meaning from text, and trying to talk and understand at the same time was very frustrating.

From this experience, a new series of questions about teaching and learning emerged: *How can I encourage kids to stretch themselves? How can I get them to understand that learning is not always easy but takes hard work and determination? But then how can I expect a student to become invested in a text when it is incomprehensible to him? How much scaffolding should I provide for a student?* Subconsciously, these were questions that I'd been struggling with for years, but in this one instance, they crystallized and the impact was tremendous. So often as teachers, we are so busy teaching and managing that we have little time for becoming reflective practitioners. Because I was focusing on one student, I could see more clearly than I had been able to before.

The struggle to be a teacher researcher—to keep a daily teacher journal—was ongoing. In spite of my spotty entries, I was able to gather more information about Ricardo than I realized. Through the oral/written interviews, I developed a fairly accurate impression of how Ricardo regarded himself as a reader and a writer. And surprisingly, the unsuccessful protocol provided a significant piece of information about Ricardo's need to make text meaningful.

Fortunately, the next event that helped me come to know Ricardo was an opportunity to present him to a group of teachers through the process of descriptive review (see Kanevsky in Chapter 7):

The primary purpose of the Descriptive Review of a Child is to bring together varied perspectives, in a collaborative process, in order to describe the child's experience in the school setting. On the basis of this description and discussion of its implications, the group comes to a fuller understanding of the child, makes recommendations for supporting and deepening the child's school experiences, and according to need, offers ways to support the teacher bearing major responsibility for the child in implementing the recommendations. An underlying assumption of this process is that by looking at one child in this manner, it is believed that teachers can learn a great deal about other children in their classrooms. (Prospect Center documentary processes, 1986)

In preparing for the descriptive review, I brought together data from a variety of sources and situations. I used my own observations, the student's work, the interview, and the think-aloud protocol. During one of our research seminars, a colleague had presented one of her special education students, Michael, through this process. At one meeting, we wondered if it was only coincidental that we both chose unassuming students for our reviews. In this conversation, we shared our struggle in gravitating toward the more demanding students and in turn "overlooking" students like Ricardo and Michael. We made assumptions that the quiet students weren't in as much need. My colleague phrased it well when she said, "In our minds we'd say to ourselves— 'that child will be all right until we get back to him.'" But we both wanted desperately for these students to do more than just survive. It was that collaborative inquiry that helped me to frame a question for the descriptive review: *How do I make Ricardo more visible to me as a student and prevent him from slipping through the cracks?*

In the descriptive review, the child is presented from five perspectives. The following are brief excerpts from the original descriptive review of Ricardo. They reflect many of the implicit questions that I wanted to explore about him.

1. Physical Presence and Gesture
   Ricardo is a handsome, rich chocolate complected 13 year old boy of African American descent. He is trim and athletically talented though small for his age. Ricardo is a "young thirteen," fairly unsophisticated, and not streetwise.

2. Disposition
   Last year Ricardo was new to Cooke Middle School and was one of the youngest students in our group. This year Ricardo is much more active, outgoing with a stronger sense of self. A little more of a "risk-taker."

3. Relationship With Children and Adults
   He gets along well with his peers though he is not at the "center" of the crowd. He shows respect to his peers and to the adults in the building. He seems to appreciate his teachers, especially if they are supportive of him and are sensitive to his needs.

4. Activities and Interests
   Ricardo loves football more than anything else. He plays with the Logan Cowboys and has practice twice a week. Outside of sports, Ricardo likes almost anything that has to do with play or games.

5. Formal Learning
   When involved in projects he considers manageable, Ricardo can be serious and focused. But when faced with a slightly more challenging situation, he frequently becomes frustrated and starts to disassociate with the task. Being "right" is very important to Ricardo, but being wrong is intolerable to him . . . being wrong in a group. The team agreed that academically Ricardo has serious basic skills deficiencies. Ricardo has consistently demonstrated himself to be an active thinker— original, though admittedly his way of thinking hasn't always been clearly understood.

In preparation for the descriptive review, information was also gathered from colleagues who had taught Ricardo. Ayesha, his math teacher, stated, "Ricardo displays a real willingness to tackle nonroutine problems. He also has a willingness to reveal himself." In social studies, Dennis recalled Ricardo's "willingness to be captured by a thought or new interest, and his enjoyment at being right." These multiple perspectives illuminated Ricardo and reinforced the value of eliciting meaningful information about students from colleagues.

The descriptive review perspective enabled me to look at Ricardo through many different lenses. In the process of working with students who have over a period of years been singled out as nonachievers and who have had negative experiences surrounding reading and writing, my primary focus has been trying to change individual attitudes by forming communities of learners. Looking globally with the descriptive review categories enriched my focus on one individual and expanded my knowledge about how effective, literate classroom environments could be created.

When the descriptive review was completed, I had conflicting feelings. I felt a sense of both accomplishment and unease. And I had begun to form new burning questions: *What are the best ways for me to support students' learning? What kinds of meaningful and manageable assessment tools can be created so that I can come to know the quiet, less assertive students in my class? How inclusive are the decision-making processes that school communities engage in around the important issues of accountability and assessment as positive tools for students and teachers?*

Although my questions as a teacher researcher keep evolving, I realize that by looking at many kinds of classroom data, I can uncover and articulate concerns that have existed in my practice for a long time. My initial questions about how students make meaning from texts evolved into new questions whose scope was much broader and encompassed other issues across children and contexts.

My initial question developed from a long-standing need to investigate why my students had such difficulty comprehending text. When I began to look closely at Ricardo, my questions regarding comprehension and inquiry were complicated by broader concerns about motivation and scaffolding in teaching and learning. While involved in the descriptive review process, the need for meaningful and manageable assessment tools became evident. My thinking evolved from: *What can I learn from my students if they engage in specific tasks?* to *What can I do for all my students if I devise and manage ways of looking not only at singular features of their literacy but instead at a richer portfolio of their literacy development?* There is little that is ingenious, particularly unique, or conspicuous about my current question: Its value lies in *how* the question was derived—a personal journey through a process that advocates systematic, intentional inquiry and collaboration—through teacher research.

. . . .

Rethinking Power

Samona Joe

SAMONA JOE *teaches sixth-grade math and science at the Barratt Middle School in the School District of Philadelphia. She is a 1991 graduate of Project START at the Graduate School of Education, University of Pennsylvania. This is her 1st year of teaching and her first solo published piece, which she also presented at the Ethnography and Education Forum in 1992. Joe is one of the coauthors of "Leaving the Script Behind" (see Chapter 8).*

I am an African-American woman teaching math and science to two classes of sixth-grade students in a large Philadelphia middle school. This is my 1st year of teaching. This essay draws on experiences I had as a teacher researcher during my student teaching year and what I have been learning during this 1st year in the classroom.

Although because of district personnel policies I was not officially to begin work until 2 weeks after the opening of school, I decided to go in on the 1st day to check out the school and the students. I approached the day with all the zest of a young child on Christmas morning. The dark and seemingly restrained appearance of the building didn't shake my zealousness one bit. After all, I was walking in there equipped with solid student teaching experience, my *Handbook for New Teachers,* and a $22,000 Ivy League degree. The plan was that I would spend the morning observing the woman with whom I was to team teach. However, that plan was short-lived.

I sat near the back of the room while my partner called roll and began talking about classroom rules and school supplies. Some of the students began to talk among themselves about who they thought I was. As the not so quiet whispers reached the student sitting closest to me, I leaned over to him and said, "No, I am not anyone's mother." He whispered to his other neighbor, "I wish she was our teacher . . . nobody want that white lady." Before I could respond or hear the rest of that conversation, I heard my partner beginning to chastise the students for talking. The response from most of the students was to suck their teeth, roll their eyes, sigh, and continue talking at a slightly lower volume. It surprised me somewhat that they would be so obviously "uncooperative" given that this was the first day with their new teacher. As I asked myself, Should she have started with a different topic and a different tone of voice? Would it have made a difference? I was called to report to Room 312.

This is where I met my homeroom or advisory class. Students were sitting on desks yelling to one another about various things, and the black substitute teacher was trying to conduct a game of seven up. Given my experience with young black people and the scene I had just witnessed, I used my most serious, most black teacher voice to call for everyone's attention. I introduced myself as their new teacher and informed them that there was business to be taken care of. With the help of the substitute teacher, we got the roll called, school rules reviewed, school supplies noted, class schedules copied, and teacher expectations stated. Fortunately for them, as I made clear, the bell rang for lunch and there was early dismissal. Breathing a sigh of relief, I asked myself, "Would my luck have held up with that black teacher voice if the day had been extended?"

My 1st day was full of questions—questions I find myself continually raising within my framework as a teacher researcher. These questions center on issues of power, goals, and assessment. Although I revisit these questions from different angles each time, I repeatedly find myself asking:

- What role does power as played out in differences of gender, race, and class have in my teaching and in my students' learning?
- What do I do as an educator to address issues of race and racism in current educational policy and practice?
- How does awareness of race and racism inform my evaluation of my students' performance and learning and my own growth as a teacher?

These questions are the main markers along my journey in teacher research, which thus far spans the academic year of my student teaching and the first semester of my 1st year. My data include essays written during my student teaching year, discussions before I became a "real" teacher, and experiences in the classroom as a beginning, employed teacher.

POWER

The first major set of questions for me centered on issues of power. I define power as the ability to guide and/or shape outcomes in one's own life and to influence others' lives. In my view, there are certain very specific, although complex, indicators and/or sources of power in this country, including race, class, and gender.

Inside the classroom, I wonder about my children: Who are they? How do they see power? Do they think I have it all? Do I? How do their views affect their learning and my teaching? How do I exercise the power I feel I have in order to help them feel empowered? These questions are related to the issues and concerns I brought with me to my student teaching. In an essay written at the beginning of my student teaching experience concerning the way that classes are organized in many schools, I wrote:

Throughout public schools students are grouped in one way or another according to ability. Borko and Eisenhart (1989) argue that reading groups represent different literacy communities in that they are characterized by different but consistent patterns of knowledge, behavior, standards of performance, expectations, and conceptions of print and uses thereof. Because the patterns are consistent and different for each reading group, movement between communities is very difficult. . . . [D]ifferences were found in the students' conceptions of reading, ways of communicating about print, and teacher expectations and evaluations of students in different ability groups.

One important question I would ask the authors would concern the role that race, class, and gender play in the way the reading groups function as literacy communities. Particularly because we live in a society laden with value judgments, presuppositions, and stereotypes, it seems that issues of race, class, and gender would play a role in some way in how we look at "ability" as well as ability-based groups (however such is defined). Therefore, it also seems very likely that these issues might affect what we might expect from different children and how we might evaluate them.

Another question I would ask these authors concerns the students' perceptions of reading and ability. More specifically: how do students' perceptions affect (and how are these perceptions affected by) differences in teacher expectations, evaluations, and other dynamics of the ability-based groups? It seems that the way a child perceives reading and the ability to do so must affect, for example, how s/he communicates about the activity of reading. This in turn affects what the teacher comes to expect from that child and how s/he is evaluated. Together, all these factors interact with how that child defines success and his/her chances of achieving what the school calls success.

The difficulty of movement from one group to another and the connection to larger school success means that these groups minimize the power children might wield over their own achievement and, in fact, set them up to fail. That is to say that the low-ability groups help to perpetuate self-fulfilling prophecies of socially constructed differences. People who have the ability to recognize, learn, and exhibit "socially appropriate" language and behavior wield more power in controlling outcomes in their lives. Similarly, children who have the ability to recognize, learn, and exhibit socially appropriate uses of oral and written language wield more power in controlling their success within a given reading group.

Those of us born outside of the group whose language, values, and norms of behavior are the basis on which schools operate are less likely to be reared according to those same norms. Partly as a function of how we as African-Americans view the world and partly as a function of how we must live daily life in this world, we raise ourselves and our children with different values, languages, and behavioral expectations. These differences are not negative in and of themselves, but it is via these differences that the likelihood of understanding, surviving, and thriving in a white middle-class normed school setting is greatly reduced. This reduced likelihood is further exacerbated by the fact that we as African-Americans disproportionately end up in the lower ability groups, slower academic tracks, and generally weaker echelons of school settings, which reinforce the negative outcomes of these differences.

I have been trying to examine the ways in which these issues affect me personally from outside (systematically and/or institutionally) as they obviously affect my children in the classroom. On a very personal level around the issue of power I ask: Who am I as an African-American woman? What power do I have? What are the historical, sociopolitical, economic, and psychological/emotional contexts that help to define who I am? How do who I am and the power I control (or don't control) affect my teaching?

My questions about power and empowerment have carried over into my classroom this year. At the public school where I teach, most of my children are, like me, African-American from poor families who are at best working class. Many of them have already repeated a grade, which as statistics show, is the leading predictor of dropping out of school before the completion of 12th grade. Being from low socioeconomic backgrounds puts my students—and me, for that matter—at risk for many negative life outcomes, which at best include remaining in a low socioeconomic class.

Given all of this, I ask myself what I can do for these children when the odds are stacked so heavily against them and against me, for that matter. I have decided that I need to exercise the power I do have to begin to at least swing the odds. I've been trying to do this by offering to my students what was offered to me: opportunities to explicitly examine issues of power. I began by putting up posters with explicit slogans, attempting to physically surround my students with issues of power. In addition, I urged my students to tell "how and why"—to give reasons for what they think—and often point out the standard English version of what they have to say. In doing this, I'm trying to find ways to make it clear to them that it is important to be able to express themselves so that anyone and everyone can understand them.

ASSESSMENT

A second set of questions that I kept coming back to as a student teacher evolved around issues of assessment. Despite images from the media and messages implied in scenarios described by fellow teachers that I should feel especially powerless as a new teacher in an inner-city school, I feel quite empowered. I've come to believe that the power I hold is partly a result of the fact that I have spent some time considering what power is all about and what its major sources are. It seems to me that one major source of power for anyone and everyone is knowledge. I was not quite sure of this until I asked my students what makes a person powerful. They said, among other things, that you have to be smart. Unfortunately, though, many of them went on to say that being smart referred to "the brains you're born with." Their concept of smart and its connection to power explain in part some of the feelings of powerlessness that I have seen them exhibit, particularly when they are faced with something they find difficult.

One of the most important ways that I think power gets played out for teachers is in their assessments: how I judge myself personally, how I judge my students, and how I judge the job that I am doing as a teacher. I refuse to relinquish control of the standards by which I make those judgments. This refusal results from a personal life experience of having been reared by strong, independent African-American women and men as well as from social, academic, and professional experiences. The principal, the school district, and the government can set the curriculum in front of me and can force me to use a standard grading guideline. However, I control the way in which I present and involve myself and my students in that curriculum, how I feel about it, and the bases on which I evaluate that involvement. Although this may not seem like much in the larger scheme of things, if nothing else it helps build resistance to those sometimes imposing forces.

In an essay for a course on language and learning during my student teaching, I reflected on how these personal issues of power related to questions about assessment:

Educators and politicians alike talk about the goals of education as being the personal growth and development of critical thinking and analytical skills with an ultimate aim of creating worthy, capable citizens of a democratic society. Even the President has gotten in on fighting the people's educational cause as he espouses theories about what schools and America's children need. I would ask those who espouse the popular platform goals for democratic education the following question: How do we reconcile the uses of restrictive assessment methods to place kids (unbeknownst to them or their families) into nearly inescapable tracks which in many ways determine their life outcomes?

I agree with the educational goals that aim to create capable participants in a democracy. However, it seems to me that all the democratic ideals of choice, equity, and equality mean very little when "the powers that be" decide for the vast majority of students whether they are bound for college, for a factory assembly line, or for chronic, persistent unemployment. Sadly enough, these "powers that be" lie overwhelmingly in standardized tests; so much so that one's junior high school math placement is a strong correlate with whether or not one will attend college after high school (J. Lytle, 1990).

This notion of assessment of what students know and its predictive value has particular value for me. My own experiences as a student as well as my experience in various teaching settings have made it abundantly clear to me that somehow someone sold the idea that you can predict what an individual is capable of based on his or her performance on a test. However, rather than focus on strengths, the tests are often used to emphasize weaknesses of the students as gauged by the tests.

Given the tie of these tests to the American fallacy of faith in untainted meritocracy and the multimillion-dollar industry of standardized test research, development, and preparation courses, it does not seem likely that the use of standardized tests is going to end any time soon. Rather than continue to expose the racial, cultural, gender, and/or class biases of the tests, I have been trying to examine tests from the perspective of their uses. In another student teaching essay, I wrote:

It seems to me that the way in which we test or assess students says a lot about the way we define learning (or whatever it is we say we are testing). It follows logically for me that if we recognize that learning is a complex, dynamic process which may be manifested in many different ways, then we should allow and insist that assessment be open to such manifestations. The idea of portfolio assessment seems to be a good response to an incongruence between what we know about the ways kids learn and how we test that learning.

A portfolio affords teachers, students, and parents a chance to examine pieces of a student's work over a period of time in order to look for trends or patterns. Although the use of portfolios allows for a much wider range of teaching and learning styles, it has not been an easy undertaking with my students thus far. Some of the main issues have been getting them used to keeping their own work, getting them used to playing an active role in their evaluation, and getting them to see why I care to see trends and patterns in their work.

Use of portfolios opens up the criteria for evaluation. In so doing it can be helpful in at least smudging the color lines marked in traditional methods of assessment. The important thing I've been realizing—besides the fact that this is more work for me—is that portfolios really can empower me to do my job better. They give me a more thorough sense of what my students can handle in terms of what I've given them and how I can best help them to handle it. As my students become more possessive of their folders and stay on my back about returning things to keep them updated, I am also realizing what an empowering tool the portfolios can be for them too.

I keep reminding myself, though, that it is important for me to know why it is we are really testing, evaluating, and assessing in the first place. Answers will vary but undoubtedly include things such as: to see what they know, what they have learned, how well they've been taught, and what they still need to be taught. Taking a more encompassing and in-depth view of a child and his/her work, as with the use of portfolios, would certainly help to answer such questions. However, it also seems quite sensible particularly in light of the currently espoused reasoning behind assessment. The assumption is that we do it all in order to predict what children are capable of and to try to help them to reach and stretch their potential. If indeed this is the reasoning behind assessment, then an additional question has to be: Are we capable of and prepared to accommodate a society full of all kinds of individuals who are realizing their various potentials? If the answer is yes, then I think we must be prepared for a truly democratic society in which more of the silent masses become educated participants and more of the "have-nots" join the ranks of the "haves." I think far fewer of us are ready for this than we want to think.

GOALS OF EDUCATION

Just as race and racism influence how students are evaluated, these issues also appear to affect general educational policy and practice. What I've been realizing is that to speak to policy and practice, I need to examine the broad picture of what education is about. In attempting to develop a set of educational goals for myself as an educator, in examining currently "politically correct" goals, and in questioning goals espoused by my colleagues, I now find myself asking again the questions I posed to my classmates and professors a year ago:

What does it mean to learn? to know? How does learning take place? What kind of learning happens best under which circumstances? What is this talk of personal growth in education? Is that what we want? How do we maximize it? How do we capitalize on what we've already got in our kids and ourselves? Can we really do it in our schools? What about the kids' "baggage"? What about my baggage? What do we mean by personal growth anyway? In what aspects do we wish to achieve it? Can we do it for all kids? Why is that what we want? Growth for what? democracy? where? when? for whom?

Exploration of these questions leads me to reflect, and I think of my own education. It began with my mother's fighting to keep me out of special education in a school in South Carolina, where I lived at the time with my grandmother. Fortunately for me, my mother did not hold the same respect for standardized tests as the white school officials in Greeleyville, South Carolina, did, who said I should be in classes for the learning disabled. Shortly thereafter, we moved to New York City, where I attended a Head Start program and, later, a public elementary school in the South Bronx.

After being identified as "gifted," I began to attend a placement and enrichment program for minority students called Prep for Prep. Upon graduating from P.S. 49, I was awarded a scholarship to the Horace Mann School for 7th through 12th grades. Given that my educational journey from Greeleyville, South Carolina, to "Happy H.M." was often interrupted with questions and allegations of racism and discrimination, I honestly believe that it was no accident that I ended up at such a school. That belief has nothing to do with the fact that Horace Mann is an academically rigorous, intellectually challenging, but posh, private school. Instead, it is based on the fact that the school is named for an educator who conceived of education as being political and moral.

While considering Horace Mann's philosophy, my own educational background/baggage, and the questions I asked a year ago in my student teaching journal, I have been seeking approaches to instruction that will maximize our potential to be a truly democratic society and capitalize on the capacities and potentials we already have in our students and in ourselves as individuals. I'm looking for approaches that address the psychological, social, intellectual, and emotional aspects of students as individual people. Such approaches could be used to eliminate the now-presumed need for tracks, ability groups, and other institutional tools that replicate social inequities. Given that I, as an educator, have what Weiler (1988) would call my own historical/sociopolitical situation and situatedness, I think that such an approach can help me to begin to rise above what constricts my view of education, policies, and practices. This approach would have to allow and demand that the student as a whole person is where I begin, remain, and finish. It supports my realization that no aspect is nonexistent, unimportant, or extraneous to the realm of school life and education.

As a teacher, I am looking for ways to come at educational material from different perspectives, including those used to help me make sense of that material for myself. I'm trying to find ways to help my students make sense of material for themselves; I want them to make connections and create a "big picture." Therefore, I try to give them a "big frame" within which to build. Working toward getting them to see a broad picture, however, forces me again to ask: What do I really want them to know? To answer this question, I need to be clear on what it means to "know."

During my student teaching, I thought I had found a real-life example of what it means to know when one of my students, who was struggling with long division, remarked:

Ms. Joe, you must got some magic power cause I can do it over here with you, but I can't do it in my seat.

I later wrote in my journal:

[A]lthough it probably shattered his image of me, I had to tell him that it wasn't my magic that I was using but the questions that I asked him as we walked step-by-step through each problem. . . . He looked totally shocked when I told him that at some point he'll ask himself those questions and won't need me at all to help him do division.

Based on this and other similar scenarios, I thought that to know meant to internalize information, concepts, and cognitive strategies. As I tried to explain to my third grader, it wasn't magic or any special power that comes with being an adult or even a teacher that made division possible. Instead, knowing how to do division or anything else is about having information, cognitive strategies, and skills in your head. However, it seems to me that even that definition does not quite cover what I feel when I consider long-term educational goals and all the things that I want my students to know.

I've been looking at curriculum to figure out what knowing is about because, theoretically, the curriculum is about learning and growth. The idea is that we as educators give the students what they should know: something with which they can connect and build. Therefore, we have, for example, a lot of African and African-American stuff included in the curriculum. However, even when we require such material to be part of the curriculum, there are still problems in terms of how such material will be approached, introduced, and covered. Essentially, such issues are left unaddressed. Often, there is no training for teachers, and they are left essentially unprepared for class. I've been finding that my colleagues and I are sometimes forced to relegate some things to secondary positions behind the "important" stuff that we are knowledgeable of and comfortable with.

CONCLUSION

These and all the other questions that I have been raising tend to overlap and cut across issues of power, assessment, and goals. For me, these issues are inextricably tied as each impacts on the other and on everything that I do. Perhaps it is in the very way that I define my job that these issues become intertwined. Thus far, I have not been able to carry out any part of my job without wondering whether I am giving my students as much as I can and helping them to stretch their limits as far as they can. With this as the framework within which I struggle to seek truth, create meaning, and generate values for them and for myself, I think that I at least begin to answer some of the questions as I focus on the sign on my classroom door, which reads: IT'S A JOURNEY . . . ALL ARE WELCOME.

Part II: References

Anderson, R. C., Hiebert, E. H., Scott, J. A., Wilkinson, I. (1985). *Becoming a nation of readers: The report of the Commission of Reading.* Washington, DC: The National Institute of Education.

Anderson, R. C., Wilson, P. T., & Fielding, L. G. (1988). Growth in reading and how children spend their time outside of school. *Reading Research Quarterly, 23,* 285–303.

Atwell, N. (1987). *In the middle: Writing, reading and learning with adolescents.* Portsmouth, NH: Boynton/Cook.

Auerbach, E. R. (1989). Toward a social-contextual approach to family literacy. *Harvard Educational Review, 59,* 165–181.

Auerbach, E. R. (1990). *Making meaning, making change.* Boston: University of Massachusetts.

Bakhtin, M. M. (1986). *Speech genres and other essays.* Austin, TX: University of Texas Press.

Baum-Brunner, S. (1990). *Talk about writing and revision of rough drafts.* Unpublished doctoral dissertation, University of Pennsylvania, Philadelphia.

Berthoff, A. (1987). The teacher as researcher. In D. Goswami & P. Stillman (Eds.), *Reclaiming the classroom: Teacher research as an agency for change.* Upper Montclair, NJ: Boynton/Cook.

Bleich, D. (1975). *Readings and feelings: An introduction to subjective criticism.* Urbana, IL: National Council of Teachers of English.

Borko, H., & Eisenhart, M. (1989). Reading ability groups as literacy communities. In D. Bloome (Ed.), *Classrooms and literacy.* Norwood, NJ: Ablex.

Britton, J. (1987). A quiet form of research. In D. Goswami & P. Stillman (Eds.), *Reclaiming the classroom: Teacher research as an agency for change.* Upper Montclair, NJ: Boynton/Cook.

Brooke, R. (1988, February). Modeling a writer's identity. *College Composition and Communication 39,* 23–41.

Bruffee, K. (1984). Peer tutoring and the conversation of mankind. In G. Olson (Ed.), *Writing centers, theory, and administration.* Urbana, IL: National Council of Teachers of English.

Carini, P. (1979). *The art of seeing and the visibility of the person.* Grand Forks, ND: North Dakota Study Group on Evaluation, University of North Dakota.

Carini, P. (1986). *Prospect's documentary processes.* Bennington, VT: Prospect School Center.

Carnegie Forum (1986). *A nation prepared: Teachers for the 21st century: The report of Task Force on Teaching As a Profession*. New York: Carnegie.

Chall, J. S. (1983). *Stages of reading development*. New York: McGraw-Hill.

Chittenden, E. (1990). Young children's discussions of science topics. In G. Hein (Ed.), *The assessment of hand's-on elementary science programs: North Dakota Study Group monograph*. Grand Forks, ND: University of North Dakota Press.

Clark, R. (1983). *Family life and school achievement*. Chicago: University of Chicago Press.

Cochran-Smith, M. (1984). *The making of a reader*. Norwood, NJ: Ablex.

Cochran-Smith, M. (1991). Learning to teach against the grain. *Harvard Educational Review, 61,* 279–310.

Connell, R. W., Ashenden, D. J., Kessler, S., & Dowsett, G. W. (1982). *Making the difference: Schools, families and social division*. Sydney, Australia: George Allen and Unwin.

Crusius, T. (1989). *Discourse: A critique and synthesis of major theories*. New York: Modern Language Association.

Davidson, J. L. (1988). *Counterpoint and beyond*. Urbana, IL: National Council of Teachers of English.

DeFord, D. E. (1980). Young children and their writing. *Theory Into Practice, 19,* 157–162.

Delpit, L. (1986). Skills and other dilemmas of a progressive black educator. *Harvard Educational Review, 56,* 379–385.

Donaldson, N. (1984). Speech and writing and modes of learning. In R. Beach & L. S. Bridwell (Eds.), *New directions in composition research* (pp. 174–184). New York: Guilford.

Dyson, A. H. (1987a). Individual differences in beginning composing. *Written Communication, 4,* 411–442.

Dyson, A. H. (1987b). The value of "time off task": Young children's spontaneous talk and deliberate text. *Harvard Educational Review, 57,* 396–420.

Edelsky, C. (1982). Writing in a bilingual program: The relation of L1 and L2 texts. *TESOL Quarterly, 16,* 211–218.

Edelsky, C., & Smith, K. (1984). Is that writing—or are those marks just a figment of your curriculum? *Language Arts, 61,* 24–32.

Eisner, E. W. (1985). *The educational imagination (2nd ed.)*. New York: MacMillan.

Emig, J. (1985). Writing as a mode of learning. *College Composition and Communication, 36,* 34–40.

Emig, J. (1987). From non-magical thinking: Presenting writing developmentally in schools. In D. Goswami & P. Stillman (Eds.), *Reclaiming the classroom: Teacher research as an agency for change*. Upper Montclair, NJ: Boynton/Cook.

Ferdman, B. M. (1990). Literacy and cultural identity. *Harvard Educational Review, 60,* 182–204.

Ferreiro, E. (1978). What is written in a written sentence? A developmental answer. *Journal of Education, 160,* 25–39.

Fish, S. (1980). *Is there a text in this class: The authority of interpretive communities*. Cambridge, MA: Harvard University Press.

Flood, J., & Lapp, D. (1987). Reading and writing relations: Assumptions and directions. In Squire (Ed.), *The dynamics of language learning*. Urbana, IL: National Council of Teachers of English.

Florio-Ruane, S. (1986, April). *Taking a closer look at writing conferences.* Paper presented at the annual meeting of the American Educational Research Association, San Francisco.

Freedman, S., Dyson, A., Flower, L., Chaffe, W. (1987). *Research in writing: Past, present and future* (Technical report no. 1). Berkeley, CA: Center for the Study of Writing.

Freire, P. (1971). *Pedagogy of the oppressed.* New York: Herder and Herder.

Freire, P., & Macedo, D. (1987). *Literacy: Reading the word and the world.* S. Hadley, MA: Bergin and Garvey.

Galda, L. (1984). The relations between reading and writing in young children. In R. Beach & L. S. Bridwell (Eds.), *New Directions in Composition Research.* New York: Guilford.

Geertz, C. (1973). *The interpretation of cultures.* New York: Basic Books.

Gere, A. R., & Stevens, R. (1985). Language of writing groups: How oral response shapes revision. In S. Freedman (Ed.), *The acquisition of written language: Response and revision.* Norwood, NJ: Ablex.

Giroux, H. (1985). Intellectual label and pedagogical work: Rethinking the role of teachers as intellectuals. *Phenomenology and Pedagogy, 3,* 20–31.

Goodlad, J. (1984). *A place called school.* New York: McGraw-Hill.

Goodlad, J. (1990). *Teachers for our nation's schools.* San Francisco: Jossey-Bass.

Goswami, D., & Stillman, P. (1987). *Reclaiming the classroom: Teacher research as an agency for change.* Upper Montclair, NJ: Boynton/Cook.

Graner, M. (1987, March). Revision workshops: An alternative to peer editing groups. *English Journal, 76,* 40–45.

Graves, D. H. (1983). *Writing: Teachers and children at work.* Portsmouth, NH: Heinemann.

Griffin, G. A. (1986). Thinking about teaching. In K. Zumwalt (Ed.), *Improving teaching: 1986 ASCD yearbook.* Alexandria, VA: Association for Supervision and Curriculum Development.

Hall, M. A., Moritz, S. A., & Staton, J. (1976). Writing before grade one: A study of early writers. *Language Arts, 53,* 582–585.

Halliday, M. A. K. (1975). *Learning how to mean: Explorations in the development of language.* New York: Elsevier North-Holland.

Hargreaves, A., & Dawe, R. (1989, April). *Coaching as unreflective practice: Contrived collegiality or collaborative culture?* Paper presented at the annual meeting of the American Educational Research Association, San Francisco.

Harris, J. (1989). The idea of community in the study of writing. *College Composition and Communication, 40,* 11–22.

Harris, S. (1986). Evaluation of a curriculum to support literacy growth in young children. *Early Childhood Research Quarterly, 1,* 333–348.

Harste, J. C., Woodward, V. A., & Burke, C. L. (1984). *Language stories and literacy lessons.* Portsmouth, NH: Heinemann.

Heath, S. (1981). Toward an ethnohistory of writing in American education. In M. F. Whiteman (Ed.), *Writing: Nature, development, and teaching of written communication.* Hillsdale, NJ: Lawrence Earlbaum.

Heath, S. (1983). *Ways with words: Language, life, and work in communities and classrooms.* New York: Cambridge University Press.

Himley, M. (1991). *Shared territory: Understanding children's writing as works.* New York: Oxford University Press.

Hirsch, S. A. (1990). New teacher induction: An interview with Leslie Huling-Austin. *Journal of Staff Development, 11*, 2–4.

Huling-Austin, L., Odell, S. J., Ishler, P., Kay, R. P., & Edelfelt, R. A. (1989). *Assisting the beginning teacher*. Reston, VA: Association of Teacher Educators.

Johnston, P. (1987). The social scenes of reading: A study of eighth-graders' talk about books. Unpublished doctoral dissertation, University of Pennsylvania, Philadelphia.

Johnston, P. (1992). Coming full circle: As teachers become researchers, so goes the curriculum. In A. Branscombe, D. Goswami, & J. Schwartz (Eds.), *Students teaching, teachers learning*. Portsmouth,NH: Heinemann-Boynton Cook.

Kanevsky, R. (1992). *Exploring values and standards: Implications and assessment*. New York: Teachers College Press.

Kroll, B. (1980). Developmental perspectives and the teaching of composition. *College English, 41,* 741–752.

LeGuin, U. K. (1989). *Bryn Mawr commencement address: Dancing at the edge of the world*. New York: Harper & Row.

Little, J. (1989, April). *The persistence of privacy: Autonomy and initiative in teachers' professional relations*. Paper presented at the annual meeting of the American Educational Research Association, San Francisco.

Long, E. (1985). *The American dream and the popular novel*. Boston: Routledge & Kegan Paul.

Lorde, A. (1989, April). Women, power and difference. Speech given at *Women in America: Legacies of Race and Ethnicity*. Georgetown University, Washington, DC.

Lytle, S. (1982). *Exploring comprehension style: A study of twelfth-graders' transactions with text*. Unpublished doctoral dissertation, University of Pennsylvania, Philadelphia.

Lytle, S. (1991). Living literacy: Rethinking development in adulthood. *Linguistics in Education, 3,* 109–138.

Mavrogenes, N. A. (1986). What every reading teacher should know about emergent literacy. *The Reading Teacher, 40,* 174–178.

Michaels, S., Ulichney, P., & Watson-Gegeo, K. (1989). Writing conferences: Innovation or familiar routine? Unpublished manuscript, Harvard University, Cambridge, MA.

Michaels, W. B. (1980). The interpreter's self: Peirce on the Cartesian "subject." In J. Thompkins (Ed.), *Reader Response Criticism*. Baltimore: Johns Hopkins University Press.

Myers, M. (1985). *The teacher-researcher: How to study writing in the classroom*. Urbana, IL: National Council of Teachers of English.

Newkirk, T. (1984). Directions and misdirections in peer response. *College Composition and Communication, 34,* 301–311.

Odell, S. J. (1989). Developing support programs for beginning teachers. In L. Huling-Austin, S. J. Odell, P. Ishler, R. P. Kay, & R. A. Edelfelt (Eds.), *Assisting the beginning teacher*. Reston, VA: Association of Teacher Educators.

Onore, C. (1989). The student, the teacher, and the text: Negotiating meaning through response and revision. In C. Anson (Ed.), *Writing and response: Theory, Practice, and Research*. Champaign, IL: National Council of Teachers of English.

Peck, M. S. (1978). *The road less traveled*. New York: Simon and Schuster.

Philadelphia Teachers Learning Cooperative (1984). On becoming teacher experts: Buying time. *Language Arts, 61,* 731–736.

Pincus, M. (1987). Sharing control. *Work in Progress, 1,* 1–13.

Pincus, M. (1988). Teacher as researcher: Conversion of a skeptic. *Work in Progress, 2*, 7–18.

Pincus, M. (1990a). Assessment in the urban classroom. *Voice, 2*, 2–3.

Pincus, M. (1990b, March). *High school restructuring: A teacher's perspective.* Paper presented at the University of Pennsylvania's 200th Anniversary Forum on Restructuring, Philadelphia.

Reither, J., & Vipond, D. (1989, December). Writing as collaboration. *College English, 51*, 855–867.

Resnick, L. B. (1987). Learning in school and out. *Educational Researcher, 16*, 13–20.

Rogers, T., Green, J. L., & Nussbaum, N. R. (1988). Asking questions about questions. In S. Hynds & D. Ruben (Eds.), *Perspectives on talk and learning.* Champaign-Urbana: National Council of Teachers of English Yearbook.

Rorschach, E., & Whitney, R. (1986). Relearning to teach: Peer observation as a means of professional development for teachers. *English Journal, 18*, 159–172.

Ryan, K. (1970). *Don't smile till Christmas.* Chicago: University of Chicago Press.

Sherman, R. R., & Webb, R. B. (1988). *Qualitative research in education: Focus and methods.* London: Falmer Press.

Shulman, L. (1986). Paradigms and research programs in the study of teaching: A contemporary perspective. In M. C. Wittrock (Ed.), *Handbook of research in teaching* (3rd ed., pp. 3–36). New York: MacMillan, .

Smith, F. (1984). The creative achievement of literacy. In H. Goelman, A. Oberg, & F. Smith (Eds.), *Awakening to literacy.* London: Heinemann.

Sommers, N. (1982, May). Responding to student writing. *College Composition and Communication, 33*, 148–156.

Stallard, C. (1974). Description of the composing processes of college freshman: An analysis of writing behavior of good student writers. *Research in the Teaching of English, 18*, 206–218..

Strieb, L. (1985). *A Philadelphia teacher's journal: North Dakota Study Group Center for Teaching and Learning.* Grand Forks, ND: North Dakota Study Group Center for Teaching and Learning.

Strieb, L. (1988). Trees. *Outlook, 3.*

Taylor, D. (1983). *Family literacy: Young children learning to read and write.* Portsmouth, NH: Heinemann.

Taylor, D., & Dorsey-Gaines, C. (1988). *Growing up literate: Learning from inner city families.* Portsmouth, NH: Heinemann.

Teale, W. H. (1981). Parents reading to their children: What we know and need to know. *Language Arts, 58*, 902–912.

Tizard, J., Schofields, W. N., & Hewison, J. (1982). Symposium: Reading-collaboration between teachers and parents in assisting children's reading. *The British Journal of Educational Psychology, 52*, 1–15.

Topping, K. (1987). Paired reading: A powerful technique for parent use. *Reading Teacher, 40*, 608–614.

Vygotsky, L. (1962). *Thought and language.* Cambridge, MA: Massachusetts Institute of Technology.

Vygotsky, L. (1978). *Mind in society.* Cambridge, MA: Harvard University Press.

Weiler, K. (1988). *Feminist methodology: Women teaching for change: Gender, class and power.* New York: Bergin and Garvey.

Wise, A. E. , Darling-Hammond, L., & Berry, B. (1988). Selecting teachers: The best, the known, and the persistent. *Educational Leadership, 45,* 82–85.

Wolf, Dennie P. (1988). *Reading reconsidered.* New York: College Entrance Examination Board.

About the Authors

Marilyn Cochran-Smith is assistant professor of education in the Educational Leadership Division at the Graduate School of Education, University of Pennsylvania, and Director of Project START, a master's program in elementary education. Dr. Cochran-Smith's scholarly interests include teacher education, children's early literacy development, and research on teaching. She is the author of *The Making of a Reader* (Ablex); and coauthor of *Learning to Write Differently* (Ablex), and numerous articles on teaching and teacher education. In her work with preservice teachers, Dr. Cochran-Smith draws on her experience as an elementary school teacher as well as a scholar and researcher. She is particularly interested in reinventing the structures of preservice teacher education so that student teachers learn to "teach against the grain."

Susan L. Lytle is assistant professor of education in the Language in Education Division at the Graduate School of Education, University of Pennsylvania; and director of The Philadelphia Writing Project and of the master's and doctoral programs in reading/writing/literacy. Dr. Lytle's research focuses on the professional development of teachers, literacy learning in adolescence and adulthood, and alternative assessment. She is the coauthor of *Adult Literacy Education: Program Evaluation and Learner Assessment* (ERIC) and *The Pennsylvania Framework: Reading, Writing, and Talking Across the Curriculum,* as well as many articles on literacy and teacher education. A former high school English teacher and Peace Corps Volunteer, Dr. Lytle works with communities of experienced teachers and other practitioners committed to inquiry and educational reform.

Dr. Cochran-Smith and Dr. Lytle are co-holders of the Joseph L. Calihan Chair in Education, established in recognition of their collaborative work on teacher inquiry and the improvement of teaching and learning. This book is based on their collaborative research and practice with Philadelphia area teachers and student teachers. They co-chair the annual session on teacher research at the Ethnography in Education Forum, held at the University of Pennsylvania.

Author Index